Counseling and Psychotherapy: A Behavioral Approach *by E. Lakin Phillips*

Dimensions of Personality *edited by Harvey London and John E. Exner, Jr.*

The Mental Health Industry: A Cultural Phenomenon *by Peter A. Magaro, Robert Gripp, David McDowell, and Ivan W. Miller III*

Nonverbal Communication: The State of the Art *by Robert G. D. Matarazzo*

Alcoholism and Treatment *by David J. Armor, J. Michael Pol*

A Biodevelopmental Approach to Clinical Child Psychology: Control Theory *by Sebastiano Santostefano*

Handbook of Infant Development *edited by Joy D. Osofsky*

Understanding the Rape Victim: A Synthesis of Research Findings *by Sedelle Katz and Mary Ann Mazur*

Childhood Pathology and Later Adjustment: The Question of Prediction *by Loretta K. Cass and Carolyn B. Thomas*

Intelligent Testing with the WISC-R *by Alan S. Kaufman*

Adaptation in Schizophrenia: The Theory of Segmental Set *by David Shakow*

Psychotherapy: An Eclectic Approach *by Sol L. Garfield*

Handbook of Minimal Brain Dysfunctions *edited by Herbert E. Rie and Ellen D. Rie*

Handbook of Behavioral Interventions: A Clinical Guide *edited by Alan Goldstein and Edna B. Foa*

Art Psychotherapy *by Harriet Wadeson*

Handbook of Adolescent Psychology *edited by Joseph Adelson*

Psychotherapy Supervision: Theory, Research and Practice *edited by Allen K. Hess*

Psychology and Psychiatry in Courts and Corrections: Controversy and Change *by Ellsworth A. Fersch, Jr.*

Restricted Environmental Stimulation: Research and Clinical Applications *by Peter Suedfeld*

Personal Construct Psychology: Psychotherapy and Personality *edited by Alvin W. Landfield and Larry M. Leitner*

Mothers, Grandmothers, and Daughters: Personality and Child Care in Three-Generation Families *by Bertram J. Cohler and Henry U. Grunebaum*

Further Explorations in Personality *edited by A.I. Rabin, Joel Aronoff, Andrew M. Barclay, and Robert A. Zucker*

Hypnosis and Relaxation: Modern Verification of an Old Equation *by William E. Edmonston, Jr.*

Handbook of Clinical Behavior Therapy *edited by Samuel M. Turner, Karen S. Calhoun, and Henry E. Adams*

Handbook of Clinical Neuropsychology *edited by Susan B. Filskov and Thomas J. Boll*

The Course of Alcoholism: Four Years After Treatment *by J. Michael Polich, David J. Armor, and Harriet B. Braiker*

Handbook of Innovative Psychotherapies *edited by Raymond J. Corsini*

The Role of the Father in Child Development (Second Edition) *edited by Michael E. Lamb*

Behavioral Medicine: Clinical Applications *by Susan S. Pinkerton, Howard Hughes, and W.W. Wenrich*

Handbook for the Practice of Pediatric Psychology *edited by June M. Tuma*

Change Through Interaction: Social Psychological Processes of Counseling and Psychotherapy *by Stanley R. Strong and Charles D. Claiborn*

Drugs and Behavior (Second Edition) *by Fred Leavitt*

Handbook of Research Methods in Clinical Psychology *edited by Philip C. Kendall and James N. Butcher*

A Social Psychology of Developing Adults *by Thomas O. Blank*

(*continued on back*)

INNOVATIVE INTERVENTIONS IN
CHILD AND ADOLESCENT THERAPY

OTHER BOOKS BY CHARLES E. SCHAEFER

Teach Your Baby to Sleep Through the Night (*With M. Petronko*) 1987

Advances in Therapies for Children *(With H. Millman, S. Sichel, and J. Zwilling),* 1986

Game Play *(With S. Reid),* 1986

Family Therapy Techniques *(With J. Briesmeister and M. Fitton),* 1984

How to Talk to Children about Really Important Things, 1984

Group Therapies for Children and Youth *(With L. Johnson and J. Wherry),* 1983

Handbook of Play Therapy *(With K. O'Connor),* 1983

How to Influence Children (Rev. Ed.), 1982

How to Help Children with Common Problems, 1981

Therapies for School Behavior Problems *(With H. Millman and J. Cohen),* 1980

Therapies for Psychosomatic Disorders in Children *(With H. Millman and G. Levine),* 1979

Childhood Encopresis and Enuresis, 1979

How to Influence Children: A Handbook of Practical Parenting Skills, 1978

Therapies for Children: A Handbook of Effective Treatments for Problem Behaviors *(With H. Millman),* 1977

Therapeutic Use of Child's Play, 1976

Developing Creativity in Children, 1973

Becoming Somebody: Creative Activities for Preschool Children, 1973

Young Voices: The Poetry of Children, 1970

Innovative Interventions in Child and Adolescent Therapy

Edited by

CHARLES E. SCHAEFER

Fairleigh Dickinson University

WILEY

A WILEY-INTERSCIENCE PUBLICATION

JOHN WILEY & SONS

New York • Chichester • Brisbane • Toronto • Singapore

0-471-63511-1

10 9 8 7 6 5 4 3 2 1

Printed in the United States of America

To Anne

About the Contributors

John A.B. Allan, Ph.D., is an Associate Professor of Counseling Psychology at the University of British Columbia, Vancouver, Canada and a Senior Training Analyst with the Inter-Regional Society of Jungian Analysts. He is on the editorial board of *Journal of Analytical Psychology* and *Elementary School Guidance and Counselling*. Dr. Allan is co-author of *Children Who Move, Class Discussions, Mainstreaming* and *Managing Common Classroom Problems*. He is currently working on *Earth, Fire, Water and Sun: Jungian Approaches with Children*.

Jerrold R. Brandell, Ph.D., is an Assistant Professor in the School of Social Work at Michigan State University. He has served as a consultant to agencies in both Michigan and Illinois, and maintains a part-time private psychotherapy practice. His recent publications have addressed clinical issues in child psychotherapy and diagnosis, and instruction and supervision in psychoanalytic psychotherapy.

Marian C. Fish, Ph.D., is an Assistant Professor in the Graduate Program in School Psychology, Queens College, City University of New York, and a member of the doctoral faculty in the Department of Educational Psychology at the Graduate Center, City University of New York. She has worked as a school psychologist and in the field of behavioral medicine. Her research interests include developing behavioral interventions, particularly self-management strategies, to remediate children's academic and social difficulties, and using systems theory to study family-school relationships. She has published work in these areas.

Mother Hildegard George, OSB, M.A., is a Benedictine nun in private practice in Bethlehem, Connecticut. Her monastery has a large farm where she is able to incorporate animals into treatment with children. She received her B.S. from Michigan State University, her M.A. from Goddard College in Vermont and is currently working on a doctorate from The Union for Experimenting Colleges and Universities. She has worked with emotionally disturbed children at Green Chimneys in Brewster, New York and at Blueberry Treatment Center in Brooklyn, New York.

Joan K. Ham, M.S.W., is a leader of a multi-disciplinary team at Unified Services for Children and Adolescents in Troy, New York. Unified Services is a component of the Rensselaer County mental health system and serves children and families with a broad spectrum of problems. She has also been for many years adjunct instructor for the State University of New York at Albany in the Nelson Rockefeller School of Public Policy.

JoAnn Harrison is a Family Services Program Supervisor with the Kentucky Cabinet for Human Resources, Department for Social Services. Her extensive work experience in adoption and foster care led her to co-author *Making History: A Social Worker's Guide to Life Books*. She also is a management consultant, providing workshops and presentations for the first-time manager.

Joop Hellendoorn, Ph.D., is a senior lecturer in the Department of Special Education at the University of Leiden, The Netherlands. As part of that job she serves as director of both a graduate course in child psychotherapy and a research program in that same field. She is (co-)author of four books and numerous scientific papers, and is a member of the editorial boards of a Dutch professional journal *(Kind & Adolescent)* and a book series *(Kinderen als Beroep)*.

Aaron Noah Hoorwitz, Ph.D., is Clinic Director of Unified Services for Children and Adolescents, a public mental health agency in Rensselaer County, New York. He maintains a private practice and is on the faculties of Russell Sage College and Albany Medical College. He has published numerous articles on court consultation, sex abuse, and strategic family therapy. His most recent publication is a book entitled *Hypnotic Methods in Nonhypnotic Therapies*.

Greg Johanson, M.Div., is a pastor, psychotherapist, editor, and writer who has published a number of works in the field of psychology and religion. He is a certified therapist and trainer of the Hakomi Institute and edits the Institute's journal, *Hakomi Forum*. His experience includes using hakomi therapy in mental health clinic, parish, college, public school, and hospital settings. He is a doctoral student in clinical psychology at the Oregon Graduate School of Professional Psychology.

George V. Neagu, M.A., is Senior Therapist at Swanson Center, a community mental health center in Michigan City, Indiana. He is an experiential psychotherapist who has used focusing with adults, couples, Vietnam veterans, children, and adolescents. Currently, he is exploring the use of focusing with chronically mentally ill patients in a day treatment program. His articles on social concerns have appeared in magazines and books. He has published articles in professional journals and newsletters on staff development and play therapy. He assumed a leading role in the three year Uptown (Chicago) Project on child abuse, is a Parent Effectiveness Training Instructor and a Focusing Trainer. He has received numerous awards in human relations and civil rights and is on the Human Relations Commission in his city. He is also a freelance writer.

Helen Payne, Adv. Dip. Spec. Ed., Cert. Ed., Laban Cert., is a senior lecturer in the Division of Arts and Psychology at Hertfordshire College of Art and Design in England. She was a co-founder of the Association for Dance Movement Therapy and serves on the Standing Committee for the Arts Therapies Professions. She is trained in Group Analysis and is a practicing Dance Movement Therapist. At present she is involved in the development of post-graduate training for dance movement therapy (DMT). Ms. Payne has presented her research on DMT for the degree of M.Phil. at the University of Manchester. This is the first research on this subject done in the United Kingdom.

Ronald H. Rozensky, Ph.D., is the Associate Chairman of the Department of Psychiatry, the Evanston Hospital, Evanston, Illinois, where he is also the Chief of the Division of Psychology. In addition, he is an Associate Professor of Clinical Psychiatry and Behavioral Sciences at Northwestern University Medical School and an Associate Professor of Psychology at Northwestern University. His private practice focuses upon the use of psychotherapy and biofeedback. Dr. Rozensky has published articles in the areas of biofeedback, self control, and behavioral medicine.

Carol R. Taylor, M.Ed., has been counseling in public schools for 15 years, developing programs for seriously emotionally disturbed students, and providing both individual and family therapy. She has training in a number of therapeutic orientations and was among the first students to study Hakomi Therapy with Ron Kurtz. She has also developed counseling skills and insights through acting as an accomplished violinist and as a teacher and university lecturer of the Suzuki Method.

Peter Tilton, M.D., is a psychotherapist in private practice using hypnosis in both brief and long-term dynamic psychotherapy with a special interest in the use of hypnosis in psychosomatic and stress-related disorders. He is a Diplomate of the American Board of Medical Hypnosis and has published articles in the *American Journal of Clinical Hypnosis* and the *International Journal of Clinical and Experimental Hypnosis* as well as a chapter in *Hypnosis: Questions and Answers*. In addition he has given many workshops and has supervised groups on the use of hypnosis in psychotherapy.

Judy Weiser, M.S.Ed., A.T.R., R.S.W., is the Director and Training Coordinator of the PhotoTherapy/PhotoExplorations Centre in Vancouver, Canada. Focusing on the non-verbal/visual aspects of communication and behavior (including cultural differences), she specializes in conducting workshops and teaching the applications of 'ordinary' snapshots and photo-interactions as adjunctive tools for therapeutic and intercultural uses. Editor of the journal, *Phototherapy,* she has authored numerous articles and several book chapters on these topics. A therapist and trainer for over 20 years, she has focused on working with many 'culturally different' or 'hard-to-reach' populations, including deaf and Native Indian clients, 'street kids', teens with alcohol/drug problems, general adolescent and family issues, etc. Fluent in a variety of Deaf Sign and nonverbal symbol languages, she is also a professional photographer with many gallery exhibits and photographic publications.

Series Preface

This series of books is addressed to behavioral scientists interested in the nature of human personality. Its scope should prove pertinent to personality theorists and researchers as well as to clinicians concerned with applying an understanding of personality processes to the amelioration of emotional difficulties in living. To this end, the series provides a scholarly integration of theoretical formulations, empirical data, and practical recommendations.

Six major aspects of studying and learning about human personality can be designated: personality theory, personality structure and dynamics, personality development, personality assessment, personality change, and personality adjustment. In exploring these aspects of personality, the books in the series discuss a number of distinct but related subject areas: the nature and implications of various theories of personality; personality characteristics that account for consistencies and variations in human behavior; the emergence of personality processes in children and adolescents; the use of interviewing and testing procedures to evaluate individual differences in personality; efforts to modify personality styles through psychotherapy, counseling, behavior, therapy, and other methods of influence; and patterns of abnormal personality functioning that impair individual competence.

IRVING B. WEINER

Fairleigh Dickinson University
Rutherford, New Jersey

Preface

The academic preparation of child therapists has traditionally included courses in major theoretical orientations and applications but not in more specialized child therapy techniques. The goal of this volume, then, is to describe a wide variety of the most promising therapeutic procedures that have been developed for children and adolescents. These are techniques that are not currently in the mainstream of clinical practice, so they would not be discussed in traditional therapy courses on humanistic, psychodynamic, cognitive-behavioral, or family approaches. They are also not likely to be taught in practicum experiences or clinical internships.

Quite comprehensive in scope, this sourcebook includes 15 original chapters by specialists who have extensive experience with the techniques. The range of specific approaches includes storytelling; hypnosis; focusing; phototherapy; fantasy play therapy; dance and video therapy; the use of pets, drawings, and rituals; relaxation and biofeedback; Hakomi therapy, and Life Story Books. The techniques, which cut across diagnostic categories and theoretical orientations, are classified for ease of reference in this book into four broad sections: "Creative Arts" Techniques; "Relaxed State" Techniques; "Altered View of Reality" Techniques; and Other Techniques: Phototherapy, Life Story Books, Animal, and Video Techniques.

The emphasis of the chapters is on clinical practice—particularly a detailed description of the "nuts-and-bolts" of the techniques. The presentation of each procedure follows a common format, in which the historical and theoretical foundations of the technique are first discussed, followed by a step-by-step account of how to carry out the technique, and finally illustrative examples drawn from actual cases are presented. These case examples provide the reader with considerable depth and richness of detail. Clearly, the procedures have been tested by the authors in the hearthstone of clinical experience over many years and have been found to be capable of producing therapeutic change.

A word of caution about the techniques described in this volume: Some of the therapeutic practices are based upon extensive empirical validation, while others appear promising but have been successful with only a limited number of cases. Consequently, a number of the techniques described in this book should be viewed with full recognition of the need for more extensive independent replication. It should also be recognized that the procedures contained herein are best used as supplements to more general theoretical orientations. They are meant to be adjunct practices rather than a clinician's primary or sole therapeutic approach. Moreover, an understanding of childhood psychopathology, child development, and personality theory is needed to effectively apply the techniques.

Clinicians and counselors from different theoretical persuasions who have an interest in enhancing their repertoire of skills should find this book invaluable.

It has been a genuine pleasure to organize and edit a volume dedicated to child therapy practices. The process has, I believe, broadened my horizons and increased my clinical acumen. I am indebted to the contributors, each a respected clinician in their own field. I find their enthusiasm for exploring innovative practices both contagious and inspiring.

CHARLES E. SCHAEFER

Hackensack, New Jersey
February 1988

Contents

INTRODUCTION

Current Trends in Child Therapy

The focus of this book is on practical techniques rather than on therapy or research. Techniques are step-by-step procedures used by practitioners to induce and guide change. This emphasis on specific techniques is not meant to disregard the importance of nonspecific factors in psychotherapy, such as the therapist's warmth, acceptance, respect, and caring for the client. However, investigations (Woody, 1971) into the interaction between specific techniques and nonspecific relationship variables in therapy have shown that the effective therapist "must be more than a 'nice guy' who can exude prescribed interpersonal conditions—he must have an armamentarium of scientifically derived skills and techniques to supplement his effective interpersonal relations" (p. 8). In a similar vein, Telch (1981) strongly suggested that techniques or interventions are at least as potent as the relationship or the therapist's interpersonal skills. Most practitioners today recognize that both therapeutic skills *and* personality factors are important for effective psychotherapy.

CURRENT TRENDS

The presentation of a variety of child therapy techniques in this book is in accord with several trends in child therapy, namely eclecticism, flexibility, differential therapeutics, specificity, combining techniques, and pragmatism.

The Eclectic Movement

The current psychotherapy Zeitgeist is one of rapprochement of various systems and an integration of therapeutic practices. Clinicians of all orientations are increasingly adopting an eclectic approach to psychotherapy, as opposed to a narrow focus. Eclecticism has already become the modal orientation of clinical psychologists (Norcross, 1986), and many psychotherapy experts predict that its use will increase in popularity in the decade ahead.

Eclecticism can best be defined as the "process of selecting concepts, methods, and strategies from a variety of current theories which work" (Brammer & Shostrom, 1982, p. 35). Eclectics, then, comprise a group of professionals who use multiple procedures and do not restrict themselves to a single theory or method. The very nature of eclecticism—the fact that its components are

1

selected from a variety of sources—mitigates against a tightly knit, integrated conceptual framework.

Flexibility

In addition to integrating knowledge and skills from different theoretical orientations, clinicians are now attempting to flexibly apply such expertise. Often, the methods that seemed so appealing in theory and proved so successful in laboratory studies turn out to be complete disasters when first applied by the clinician. In the real world, there are simply many more uncontrolled and uncontrollable factors. Thus, the child therapist discovers that the bell-and-pad apparatus does not work because children either sleep through the alarm or remove the plug every night before they go to sleep. Only after more extensive preparations or adaptations does the procedure prove successful in such cases. To be successful in practice, then, clinicians are discovering that they need to develop creative problem-solving skills: to become keen observers, flexible thinkers, creative adaptors of methods, and effective collaborators with others, and to become self-confident and persistent in the pursuit of more effective practices.

Differential Therapeutics

The trend toward eclecticism has grown out of the realization that no one therapeutic approach is equally effective with all psychological disorders of children and adolescents. Following a prescriptive approach, eclectic therapists attempt to adapt their intervention to meet the needs of the particular case. The long-term goal of this approach is to refine therapeutic methods so that one can eventually say what technique is best, given certain child, therapist, and situational variables. Physicians operate in this manner when they write an individualized prescription for a physically sick child. Rather than attempting to force a child into one all-purpose therapeutic mold, therapists are now trying to individualize, to fit the remedies or techniques to the needs of the specific child. Ideally, the prescriptive approach will result in maximum therapeutic effectiveness in the briefest possible time period.

Differential therapeutics (Francis, Clarkin, & Perry, 1984) is another name for this prescriptive approach that has come to the forefront as an essential aspect of treatment planning. Under this approach, a treatment modality is selected based upon the latest research evidence about the effectiveness of various therapies for the particular problem, one's clinical experience, and the desires of the client. Flexibility in selecting interventions is the essence of the prescriptive approach.

The skillful application of the prescriptive approach involves the development of expertise in a wide variety of therapeutic methods, such as behavioral, cognitive, and dynamic approaches. This means adopting an eclectic, pluralistic, or generalist position rather than relying on one or two approaches. Concomitant with an increased interest in developing a broad spectrum of clinical skills has been a decreased interest in fostering specialty fields, such as counseling, clinical, and school psychology. Professionals are showing more and more interest in developing clinical skills that cut across disciplines, theories, and specialty fields. Consequently, there seem to be fewer distinctions and more cooperative interplay between the various professional and therapeutic camps.

Specificity

The prescriptive approach has led to a greater interest in the specifics of therapeutic practice; that is, in the concrete application of general principles. Professionals working directly with children want to offer more than a general diagnosis, global approach, or analytical explanation of etiology; they seek to offer a practical approach for alleviating a child's problems. For example, they want to suggest concrete actions when the child has another temper tantrum. It is the techniques, not the theories, that are actually used on children. Study of the effects of psychotherapy is always the study of the effectiveness of techniques.

Technical eclecticism (Woolfolk, 1976) is an approach that draws on all effective techniques without necessarily subscribing to the theories or systems that gave rise to them. The basic assumptions of this type of eclecticism are that (1) all or most psychotherapy approaches are potentially beneficial to some individuals; and (2) therapeutic procedures are capable of being implemented independently of their originating theories.

The state of the art in child therapy has advanced in recent years to the stage that behavior modifiers, nondirective counselors, and others can now give specific how-to's rather than teaching only process or general goals and principles. Of course, child therapy is far from being an exact science. Clinical judgment and skills based on extensive training and experience are still needed to effectively select and apply the available therapeutic tools and to avoid using them in a standardized or mechanical fashion.

Combining Techniques

Another trend in eclectic practice is to combine techniques that complement each other and add to therapeutic power. Comprehensive multimethod interventions are often the rule now, wherein several interventions (e.g., cognitive, behavioral, and psychopharmacological) are combined with the goal of increasing therapeutic effectiveness. Of course, the synthesis of different techniques must be constantly revised to keep abreast of the latest developments and research.

Systematic, multimethod eclecticism attempts to selectively choose interventions based on a comprehensive assessment of the needs of the individual case. Etiologies of a behavior disorder are often multiple, and a thorough assessment is the key to identifying the underlying causes and, thus, the needed interventions. Combining techniques recognizes the complex and interrelated nature of human functioning.

In this regard, psychologist Arnold Lazarus (1976) has developed a therapeutic approach called multimodal therapy. It assumes that lasting therapeutic change can only result if the therapist assesses and, where appropriate, alters seven different modalities (the behavioral, affective, sensate, imagery, and cognitive modalities in the context of interpersonal relationships and, sometimes, in conjunction with medical professionals), in administering drugs and other medical procedures. Rather than stressing a single panacea, core construct, or critical mode of functioning, the multimodal approach asserts that people experience a multitude of specific problems across the various modalities that can best be treated by a variety of specific techniques.

Pragmatism

Pragmatism means a commitment to be guided by what works in practice. This commitment takes precedence over adherence to any theoretical orientation. Openness and flexibility are required (on the part of practitioners) for this orientation, as well as a continued review of outcome research.

The pragmatic therapist tries to ascertain what works best by analyzing empirical research findings and clinical experience rather than by relying on pet theories or the personal appeal of certain techniques. This approach uses the practical consequences of a therapeutic intervention as the standard for evaluating its usefulness.

An empirical orientation is one basic foundation of this approach; that is, basing one's intervention on evidence from experimentation, observation, and measurement, and not on theoretical speculation.

FINAL THOUGHTS

Hopefully, the following chapters will help broaden your therapeutic horizons, assist you in keeping abreast of current trends, and aid you in adapting your clinical interventions to the particular needs of each child.

REFERENCES

Brammer, L.M., & Shostrum, E.L. (1982). *Therapeutic psychology: Fundamentals of counseling and psychotherapy* (4th ed.). Englewood Cliffs, NJ: Prentice-Hall.

Francis, A., Clarkin, J., & Perry, S. (1984). *Differential therapeutics in psychiatry*. New York: Brunner/Mazel.

Lazarus, A. (Ed.) (1976). *Multimodal behavior therapy*. New York: Springer.

Norcross, J.C. (Ed.) (1986). *Handbook of eclectic psychotherapy*. New York: Brunner/Mazel.

Telch, N.J. (1981). The present status of outcome studies: A reply to Frank. *Journal of Consulting and Clinical Psychology, 49*, 472–478.

Woody, R.H. (1971). *Psychobehavioral counseling and therapy*. New York: Appleton-Century-Crofts.

Woolfolk, R.L. (1976). The multimethod model as a framework for decision making in psychotherapy. In A. Lazarus (Ed.), *Multimodal behavior therapy*. New York: Springer.

PART 1

Creative Arts Techniques

Techniques Involving Imaginative Expression
by Children and Adolescents

CHAPTER 1

Storytelling in Child Psychotherapy

STORIES AND STORYTELLING IN NORMAL
CHILD DEVELOPMENT

The age-old and universal appeal that stories and storytelling have for children makes them an undeniably powerful source of dynamically meaningful information as well as an effective medium for therapeutic communication. Since time immemorial, parents, teachers, and other adult caregivers have well understood the special affinity that children have for imaginative stories. The undiminished popularity of fairy tales and legends in modern times attests to the unique place such stories appear to have in children's fantasy lives.

Bettelheim (1977) has discussed the importance of children's stories from the viewpoint of developmental psychology. He believes that fairy tales appeal to children because they address the most difficult problems of growing up, and provide new dimension to children's efforts to resolve the inevitable disappointments, frustrations, and conflicts that are concomitant with psychological maturation. The psychological process whereby mastery over oedipal conflicts, sibling rivalries, and narcissistic disappointments is attained does not evolve out of children's rational understanding of their own unconscious. Rather, children's ruminative fantasies and daydreams are continually reworked and developed in response to demands from both the unconscious and the external environment. Bettelheim believes that fairy tales possess an unequaled value for enriching a child's imagination and providing new solutions to the dilemmas of childhood.

While Bettelheim has focused somewhat narrowly on the psychological meaning of the fairy tale and the contributions it can make to the child's ef-

The author wishes to acknowledge the following publications, in which earlier versions of portions of this chapter have appeared: Autogenic stories and projective drawings: Tools for the clinical assessment and treatment of severely disturbed and at-risk children. *Journal of Independent Social Work*, *1*, 19–32; Using children's autogenic stories to monitor therapeutic progress. *Journal of Child and Adolescent Psychotherapy*, *3*, 285–292; Using children's autogenic stories in dynamic clinical assessment. *Child and Adolescent Social Work Journal*, *2*, 181–190; Stories and storytelling in child psychotherapy. *Psychotherapy*, *21*, 54–62.

forts to master intrapsychic conflicts, others have explored aspects of the child's fantasy life through the medium of children's autogenic stories. Pitcher and Prelinger (1963) elicited stories from 137 children of nursery school and kindergarten age in the most extensive study to date of spontaneously told stories of normal two-to five-year-olds. Since they were primarily interested in stories emerging from the child's own creative imagination, only autogenic material was utilized.

Pitcher and Prelinger examined formal story dimensions, content categories, psychosocial modalities, and dynamic themes and defenses. They found that the implicit story themes of their subjects included such phase-specific issues as abandonment and separation, pregnancy, sibling rivalry, sex, and several other gender-related themes. Pitcher and Prelinger also discovered that it was possible to identify a wide range of defensive adaptations in the children's stories, although the authors encountered some difficulty in differentiating between defensive operations as solutions to conflict and the role of defensive operations in the actual construction of the story. The selection of an animal as the child's "personal representative" in a story may reflect one of several defensive operations (e.g., projection, displacement, or symbolization), inasmuch as it disguises wishes and concerns of the storyteller. Such censorship or distortion, however, does not represent an effort to make either a compromise or a neurotic adaptation. Mechanisms such as denial and undoing comprised this second, more restrictive category of defensive operations.

Ames (1966) has also studied and analyzed the spontaneously told stories of preschoolers. In the Ames study, the stories are treated as objective data, rather than as constitutive examples of fantasy. Ames used 270 stories from an equal number of subjects, half of whom (135) were female and half male. The thrust of the Ames study was in analyzing manifest story content with an eye toward discovering prevalent thematic concerns and their relationship to the child's age and sex.

Violence was found to be a pervasive story theme for both sexes and all age groups. At most ages, however, violence was mentioned more frequently by boys than by girls. In comparing her research with Pitcher and Prelinger's earlier study, Ames concluded that the similarities are fairly pronounced. The two studies are in close agreement as to the particular themes emphasized and the degree of their occurrence. Ames noted that the "four leading themes at every age are chosen from among violence, sibling rivalry, crying, food and eating, personalization of animals, goodness and badness, and castration" (Ibid., pp. 394–395).

Ames's findings differ in two major areas from those of Pitcher and Prelinger: Ames feels that there are quite distinct trends according to both the child's age and sex, while Pitcher and Prelinger have apparently largely ignored these differences. Other comparisons between the two studies are made with greater difficulty since Pitcher and Prelinger did not limit their study to the manifest story content, as Ames did.

THE AUTOGENIC STORY IN PSYCHODIAGNOSTIC ASSESSMENT

Although stories and storytelling hold a time-honored role in therapeutic work with children, the elicitation of an autogenic (stimulus-independent) story for diagnostic purposes has generally not been advocated as a useful diagnostic technique.*

Children's stories have long been recognized as an important source of information about the child's intrapsychic structure, characteristic conflicts, and defensive adaptations. In addition, children's stories can also provide information about disturbing wishes and fantasies, interpersonal relations, the development of the self, and other aspects of the child's character. Several projective instruments, most notably Bellak's Children's Apperception Test (CAT), Blum's Blacky Pictures, and Roberts' Apperception Test, have made use of pictorial stimuli suggesting various themes to elicit data from children in story form (Bellak & Bellak, 1949; Blum, 1950, 1960; McArthur & Roberts, 1982). While the projective story told in response to a pictorial stimulus is a valuable indicator of "the child's structure, defenses, and his dynamic way of reacting to, and handling his problems of growth" (Bellak, 1954, p. 149), it constitutes a very different sort of clinical communication than does the autogenic story.

The autogenic story has been described as the product of an interplay of forces bearing a certain phenomenological similarity to the dream (Pitcher & Prelinger, 1963):

> These forces consist on the one hand of unconscious wishes striving for expression and fulfillment, and on the other of forces aiming to disguise these wishes and to produce a story which is reasonably conforming to standards of realism and social acceptability. Each story thus represents a compromise solution to a conflict. (pp. 216–17)

Richard Gardner's Mutual Storytelling Technique (1971a; 1971b) was specifically designed as a means for eliciting children's autogenic stories in the context of dynamic child treatment. Gardner has asserted that the stories provide children with the opportunity to give expression to their wishes, fears, and defensive adaptations in an unconscious, metaphorical form. The therapist then discerns the dynamic meaning of the story, and responds within the story metaphor with a corrective version. The responding story provides healthier, relatively conflict-free solutions for the maladaptive solutions to conflict that have presumably characterized the (child's) original version of the story. This reciprocal storytelling process, which establishes an intersubjective discourse that can be maintained throughout treatment, is an undeniably powerful therapeutic tool for the clinician. Whether or not it can function with

*An exception to this general rule is Pearson (1984) who nevertheless advocates the use of play materials such as plastic animals or people, pictures, and drawing materials to stimulate story-making in children who seem otherwise unable to compose autogenic stories.

comparable effectiveness during the diagnostic phase, prior to the formation of a therapeutic alliance and the establishment of an intersubjective discourse, is an inherently more ambiguous issue.

Gardner (1971a) strongly suggests that the child's first story told in treatment receive a therapeutic response. He advocates this in spite of his observation that "one may not know enough about a child to ascertain the psychodynamics of his first story and it may be difficult to create a meaningful story in response" (p. 33). Gardner's procedure is to attempt a therapeutic story-response regardless, in the hope that one of the early responding stories communicated to the child will be "on target."

There are several significant drawbacks to Gardner's recommendation that the therapist attempt a therapeutic response to the child's earliest autogenic stories. He has already observed that the responding story in such a case may be tangential to the meaning of the child's story, inasmuch as the therapist may simply not have enough clinical data to construct a meaningful response. A second problem inheres in the use of what is essentially a therapeutic technique for diagnostic purposes. In the assessment phase, one is interested in learning about the nature of the child's conflicts, although not in providing a therapeutic response to them. While a sort of nonspecific treatment frequently begins with the initial diagnostic interview—if only in consequence of the clinician's empathic attention to the child—the distinction between assessment and treatment needs to be maintained. It is only as a result of the clinician's thorough understanding of the various dynamic, structural, genetic, environmental, and other relevant clinical features that useful recommendations can be made and treatment initiated (McDonald, 1965).

Gardner's recommendation becomes even more problematic when two different clinicians are involved in diagnostic assessment and treatment, respectively. Obviously, one would wish to be even warier of injecting questionable therapeutic communications when another clinician will assume responsibility for conducting the treatment. A final objection to Gardner's recommendation rests primarily on the writer's belief that the child's first autogenic story is a unique communication that does not require an immediate response. It seems to be a general observation in diagnostic work with children that certain kinds of clinical material can be very near the surface in early interviews, only to become inaccessible once treatment has been initiated (Lourie & Rieger, 1974). Frequently, children may give expression to their deepest fears and conflicts, albeit in an oblique and metaphorical manner. Such a clinical communication can serve as a sort of narrative statement of the child's nuclear conflict, illustrating the particular issue that is of greatest concern and import to the child. (The first dream recounted in adult psychotherapy has a similar significance, according to Fromm-Reichmann [1950] and others.) When the child makes such a communication in the form of an autogenic story, it can provide the clinician with information that is unsurpassed—and perhaps unequaled—in its richness and meaning.

Eliciting the Autogenic Story

Gardner (1971a) and others have asserted that storytelling is, for most children, a mode of communication that is both natural and stimulating. Although a certain degree of satisfaction in listening to the clinician's responses may be absent when the story is used for diagnostic purposes and there is no responding story, most children are more than pleased to provide an autogenic story at the clinician's request. The clinician must impress upon the child the need to present an entirely original, made-up story. (There is undoubtedly some contamination of the content from exposure to movies and television although this is generally not pronounced.) Gardner's suggestion that the therapist request a beginning, a middle, an end, and a moral can be followed, although most children over six or seven years of age are able to provide reasonably well-integrated stories without specific direction from the clinician. (The moral or lesson can be of special usefulness when story content is ambiguous.) The use of a tape recorder frequently serves to enhance the child's storytelling, and can provide the narcissistic satisfaction of hearing his or her own voice played back. Some children are, however, resistant to the idea of the tape recorder, and may experience its use as intrusive or anxiety-generating. The audio recording of stories and perhaps even the therapist's note-taking may be contraindicated with children who exhibit paranoid ideation or fears.

The story in most instances should not be elicited until midway through the initial diagnostic interview, or until the clinician feels that some measure of rapport with the child has been achieved. For the child who wishes to know the clinician's reasons for requesting a story, a reasonably direct answer an be given. The child can be told that stories, like pictures and other play activities, can help the clinician to better understand the nature of the child's problems and the ways in which the child can be helped in solving them. The self-conscious or shy child may be assisted in starting the story ("Once upon a time, there was a . . . ") although the clinician must be especially careful not to suggest content.

Clinical Examples

The following clinical vignettes illustrate the kinds of information that can be derived from the child's first autogenic story.

CASE 1

David was an attractive nine-year-old who was referred because of escalating physical aggressiveness with peers, poor school performance, pathological lying, and generalized anxiety. David's parents had been divorced less than a year before his mother brought him in for treatment, and his problems greatly intensified shortly after custody was awarded to her. David's father was a seriously disturbed individual who was subject to periods of psychotic depression. Shortly before his parents were divorced, David walked into the garage to discover his father, barely alive, hanging by a necktie from one of the support beams. David's swift response to his father's attempted suicide was credited with saving his life. The psychological sequelae, however, were awesome. Most of David's symptoms, including recurrent nightmares in which this terrifying event was relived over and over again, dated to the circumstances surrounding the father's psychotic breakdown and subsequent hospitalization. David told the following story during the first diagnostic interview:

How Frogs Got Bulgy Eyes

Once upon a time, there was a frog on the sidewalk. There was also a big cat, and the cat saw the frog and started running after him. The little frog managed to escape, but he was taking real big breaths. He wasn't really looking out, and someone came along and stepped on top of him. Then his eyes got all bulgy. Moral: It's a dangerous world.

This is the story of a child who has come to experience life as a recurrent bad dream, and whose self-experience is that of a passive actor who barely has enough time to draw a deep breath between the blows. The frog, which can be understood as David's personal representative in the story, is depicted as vulnerable, although not completely helpless in its dramatic efforts to protect itself from the dangers of a malevolent and cruel environment. In fact, David himself had also managed to survive in spite of the painful traumata he had sustained. While his school performance had deteriorated, he had maintained close friendships with several peers, and continued to participate enthusiastically in after-school activities.

David's strength and partial success in coping with his difficult family situation was probably due in large measure to the essentially positive relationship he had with his mother. Mrs. B. was a sensitive and generous individual who derived a great deal of satisfaction in raising David and his older sister. She was usually able to provide both affection and maternal attention in a way that was well-matched to her children's psychological needs.

Autogenic stories, like dreams, are subject to the principle of multiple determination. It is the rare story that seems to permit of only a single interpretation or explanation. One can, for instance, alternatively understand both the cat and the person who inadvertently steps on the frog as David's personal representatives. The frog could be seen as a father-representative toward whom David feels considerable anger, guilt, and disappointment. The frog's bulging eyes and breathlessness then come to represent the ghastly image of David's father as he hung from the beam gasping for air.

While the "world is a dangerous place" according to David's moral, the greatest dangers appear to lie within. David's repressed guilt and his maladaptive expression of anger made the world feel much more dangerous as he projected his most disturbing wishes and greatest fears outward.

As might be expected, the rage and guilt David experienced over his father's suicide attempt and his parent's divorce, and the ambivalent relationship that had evolved between David and his father, became important foci of his treatment.

CASE 2

Carl, an eleven-year-old boy, was referred by his school psychologist to a family service agency for diagnostic assessment. At the time of referral, his symptoms included secondary encopresis, antisocial behavior, multiple facial tics, aggressive behavior toward his siblings and peers, school refusal, and suicidal threats and gestures. In the first diagnostic interview, Carl told this story:

> Once upon a time, No. 47's house caught on fire. Her kitchen and living room roof collapsed. All the people managed to get out of the house before it burned down. My neighbor, Sue, burnt to a crisp, though. Everyone was sad to see the house go, but there was a good part of it, because the house was rebuilt one month later. Moral: Never play with matches or with a stove.

Carl was a severely troubled borderline child, who presented a disturbing range of severe symptomatology. Relationships between Carl and both of his parents were exceedingly poor, with Carl's provocative behavioral style often engendering punitive and sometimes abusive responses from his mother and his father. Carl was nearly incapable of tolerating even minor frustrations and had very little control over his aggressive impulses. Psychological testing failed to reveal any specific learning disabilities, although IQ testing placed him on the borderline between dull normal and minimally retarded. Carl frequently told his parents how much he hated them, and threatened to kill himself in order to get even with them. On at lease one occasion he was treated and released from a community hospital following a minor self-inflicted knife wound.

Carl's story is especially helpful not because it provides new or revealing information about this child, but because it confirms the clinical intuitions the examiner had already begun to form. The story dramatically illustrates not only the magnitude of this child's hostile-aggressive wishes, but the paucity of solutions available to his ego. Hyperaggressive children frequently make use of the mechanism of undoing ("the house was rebuilt one month later") to defend against their destructive wishes. The story also reflects the degree to which Carl's ego integrity is compromised by the expression of his rage. There is a blurring of primary and secondary process content that is revealed by Carl's remark about his neighbor, Sue, "burning up." (Several days prior to the interview, he had been reprimanded by this neighbor for beating up on a smaller neighborhood child.) Although Carl had been asked to compose a story that had make-believe characters as well as imaginative content, his use of the possessive pronoun and his neighbor's name suggests that fantasy and reality are continuous for him, rather than existing as two distinct modes of experience.

The structural deficiency of Carl's superego becomes quite evident when one examines the moral to his story. The moral, which makes the story sound like a cautionary tale, reflects neither self-awareness nor a truly internalized sense of right and wrong. It speaks to the story in much the same way that a parent speaks to a three-year-old child: "Don't play with matches because you can hurt yourself." The moral has a false ring to it, and is no more than gratuitous offering to the clinician in the interest of making the story somewhat more socially acceptable.

STORIES AND THE STORYTELLING PROCESS IN CHILD PSYCHOTHERAPY

An extensive review of the child psychotherapy literature reveals relatively few instances in which storytelling is used systematically and independently of other psychotherapeutic techniques. Stories and storytelling nevertheless constitute an important activity of the psychodynamically oriented child therapist. Often, stories are elicited by the child therapist in conjunction with other therapeutic activities, such as puppetry (Bender & Woltmann, 1936; Gondor, 1957; Woltmann, 1951, Hawkey, 1951); finger painting (Arlow & Kadis, 1946); drawing and watercolor painting (Rambert, 1949); costume play (Marcus, 1966); and clay modeling (Woltmann, 1950). Doll play has also proved to be a rich source of stories and fantasies (Millar, 1974) and is generally regarded as an indispensable tool for the child therapist.

Most techniques utilized in child psychotherapy are designed to elicit fantasies, however, and not necessarily stories. Exponents of the Kleinian school of play therapy (Klein, 1955) might even object to a technique that required the child to produce an autogenic story on the grounds that it imposes an unnecessary structure on the flow of material from the unconscious, or that it restricts expression to the level of verbal communication. Other writers, such as Gondor (1957), have asserted that the selection of a mode for communicating fantasies should depend entirely on the child's own preference and the therapist's motivation and ingenuity in helping the child discover the best way to express those fantasies. Gondor illustrates this process with a clinical examples of a very withdrawn 10-year-old client who found direct verbal communication most difficult. Gondor soon discovered that her young client was able to express herself much more easily through the medium of a story told to the therapist in weekly installments.

Despite the relative paucity of techniques making prominent use of stories and storytelling reported in the literature before the mid–1960s, the value of stories in both treatment and evaluation was recognized earlier. In 1936, Despert and Potter reported on a study they undertook to evaluate the story as a means of investigating psychiatric problems in children. Their subjects were 22 institutionalized children ranging in age from 4 to 13 years. Although their research was not methodologically rigorous, Despert and Potter offered several conclusions based upon the evidence they amassed:

1. The story is a form of verbalized fantasy through which children may reveal their inner drives and conflicts.
2. A recurring theme is generally found indicating the principal concern or conflict; this may be corroborated with other clinical evidence (e.g., dream material).
3. Anxiety, guilt, wish-fulfillment, and aggressiveness are the primary trends expressed.
4. The use of stories appears to be most valuable when children determine the subject matter of their stories.
5. The story can be used as both a therapeutic and an evaluative device.

Storytelling and story materials sometimes are associated with highly specialized techniques used in the psychotherapeutic treatment of children. One such technique is psychodrama, where children are called upon to utilize sociodramatic play in order to achieve insight into their behavior and to enable them to learn other, more appropriate roles for meeting the challenge of different interpersonal situations (Starr, 1977).

Children's stories sometimes have been reported in the psychotherapeutic literature simply as "clinical material," rather than as a means of illustrating the operation of a specific technique. One example is Liebowitz's study (1972) of a severely disturbed seven-year-old whose use of storytelling was less a means of communication than a way of holding on to the relationship with the therapist. This child's stories had no plot or meaning, and the characters had no apparent relation to each other. Puppets and graphics were used freely to assist in the continuing therapeutic work with this child, and the therapist participated directly in altering or adding material to the child's autogenic stories.

Robertson and Barford (1970) have found therapist-constructed stories useful in therapeutic work with a chronically ill child hospitalized with respiratory failure. The stories were composed on a daily basis and incorporated the child's view of his world as well as the therapeutic team's perspective. The authors believed that the stories read to this child ultimately equipped him to involve himself "both psychologically and physiologically in the world beyond the hospital," culminating in his separation from the respirator and his eventual discharge (1970, p. 106).

Kestenbaum (1985) has also described a storytelling technique that involves the therapist's participation in the storytelling process. The central ingredient in this technique appears to be dictation of these collaborative stories into a "story book." She feels that this process can provide a high degree of continuity between sessions, and also can enable the child to work through neurotic conflicts in a smoother and more synchronous fashion than many other techniques permit.

The Structured Therapeutic Game Method of Child Analytic Therapy and the Mutual Storytelling Technique

Nathan Kritzberg (1975) and Richard Gardner (1971a) have made the most extensive contributions to the modern child psychotherapy literature on the therapeutic uses of stories and storytelling. Each has developed a specialized procedure based on the principles of psychoanalytically oriented child psychotherapy in which storytelling is used in a systematic way and constitutes a prominent focus of the therapy. The similarity between the authors appears to end there, however (see Table 1.1).

Storytelling as a Method in Child Psychotherapy

Kritzberg's use of storytelling is a richly innovative one, although it constitutes a method rather than simply a technique of child psychotherapy. It is envisaged by its author as a means of affectively engaging the child whose "ego resources, character trends, and defenses make him uncomfortable, stilted, and generally unproductive in a free play situation" (Kritzberg, 1971, p. 232). Such children, the author observes, have constricted verbalizations, play, and other activities whose narrow range makes therapeutic utilization exceedingly frustrating and difficult.

TABLE 1.1.   **Major Technical Distinctions between Kritzberg's Structured Therapeutic Game Method of Child Analytic Therapy and Gardner's Mutual Storytelling Technique**

Kritzberg	Gardner
a. Stories are stimulus-dependent; require use of therapeutic game(s).	Stories are stimulus-independent stories composed by child *without* pictorial stimulus
b. Constitutes a "new method of dynamic analytic psychotherapy"	Constitutes one technique in the therapist's armamentarium
c. Utilizes concrete rewards (tokens)	Utilizes no system of extrinsic rewards
d. Sociodramatic play a regular therapeutic maneuver	Sociodramatic play employed as an adjunct
e. Content of therapist's story need not be restricted to themes and conflicts in the child's story	Therapist's story must utilize same thematic content and represent same intrapsychic conflicts as child's story
f. Stories are recorded manually	Stories are recorded both manually and mechanically; playing stories back is an important technical component
g. Analytic inquiry is categorized and highly structured (*referentiation operations*)	Analytic inquiry is used as a general means of clarifying material where meaning is unclear
h. Specific varieties of therapist response (i.e., stories) are described (*suggestive, confrontative, indirect interpretation, reflective, etc.*)	Therapist's responses are not typed or classified
i. Neither the child's nor the therapist's stories necessarily contain a lesson or moral	Both the child's and the therapist's stories conclude with a lesson or moral

Source: Reprinted, with permission of the publisher, from J. Brandell, "Stories and storytelling in child psychotherapy," *Psychotherapy, 21,* (1984):56.

Kritzberg has developed two therapeutic games, TISKIT and TASKIT, to serve as a means of systematically eliciting and therapeutically processing the stories told by his young clients. TASKIT (Tell-A-Story-Kit) is a therapeutic storytelling word game designed for use with children 7 to 13 years of age. TISKIT (Therapeutic Imaginative Storytelling Kit) is similar to TASKIT, but contains iconic objects instead of word cards, and is designed for use with nonliterate children younger than seven years.

The TASKIT game consists of a two-sided board composed of interlocking words selected because, in the author's words, they are "loaded":

> The words . . . can be seen to be derived from clusters of words (1) related to psychosexual levels of development, e.g., oral, anal, phallic, etc., and parallel levels of psychological adaptation. Some are derived from (2) nuclear themes in child rearing and personal development, e.g., separation anxiety, object loss, loss of love, castration anxiety, etc., and others from (3) certain generally interpersonally significant situations, e.g., relation to social authorities, etc., and still others owe their selection and presence in TASKIT to (4) relatedness to significant aspects of the self, ego, superego, and ego-ideal. Finally, others are there from sundry and miscellaneous categories of psychological experience. There is an attempt to cast a net, metaphorically speaking, over the whole psychic domain.
>
> *(Kritzberg, 1975, p. 98)*

Kritzberg suggests that storytelling is a particularly effective means of therapeutic communication for two important reasons. First, he observes that listening to and telling stories is associated early in development with "important emotionally charged bodily activities such as feeding, eliminative actions, and hypnogogic activities" (Ibid., p. 122). Second, various early school activities ("show and tell," "what I got for my birthday," "where I went for vacation," etc.) are also associated with listening to or telling imaginative stories.

Storytelling as a Technique in Child Psychotherapy

Richard Gardner's Mutual Storytelling Technique (MST) (1968, 1969, 1970, 1971a,b, 1972, 1973) was designed by its author as a means of utilizing psychotherapeutic insights in a mode of communication that is both natural and stimulating for children. Gardner has observed that children's stories and fantasy productions generally contain less distortion, obscurity, and misrepresentation than one characteristically encounters in the dreams, free associations, and other productions of the adult client (1971a). The problem occurs when the child therapist attempts to use the information therapeutically. Gardner asserts that it is a relatively unusual child who is interested in arriving at a conscious understanding of the unconscious process, leaving aside the secondary issue of using such insights therapeutically. Since storytelling is a popular mode of communication for most children, Gardner reasoned that it might be effective for the therapist to utilize the same mode of communication for therapeutic messages. The use of stories to convey insights or transmit values is evident in the ancient and universal appeal of fable, myth, and legend (1971a, p. 20).

Gardner has found the MST to be an effective therapeutic device for the treatment of a wide range of emotional disturbances and behavioral disorders. He has advocated its use in the treatment of Oedipal problems (1968), anger-inhibition problems (1971a), problems in the regulation of self-esteem (1971a), superego deficiencies (1971a), situational or reactive disorders (1971a), psychogenic problems secondary to minimal brain dysfunction (1972), school phobia (1971a), posttraumatic neurosis (1970), and learning disorders (1971a). Favorable therapeutic results have been reported for the MST in the pastoral treatment of children hospitalized with both acute and chronic physical problems (Schooley, 1974). The MST has also been adapted for use with preschoolers in a group situation (Eberhardt, 1979).

Unlike Kirtzberg's mother, Gardner's technique is not a therapeutic system as such, and constitutes but "one technique in the therapist's armamentarium" (Gardner, 1971a, p. 939). Its use is not always indicated for every child client, and it may have variable therapeutic effectiveness even for the same client at different points in time.

Other Major Differences Between the Structured Therapeutic Game Method and the Mutual Storytelling Technique

AUTOGENICITY VS. STIMULUS-DEPENDENCE. The Mutual Storytelling Technique utilizes only autogenic (stimulus-independent) stories. Gardner feels this technical requirement is necessary to ensure that the child's stories are not contaminated by other play modalities that might serve to artificially restrict story content or directionality. The therapist using the MST is, however, permitted to help a child get started by providing a brief introduction ("Once upon a time, there was a _____, and this _____ . . ."), as long as the assistance is confined to structural elements in the story and does not suggest content to the child.

Kritzberg describes the storytelling process as an intermediate level of organization somewhere between "the more fluid primary process-like ideational activity of genuine free association, and the more orderly, secondary process thinking of logical, conscious syntactical communication" (1975, p. 92). Because of their proximity to primary thought processes, similar resistances to those activated in adult free association occur. Kritzberg contends that the requirement of autogenicity adds yet another factor to the strength of the collective forces that resist the child's efforts to produce and convey fantasy materials. Therefore, he generally does not utilize autogenic stories in either the TISKIT or the TASKIT methods.

USE OF CONCRETE REWARDS. Kritzberg utilizes concrete rewards (tokens) that are regularly made for word completion, storytelling, replying to analytic inquiry, and participating in sociodramatic play. Since the rewards are not made contingent upon the demonstration of an appropriate behavior, but constitute an integral part of the game and are much more closely associated with the disclosure of meaningful intrapsychic information, Kritzberg does not feel that they serve as reinforcers in the traditional behavioral sense.

Gardner has used the MST in conjunction with several therapeutic games that he has developed, although there exists no built-in reward component in the MST.

SOCIODRAMATIC PLAY.   Sociodramatic play is employed by Kritzberg's method as a regular therapeutic procedure for which the child receives reward tokens. Although Gardner has recently suggested that sociodramatic play may prove valuable in work with certain children, it is viewed as a discretionary rather than an integral feature of the MST.

CONTENT OF THERAPIST'S RESPONDING STORIES.   Kritzberg's Structured Therapeutic Game Method (STGM) requires the participation of both the child and the therapist in the storytelling, but does not restrict the content of the therapist's responding story to the themes and conflicts that emerge in the child's story. The therapist is free to impart any therapeutic message that has general relevance for the child, whether or not it bears on the content of the child's story.

The MST requires that the therapist always use the same thematic material as the child, although the conflicts that are either unresolved or unsuccessfully resolved in the child's story are given healthier, relatively conflict-free solutions in the therapist's tale (Gardner, 1971a).

USE OF MECHANICAL RECORDING DEVICES.   Gardner correctly observes that storytelling rarely has been a separate and distinct therapeutic procedure in child psychotherapy, but usually occurs in relation to other therapeutic modalities, such as puppets, toys, and dolls (1971b). The MST requires only the use of a tape recorder, which Gardner has suggested possesses certain advantages over the more conventional storytelling "props." One advantage lies in the fact that there is a "total absence of stimuli which might restrict the story or channel it into specific directions" (1971b, p. 254). A second major asset is the delight that children almost invariably take in hearing the playback of their own voices, which serves to enhance interest and participation. The playback is a useful therapeutic procedure as well, since it gives the therapist two opportunities to convey each therapeutic story message.

The Kritzberg storytelling method does not require use of a recording device, although the therapist is free to take notes on the child's story.

USE OF ANALYTIC INQUIRY.   The STGM utilizes a systematic form of inquiry called Systematic Analytic Inquiry and Interpretation (SAIAI), which is designed to answer questions concerning affects, feelings, self-and object concepts, motives, consequences of actions, and object relationships in the story. Kritzberg has developed an extensive and complex network of *referentiation operations* to direct the therapist in the poststory SAIAI section. Referentiation operations are defined as questions designed to link symbolic material from the stories to the child's real-life experiences. These formalized referentiation procedures assist the child and the therapist in their mutual endeavor to translate or decode symbolic and metaphorical story elements "into their referent objects (self and others), actions (and events) and affects, etc." (Kritzberg, 1975, pp. 154–156).

Gardner's poststory analytic procedure is considerably less structured and formulaic then the SAIAI referentiation operations. Poststory inquiry is used primarily to clarify unclear elements in the child's story. Gardner (1971a) observes that the child's story, while less difficult to understand than the dream of the adult, is analyzed according to similar principles, a long-accepted practice of child psychotherapy and psychoanalysis. An effort is made initially to determine which figure or figures represent the child and which stand for other people in the child's environment. It is also suggested that two or more figures (the "good girl" and the "bad girl," for example) may represent various aspects of the same individual's personality.

THERAPIST-RESPONDING STORIES.   The function of the therapist's story also receives an exhaustive exposition in Kritzberg's book (1975). Four major types of therapist stories are described (*preservative* or *reflective* stories, *indirect interpretation* stories, *suggestive* stories, and *confrontative* stories) together with specific indications for their use.

Preservative or reflective stories
are useful when referentiation and interpretation are contraindicated (or simply unproductive), and the theme of the child's story is relatively clear and can therefore be replicated (Ibid., p. 230). The therapist's object in telling such stories is to enhance the unfolding of therapeutic interaction and the development of therapeutic rapport.

Indirect interpretation stories
are used to convey the therapist's understanding and interpretation of material from the child's unconscious. The interpretations are disguised in greater or lesser degree according to the therapist's judgment as to the usefulness of open interpretation. There are two specialized variants of the indirect interpretation story, referred to respectively as the *indirect transference interpretation* story and the *counter-resistance* story.

Suggestive stories
are the metaphoric equivalents of the important exhortations and reassurances that the therapist is occasionally called upon to make: "keep pushing on ahead," "don't be discouraged," "beginnings are always difficult," "talking is helpful," "explore further," and so on. Kritzberg imputes an important facilitating function to the suggestive story, but simultaneously cautions against its misuse (Ibid., pp. 232–239).

The confrontative story

is somewhat less frequently used by therapists due to its extra-analytic nature. It is described as a way of actively introducing an important part of the child's life or experience ("especially impending significant events"), which for one reason or another the child may have been unwilling or unable to introduce in the story (Ibid., pp. 263–264).

Several special varieties of therapeutic response are also described. These include the *therapist's role definition* story and the *beginning* story. These stories are both primarily informational or instructional, and can be employed to begin a story sequence as well as to continue a sequence begun by the child.

While the responding stories Gardner uses to illustrate his storytelling technique sometimes appear to have been derived from a typology similar to Kritzberg's, there is no effort either to formally classify them or to provide any set of guidelines for their use.

THE LESSON OR MORAL.   In the MST, the child is asked to tell a story that contains an introduction, a middle, an end, and a moral (Gardner, 1971a). While the general feeling or tone of the story, where it takes place, and the child's nonverbal cues and emotional reactions while telling it all contribute to the therapist's dynamic understanding of the story, the moral or lesson also serves an important function. Gardner believes that the moral or lesson the child provides frequently can help to narrow the therapist's focus and enable selection of the theme "most pertinent for the child at that particular time" (Ibid., p. 29). The therapist's use of lessons or morals in the responding stories is equally valuable, for it provides the therapist with an additional opportunity to demonstrate the mechanisms through which conflicts are successfully and adaptively resolved. The STGM requires neither the child nor the therapist to conclude their story with a lesson or moral.

The basic mutual storytelling process described above is illustrated in the clinical case material that follows.

CASE ILLUSTRATION

Sean was a coresident of a group home at the time treatment began. He was eleven years old, and had spent nearly six of those years being shuffled from one foster or group home to another. He was a bright child with a fanciful imagination, but already demonstrated a moderate degree of emotional disturbance. Sean suffered mild to marked impairments in his interpersonal relatedness; had great difficulty in controlling his temper, which resulted in frequent rageful outbursts against the other children and staff members at the group home; exhibited moderate to marked mood lability and behavioral unpredictability with a corresponding difficulty in modulation of affect; and was impulsive. In addition, there were marked developmental lags and other deviations and abnormalities in the history that, in combination with the clinical signs and symptoms, strongly suggested a nascent borderline personality organization. When Sean was five, his natural parents relinquished custody in order to have him placed in a foster care home. It is probably an understatement to describe the nature of his relations with both parents—particularly his mother—as "malignant" by that time. Sean was completely out of control, destroying furniture and urinating at will on the carpet and walls. His hatred was, however, equal in intensity to that of his parents, who urgently requested foster placement in the interest of their survival as well as his. It was probably of no small import that Sean was born with pyloric stenosis, which went undiagnosed for at least six to eight weeks. His mother's frustration in feeding him and her deep sense of maternal inadequacy and imcompetence were most certainly mirrored in the disturbed symbiosis that followed. Perhaps it is not really an exaggeration to suggest that this early and painful experience was retained as a sort of template that was repeatedly and unconsciously applied to later experiences. Sean, on the other hand, was a difficult baby whose physical problems and temperament brought few gratifications to his parents.

The story that appears below was told early in the middle phase of treatment. While this story was thematically centered around an abandonment/rejection motif, as were many of Sean's stories and productions, it was also quite directly linked with a specific environmental event. During the several weeks preceding the time that this story was told, relations between the "foster" parents and the rest of the staff at Sean's group home had deteriorated to such a degree that the couple no longer attended staff meetings or functions. In addition, they generally absented themselves from meals at the house as soon as the food was prepared.

Amidst a significant amount of controversy over their inability and unwillingness to meet certain requirements that other staff members held to be essential in the treatment of children in the home, the couple announced their decision to resign. With such strong negative feelings against the couple, no thought was given to preparations for the customary farewell dinner. Given the overall staff sentiment, such an endeavor—had it been undertaken—would perhaps have more closely approximated a gesture of "good riddance."

Consequently, it came as a bit of a surprise that a small farewell party had been planned and executed by the children on the evening prior to the couple's departure.

The story that follows was told by Sean in a therapy session held the evening before the departure of his treatment parents:

CHILD: Once upon a time, a long, long time ago . . . many virtues [sic] of centuries ago . . . I mean just far, far back . . . way, way, way, way, back . . . actually, it's about a couple days ago (laughter) . . . there lived a [pause] small king and his wife, the queen. They lived in England. They were living happily . . . you know . . . they lived happily ever after, meaning as . . . when they first became King and Queen, they were completely new to the . . . you could say occupation, vocation . . . job, or their specialty, in a way . . . or their dream. Well, anyways these people, they had seen a lot of . . . [has difficulty pronouncing the word "harsh"] weird things . . . happen to people . . . from other kings . . . kings would get . . . lots of people after one person . . . or, they'd get a dragon—you know, "dragon spirits," as they say—after a person, and you know, just incredibly, that really happened.

They became King and Queen and they set the world at peace and they didn't make taxes or anything . . . and about four years after that, when the King resigned—you know, he'd turned sixty . . . eight . . . he was sixty-five when he . . . no, sixty-four when he first started and he turned sixty-eight and he decided it was time to quit. So the people gave off a big surprise party. The King and Queen and everybody in the castle—or just the King and Queen—didn't know about this party. The whole country came to the castle and they wished the King good luck on his future. They made a super giant cake. They made two, four, six of them about the size of a room. And everybody got a piece. And everybody got some wine or milk, or cherry juice, or whatever they please [pause].

Well, the King and Queen were really surprised and from that day on, they really didn't brag about being the fairest or anything else.

So, from that day on, the King and the Queen were not the King and the Queen. They were man and wife, and the people liked them very much [admonishes the therapist to take notes more rapidly]. They were known well after that.

The King and the Queen coincidentally died on the same day . . . meaning as the Queen died the same day as the King, and the King died the same day as the Queen, or reverse otherwise. And they died, and everybody who was at the party, or everybody who lived in the country came to that party . . . er . . . that came to the funeral . . . and the people were really upset. Some of the people cried, some of the people were sad, but they didn't think it was really worth cryin'. I mean, you know, they were really sad, but they didn't want to cry, and other people . . . felt that . . . you know, they were kind of glad that the King died, and those were the people with the negative side. Those were the people that were hated, and they took it out on the King.

So from then on, the King and the Queen cherished [sic] off in another world so far, far away. I mean, just billions and billions and quadrillions of miles away. I mean, centuries of miles away . . . thousands and billions, etc. . . . zillions of miles. I mean, really actually it was just next door. The end.

Moral: Do unto others as . . . you would expect them to do unto you.

THERAPIST: Once upon a time, there lived a King and his wife, who was the Queen. They lived in a far-off land, and this story takes place a long time ago.

Well, anyway, this King and Queen began their reign when they were both pretty old, and the kingdom that they reigned in was having a lot of problems. There were all kinds of things that were going wrong with their subjects—with the people who lived in the Kingdom—and they needed good and fair rulers, both a King and a Queen . . . they needed fair people to come and to help them. When the King and the Queen came, they had very good intentions, and they wanted very much to help the people in the kingdom as best they could.

And, at the beginning, things were really well. They had some very high ideas of what they wanted to do. They had goals, kind of high goals of what they wanted to achieve with the people in their kingdom. At the beginning of their reign, when they first started to rule, everything went really well, and people were happy, in general.

But after a while, they started to do . . . sort of strange things, and they became unpopular with not only their subjects in the Kingdom, but also with what we call the parliament, other people who . . . made the laws and helped the King and Queen. The King and Queen were both pretty old, they were in their sixties. Finally, all the problems that they were having sort of came to a head, and the conflict became very open between the parliament and the King and Queen, and between the King and Queen and the subjects they ruled over. The King and Queen finally announced that they would have to leave; that they couldn't rule anymore, they didn't feel that they were being effective. . . . They didn't want to rule anymore, either. And so, they made the announcement to the people and to the parliament, and everybody reacted a little bit differently. Some people were very . . . well, first they felt really rejected and hurt, and then they became angry. Some people just became really sad and depressed and . . . some of them cried, and some of them couldn't cry. They couldn't bring themselves to cry because it hurt so much. And some of the people just felt that . . . well, they'd seen so many kings and queens that it really didn't even matter. They couldn't care less, because there'd be another set of rulers in a little while, and . . . so, there was a whole range of feelings about the King and Queen leaving.

Despite a lot of the . . . negative feelings that people had about the King and Queen leaving, they decided to have a surprise party in the castle . . . right before the King and Queen left the kingdom. And the subjects brought all kinds of exotic and delicious foods from far-away lands, and they brought all kinds of drinks . . . of every variety: liquor, wines, and beer; juices and milk; and all kinds of things that people like to drink. And, they decided that even though they felt bad and were angry—many of them—that the King and Queen were leaving, that they'd have a party to show that they had appreciated the little period of time that the King and Queen had ruled over them.

So the King and Queen left. And at about the time they left, some of the people in the kingdom who really hadn't gotten over a lot of their feelings kind of wished in the backs of their minds that the King and Queen would die, and they had fantasies about the King and Queen dying, that somehow making up for the fact that they . . . in a way, that they deserted their subjects. They left, and they hadn't finished their job. But, after a time, a lot of the subjects felt different, and they realized that those feelings—wishing that the King and Queen were dead—were pretty normal feelings to have at the time . . . that really, the King and Queen hadn't done what they said they would. They hadn't been fair and just rulers in some circumstances, and in a lot of ways, they deserved to have the hatred and the anger of their people.

So, they may or may not have lived happily ever after. No on really knows because they left the kingdom, and they went far away, and they came back to visit very infrequently, so no one had much contact with them.

I guess the moral of my story is that sometimes even kings and queens aren't necessarily fair and just rulers, and kings and queens have problems, too, that oftentimes they can't solve themselves.

And, there's a second moral, too, which is that—it concerns their subjects—under certain conditions, sometimes people can feel an uncontrollable anger and hatred, and think things like, "I wish the King was dead," or, "I wish the King and Queen were dead because they left us and rejected us," and in some ways, that feeling is justified, but part of growing up is learning to accept that . . . kings and queens have problems, also . . . just like subjects do. I guess that's the end.

Analysis. Sean's story is about object loss, and dramatically illustrates the whole character of the separation reaction. Separation is the most basic of all anxiety-generating situations, and accounts for a number of the different emotional responses evinced in the story.

The separation is portrayed in a fairly dramatic way, for several reasons. Ultimately, a separation may be seen as a death, although this point of view corresponds more closely to the sort of reaction an infant or a very young child might have (i.e., *all* separations from one's parents are permanent). The death of the King and Queen in the story is most likely an overdetermined element, in that it also represents defensive hostility ("If you leave me, then I hope you die.").

One must also bear in mind when interpreting these stories that they are largely egotistical. This becomes apparent when one examines, for example, the reactions that the people in the first story have to the "coincidental" death of the King and the Queen.

Some of the people cried, some of the people were sad, but they didn't think it was worth crying . . . they didn't want to cry, and other people . . . felt that . . . they were kind of glad that the King died, and those were the people with the negative side. Those were the people that were hated, and they took it out on the King. . . .

Such a range of feelings and emotional responses might just as easily be attributed to the storyteller himself.

In an effort to ward off both the anxiety and the ensuing depression, mechanisms of defense such as projection, rationalization, and distantiation are employed. The storyteller also attempts to convince the therapist that he bears no real or imaginary responsibilities for the deaths of the King and Queen: It is, instead, the "people with the negative side" who are responsible for such monstrous thoughts. The storyteller's use of the dimensions of time and distance is also very interesting. It is almost as if he were saying, "I'm trying as best I can to defend against the pain of yet another separation by distancing myself. I wish this *had* happened millions of years ago, in a faraway land, and to someone else."

It is also worth noting that the moral—here seen as a reworking of the Law of Talion, the origins of which are to be found in the Mosaic code—has the effect of undoing some of the feelings represented earlier. In view of the storyteller's anger toward the King and Queen, he might just as well have concluded with "an eye for an eye, a tooth for a tooth."

Although the group response to the departure of the treatment parents was overtly represented in Sean's story, there was an equally clear intra-individual attempt to compensate for yet another loss in this child's life. Because Sean was unable to openly discuss his feelings about the crisis in the group home, the projective nature of the storytelling technique permitted him a relatively safe way of giving expression to these feelings.

The therapist's story is fairly transparent, and simply attempts to convey two related messages extracted from the content of the child's story. The first is that although as children we sometimes think of adults as having the wisdom to solve even the most difficult problems, this certainly cannot always be the case. The second is that although it is sometimes painful, part of growing up is learning to accept separations and losses with equanimity, and to accept the shortcomings of others with compassionate understanding.

Sean's stories exhibited a clear progression from almost exclusive reliance on unsuccessful mechanisms for conflict resolution early in treatment, to prominent use of adaptive, relatively conflict-free solutions as the treatment neared termination. These changes appeared to be primarily the result of the child's successful incorporation of the therapist's story-messages, but may also have reflected a more generalized treatment effect.

STORY-DRAWINGS AND OTHER VARIATIONS ON THE STORYTELLING PROCESS

Although most children—including those who are initially highly resistant and certain children with nascent or manifest characterological disturbances—can frequently participate in autogenic storytelling, some children find this to be too difficult and anxiety-provoking. For such children, it is possible to elicit stories if the storytelling is not completely autogenous in nature, without resorting to the highly structured and formulaic method of treatment (STGM-CAP) described above. This may be accomplished through a combination of Winnicott's (1971) *squiggle technique* (essentially a drawing completion game) and imaginative storytelling. (See Claman, 1980, and Gabel, 1984, for descriptions of similar therapeutic procedures.) The squiggle technique calls for the clinician and the child to take turns drawing squiggly lines and then completing the other person's drawing. The squiggle is made with the eyes closed, although the picture is always completed by the other subject with open eyes. Winnicott characteristically used the squiggle content as a springboard for analytic investigation, and did not always work within the metaphor of the drawing in the discussions that followed. Neither did he ask the child to use the picture in composing an original story, although some of his subjects did this spontaneously. The child, however, may be asked to make up a story about the picture just created with the ground rules described above: The story must be original, the characters must be imaginary, and there must be a beginning, some development of the story, and an ending.

CASE ILLUSTRATION 1

The squiggle and accompanying story in this example are derived from an early interview with a six-year-old boy named Danny. Danny was referred for evaluation and treatment following a report of physical abuse made against his father. Although there was a long history of violent marital arguments and psychological abuse of both Danny and his younger sister by their father, neither child had ever been seen for assessment or treatment. Danny had sustained several facial cuts and a black eye when his father pushed him down against the bathtub, and still had discoloration around his eye and scars from the facial lacerations when he arrived for the initial interview. Danny was slow to warm up, and participated in the first couple of sessions in a somewhat suspicious and rather tentative way. He refused to tell a story, and didn't seem particularly interested in other play modalities, either. After a couple of frustrating sessions with Danny, the examiner managed to interest him in the squiggle game, although the child's enthusiasm was of a less-than-optimal degree.

The squiggle portion of the drawing (Figure 1.1) was the examiner's; Danny turned it into a snail (Figure 1.2). He then told the following story:

> Once upon a time, there was a snail running through the grass. Then he stopped at a hole. He looked inside of it and saw nothing but black dark. Then, "Boo!" He fell into the hole. Then a little kitten came and got him out, and ate him.

This story proved to be a very important early communication for Danny. One can recognize several important elements in it almost immediately. It is told with a depressed and hopeless tone, and describes the self-experience of

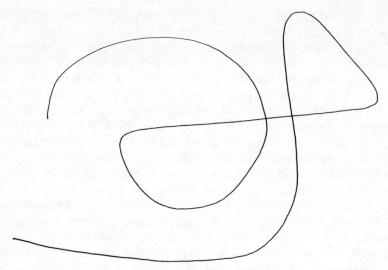

Figure 1.1. Examiner's squiggle.
Reprinted with permission from Brandell, J.R. (1987). Autogenic stories and projective drawings:
Tools for the clinical assessment and treatment of severely disturbed and at-risk children. *Journal
of Independent Social Work, 1*,(2), 24.

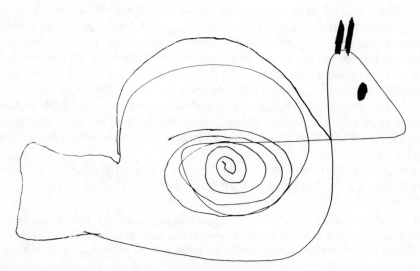

Figure 1.2. Danny's snail drawing from the examiner's squiggle.
Reprinted with permission from Brandell, J.R. (1987). Autogenic stories and projective drawings:
Tools for the clinical assessment and treatment of severely disturbed and at-risk children. *Journal
of Independent Social Work, 1*(2), 25.

a child who has come to regard the world as a place filled with dangers and malevolent forces which threaten both his psychological and physical integrity. He is finally at the mercy of a little kitten, who easily pulls him out of the hole into which he has fallen, and eats him whole. The choice of the snail as a personal representative, which is evidently not an unusual one for children who have been traumatized, speaks both to his smallness and fragility and to a prominent defensive mode: psychic withdrawal. The fear of being devoured, which can be understood as Danny's profound fear of his own father's aggression and his helplessness in the face of it, has another dynamic meaning. The kitten is an overdetermined representative, in that it can also give expression to Danny's own unexpressed rage toward both his mother and his father, and perhaps even of his father toward his mother.

Danny has made a number of subsequent squiggle stories since this early production, although he is still resistant to producing an autogenic story in the manner previously illustrated. He is significantly less anxious and depressed, and at present continues to make clinical progress despite persistent uncertainties and environmental deficits in his family life. (His father is on probationary status, and Danny no longer has any contact with him.)

CASE ILLUSTRATION 2

Although Gardner has not specifically addressed the treatment of children with borderline personality disorders in his Mutual Storytelling Technique, it can be used meaningfully with some accommodations in work with this increasingly large clinical population.

The following illustration involved a ten-year-old boy named Harry.

Harry exhibited markedly disturbed interpersonal relatedness, paniclike anxiety and occasional paranoid ideation, moderate impulsivity, tendency toward regressive behavior, aggressive outbursts and primitive behavioral displays (e.g., kicking, biting, and urinating), and frequent shifts of mood. He also lied often, and tended to localize all responsibility and conflicts outside of himself. Harry's mother was a severely disturbed individual, who had been hospitalized several times during acute depressive episodes. She had recently been diagnosed as borderline, and was a very unstable and highly dependent person. She was given to protracted outbursts of rage, during which she remained almost completely refractory to the efforts of all around her to calm and soothe her. Harry's father was a good deal more stable and dependable, although sometimes very ineffectual in dealing with Harry's mother. Harry's involvement with him was much healthier, and this relationship became extremely important during those times when his mother was enraged, withdrawn, or hysterical.

In working with the borderline child, the therapist is faced with myriad clinical and transferential difficulties not characteristically encountered in work with higher-functioning children. Such children are frequently found to exhibit significant impairments in reality testing and markedly poor judgment;

massive shifts in the level of ego organization in response to anxiety, which is not well-tolerated; and, generally speaking, considerable internal disorganization that is the result both of structural deficiencies and of pathogenic and disorganized environments. Harry was an unattractive, undersized child with poor coordination, who wore thick corrective lenses with a strap so as not to lose them. He spoke with a nasal voice, and often peppered his pressured speech with an inappropriate laugh and smile, which he used a little like punctuation at the end of a sentence or phrase. He had no close friends, and his primitivity, at the levels of both affect and ideation, made him less than desirable to work with initially.

A story Harry told early in treatment appears below, along with the therapist's responding story:

CHILD: Once upon a time there was a man who was an explorer and had a ship. He lived on an island, but no one lived there with him. He was stranded. (No one was able to help him get home.) He found a hole in the earth that someone else had dug. There was a genie down there, whom he saw. The genie was way, way, way down there. He was beyond the lava and all of the other rocks. The genie said he couldn't come up because of the oxygen and hydrogen in the air, but he did have assistant genies who also had magical powers. All 10 of the assistant genies helped the man. All the man had to do was steer the boat. The machine-made men, who were made by the assistant genies, did *everything else*. The genies then went back into the hole. The man, who was in his late twenties, went back and found his parents in Pleasantville, and lived with them forever after.

    Moral: Never go out too far all alone when you explore.

    Moral: Never go out by yourself in a far, far away place.

THERAPIST: Once upon a time there was a explorer who had gone far away from home and got stranded on a desert isle. He was very, very upset and very sad because he feared he would never see his parents again. He discovered a hole, went down and found it was very warm and dark, and there was a genie who spoke to him and made him feel much better. He asked the genie if there were assistant genies who could help him get what he needed in order to find his way back to his parents, but the genie said that both he and his assistants were powerless outside of the hole that they lived in. The man finally had to leave the hole, in search for others to help him fix his ship. He was successful, and he went back to Pleasantville, found his parents, and wanted to live with them forever. However, he also wanted to be an explorer, and decided finally to go out again with another person he had met who also liked to explore.

    Moral: It's dangerous to be an explorer only if you take unnecessary chances. As long as you follow the rules, you can explore anywhere.

    Moral: There are no magical solutions to problems. Solving problems requires hard work.

Analysis. Harry has represented himself in this story as the explorer who has become stranded on an island. Harry frequently told stories in which the protagonist (his personal representative) would venture too far and either be unable to return, or face dangers that were invariably of a life-threatening sort. It may be possible to understand such stories as a metaphorical equivalent for the earliest, affectively charged experiences of exploration, that is, what Mahler has termed *practicing*, or the early attempts to move beyond the orbit of the symbiotic relationship. In the case of normal development, the practicing period gives way to *rapprochement* and to the *rapprochement crisis*, and through a difficult and laborious process, finally to the consolidation of self-identity and the attainment of object-constancy. In the case of a child such as Harry, for reasons which in and of themselves could be the topic of a lengthy presentation, neither object-constancy nor a consolidated sense of self has been achieved. Harry is metaphorically suspended in the rapprochement crisis, making efforts to move beyond the pathological relationship with his mother, but doing so without the intrapsychic structure to sustain his forays out into the world. In Harry's story, the therapist is depicted in a magical and idealized manner as the genie whose assistants rescue the stranded explorer and send him back home. It may further illuminate the significance of Harry's story to learn that for several weeks (Harry was in twice-weekly psychotherapy) Harry had been representing the therapist in his stories as a genie who magically solved everyone's problems. In his therapeutic responses to these stories, the therapist had emphasized the limitations of the genie's magic. Harry's compromise solution here is to acknowledge the genie's limitations (he can't go above ground) and to simply imbue the 10 assistants with the same magical and idealized transference features that had previously been associated with the genie (hardly a more adaptive resolution to the conflicts represented in the story). The solution presented at the conclusion of the story is a categorically maladaptive one, reflecting Harry's tendency toward massive regression in order to avoid paniclike anxiety.

In the responding story, the therapist first made an effort to introduce the affect which is frequently isolated or otherwise primitively defended against in many borderline children. There is an effort to identify and discuss the explorer's sadness over becoming lost and his fear that he might never see his parents again. The therapist's explorer is frightened, although Harry's explorer never talked about feeling anything. The responding story also uses the symbolism of the cave, highlighting it as a retreat from the outer world where he could come to feel better, but also emphasizing the limitations of both the genie and the genie's assistants. One finally must seek help and work on problems; there is no magic, nor is there someone who can do the work for you. The therapist also tried to capture Harry's struggle over his wish to explore and his fear of annihilation. In the "corrective" version of the story, the wish to explore is more powerful than the regressive retreat, and there is also the intimation that one doesn't always have to explore alone; the explorer in the responding story finds a partner with whom to sail his ship.

RESEARCH ON THE THERAPEUTIC USE OF CHILDREN'S STORIES

Research in the child psychotherapy field has tended to focus upon the evaluation of treatment effectiveness or therapeutic outcome, where treatment tends to be somewhat globally defined. There has been relatively little interest among researchers in investigating therapeutic process in clinical work with children. This seems to be true in spite of the fact that such investigations are the only reliable method of understanding how the various techniques of child psychotherapy actually work—indeed, *if* they work.

Children's stories are currently used in assessment and in treatment, generally in conjunction with other diagnostic instruments and play modalities. Although the predictive validity and reliability of autogenic stories used in psychodiagnostic work remains unconfirmed (Pearson, 1984), there has been some research on the therapeutic use of children's autogenic stories.

Despert and Potter (1936), as described earlier, first advocated the imaginative story as a means of assessing the child's progress in treatment a half-century ago. Gardner (1971a) also has suggested that the child's progress in psychotherapy can be monitored impressionistically by carefully noting whether the child's solutions to conflict become more adaptive and are used more often over the course of treatment. Others (Pitcher and Prelinger, 1963) observe that the autogenic story can be readily used to assess the level of defensive operations, the extent of object-relatedness, and the type of prevalent dynamic themes and defenses, although they do not actually advocate using the story told in treatment as an evaluative instrument per se.

Impressionistic data (Gardner, 1971a; 1973) and clinical wisdom suggest that as children are able to expand their repertoire of adaptive solutions to conflict, their projective stories will provide the clinician with confirmation of therapeutic progress. The author tested this formulation recently in a single-case exploratory study that also utilized several instruments for analyzing patient process variables. (See Brandell, 1986, for a more complete discussion of this investigation.)

The subject in this research was a ten-year-old boy named John, who had been diagnosed as suffering from an oppositional disorder. John was in treatment for slightly less than three months, during which time he told 20 stories. Some of his stories reflected preoccupation with separation-individuation issues; others portrayed Oedipal ambitions and conflicts, and sibling rivalries; still others gave expression to John's resistance to treatment, or to his transference fantasies about the therapist. John's stories exhibited a wide range of content and several different focal conflicts. Despite these differences, however, each of the stories also revealed thematic concern with the problem of expressing anger.

Accordingly, outwardly directed hostility was selected as a major patient process variable, and was measured in John's stories by the Gottschalk-Gleser Hostility Directed Outward Scale (Gottschalk & Gleser, 1969; Gottschalk, Gleser & Winget, 1969). For the purpose of analysis, the child's treatment was then broken down into three phases representing the beginning, middle, and end of treatment. Outwardly directed hostility was then measured for each session and averaged according to the phase of treatment. Although there were substantial variations in the hostility-directed outward scores within all three of the treatment phases, there did appear to be a downward trend in the expression of outwardly directed hostility across the three treatment phases. This change was also noted on a more impressionistic level by the child's psychotherapist (see Figure 1.3).

A second instrument, the Therapist Influence Scale, was an original instrument developed specifically to determine the influence of the therapist regarding the child's selection of adaptive story elements. Operationally, this meant that the two raters were provided with transcribed copies of both the child's and the therapist's stories in their original (i.e., chronological) order. They were then asked to decide which of the child's stories displayed evidence of adaptive elements which appeared in homologous but not identical form in earlier responding stories of the therapist. For example, the therapist may have suggested in a responding story told early in treatment that "angry thoughts can't harm." Several sessions later, the child may have demonstrated that he understood this therapeutic message by resolving a story situation similar to that in his earlier story, perhaps by concluding that "just wishing somebody dead can't really make it happen." The child's moral was quite similar, but not identical, to the earlier version presented by the therapist. If the moral or lesson was either inappropriate to the content of the child's story or appeared to be an exact replication of the earlier moral or lesson of the therapist's, the story was not considered to have been genuinely adaptive. The raters agreed that there was increasing evidence of the therapist's corrective influence in John's selection of story adaptations, as well as evidence of change in a wide range of symptom and behavior areas.

In addition, two pre/posttest measures, The Parent's Behavior Check List (Embry, Leavitt, & Budd, 1975) and the Children's Psychiatric Rating Scale (DHEW, 1973) were used in the study. The Parents Behavior Check List, a 45-item inventory designed to assess the frequency and severity of problem behaviors, was administered to John's parents both prior to the beginning and at the termination of their son's treatment. Visual comparison of pretest and posttest scores in items where any change was noted revealed improvement in 18 of 21 areas (see Figure 1.4).

The Children's Psychiatric Rating Scale was used to assess the degree of clinically measurable psychopathology both before and after treatment. It was administered by a separate examiner who was not involved in the child's treatment. Inspection of pretest and posttest scores once again reveals improvement in a wide spectrum of symptom areas (see Figure 1.5).

These findings tended to serve as confirmatory evidence that the quantitative and impressionistic changes observed in John's stories accurately reflected his overall adjustment. In addition, John's parents reported a significant attenuation in virtually all of the original symptomatology at the conclusion of

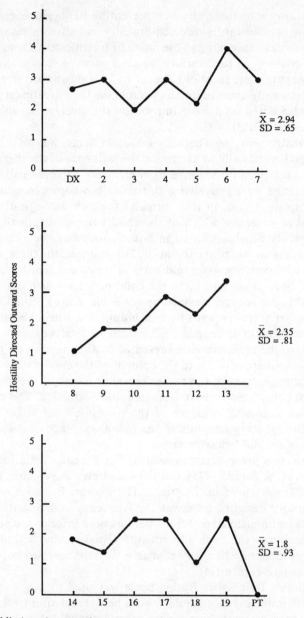

Figure 1.3. Child's (gross) autogenic story scores.
Reprinted with permission from Brandell, J.R. (1986). Using Children's Autogenic Stories to Assess Therapeutic Progress. *Journal of Child and Adolescent Psychotherapy, 4*(3), 228.

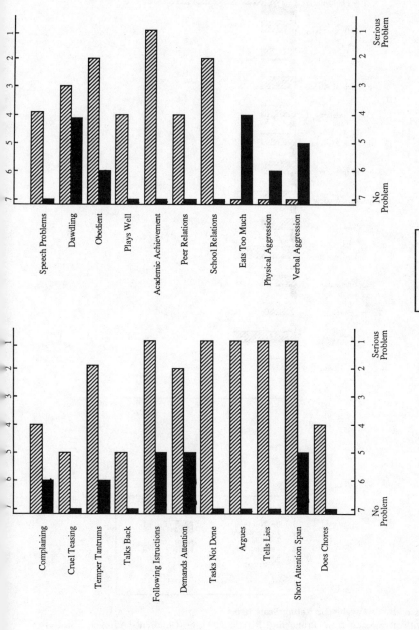

Figure 1.4. Parent's Behavior Check List items.
Reprinted with permission from Brandell, J.R. (1986). Using Children's Autogenic Stories to Assess Therapeutic Progress. *Journal of Child and Adolescent Psychotherapy, 4*(3), 288.

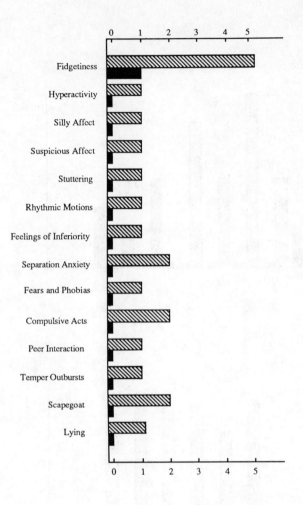

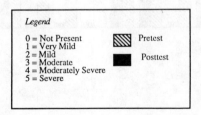

Figure 1.5. Children's Psychiatric Rating Scale Items.
Reprinted with permission from Brandell, J.R. (1986). Using Children's Autogenic Stories to Assess Therapeutic Progress. *Journal of Child and Adolescent Psychotherapy, 4*(3), 288.

their son's treatment. Informal follow-up several months later revealed that John was continuing to make a good adjustment both at school and at home. Some oppositional trends in John's personality did persist in a milder form, but his parents felt that these trends were primarily adaptive and age-appropriate.

In effect, the stories told by this subject proved to be fairly reliable indicators of the magnitude of his hostile-aggressive feelings, as well as of the extent to which he was able to successfully incorporate the therapist's corrective responses to his less successful efforts at conflict resolution. Although one must be careful in generalizing from a single case, a tentative conclusion of this investigation is that children's autogenic stories appear to provide the therapist with valuable impressionistic data about the child's progress in treatment that can be confirmed through the use of more quantitative procedures.

Clearly, much research remains to be conducted on the psychodiagnostic and psychotherapeutic uses of children's stories, as indeed, there remains to be done in the child psychotherapy field as a whole. With the resurgence of interest in the process-research arena, perhaps neglected areas such as autogenic stories and the contribution they make to our understanding of children as well as to our efforts to treat them, will finally receive the attention they deserve.

CONCLUSION

Stories and storytelling activities are a time-honored tradition in both psychodiagnostic and psychotherapeutic work with children. Although this is partially true because of the valuable contribution stories make to the clinician's understanding of young patients, it is equally a function of the interest and enthusiasm that children almost universally exhibit for stories and storytelling, both inside and outside of treatment.

In this chapter, various means by which stories can be utilized in child treatment were explored, including storytelling as a treatment method (Kritzberg's Structured Therapeutic Game Method of Child Analytic Therapy); storytelling as a treatment technique (Gardner's Mutual Storytelling Technique); autogenic stories as a diagnostic tool; story-drawings (squiggle-story productions); and the use of reciprocal storytelling in work with the clinically borderline child. A research investigation was also reviewed that examined children's autogenic stories as a means through which progress in dynamic child treatment can be monitored.

REFERENCES

Ames, L. (1966). Children's stories. *Genetic psychology monographs, 73,* 336–396.

Arlow, J., & Kadis, A. (1946). Finger painting in the psychology of children. *American Journal of Orthopsychiatry, 16*, 134–146.

Bellak, L., & Bellak, S. (1949). *Children's apperception test*. New York: C.P.S. Co.

Bellak, L. (1954). *The TAT and CAT in clinical use*. New York: Grune and Stratton.

Bender, L., & Woltmann, A. (1936). The use of puppet shows as a psychotherapeutic method for behavior problems in children. *American Journal of Orthopsychiatry, 6*, 341–354.

Bettelheim, B. (1977). The uses of enchantment: The meaning and importance of fairy tales. New York: Vintage.

Blum, G. (1950). *The blacky pictures: A technique for the exploration of personality dynamics*. New York: The Psychological Corporation.

Blum, G. (1960). The blacky pictures with children. In A. Rabin & M. Haworth (Eds.), *Projective techniques with children*. New York: Grune and Stratton.

Brandell, J. (1984). Stories and storytelling in child psychotherapy. *Psychotherapy, 21*, 54–62.

Brandell, J. (1986). Using children's autogenic stories to assess therapeutic progress. *Journal of Child and Adolescent Psychotherapy, 3*, 285–292.

Brandell, J. (1987). Using children's autogenic stories to monitor therapeutic progress. *Journal of Independent Social Work, 1*, 19–32.

Claman, L. (1980). The squiggle-drawing game in child psychotherapy. *American Journal of Psychotherapy, 34*, 414–425.

Department of Health, Education, and Welfare (DHEW). (1973). Pharmacotherapy of children [Special issue]. *Psychopharmacology Bulletin*, Rockville, MD: DHEW (HSM No. 73-9002), 196.

Despert, J., & Potter, W. (1936). Technical approaches in the study and treatment of emotional problems in childhood. *Psychoanalytic Quarterly, 10*, 619–638.

Eberhardt, A. (1979). Therapeutic storytelling with pre-schoolers. *Journal of the American Academy of Child Psychiatry, 18*, 119–127.

Embry, L., Leavitt, S., & Budd, R. (1975). Parent training check lists. Unpublished manuscript.

Fromm-Reichmann, F. (1950). *Principles of intensive psychotherapy*. Chicago: University of Chicago Press.

Gabel, S. (1984). The draw-a-story game: An aid in understanding and working with children. *The Arts in Psychotherapy, 11*, 187–196.

Gardner, R. (1968). The mutual storytelling technique: Use in alleviating childhood oedipal problems. *Contemporary Psychoanalysis, 4*, 161–177.

Gardner, R. (1969). Mutual storytelling as a technique in child psychotherapy and psychoanalysis. In J. Masserman (Ed.), *Science and psychoanalysis* (Vol. 14) (pp. 123–125). New York: Grune and Stratton.

Gardner, R. (1970). The mutual storytelling technique: Use in the treatment of a child with posttraumatic neurosis. *American Journal of Psychotherapy, 24*, 419–439.

Gardner, R. (1971a). *Therapeutic communication with children: The mutual storytelling technique*. New York: Jason Aronson.

Gardner, R. (1971b). Mutual storytelling: A technique in child psychotherapy. *Acta Paedopsychiatrica, 38*, 253–62.

Gardner, R. (1972). Psychotherapy of psychogenic problems secondary to minimal brain dysfunction. *International Journal of Child Psychotherapy, 2*, 224–256.

Gardner, R. (1973). *The mutual storytelling technique* [12 one-hour tapes]. New York: Jason Aronson, Inc.

Gondor, L. (1957). Use of fantasy communications in child psychotherapy. *American Journal of Psychotherapy, 5*, 323–35.

Gottschalk, L., & Gleser, G. (1969). *The measurement of psychological states through the content analysis of human behavior.* Berkeley: University of California Press.

Gottschalk, L., Gleser, G., & Winget, C. (1969). *Manual of instructions for using the Gottschalk-Gleser content analysis scales: Anxiety, hostility, and social alienation-personal disorganization.* Berkeley: University of California Press.

Hawkey, L. (1951). The use of puppets in child psychotherapy. *British Journal of Medical Psychology, 24*, 206–214.

Kestenbaum, C. (1985). The creative process in child psychotherapy. *American Journal of Psychotherapy, 39*, 479–489.

Klein, M. (1955). The psychoanalytic play technique. *American Journal of Orthopsychiatry, 25*, 233–237.

Kritzberg, N. (1971). TASKIT (tell-a-story-kit), the therapeutic storytelling word game. *Acta paedopsychiatrica, 38*, 231–244.

Kritzberg, N. (1975). *The structured therapeutic game method of child analytic psychotherapy.* Hicksville, NY: Exposition Press.

Liebowitz, J. (1972). Storytelling in search of a plot. *Reiss-Davis Clinical Bulletin, 9*, 112–115.

Lourie, R., & Rieger, R. (1974). Pyschiatric and psychological examination of children. In S. Arieti (Ed.), *The American handbook of psychiatry* (Vol. 2) (pp. 1–36). New York: Basic Books, Inc.

Marcus, I. (1966). Costume play therapy: The exploration of a method for stimulating imaginative play in older children. *Journal of Child Psychiatry, 5*, 441–452.

McArthur, D.S., & Roberts, G.E. (1982). *Roberts apperception test for children: Manual.* Los Angeles: Western Psychological Services.

McDonald, M. (1965). The psychiatric evaluation of children. *American Academy of Child Psychiatry, 4*, 569–612.

Millar, S. (1974). *The psychology of play.* New York: Jason Aronson.

Pearson, G.S. (1984). The use of storytelling in the psychiatric assessment of children. *Journal of Child and Adolescent Psychotherapy, 1*, 101–106.

Pitcher, E., & Prelinger, E. (1963). *Children tell stories: An analysis of fantasy.* New York: International Universities Press.

Rambert, M. (1949). *Children in conflict.* New York: International Universities Press.

Robertson, J., & Barford, F. (1970). Story-making in psychotherapy with a chronically-ill child. *Psychotherapy: Theory, Research, and Practice, 7*, 104–107.

Schooley, C. (1974). Communicating with hospitalized children: The mutual storytelling technique. *Journal of Pastoral Care, 28*, 102–111.

Starr, A. (1977). *Rehearsal for living: Psychodrama.* Chicago: Nelson Hall.

Winnicott, D.W. (1971). *Therapeutic consultations in child psychiatry.* New York: Basic Books, Inc.

Woltmann, A. (1950). Mud and clay: Their functions as developmental aids and as media of projection. In N. Wolff (Ed.), *Personality: Symposium on topical issues* (pp. 35–50). New York: Grune and Stratton.

Woltmann, A. (1951). The use of puppetry as a projective method in therapy. In H. Anderson & G. Anderson (Eds.), *An introduction to projective techniques and other devices for understanding the dynamics of human behavior* (pp. 606–638). Englewood Cliffs, NJ: Prentice-Hall.

CHAPTER 2

Imaginative Play Technique
in Psychotherapy with Children

JOOP HELLENDOORN

INTRODUCTION: PLAY IN CHILD THERAPY

All methods of individual psychotherapy with children make use of imaginative play, although the use of play may differ from a central to a more marginal role. In psychoanalytic child therapy, play is considered important for several reasons: (a) it gives the child an opportunity for symbolic reenactment of conflict-laden content, which may, through interpretation by the therapist, be grasped by the child's conscious; (b) it offers the possibility for vigorous expression of repressed primitive wishes in "make-believe," without repercussions from daily reality; and (c) it provides a means for engaging children in a therapeutic relationship.

In client-centered therapy with children, play has always had a special place because it gives children a natural medium both for expressing themselves in a truly personal way, and for experimenting with the ideas, feelings, and roles of others. It is the therapist's task to emphasize the children's autonomy and separateness, thus helping them to acknowledge their own emotions and to discover their own sense of identity and personal value.

From its start, behavior modification has made use of imagery and role play for specific purposes. In cognitive therapy in particular, there is growing interest in training programs featuring model-learning through skills-oriented role play (Meichenbaum, 1977; Urbain & Kendall, 1980; Spivack & Shure, 1982). In most programs, the therapist actively models good coping strategies, which the child then exercises in role play situations with the therapist providing feedback.

Until now, play has not been a very important aspect of family therapy. It may be introduced to keep younger children busy and reasonably quiet while older family members talk, or as a safe haven, for relaxation when the therapy situation becomes too threatening (Dulcan, 1984). Joint play may also clarify family transactions, and can therefore be used for family assessment (Guttman, 1975; Klijn, 1980) as well as for restructuring interventions (Safer, 1965). Recently there also have been some attempts to incorporate imaginative play in family sessions as a joint expression of feelings and experiences (Ariel, Carel & Tyano, 1985; Ariel, 1986).

In the Netherlands in the 1950s, another method of child therapy (called imagery interaction) was developed that puts special emphasis on the therapeutic implications of imagery and imaginative play. Its roots lie in European phenomenological psychology. This school of thought emphasizes the continuous interaction of people with both their environment and their daily living reality. People can never be studied either just on their own or as completely separate intrapsychic units. They must be seen in relation to their daily world, to everything that happens and exists in which they actively participate, and to which they constantly give meaning in accordance with personal perceptions. Meanings can be roughly distinguished into two groups: The first comprises "open or common meanings"—those meanings we have in common with others in our daily environment. By these common meanings we can be sure to understand one another, once we have learnt them: A chair is a chair to all of us. The second group are "personal meanings"—those meanings which are individual and specific, and, therefore, can only be understood if one is deeply interested in the other's personal existence.

People are psychologically healthy if interaction with their world comprises a reasonable proportion of common meaning, if their personal meanings cover a wide range—positive as well as negative—and if these are sufficiently understandable to others.

Personal meaning is formed by experience and applied to actual occurrences. A preponderance of negative life experiences renders people less trustful about that which will happen today. This means that they become less open to the meaning a particular situation might suggest or evoke. Thus, the range of meaning becomes narrower and less *weltoffen* (open to the world), until, at last, only negative-affective meaning can be attributed. At the same time, this person's meanings become less accessible to others—a fact that courts misunderstanding and conflict. If this situation goes on long enough, one will probably develop serious personal problems and need professional help.

In treatment, these personal meanings are clearly of prime importance. Of course, language is a powerful tool in communication, but the full depth and subtlety of human experience are difficult to express and capture in verbal exchanges. In many ways, experiences are beyond words. However, in creative work and in play, where at least some of the limitations of language do not apply, many adults and children find ways to express their ideas and feelings in analogous form (in metaphor or image). These can be felt, co-experienced, and shared by others.

For children, this point is of special import because communication about their personal experiences poses two additional problems (Langeveld, 1955, 1964). In the first place, the younger the children, the more limited their language mastery, vocabulary, and ability for self-reflection. In the second place, and perhaps even more important, is the special position of children. Open discussion of their problems may create a serious loyalty conflict, because the problems of children almost always relate to their parents on whom they depend both physically and emotionally, and with whom they feel solidarity and alliance. Therefore, for therapeutic communication, less open and more covert ways of expression (metaphoric or symbolic) may better suit the purpose. For children, imaginative play is one such covert way to handle emotional experiences.

The themes a child develops in play are believed to be expressions of thoughts and feelings. Expression itself (in the presence of a therapist) may already be therapeutic, insofar as it reopens communication of experiences that have long been sealed off. However, in imagery interaction the therapist also actively helps the child (a) to fully develop his or her own play themes, and (b) to work through those play themes, differentiating and shading them, and gradually influencing them in more desirable directions. The working hypothesis is that by influencing the expression of experiences, one influences the experiencing itself. That is why the therapist stays within the play level and tries to give all interventions a play format. According to Singer (1985), one might also state that this way of working gives children the opportunity to process adverse or conflicting stimuli on their own level, within their own intellectual grasp.

The role of the therapist is an active one that should include joining the child in play. This is thought to serve several purposes:

1. It facilitates the involvement of the child in play. The therapist, by joining in or by initiating play, creates a child-centered situation in which childlike play expression counts as desirable and even important. Additionally, the therapist may, through direct involvement, help develop and deepen the initially superficial and implicit play world.

2. The therapist models not only the importance of play, but also its many possibilities.

3. Through involvement in the play world, communication between therapist and child evolves in a nonthreatening way, thus opening up experiences that had been sealed off.

4. As a partner in play, the therapist is better able to influence the form and content of play in the direction of therapy goals.

Imaginative play is the essential therapeutic ingredient of imagery interaction, actively used by the therapist to bring about change. Therefore, we feel justified, in the context of this chapter, to give special attention to its techniques. In subsequent sections therapeutic practice will be described in more detail and with a number of case illustrations.

SOME RESEARCH FINDINGS

It may safely be said that much more is known empirically about play than about play therapy. Most researchers on imaginative play agree that it is an important aspect of child development with beneficial effects on emotional as well as cognitive and social development (Fein, 1981; Rubin, 1980; Singer, 1973, 1986; Vandenberg, 1980; Yawkey, 1981; and others). Going one step further, play training programs have been designed to stimulate development, especially in socially deprived children. Although there has been some criticism on methodology (e.g., Smith & Syddall, 1978), these programs are not found less successful than other, less child-friendly programs.

Play therapy has been used with all kinds of problems and with all kinds of children, although it is generally believed to work best with neurotic children. However, all children may not be equally responsive to play. Fein (1975), Lieberman (1977), and Singer and Singer (1981, 1985) all found that children differ in imagination and playfulness, a fact that may have its correlates in family atmosphere and involvement. All the same, that does not necessarily have direct consequences for their accessibility to therapy. Children who are poor in imagination because of lack of support or stimulus may be trained to develop their ability in this respect (Baron & Cautella, 1983; Singer & Singer, 1985). A recent study by the author (Hellendoorn, 1988) corroborates this tendency.

Although much has been written about different forms of play therapy, and many case histories have testified to its individual effectiveness, actual controlled outcome research in play therapy from different theoretical backgrounds is notably scarce. In many settings, the number of cases per annum is low and/or the organizational prerequisites (pre-, post-, and follow-up assessment at the very least) are lacking, not systematically observed, or even judged unacceptable by practitioners—all of which preclude outcome research. For their meta-analytic investigation, Reams and Friedrich (1983) found not more than 25 more-or-less controlled studies, of which only 15 were suitable for use. Their main conclusion is that play therapy has more effect than no treatment at all, but the effect is limited to only general adaptation and intellectual skills. Although these results are perhaps somewhat disappointing, in theoretical scope there is one encouraging aspect that is supported by an earlier study of Wright, Moelish, and Pollack (1976): The effects of play therapy increase over time, and follow-up gains are larger than gains at termination of therapy.

In an explorative study by Harinck and Loeven (1985a,b), 18 therapists gave extensive information about their own practice of imagery interaction. Their success ranges from 65 to 90 percent, with better results in outpatient settings, with younger children (under 10 years old), and by therapists who keep well-documented files, with clearly formulated goals and strategies.

Perhaps more illuminating is the research about the play therapy process. There are some descriptive studies on specific therapy ingredients (like the well-known study on play therapy limits by Ginott & Lebo, 1961; recently replicated by Rhoden, Kranz & Lund, 1981). The importance of realistic expectations about what is going to happen, and thus of a good preparation for therapy, both of parents and children, is emphasized by Day and Reznikoff (1980) and Adelman, Kaser-Boyd, and Taylor (1984). The process of change in client-centered play therapy has been studied by Borke (1947), Moustakas and Schalock (1955), Hendricks (1971), Schmidtchen, Wörmann, and Hobrücker (1977), Schmidtchen and Hobrücker (1978), Schmidtchen and Rahlf (1982), and Mook (1982a,b), and others. A main difficulty in this field is formed by varying ideas about what behavior is important to study (verbal, nonverbal, expression of affect, insight, etc.). That means that almost all researchers develop their own (new) instruments, in which only some include interaction with the therapist. A thorough overview of the different methods and results is given by Schmidtchen (1986).

My own research is concerned with microanalysis of the interaction between child and therapist in imagery interaction play therapy (Harinck & Hellendoorn, 1983, 1987). One result seems crucial; that is, that of all possible child behaviors, imaginative play is the most influenced by therapist intervention in the sense that it is strongly facilitated by imaginative play behavior of the therapist and repressed by all other therapist behaviors. Consequently, if imaginative play is considered therapeutically important, as in imagery interaction, the therapist should actively model this kind of behavior.

IMAGERY INTERACTION PLAY TECHNIQUE

In imagery interaction, the tenet that the therapist join actively in the child's play is implemented by the basic technique of verbalizing. This means putting into words whatever happens in play. Its starting point lies in the play events created by the child. By verbalizing these the therapist gives them special meaning. Two examples follow:

Sacha chose toy animals to play with and put them in the sandbox. She separated the different species by strong fences. Therapist: "That's the elephant's den . . . and there the lions' . . . and the horses' . . . they all have their own compartments."

Peter took a toy airplane, circled it over his head for some time, then put it down. Therapist: "The plane takes off . . . higher . . . still higher . . . down he goes again . . . landed."

These examples illustrate the principle that the therapist does not talk about the child and his or her feelings or ideas, but about the play world and the play persons and *their* thoughts and feelings. By verbalizing, the therapist tries to come close to the action and feeling tone of the child at the level where he or she is playing and, at the same time, expresses implicit acceptance of whatever is happening. There is, however, even more to it: In both examples we see that verbalization makes a simple play act more meaningful. At the start of play, most children do not have a definite plan. Rather, they are attracted—for whatever personal reasons—to certain playthings, and by looking at them and manipulating them the personal "imaginative quality" of the material gradually emerges. This may be strengthened by the therapist's verbalization. It is quite conceivable that Sacha continued: "Yes, and they may not come together," which opens new play possibilities. Verbalizing structures a play act, making it less superficial or incidental. This may also promote its extension and differentiation into a more encompassing imaginative play world where anything can happen. And last but not least, it assists therapists in shaping their roles as coplayers by giving them a definite task close to the child, a task that is both observant and participatory.

Evidently, the quality of a verbalization is determined by its "fit"; that is, the way it grasps the essence of what happens in play through tone of voice, tempo, and vocabulary. A short utterance like, "There they go," can be pronounced in many different ways, from coldly disinterested to heavily overacted. The best way is always determined by the play context. "There they go," may express tense anticipation (e.g., a puppet family goes on a dangerous exploring trip); relief (e.g., the policeman caught the thief and takes him away); a sober statement (e.g., the children go to school); a feeling of wellbeing (e.g., the client joyfully moves about with two cars); and so forth. Note also the expressive quality of tempo: A slow verbalization may sound dreamy or very tense, a rapid voice may sound joyful but also vehement or chaotic, and so on. Lastly, the therapist's choice of words should always be adapted to the individual child and that child's play world. Verbalizations should, as much as possible, underline the imaginative quality, the "make believe," the "almost real" of what happens. Therefore, we never talk about "the doll house" or "puppets," but always about "the house," or "people, father, mother, children," and so on.

Thus, language is not used to translate play content and meaning into reality meaning, to bring such meaning into consciousness, or to offer rational insight. It does, though, play an important role in the sense that it structures and brings order to activities, feelings, and meanings, even though these belong to the play persons. Verbalization by the therapist may also encourage children to join in and to talk more about what they are doing, which often facilitates further communication. Singer (1985) also points out that the therapist, in this way, may subtly broaden the child's vocabulary and language usage, thus furthering differential expression of experiences and information processing.

Verbalization can be varied in many ways to strengthen and deepen play experiences. Structuring was already mentioned, because most verbalizations have that effect. But this quality may also be used specifically for children with chaotic thinking and acting.

It is also possible to strengthen meaning by accentuating certain aspects of play, through increasing tension or by using accompanying sounds (cracking of guns, tooting, grumbling, groaning, etc.). In this way, play can at times become very lively, mysterious, fanciful, or whatever.

Going one step further, we can anticipate future events, to bring about more continuity in a play story that tends to stall. An example:

Together with the therapist the child built an animal farm in the sandbox. On the floor around it a road was chalked, which at one point almost touched the (doll) house. A car was put on the road. The child hesitated and leaned back. The therapist linked the doll house to the sandbox situation and anticipated: "The children in the house see that car on the road . . . Maybe they go drive in it, to the animal farm."

Deeper and more personal involvement in play can be fostered by verbalizing thoughts and feelings of the play people. In the example above, the therapist could add: "They think about how much they would like to go there." Further examples:

Roy (eight years old) had one boy doll throw all people out of the house, playing intensely. Therapist: "He was so mad . . . at all of them . . . out you go . . . and you . . . out with you . . . I'll kill you . . . all of you . . . "
Jean (five years old) drove a large train very fast, obviously enjoying the speed, and its being faster than another. Therapist, speaking for the train: "Huh, look at me, I am the fast fast fastest of all . . . Huh, nobody can go as fast as me . . . !"
Later on, Jean shut a little horse in a cage. Therapist: "The little horse is thinking, if only I could get out . . . "

Note that in all these cases verbalization maintains the imaginative level. Children are not obliged to acknowledge or openly admit that their own thoughts or feelings are being talked about. These remain under the safe cover of play.
    In this same way, all kinds of therapeutic messages can be woven into play. A therapeutic message goes even further in adding meaning to what happens in the play world; in this case, a meaning that is specially geared to clarify or work through the child's problems. Again, a few examples:

Eight-year-old Monica was in therapy for problems that were related to the overstressed ideal-child image of her parents and herself, forcing her to be always nice and good. Playing with the baby doll, she took the role of mother and spanked the baby good and hard: "She is bad, bad, bad. . . ." The therapist took the role of mother's friend who was coming to tea: "How mad you are at that child of yours, she must have done something terrible. Mine too; sometimes they are just horrible. But that is just how children are: sometimes they are very good, and sometimes not."
Peter (six years old) was in therapy because of an emotionally determined retardation in development, with a history of child abuse, parental divorce, and

family conflict. With Playmobile figures he played a man being thrown into jail, who escapes but is caught again. The therapist tried to find out the reason for his jailing, but the man does not know why. The therapist knew that in his daily life Peter felt constantly overwhelmed by things that happened that he could not control. That is why in this play story he took the role of the prisoner and screamed: "I want to know why I am here! You cannot put me in prison without a cause! You have to tell me what I have done. I have a right to know."

We already met Sacha, (age seven) who so clearly set her animal families within strong fences. Therapy was indicated because of strong inferiority feelings, overadapting behavior, and too little trust in her family and her parents. In the course of a few sessions the fences became thicker and stronger, until they were like unpenetrable stone walls. Then she chose a toy bird—which might be able to get over the walls—but she put it on a chain. The therapist tried to verbalize the ambivalent feelings of the animals: "Mmm . . . at last it is really safe, those walls . . . nothing can happen now . . . but on the other hand they can't do anything . . . just no way . . . they can only stay where they are. . . . "

These therapeutic messages or interpretive play interventions come close to interpretation in a psychodynamic sense, because they relate the play events to aspects of the child's reality. But even here, the play cover is maintained: These things happen to and are said by or about play people, within roles. This possibility of leaving concealed what is at the same time revealed, is the strong point of this imaginative technique, because it enables the child to communicate about things that cannot or may not be said aloud. Still, these interventions should not be made without careful consideration of individual therapy goals, about which more will be said in a moment.

The basic technique of verbalization and its many variations open all sorts of opportunities to help the child develop play and become more personally involved in therapy. But the therapist, as a coplayer, has more strings to the bow. Some children do not have ready access to imaginative play and may need strong stimuli to get started. In that case suggestions about possible play material, and the modeling of play actions might help. In the course of a story, extension of materials, places, or play content may also be suggested. A very important sort of intervention in this class is the introduction of specific sensations: actual or imaginary sensory and bodily involvement, such as things that can be heard, tasted, smelled, or touched.

For example, have you ever felt what happens to sand when it gets wet? First, take some dry sand. Feel it; let it slip through your fingers and fall onto the bottom of the sandbox. Do you hear its sound? Do you feel its texture? Its temperature?

Now get some water, and sprinkle it on the sand, like rain. At first you see the separate drops, which darken the sand. Gradually all the sand gets darker and harder. Take it in your hand again; it does not slip out and you can even make it into a hard ball.

Drop more water on the sand and feel how it again loosens up into mud that is soft and probably cold to the touch. The wetter it gets, the more it slips away: You can no longer use it to make balls or hills. If you do not like this slippery mud (and for many children this can be extremely threatening), you have to get more dry sand and mix it in. Gradually it gets firmer and harder so that you can do something with it again. But it is impossible to get it dry unless you leave it in a warm place for a long time.

If you tried this out for yourself, you may have discovered that the different sensations evoke different emotions and different associations to situations or people. It may also have reminded you about the joys and/or awfulness of "being dirty." This way of tactile involvement is basic to all of us, including children. Therefore, it can be a powerful tool to evoke personal meaning and more involved play.

Almost all children meet specific blocks at one time or another, which the therapist may help them overcome. These blocks may have to do not only with specific sensations (e.g., feeling dirty), but also with play content. In these situations the therapist's joining in the play is especially important because of the implicit acceptance of what is happening: If the therapist joins in, the action it is not forbidden, but permitted by at least one adult. If this does not enable the child to cross the barrier, further suggestions must be carefully spaced and worded. Trying to force children through a block usually has the opposite effect: As likely as not they will entrench themselves further. It is the experience of many therapists that even very good and carefully formulated suggestions may have a long-term impact. Sometimes they take minutes or even sessions to be effected.

Another category of intervention is limit setting in a more or less gentle way. Frequently the simplest form of limit setting can be integrated in play.

Mike, a rather chaotic six-year-old, put some animals together at the farm door "because they are so thirsty." He went to the tap to get water, but got carried away by a spray can he found there. The therapist let him experiment for some time, then gently nudged: "Those cows are still waiting for their drink, they are so thirsty." If the child does not react and is not engaged in another important action, the therapist might intervene more crisply: "Come on, Mike, let's bring these cows their water first."
Sheila made "a landscape" in the sandbox, adding more and more trees, fences, and people until there was almost no free space left. Therapist: "Mmm, it is so busy here, they can hardly breathe or move anymore. Maybe this is enough of a crowd now."

Sometimes, of course, this is not enough, and more definite limits (time, no hurting each other, etc.) have to be set, but in those cases the therapist will leave the play world, and clearly tell the child what is wanted.

Effective psychotherapy is only possible on the basis of a thorough assessment of both the child's and the family's problems. In the first place, we need to know whether therapy—more specifically, this kind of therapy—is indicated for the child. The second question is what specific goals therapy should accomplish in this individual case. Finally, we want to determine what therapeutic strategy, or what composition of techniques, would be most effective in approaching these goals.

By careful consideration and formulation (in writing) of such a treatment plan, the therapist will be better able to choose and account for intervention at each moment during a session. The treatment plan also provides the searchlight for evaluation of every session and for the treatment process. Sometimes, in doing so, new facts come to light which ask for rewording of goals or strategies. We also feel that, if kept up to date, the treatment plan is a most important tool in determining the phase of termination.

CASE STUDIES

In this section, some action examples of play techniques are discussed. The presentation of case material always poses the problem of brevity versus completeness. It is clear that describing the intricacies of an individual case requires too much space, while the choice of a few interesting sequences may put these too much out of context. Here, we aim for a compromise in order to illustrate specific themes or problems. Some examples are just short fragments; others try to give more of an overview of the therapeutic process. With all of them, the reader should keep in mind that much more happened during the therapy hours than can be discussed here. For instance, most of the slow and gradual building of a therapeutic relationship; the work with parents; the painstaking case analysis, goal setting, and treatment planning of the therapist; and the many immediate and sometimes difficult decisions made during even a single hour, are all taken for granted and left out of this account.

Talking about Problems in Play

In the case of John, reported by Tiemensma and Schokking-Kanij (1985), a rather direct illustration can be found of how children are able to express a problem that they are unable to talk about. John was twelve years old and had been in residential treatment for two years. The disrupting acting-out behavior that necessitated his admittance had greatly improved, but much of this improvement was believed to be no more than surface adaptation. Talking about himself and the problems he still experienced was almost impossible, which is why play therapy seemed indicated. At about the same time, his placement was evaluated and extended for one year to allow time for finishing primary school (where he was doing much better), as well as for therapy. The following fragment is from the 18th session.

In role play John was a thief who hates the policemen and their boss (a role played by the therapist, under John's direction), because they imprisoned his best friend, without his knowing why. The therapist, in the role of chief-of-police, expressed understanding of John's anger and distrust.

J: Can my friend be released then?

TH: Well, I can't answer yes or no. That depends on the reason for it all, what he did. But the least I can do is find out more about that.

J: Now I am my friend, in prison, and you ask me.

TH: Can you tell me, why you got into jail?

J: I do not remember, I have to talk with the judge. (To therapist:) You are the judge now.

TH: I heard from a policeman that your friend is very angry because of your being jailed. It seems you do not know why you are in prison. Is that correct?

J: Yes. But do you know yourself? There has to be a file, all kinds of papers. If you don't have them, then there is no evidence, and you must release me.

TH: If there is no file . . . But if that were true, you would be here unlawfully. If that were true, I can imagine your being dreadfully angry.

J: (Screaming) Then why did you keep me here? Let me go, I tell you, let me go!!

TH: Look here, I have to find out. Can't you remember anything from that time? For instance, what did you do for a living?

J: I was a carpenter. I had my own workshop. (TH: Your own workshop. . .) And that still is mine. The police said they'd guard it for me. That is true, isn't it? Then you said: Yes that is correct.

TH: That is correct, yes.

J: They'd keep it for a whole year, because I'd be in prison for a whole year . . . And then you saw all at once that I had been in prison for three whole years!

TH: For three whole years? But that is impossible. If you had a sentence for just one . . . That is terrible . . .

J: You came to say you were sorry, bring me some nice cake, and a drink for my health, that you were sorry . . .

TH: Well, this is certainly something that has to be looked into, very carefully.

Comment

It is clear that the extension of placement was an important source of anger to John. Later it transpired that this decision was extensively discussed with his mother, but not with John himself. He had spoken to nobody about his anger; but he spoke to the therapist in the context of play. Some weeks later, after talking this over with John, the therapist took the problem to a staff meeting.

Controlling the Relationship

Philip (six years old) is difficult to handle, both in his daily life and in the therapy hour. He constantly directs the therapist and when she does what he wants he changes the orders. This poses the problem as to who controls the relationship. Most therapists consider it very important that they themselves feel in control all the time. If possible, it should be accomplished without the child's noticing, and, at least, without undue pressure. A short sequence from one of Philip's early sessions follows.

Philip assembled all the toy guns he could find. He took the role of a thief and gave one gun to the therapist, who was to be another thief.

TH: Is that for me to use, or shall I keep it for you in reserve?

P: You decide that.

Th: Well, we will see what happens.

P: (All of a sudden, Philip turned toward the therapist and shot her.) You were dead! You have to fall dead!

TH: (Following directions and falling down "dead") Oh, how terrible this feels, I am dead, I am dead.

P: And then you were alive again, and you tried again to attack me.

TH: (Came alive, looked around and talked to herself) How strong he is. This becomes very difficult for me. (Therapist went in Philip's direction.)

P: (Immediately jumped forward and shot her) Dead again, ha ha! (This same event happened once more. Therapist again fell down.)

TH: Well, perhaps that was a little bit stupid of me. I know by now that he will shoot me again, and still I try again. It seems I am rather a pig-head to attack him over and over again.

Comment

By following the child's directions, but at the same time commenting on them in her role, the therapist does not lose control even though she is "dead" on the ground. Simultaneously, she is also making significant interventions.

Another way to deal with a controlling child is for the therapist to take the role of a servant ("You tell me what to do"), thus nicely directing the situation in such a way that the child feels in control. The therapist, who is constantly criticized for doing bad things in play might also say: "It is just terrible today. This thief is so clumsy (or pig-headed or difficult), he does everything wrong. No wonder the other one is so angry." Or alternatively (but more accusingly): "How angry this other man is. I wonder what happened to him. It cannot be just me, I was really not all that clumsy (or pig-headed, etc.).'' It is clear that this approach demands much self-confidence and creativity from the therapist.

Friend or Foe

A recurrent theme in many therapies with children is the uncertainty about trust. Of course, this is an essential life theme, and many therapy clients have reason to distrust those nearest them because of abuse, rejection, and other forms of dysfunctional parenting. While we take Peter (6 years old) as an example, we could just as well look at many others who play the same themes in slightly different form.

Peter, as will be remembered, was referred because of delayed development on emotional grounds. His parents divorced two years before, after a history of child and wife abuse. Afterwards, his mother took him to live with her own mother.

"Friend or foe" was a central theme in Peter's play sessions. For instance, in his first session he set up two parties of soldiers: the red ones in the sandbox, the blue ones on the floor. "The blues are going to attack." He took his time ordering the toys, and as his attention was rather easily distracted, the therapist tried to keep him to the subject with her verbalizations: "How strong they are with all those guns and cannons . . . They are thinking, when would it be time for the attack? . . . This one is taking one step toward them . . ." and so on. After a long look at the therapist—silently asking whether it really was okay to fight—he started the battle. It seemed that the red soldiers were winning. But all at once, two red ones started fighting each other, a blue one came to help, and then, in total confusion, all the soldiers shot one another.

All the soldiers laid dead; then he quickly picked them up: "They were not really dead, they start all over again." The therapist, rather overwhelmed by the confused happenings, was now warned, and quietly tried to verbalize: "How unsafe that must feel, not knowing who is friend and who is enemy . . . That one he thought was a friend, was not after all . . . Look, there he starts shooting at him, take cover! . . . " After the end of the battle the pervading feeling of uncertainty was verbalized again.

In another session, the uncertainty was made more concrete in a father figure who dangled from the roof of the doll's house swinging like Tarzan, appearing and disappearing in front of the windows. He laughed and wanted to play with the children; but, all at once, he turned angry and hit them. Gradually the therapist introduced the possibility that something had happened to the father that had caused this sudden change: a headache, dizziness, a very painful memory. This intervention was chosen to stress the fact that the father's moods were not the children's fault—although sometimes, of course, they can be very nasty—but rather something beyond control, something you can understand but not do anything about.

Still later, Peter worked out this theme in a play story about thieves and policemen, all of whom took turns at being bad and good. Then the therapist introduced a boy who was confused all the time: Could he go with the police without risking being caught as "bad" after all? Peter thought this a good game and tricked the boy a few times before he caught on to its meaning: Some people can really be trusted, some cannot, and you have to find out which people are which for yourself. So long as you are not sure, it is best to be careful. This idea was then played out in several variations.

Overcoming Trauma in Brief Mother-Child Treatment

Freddy (three years and eight months old) was presented for treatment by his parents because of delayed language development. He spoke baby talk and often just mimicked sounds. Several consonants were not well pronounced. An earlier counselor saw this as being caused by an insufficient mother-child relationship, and applied a "holding therapy." This had no effect on Freddy's language. Mother, feeling guilty, was unsure of her parental role, and father was hardly motivated for further help. Still, they tried again because of their anxiety about Freddy's reaction to the approaching birth of a sibling. Because of his age, Freddy's assessment took the form of a play observation. He looked like a vital, exploring preschooler, accepting the therapist as a matter of course. The content of his play indicated a feeling of "not being able to go on" and "being stuck" (in mud and sand). It was also full of aggression (hitting and kicking). The therapist felt that there was not very much wrong with the child, open and trustful as he was toward her. Therefore, she and the parents decided upon a brief treatment: two discussions with them and four play sessions with Freddy. Her goals with Freddy were to (a) clarify his discontent, and (b) to influence the mother-child relationship in a positive direction. With the parents, her goals were to (a) take up the parents' presenting problem by discussing and implementing playful ways of stimulating language use; and (b) support the mother in her parental role, toward a more secure and assertive position.

In all, this treatment took two individual play sessions, two talks with the parents, and one mother-and-child play session, over a period of 10 weeks. The first play session took place at Freddy's home. Mother had just given birth to a second son. Freddy was again active and lively. He chose cars to play with. In one particularly important sequence, a crane swung a small car about; Freddy forcefully called this the "bang-car."

A discussion with both parents, directly after the play hour, gave important new information: Two years previously, Freddy and his mother had been in a car accident in which a crane was involved. There had been only material damage, but on coming home the question of who was to blame for the accident became so all-important that neither of them had much chance to work through the shock and emotions.

The parents had accepted the therapist by now. Both seemed rather overindulgent and protective in their attitude toward Freddy. Before her marriage, his mother had been trained for child care, and her possible fear of not doing well with her own children was addressed by the therapist. Subsequently, the parents wanted to discuss how to be more assertive with Freddy, who really needed that.

In the next play session, the therapist tried to further develop the "accident" theme, but in vain. Instead, Freddy returned to the "being stuck" image of his diagnostic hour. He hardly spoke at all during this session. The therapist seemed to have run against a definite block. To overcome this, she decided to invite the mother to join in the next session in order to attack more directly what seemed, by now, the crux of the problem.

In that joint session, Freddy's mother was asked to play with the cars and to stage the accident. Simultaneously, the therapist evoked and verbalized the emotions mother and Freddy must have felt: the sudden fear, trembling, and so on. Freddy burst into tears. Together the adults verbalized how terrible this accident was and how awful it is if people don't watch out. Mother seemed well able to integrate the suggestions of the therapist into the play.

Then Freddy joined in. He picked up the crane-driver and wreaked a terrible vengeance on this little toy figure. At the end of the hour he was more relaxed and floated a toy boat in water. A family with two little children sailed in the boat. During this last episode, Freddy talked cheerfully about what was happening: They sail and stay dry.

Two weeks later the parents came in for their last session. They reported considerable improvement in Freddy's language usage. Whereas formerly he had had difficulty in playing by himself, that problem was definitely over. Mother also judged herself as much more assertive and sure of herself. At long last, she understood what went wrong with Freddy and she no longer felt guilty. No further help was required. Shortly afterward, Freddy entered nursery school. Reports about him remain positive.

Comment

It seems clear that in this case the problems were solved by the joint reexperiencing of a traumatic event by mother and child. By playing together, this fearful event was brought back into communication on the imaginative level, thus losing its compelling force of being something that could be neither talked about nor lived with. Because of her active involvement, the mother felt more secure in dealing with her son, which was also positively influenced by the talks of both parents with the therapist.

Grief Work in Play

For this section, a case reported by Donker-Raymakers (1982) was chosen. Gerald (10 years old) was referred for play therapy by his teacher who was worried about his inability to communicate with the boy. In class, Gerald was very quiet and retiring, day-dreaming a lot. He had almost no peer contacts and he had been underachieving for the last year. He was the youngest in a family of four children living with their father. A year-and-a-half previously, his mother had died. During the last days of her illness, the children visited her regularly, but they did not know the full gravity of her condition. After her death, Gerald was the only one showing no emotion at all, even at the funeral. Half a year later, the family moved to another town, which also ended most of the visits and help from other family members. Father was still engrossed in the mourning process. Talking did not come easily to him, and he did not discuss his late wife with the children; he feared that that would only be an extra burden on them: "They are children, life goes on for them." He did not understand why Gerald should have problems at that time, as he had always seemed the least affected.

In therapy, Gerald played a lot with sand, but not in a joyful way. Rather, sand seemed to have a threatening quality, as he showed by letting his favorite toy truck be almost buried in it. Again and again, things were almost buried in the sand, and always afterward—when they were saved at the last moment—the sand was smoothed again and pressed down well. In his third hour, he introduced a mother figure in the doll's house, who was warm, caring, and supportive toward the children. If she was not there, the children became anxious.

Time and again these themes were played out in the same way. There seemed to be no progress. Gerald was stuck in the negation of his mother's death and the idealization of her continued presence. The therapist, after careful thought, decided to confront him more directly with the facts. At the start of each session she prepared the play room for Gerald by putting a few playthings in the sandbox and in the doll's house. Then she staged a small burial ground in one corner of the sandbox by means of a little cross, two trees, and some flowers.

Of course Gerald immediately saw it: "That cross is for a dog who died." In spite of this seeming negation he continued playing with the sand, loading and unloading it. Then, without warning, two men were caught in the sand and died a terrible death. A little boy who was looking on screamed heartrendingly: "No!," but to no avail. For the rest of that session Gerald was busy with the sand transport.

The subsequent three play hours made clear that this direct confrontation had been very threatening to Gerald. He made the doll's house safer by putting a wall of blocks up: nobody was allowed to pass. However, he also stated that none of the people in authority, not even the police, could do anything when the enemy actually comes. Gerald also avoided the therapist: Joint play was almost impossible. The therapist, understanding this, did not force him. Instead, for the time being, she emphasized the constructive side of play by helping him build a sand castle.

Gradually, their interaction reached firmer ground where imaginative play again became possible on a new level: The mother figure disappeared (although in one play she could be called by phone), and the father figure took over her role. That was a healthy sign, but all was not yet well: The father did not offer enough security. From all sides there were threats and dangers. A father and son threatened to become buried in the sand but, after all, "They came out alive." All other people died in the sand. The therapist and Gerald grieved for the dead. They solemnly made a burial ground for them which was decorated with trees and flowers to make it look less fearful.

In the last sessions the father figure received a more central, active, and protective role. Father and son built a new house for themselves that, at termination (24th session), was opened with much ado and much happiness. Gerald looked at the building and, for a moment, showed that he found it hard to terminate treatment: "The garden is yet to be done." Then for the first time Gerald and the therapist openly talked about his mother and how much he still missed her.

Comment

In this therapy a directive intervention was used to overcome the negation stage, which blocked Gerald's grief work about the death of his mother. Although this was rather a drastic move, the therapist felt her relationship to Gerald of good enough quality at that time to take the risk. From that point, the process of mourning could go on although it still needed six months until termination. Only at termination was open discussion of the problem possible. Therapy itself stayed completely on the imaginative play level. For a reticent child like Gerald, who had great difficulty expressing himself (except in play), this seemed an enormous advantage. His facial and bodily expression, the tone of his voice, the way he looked at the therapist, and so on, all bore clear evidence of the intensity of his personal involvement and experiencing.

It is important to note, however, that not only the child was helped. Much work was done with the father, often on the basis of what happened in the play sessions. For instance, in an early session Gerald expressed, in a puppet play, his anger that Santa Claus did not come any more. Understandably, the father did not feel up to joyous family parties. Still, for the children, this meant another step away from everything that had been normal and pleasant before. Too much had altered for them in too short a time and there seemed almost no continuity left. Father himself needed to talk about his own loss before he was able to take the parental protective role Gerald had ready for him. He started to talk with the children about their mother and resumed visiting her grave with them. In this way the individual grief work in play therapy was expanded to the family as a whole.

A Silent Growing Experience

Minca (eight years old) is an adopted child of Asiatic origin. She was referred because of severe language learning problems at school where she was overly quiet. In contrast, at home, she was fussy and meddlesome and sought constant attention. She was the youngest in a warm and talkative family consisting of her adoptive parents and their own two children. She arrived in the Netherlands from Asia when she was almost two years old. The last half-year there she spent in a children's clinic after being abandoned by her unwed mother. Her natural father was unknown.

On arrival here, her physical condition necessitated immediate hospital treatment for a few weeks. This was an extremely strenuous time for her new parents and herself. Minca cried almost incessantly. After her discharge she required much attention for a long time, but her development was favorable. Language development, seemingly absent at first, proceeded rapidly. In kindergarten she did well, but after the family moved to another town she had difficulty adapting to a new school. She started out well in first grade, but gradually her results deteriorated. She was not a popular child and had no friends at school.

Assessment showed a normal intelligence with the verbal subtests a bit lower than performance. Language achievement results were on the low normal side but not nearly low enough to explain her unsatisfactory school performance. These could much more easily be understood from her chaotic way of experiencing and thinking. Projection tests showed conflicts between growing up and staying small, between togetherness and rejecting others, and between a strong repressed aggression and all kinds of vague threatening feelings. During assessment she seemed joyless and low-spirited. A family observation did not yield specific family problems.

In her first play session every situation she created ended in chaos and destruction. Cows broke loose and crushed all other animals and people, an island where people lived collapsed, trees caught fire, and so on. The only time she was able to relax a little was when, at the end of the hour, she made a large quantity of mud and stirred it with her hands. In the next session, the threat became more concrete: "Thieves, who take everything . . . and then they had nothing left. . . . They went flying, to sleep with a family." Interestingly, she took away the father figure from the doll's family: He did not return for some months.

The different themes in her first plays made it clear that her problems had to do with her early history. Her feelings of loneliness and need for closeness, the threats, all the things that overwhelm one without any control, the flight to a family—were all definite references to her past. The parents, too, reported that Minca was very much involved with her past. For instance, she wanted to be told again and again about the process of being born and about the role of the father. Therapist and parents all felt that the traumatic time before and around her transfer had left a "black hole" in her existence which became more of a hindrance to further development now that her basic survival needs had been met. This way of thinking took a weight off the parents (whose helplessness in dealing with the problems had caused a lot of guilt feelings) and freed their undeniable potential for normal parenting.

The most striking element in Minca's therapy was her taciturn behavior. After speaking during the first sessions, she hardly ever talked until near termination although she played imaginatively all the time. The therapist had a difficult time: If the child tells you nothing about what happens, only scrupulous observation and empathic understanding make it possible to follow what happens and to continue verbalizing in a meaningful way. The therapist in this case felt that Minca's chaos in thought and feeling necessitated full use of the structuring effect of verbalization. Therefore, she tried to make some sense out of every play situation. More and more often, if she could not follow the story, she said so: "So much is happening at the same time, it looks like those people can't understand it at all," or words to that effect.

Comment

In this therapy, suggestions and interventions directed toward change of play content were inadequate. From the beginning, Minca herself developed and changed the play themes, using different material in almost every session. She also showed a need for control by clearing away the playthings herself when she felt a play story was ended. She accepted the therapist's verbalizations, sometimes even by a slight but explicit nod, but did not let her play a more active role: Minca played, the therapist verbalized. In this way, her treatment was very much an inner process, supported by a trusting relationship with, and prudent wording by, the therapist—but certainly not brought about by direct interventions.

Near the end of the therapy, when things improved perceptibly at home and at school, her way of playing changed. She started talking again, and she discovered other play materials: a ball, building blocks. She then started playing creatively and joyfully, and wanted the therapist to join in. It appeared that only now that the "black hole" was filled, could she start being a child again.

Working with Mentally Handicapped Children

In the past five years, more and more work has been done on play therapy with the mentally handicapped. Although the classical authors on psychoanalytic and client-centered play therapy usually require the child to have at least normal intelligence (because of the emphasis on insight and self-reflection), experiments with mildly to moderately mentally retarded children have worked out satisfactorily. Indeed, some authors contend that play therapy is particularly geared to this group of clients because most of them enjoy playing until much older than normal subjects (Scholten, 1979; Goessens, 1985).

Considering play psychotherapy for mentally handicapped children supposes, first of all, that psychological disturbances in their lives are comparable to those in the lives of normal people. Although some researchers feel that the mental life of feeble-minded persons is different, this view is not universally supported by research, particularly not in the case of mild and moderate retardation (Dosen, 1983). In the author's own research (Hellendoorn, Hockman, & Noordermeer, in press), small but not significant differences were found in the play of normal and mentally retarded children of the same mental age (four to five years).

Goessens (1984, 1985) published two case studies on institutionalized mentally retarded boys. She contends that for the elaborate fantasy play one works with in imagery interaction, a mental age of 5 to 6 years is indispensable, regardless of the child's chronological age. The best results were obtained with 12- to 18-year-olds. Goessens calls attention to some special features, which she feels are characteristic of the institutionalized retarded children she works with:

1. The children are very eager to play and have no trouble proceeding quickly to deeply personal play. It seems they are less resistant than some normal children.

2. Since many children have problems with organizing their world, the therapist should not be afraid of being directive (e.g., suggesting suitable play material and play themes). In many cases the suggestion to stage a television show together works well.

3. Institutionalized children always have conflicting feelings about their family home environment, and a lot of attention is required to work these through. In this context, it is striking that many of these children create a play world with two or more houses. It seems a good idea to allocate a lot of time to the concrete designing or building of such dwellings.

4. Another recurrent theme is that of growing up versus staying small—understandable since they experience that their growing up is not the same as that of their normal counterparts.

5. If one wants children to accept life in a fully humane sense, it is not only necessary to work through the past, but also to provide a future, a perspective. This is not always easy to do for mentally retarded children; it is further complicated because most of them will be permanently dependent (at least partially) on others.

Combining Imaginative Play Therapy with Behavior Modification Techniques

Often children are presented with problems that can only be relieved by a multifaceted approach. One of the criticisms often made about behavioral techniques is that they alleviate only certain symptoms but not the underlying problems, so that sooner or later another symptom will crop up. On the other hand, when deep-seated problems are worked through, sometimes long-standing behavioral symptoms persist, even though their original causes are gone. The author believes that if a behavior problem is not only a daily hindrance but also a sign of more serious problems, it may be a good idea to use more than one approach.

Lub (1985) reports about a boy with serious writing problems: Mark (eleven years old, in the fifth grade), was referred by a neurologist who found no neurological cause for the totally distorted writing. Mark had always been an easy and diligent pupil. In first grade he had encountered some problems in learning to write until a physiotherapist discovered his left-hand preference. A psychological examination revealed a good intelligence. Mark spoke quite openly about his bad writing. That was the only problem he had. In free situations he showed strong defenses. He was easily distracted and did not want to play. He consented only to paint a picture. A fear of accidents appeared in his painting and in his projective stories. Also evident were feelings of not being able to grow, of not being able to conform to high demands, of anxiety about the future, and of confusion about his body. It looked as if, through his symptoms, he was able to avoid most of these problems: Since he could not do any schoolwork, nobody could make any demands on him.

In his family, tension ran high: There was great anxiety about Mark's future if his writing did not improve. The parents valued school achievement. Father himself had had learning problems as a child, and an older brother was dyslectic.

The therapist devised a three-fold treatment plan. First, she felt there should be direct attention for the writing problem, which to Mark and his parents was explained as a symptom of overfatigue. Mark had indicated himself that his fingers felt tired. A rest cure in bed was prescribed, during which time he was not allowed to write at all. He was permitted to do only gentle relaxation exercises with his fingers three times a day. Every evening he was required to indicate his level of tiredness on a ten-point scale. When the tiredness disappeared for three days, careful exercises in the further use of his fingers started. Only then were visitors admitted to his bedroom.

Second, play therapy was indicated to work through Mark's feelings of inadequacy and high demands on himself. As Mark himself had chosen such a hidden symptom, an indirect therapy method (imagery interaction) seemed best. Although he did not want to play during assessment, the therapist felt it worth a try. From the first, Mark's play was a perfect example of meaningful imaginative play.

The third part of the treatment plan was intensive counseling of the parents. Their demands on Mark's school achievement had to be tuned to his capabilities, while at the same time their overly concerned, overprotective and permissive attitude in other fields needed discussion and alternative action.

The plan worked well. Writing exercises were begun (but carefully spaced) after one-and-a-half weeks of rest. At about that time he also came for his third play session, at the beginning of which he could not find anything to do. It soon became clear that he was afraid he might lose the therapist now that his writing was getting better: That had happened with the physiotherapist when Mark was six years old. Once reassured, he resumed play, and, in the muddy quicksandlike world of his first sessions, he now created firmer ground by means of dams and dikes. There remained many dangerous places, but there were also safe ones. A little monkey Mark had played with before that had always stayed close to its mother now dared to go exploring. Within the next few hours, the little monkey and a boy puppet Mark added were experimenting with all kinds of unknown situations.

Particularly beautiful play imagery was seen in the 12th session. In the large sandbox Mark created two countries, separated by a dike. One country was fertile, full of trees and water; the other country was dry and barren. The latter was inhabited by a boy and a girl. They were hungry, but not clever enough to climb over the dike. One day, the boy dug in the dike and found a tunnel to the other side. He returned later, closed the gap, and reported that the other side was just as bad. The girl and the animals were very disappointed. But still the girl was curious. With the help of a strong animal, she reopened the tunnel and found the good country. The animals followed and they all enjoyed the plentiful food and drink. The boy was punished for his lie and shut in the tunnel for seven years. After his release, he joined them in the good country.

This play image was seen (apart from the biblical theme) as indicating the possibility of a new start, which the boy did not dare to take on his own. He left the actual breakthrough to others. Only after doing penance could he himself start anew.

In the rest of his therapy, which took twenty-four sessions, Mark worked through the relationship with his parents. At first he painted this all in black and white: There were a father and a mother who were perfect, and another couple who were completely bad. Gradually this picture took on more shades, which enabled Mark to better identify with his father.

Comment

This case is a good example of an effective combined strategy, focusing on the symptom with behavioral techniques on the one hand, and working out the underlying problems on the other. It seems that covert techniques work especially well with children who have covert symptoms, as in conversions. Note that the behavioral techniques also had a covert and paradoxical form.

CONCLUSION

The techniques described and illustrated above call for an empathic and creative therapist who may sometimes act highly nondirective and at other times act highly directive. Directiveness is necessary when therapy stalls, when the child seems unable to overcome a barrier, and when limits are transgressed. It is also called for (in a milder way) when progress is slow and the child needs support. Therapeutic "messages" also have a clear directive component.

Interventions with a directive character are not without risk. If they clash with the level of experiencing of the children, these will feel forced. This is only adequate in extreme cases of limit-breaking. But if the interventions are subtly geared to the child's capability of processing, they may work very well. For such an intervention to succeed, three conditions must be met: (1) the therapist must be a real partner for the child by showing an accepting, empathic, and playful attitude; (2) the therapist must be well trained in the interpretation of personal meaning and during each session should constantly be aware of the meanings being worked on; and (3) the therapist must continually keep track of the therapy goals and of the specific end any intervention is to serve. This points to the importance of careful setting of goals, as discussed earlier.

When working with a child, the goals should be reviewed regularly: New material may arise necessitating alteration or adjustment. However, there is more to do between sessions. Analyzing the themes and meanings, the therapist is advised to prepare interventions. The more the therapist becomes acquainted with a child and the child's ways of playing, the easier it will be to think up creative ideas beforehand—to be used when the opportunity arises. For this purpose, supervision and—for the more experienced therapist—intervision are indispensable. Both supervision and intervision are forms of professional guidance or consultation, the difference being that supervision is provided by a colleague with more training and/or experience, while intervision is given by colleagues (usually in a small group) of about the same level of training.

REFERENCES

Adelman, H.S., Kaser-Boyd, N., & Taylor, L. (1984). Children's participation in consent for therapy and their subsequent response to treatment. *Journal of Clinical Child Psychology, 13,* 170-178.

Ariel, S. (1986). Family play therapy. In R. van der Kooij and J. Hellendoorn (Eds.), *Play, play therapy, play research* (pp. 153-160). Lisse/Berwyn: Swets and Zeitlinger.

Ariel, S., Carel, C.A., & Tyano, S. (1985). Uses of children's make-believe play in family therapy: Theory and clinical examples. *Journal of Marital and Family Therapy, 11,* 47-80.

Baron, G., & Cautella, J.R. (1983). Imagery assessment with normal and special needs children. *Imagery, Cognition and Personality, 3,* 17-30.

Borke, H. (1947). *Changes in the expression of emotionalized attitudes in six cases of play therapy.* Master's thesis. University of Chicago.

Day, L., & Reznikoff, M. (1980). Social class, the treatment process and parents' and children's expectations about child psychotherapy. *Journal of Clinical Child Psychology, 9,* 195-198.

Donker-Raymakers, Th. (1982). Beeldcommunicatie bij een rouwproces. *Kind en Adolescent, 3,* 94-99.

Dosen, A. (1983). *Psychische stoornissen bij zwakzinnige kinderen.* Lisse: Swets & Zeitlinger.

Dulcan, M.K. (1984). Brief psychotherapy with children and their families. *Journal of the American Academy of Child Psychiatry, 22,* 544-551.

Fein, G.G. (1975). A transformational analysis of pretending. *Developmental Psychology, 11,* 291-296.

Fein, G.G. (1981). Pretend play in childhood: An integrative review. *Child Development*, *52*, 1095-1118.

Ginott, H., & Lebo, D. (1961). Play therapy limits and theoretical orientation. *Journal of Consulting Psychology, 25,* 337-340.

Goessens, T. (1984). Het huis met het gouden dak. *Kind en Adolescent*, *5*(2), 30-36.

Goessens, T. (1985). Beeldcommunicatie met zwakzinnige kinderen. In J. Hellendoorn (Ed.), *Therapie, kind en spel* (pp. 188-204). Deventer: Van Loghum Slaterus.

Guttman, H.A. (1975). The child's participation in conjoint family therapy. *Journal of the American Academy of Child Psychiatry*, *14*, 490-499.

Harinck, F., & Hellendoorn, J. (1983). Procesresearch in de kinderpsychotherapie. In C. de Wit (Ed.), *Psychotherapie bij kinderen en jeugdigen* (pp. xx-xx). Leuven/ Amersfoort: Acco.

Harinck, F., & Hellendoorn, J. (1987). *Therapeutisch spel: Proces en interactie*. Lisse: Swets & Zeitlinger.

Harinck, F., & Loeven, L., (1985a). Beeldvorming over de beeldcommunicatie. In J. Hellendoorn (Ed.), *Therapie, kind en spel* (pp. 239-256). Deventer: Van Loghum Slaterus.

Harinck, F., & Loeven, L. (1985b). Praktijk in beeld. In J. Hellendoorn (Ed.), *Therapie, kind en spel* (pp. 257-273). Deventer: Van Loghum Slaterus.

Hellendoorn, J. (1988). *Een preventief spelprogramma*. Paper presented at the PAOS-BC conference, Leiden.

Hellendoorn, J., Groothoff, E., Mostert, P., & Harinck, F. (1981). *Beeldcommunicatie: Een vorm van kinderpsychotherapie*. Deventer: Van Loghum Slaterus.

Hellendoorn, J., Hockman, J., & Noordermeer, G. (In press). Verstandelÿk gehandicapte kinderen en verbeeldend spel. *Tÿdschrift voor Orthopedagogick*.

Hendricks, S. (1971). *A descriptive analysis of the process of client centered play therapy*. Dissertation, North Texas State University, Denton.

Klijn, W.J. (1980). Gezinsspelen, een methodiek voor het vaststellen van gezinsinteracties. *Kind en Adolescent*, *1*, 129-141.

Langeveld, M.J. (1955). Bevrijding door beeldcommunicatie. *Nederlands tijdschrift voor de psychologie*, *10*, 433-455.

Langeveld, M.J. (1964). De mens en de beelden. *Nederlands tijdschrift voor de psychologie*, *19*, 89-110.

Lieberman, J.N. (1977). *Playfulness*. New York: Academic Press.

Lub, M. (1985). De behandeling van een kind met een schrijfstoornis. In J. Hellendoorn (Ed.), *Therapie, kind en spel* (pp. 205-219). Deventer: Van Loghum Slaterus.

Meichenbaum, D. (1977). *Cognitive behavior modification: An integrative approach*. New York: Plenum Press.

Mook, B. (1982a). Analyses of therapist variables in a series of psychotherapy sessions with two child clients. *Journal of Clinical Psychology*, *38*, 63-76.

Mook, B. (1982b). Analyses of client variables in a series of psychotherapy sessions with two child clients. *Journal of Clinical Psychology*, *38*, 263-274.

Moustakas, C.E., & Schalock, H.D. (1955). An analysis of therapist-child interaction in play therapy. *Child Development*, *26*, 143-157.

Reams, R., & Friedrich, W.N. (1983). *Play therapy: A review of outcome research.* Seattle: Department of Psychology, University of Washington.

Rhoden, B.L. Kranz, P.L., & Lund, N.L. (1981). Current trends in the use of limits in play therapy. *Journal of Psychology, 107,* 191–198.

Rubin, K.H. (Ed.) (1980). *Children's play.* San Francisco: Jossey-Bass.

Safer, D.J. (1965). Conjoint play therapy for the young child and his parents. *Archives of General Psychiatry, 13,* 320–326.

Schmidtchen, S. (1986). Practice and research in play therapy. In R. van der Kooij & J. Hellendoorn (Eds.). *Play, play therapy, play research* (pp. 169–195). Lisse/Berwyn: Swets & Zeitlinger.

Schmidtchen, S., & Hobrüsker, B. (1978). Effektivitätsüberprüfung der klientenzentrierten Spieltherapie. *Praxis der Kinderpsychologie und Kinderpsychiatrie, 26,* 117–125.

Schmidtchen, S., & Rahlf, A. (1982). *Analyse der Therapeut-Klient-Kommunikation in der Spieltherapie.* Berlin: Vorlesung Kongress Psychotherapie.

Schmidtchen, S., Wörmann, D., & Hobrücker, B. (1977). Verlaufsanalyse des Spielverhaltens in der Kinderpsychotherapie. *Praxis der Kinderpsychologie und Kinderpsychiatrie, 26,* 208–217.

Scholten, U. (1979). *Spel en speelgoed bij geestelijk gehandicapte kinderen.* Den Haag: Staatsuitgeverij.

Singer, D.G., & Singer, J.L. (1985). *Make believe.* Glenview, Ill.: Scott, Foresman and Company.

Singer, J.L. (1973). *The child's world of make believe.* New York: Academic Press.

Singer, J. L. (1985). Verbeeldend spel: implicaties voor preventie en kinderpsychotherapie. In J. Hellendoorn (Ed.), *Therapie, kind en spel* (pp. 28–43). Deventer: Van Loghum Slaterus.

Singer, J.L. (1986). The development of imagination in childhood. In: R. van der Kooij and J. Hellendoorn (Eds.), *Play, play therapy, play research* (pp. 105–131). Lisse/Berwyn, Swets & Zeitlinger.

Singer, J.L., & Singer, D.G. (1981). *Television, imagination and aggression: A study of preschoolers.* Hillsdale, N.J.: J.J. Erlbaum.

Smith, P.K., & Syddall, S. (1978). Play and non-play tutoring in pre-school children: Is it play or is it tutoring that matters? *British Journal of Educational Psychology, 48,* 315–325.

Spivack, G., & Shure, M.B. (1982). The cognition of social adjustment: Interpersonal cognitive problem-solving thinking. In B.B. Lahey and A.E. Kazdin (Eds.), *Advances in clinical child psychology* (pp. 323–372). New York: Plenum Press.

Tiemensma, A., & Schokking-Kanij, L.J. (1985). Gesprek in beelden. In J. Hellendoorn (Ed.), *Therapie, kind en spel* (pp. 161–173). Deventer: Van Loghum Slaterus.

Urbain, E.S., & Kendall, P.C. (1980). Review of social-cognitive problem solving interventions with children. *Psychological Bulletin, 88,* 109–143.

Vandenberg, G. (1980). Play, problem solving and creativity. In K.H. Rubin (Ed.), *Children's Play* (pp. 49–68). San Francisco: Jossey-Bass.

Wright, D.M., Moelish, I., & Pollack, L.J. (1976). The outcome of individual child psychotherapy: Increments at follow-up. *Journal of Child Psychology and Psychiatry, 17,* 275–285.

Yawkey, Th.D. (1981). Role play and language growth: Strategies for imaginative experiences. *Contemporary Education, 52,* 223–227.

CHAPTER 3

The Use of Dance Movement Therapy with Troubled Youth

HELEN PAYNE

INTRODUCTION

This chapter describes a study (Payne, 1987) that used dance movement therapy (DMT) with adolescents who were placed in care and educated in residential schools. These young people were frequently labelled delinquent and had usually been referred to the courts for being out of parental control and had often engaged in antisocial acts. The teenagers were mostly male with an average age of thirteen to fifteen years.

Historical Background

The *I Ching,* perhaps the oldest book ever written, links movement and emotion: "Every mood of the heart influences us to movement" (Wilhelm, 1968, p. 124). Bender and Boas (1941), Laban (1951), Bainbridge (1953), Chace (1953), and Rosen (1954) were among the first authors to write on the subject of DMT, the latest of the arts therapies to develop in the United Kingdom. In the United States, the source of most of the literature, the terms *dance therapy, movement therapy,* and *dance/movement therapy* are used interchangeably and the professional association incorporates them all under the term *dance therapy.* In the United Kingdom, DMT appears to be allied more with the other arts therapies, such as art therapy and dramatherapy (Holden, 1980; Sherborne, 1974; Shirley, 1980), than with psychotherapy.

The term *dance movement therapy* has been adopted in the United Kingdom to avoid confusion between dance therapy and movement therapy and to be specific that it is a particular form of movement, namely dance—the creative or expressive movement form. This enables DMT to be consistent with the other arts therapies.

Dance has been part of all cultures since ancient times when Shamanism used dance to heal. Wright (1980), an anthropologist, drew our attention to exorcism ceremonies in Malaysia where dance, particularly trance-dance, serves as both a strategy for healing and a sign of health. She described how dance becomes an integrative force for some societies. Authors in Spencer's source book (1985) analyzed the place of dance in several societies, interpreting the dance as an aspect of ritual behavior which serves a variety of purposes. These aspects of dance form a vital link with present day DMT.

Early DMT literature refers to the goals of physical activity, social interaction, group rhythmic activity, and relationships with others. All these are valid but can also be accomplished via sports, dance, music, drama, folk dance, and so on. Chace (1953), in one of the earliest reports, claimed DMT was affecting and alleviating the isolation felt by her depressed, psychotic, and schizophrenic patients.

Bartinieff (1971), an American physiotherapist, suggested that dance therapy could be used to help the emotionally disturbed or could be concerned with movement distortions. She stated, "Dance is a non-verbal medium of emotional expression as well as the joy of action through bodily emotion, (p. 20). This implies that the approach can celebrate the client's interest in dance or can use dance as a way of fostering emotional expression.

Other studies and a large amount of literature in the area of movement and special needs have concentrated on the cognitive connections with movement Frostig, 1967; Kephart, 1971; Cratty, 1979. Condon and Ogston (1966) and Condon (1968) showed how much synchrony there is in everyday encounters, specifically in speech and nonverbal communication. This research relates to the view of dance as an interactive rhythmic encounter (Fraenkel, 1983). There is far less controlled research in the existential approach, which uses humanistic or psychoanalytical theories. That is, the process aspect, rather than the product, is seen to be fundamental to the therapy. The whole area of psychotherapy research has been struggling with the common problem of evaluating the therapy.

Dance movement therapy literature is scant and published studies concentrate, in the main, on effects in relation to body image, perceptual motor development, and affective states such as relief of anxiety. Descriptive accounts cover a range of populations although disturbed adolescents and delinquents are rarely mentioned.

According to Mason (1974), many leading DMT practitioners advocate the value of DMT for special needs groups, such as the autistic, deaf, visually impaired, elderly, minimal brain dysfunctioned, and school phobic. In this literature many approaches are utilized. The main ones seem to be corrective and existential. The former uses a medical model and has produced some controlled research studies. It is more analytical than the existential approach and evaluates projects in which movements are provided in a programmed way, systematically treating dysfunctional aspects.

Theoretical Foundation

A basic principle of DMT is the notion that bodily movement is related to emotion and that by working on the movement level in conjunction with the emotional level there is an immediate response at a feeling level (Gendlin, 1962a; Bowlby, 1982). This provides an opportunity for emotion at a preverbal level to be re-experienced and integrated through the symbolism of dance.

A second basic principle is that by enabling the client to explore and become familiar with an extended and more balanced range of movement, one fosters a greater adaptability in response to the environment.

A recent description of DMT, to which the author contributed, has been adopted by the Association for Dance Movement Therapy (founded in 1982) and the Standing Committee of the Arts Therapy Professions. It embodies these two fundamental principles:

> Dance Movement Therapy is the use of expressive movement and dance as a vehicle through which the individual can engage in personal integration and growth. It is founded on the principle that there is a relationship between motion and emotion and that by exploring a more varied vocabulary of movement people experience the possibility of becoming more securely balanced yet increasingly spontaneous and adaptable. Through movement and dance each person's inner world becomes tangible, individuals share much of their personal symbolism and in dancing together relationships become visible. The dance movement therapist creates a holding environment in which such feelings can be safely expressed, acknowledged and communicated. (Standing Committee of Arts Therapy Professions, 1987, p. 3)

Both these principles are related to the concept that a person's body is the self and that feelings about the body and the use of it in stillness and in movement are expressive of the person's inner world. This inner world (Wickes, 1968) becomes accessible not only through individual movement and personal symbols, but also in the interaction with the therapist and the group members. Dance movement therapy claims that through the dance or movement structures, relationships emerge manifesting themselves in, for example, the sharing of opposing rhythms, the use of space, willingness to support others or trusting enough to be supported, and leading or following. In this way, DMT can provide for change, awareness, and exploration, as well as being a diagnostic tool. The emphasis is on individual creativity and the personal statement of dance. The making of the movement is a creative process and engages the healthy part of the client in the journey toward individuation (Jung, 1966).

These inherent principles are the same for all populations although different emphases are applicable with different groups. Dance movement therapy has been applied through a broad spectrum of therapeutic activities that encompass, at one extreme, the use of movement and dance, movement structures, games, and relaxation techniques as media for individual psychotherapy, and, at the other, the organization of more informal groupwork or developmental movement work with the elderly or people with physical, social, emotional, or mental handicaps. Specific treatment programs may be undertaken as interventions for a variety of groups and individuals in social, educational, health, and other rehabilitative settings. Thus, it is difficult to find one definition that embraces the details of such varied applications.

There are several references in the literature to the underlying principles in DMT. Darwin (1872) recounted an infinite number of postural changes that are the distinctive aspects of the expression of feeling. Reich (1945), Schilder (1955), and Lowen (1975) all recognized the interrelationship of soma and psyche. The literature on humanistic psychology also makes reference to the body-mind approach and it has been only since its inception that study and treatment approaches have been seriously considered. A German publication by Gunter (1984) referred to the body and dance therapy in humanistic psychiatry. In the United Kingdom, this nonmechanistic, positive approach to exploring the self has had an influence on the development of DMT. The present attention on the body, dance, and fitness has enabled DMT to become more acceptable to the public. In the United States, Feder and Feder (1981) noted the impact humanistic psychology has had on the creative arts therapies (CAT) generally. They also point out the common ground between art, drama, music, and dance movement therapy: First, they all use the creative process; and, second, they all focus on nonverbal media. For DMT, theoretical models are derived from the psychological school of the individual practitioner and that practitioner's philosophy. Some popular models are psychoanalytical (Siegal, 1984; Bernstein, 1971; Jungian (Whitehouse, 1977); Gestalt (Serlin, 1977); and behavioristic and developmental (Espenak, 1981; Bainbridge-Cohen & Mills, 1979). Dance movement therapy theories and Reichian theories may contribute to a more general theory of body psychotherapy.

Unblocking resistance to growth as subjects hold frozen movement patterns, muscular tensions, or postures enables a greater breadth of feeling expression, perception, and interpersonal relating responses (Reich, 1945). It is claimed that problems manifested in emotional, social, or behavioral disturbance are invariably reflected in movement range, in abilities to express and communicate emotions, and in choices in thinking and abstracting. The fundamental belief that movement expression is reflective of the inner self gives access to intervention through body-mind interaction and expression, allowing another level of development to be released. One approach found in DMT literature suggests that a change in movement expression will result in a personality or behavioral change (Leventhal, 1980). Another approach stresses that it is the movement activities that are the vehicle for the therapeutic relationship (Delaney, 1973). There seems to be a common dichotomy here that is similar to that found in the other arts therapy literature; that is, whether it is the movement experience or the relationship that is the agent of change.

Gendlin (1962b), an American psychologist, has done much research on the phenomenological experiencing process that has been used in theoretical papers on DMT. He described two levels: the felt body level and the symbolic level. Ornstein (1973) claimed a physiological basis for this distinction, that of right and left brain respectively, but referred to two levels of experience as unique types of human consciousness: the intuitive and the rational. This is a polarity that has some correspondence with concepts such as subjective and objective. It is claimed that we mostly regard the world from an intellectual perspective because our culture exalts the rational-cognitive side and disparages the physical-emotional side (Mahrabian, 1972). Consequently, when we become strongly aroused we respond in either a constricted or a vague way. There is a lack of familiarity with our affective-motor systems, our control over our bodies, and bodily derived emotional responses. Most verbal therapies fail to recognize that the bodily derived felt level of experience must precede the conceptual level if a person is not to remain out of touch with his or her kinesthetic-affective reactions.

Schaefer (1976), in a description of the therapeutic use of child's play, stressed the need for body release action to recreate flexibility lost in former years. Play therapy is noninterpretive and essentially of a nonverbal nature that makes links with DMT. Schaefer highlighted the fact that parents may restrict body movement when the child is between one and three years of age (for example, by too early toilet training, confinement to playpens, or deprivation of space to creep, toddle, crawl, or climb). Children may develop cramped control to protect themselves from outer pressures and continuous demands. This can affect the whole psychophysical system and could lead to compulsive neurotic character structures. Schaefer pointed out that the latency-age child has a particular need for activity, both motor and muscular, and that this—combined with the cognitive—provides equipment for the acquisition of skills (Kephart, 1971). "Acting up" is a normal part of any schoolage child. "Acting out" is material dispersed through actions making it unavailable for therapy. Schaefer advised not to battle against action patterns but to use them as material, channeling a freedom of action to aid in the discovery of the body-self.

It may not be a prerequisite, as in adult therapy, that the child be aware that it is therapy he or she is engaged in. Indeed, adolescents labeled troubled or troublesome may find it difficult to accept sessions on such a basis. Nicol (1979), in his descriptions of play therapy, confirmed that the child does not need to know he or she is engaged in therapy.

Research Findings

The very recent development of DMT means that there is a dearth of rigorous research in the field. Most of the published writings come from the United States and consist of descriptive and theoretical or case study approaches. As there are very few controlled studies evaluating the effectiveness of DMT, it tends to be neglected in clinical or educational psychological literature, although nonverbal behavior has been the focus of attention in psychiatric literature for some time. There has been some contribution from the nonverbal literature to the fields of both dance and DMT, for example, Kestenberg (1971), Davis (1973), and Hunt (1978). Individual DMT practitioners have begun to record their work but there are few systematic and ordered studies, most being merely descriptive and journalistic in style. Most research is limited to outcome studies of one group or one subject pre- and posttest design. Other research has begun to look at the dance movement role (Schmais & Felber, 1977; Johnson & Sandel, 1977).

Although findings have shown favorable therapeutic outcomes in practice, any research to date has been more exploratory than definitive. Most of the case studies, theoretical material, and writings about DMT and special populations have come from the United States, although a few descriptive accounts in the United Kingdom are now appearing (Penfield, 1978; Meier, 1979; Meekums, 1981; Payne, 1979b, 1981, 1984, 1985).

Ling (1983), in a related descriptive account, gives the goals of her work in DMT with women prisoners in the United Kingdom as improving self image and communication, release of tension, and developing a positive regard for the body.

The literature includes several accounts relevant to work with adolescents. For example, Silberman (1973) tells of her experience working with disturbed late adolescent boys in a city prison hospital. She describes the slow process and her frustration when the offenders found themselves back in prison after release, showing her that the work rarely generalized. Sandel (1973) describes a videotape of work with troubled adolescents and young adults at a psychiatric institution. There is no indication of possible benefits or behavioral changes in these descriptions. Hecox, Levine, and Scott (1976) claim dance works well with adolescents in rehabilitation since there are many social motivators and reinforcers for dancing at this age. Apter, Sharir, Tyano, and Wijsenbeck (1978) studied movement therapy with psychotic adolescents and claimed positive outcomes.

Some research has been concerned with the use of the arts with children and adolescents. Torrance and Torrance (1972) undertook to teach the three Rs to disadvantaged young people through drama, creative writing, and dance. Using the Torrance Tests of Creative Thinking before and after the project, they found statistically significant gains in the ability to produce ideas. This study argues that most remedial programs were not successful because they were based on deficiencies rather than on strengths.

Torrance and Torrance did not define "disadvantaged," nor did they identify children's strengths prior to the program. They did not provide a control group either. However, the study stressed the use of creative possibilities, for example, enjoyment of music, rhythm, and inventive dance; ability to express feelings and emotions; use of gesture and humor; and responsiveness to the concrete and the kinesthetic. The researchers did not articulate what specific effects each of these activities had on the subjects. Possibly more balanced views may have been gained if the young people had been asked for their thoughts.

Hazelton, Price, and Brown (1979), in a British study with learning disabled (mild) secondary school children of 11 to 13 years of age, stated that there was improved reading success and important personality growth with the implementation of psychodrama, creative movement, and remedial arts over several years. This was studied in contrast to remedial reading techniques which were found not to improve reading. The Cattel Personality Questionaire was used to measure effects. A control group, a psychodrama group, a remedial arts group, and an unstructured movement group were all used. However, they do not say which aspects improved reading success as measured by ITPA, nor which personality aspects changed.

Dunne, Bruggen, and O'Brian (1982) have reported group body therapy approaches with hospitalized adolescents in the United Kingdom that resulted in reduced sexual behavior and violence, increased verbal interaction, and deeper concern for each other. However, the authors do not make their approach clear.

Hilyar et al. (1982) researched the use of physical fitness with young offenders in a program led by skilled counselors. From their study it can be seen that relationship variables were more important in promoting self-esteem and reducing anxiety and depression in the young people than was the activity of the physical training itself.

The present author often selects adolescents for DMT on the basis of high anxiety scores. This is because there is evidence from DMT literature and other sources from delinquency and psychotherapy that these young people are more likely to benefit from therapy.

In a study by Peterson and Cameron (1978), body movement is recommended for preparing high anxiety adult patients for verbal psychotherapy. They found that patients were more able to control their anxiety as a result of such activity. Rutter, Tizzard, and Whitmore (1970), in discussing delinquency, suggest that only highly anxious adolescents who want help would benefit from psychotherapy. Johnson (1984) claims complex feeling states that created tremendous anxiety could be expressed and explored within the therapeutic relationship using movement and dramatherapy with an 18-year-old male catatonic schizophrenic.

Leste and Rust (1984), in a British study, explored modern dance training on levels of anxiety in 114 19-year-old college students. Findings showed significant reductions in anxiety for the dance group and not for the other groups of sport or music. The authors concluded that the effects of music and physical exercise alone were less than when combined in dance. The study also found that the more interested the subjects were in dance prior to the program, the more favorable were the effects. This implies that attitude towards dance may dictate the degree to which it, or DMT, can be useful for the client.

There seems to be some evidence, therefore, that DMT could be of benefit to anxious young people with delinquent behaviors, since it incorporates dance and relaxation. In particular, this author's research found that such young people have limited language skills and are often functioning as learning disabled. Dance movement therapy may reduce their anxiety and increase their verbal skills, especially if they have a favorable attitude to dance already. It is the above literature and studies which provide the rationale for using DMT with this population of young people.

Lovell (1980) suggested that DMT may be significant for use with adolescents because of the particular body-related issues of puberty, making DMT a modality suited to resolving the body image concerns of adolescents. Examples include supporting the transition from child to adult by exploring the psychosexual issues relating to body image via movement processes; developing an acceptance of the differences between child and adolescent which are intrinsic to the adolescent phase of development; increasing awareness of the psychological and physical changes of adolescence through verbal and nonverbal means; and heightening body awareness through proprioceptive and tactile stimulation.

Brown, McDowell, and Smith (1981) mentioned that dance therapy is suitable for adolescents with behavioral problems since there are many social motivations and reinforcers for dancing at these age levels. They reported a study by Merek (1976) which compared a DMT group with a control group receiving verbal therapy for 6 weeks. Self-concept and movement scales were used, the latter including self-reports and ratings by others. Although results did not differentially support DMT as superior to verbal therapy, both groups showed gains in physical expressions. These findings support the claim that DMT enhances expressive qualities.

The Author's Study

The following is a description of a study this author recently conducted of the perceptions of male adolescents labeled delinquent towards a program of dance movement therapy (DMT).

Of special interest in this research was the aspect of clients' perceptions toward the experience of DMT. The author was unable to discover any literature in this area apart from a few descriptive accounts. For example, Rosen (1957) quoted an essay by a patient on her reactions to dance therapy on an open ward in a psychiatric hospital. Dickinson (1957) mentioned an article (Keleher, 1956) which described a beginning session at a New York psychiatric hospital for small boys. It began:

> They didn't want to dance, they kicked the locked door trying to get out. The psychiatrist persuaded, the dance therapist kept up a rhythmic beat on the drum, but the boys would have none of it. "We want to go home," they shouted, stomping round the room. But feet fell into step with the dance rhythm and the session was on.

The research was pioneering for several reasons. Little research has been undertaken on DMT in the United Kingdom and the author is not aware of any material on clients' perceptions towards DMT or on DMT with adolescents labeled delinquent.

Three stages of experimental fieldwork were undertaken: preliminary, pilot, and final. The preliminary fieldwork took place in a community home with education on the premises (CHE) in the Northeast of England. Subjects were 13 to 15 years old, male, and in care. The pilot study, which was based on recommendations made in the preliminary fieldwork, took place in the same setting with another similar group of young people. One theme was selected from the analysis of pilot study results for the final fieldwork, which aimed to discover how the young people, in particular, perceived and experienced the process of DMT.

The final fieldwork was undertaken in Scotland in a different but comparable setting to the pilot study. A DMT intervention program was designed, based on pilot study recommendations and was implemented over a 3 month period. Two weekly sessions took place with 4 volunteer male adolescents. The primary data collection was by semistructured interviews conducted by trained interviewers over the duration of the program and at follow-up.

The limitations of this research must be recognized, hence caution needs to be employed when drawing conclusions. The following are the seven main conclusions drawn from this research.

1. The young people's experience and world view can be seen to be concerned with a dimension encompassing enjoyment and boredom. Enjoyment was linked to "good" and boredom to "bad." They enjoyed group sessions but not individual sessions when prior to group sessions. They found the latter more embarrassing and felt "stupid."

2. The young people stressed a variety of experience in concrete terms in order to conceptualize DMT. They labeled movement games, dance, exercise, relaxation, and improvisation. They also named apparatus, music, verbalization, and vocalization.

3. In order to evaluate their experience, the young people contrasted it with their other activities in school, for example, the simplistic comparison of "skive" with "hard work." They judged the therapist's approach to be nondomineering and responsive.

4. A pretreatment interview was found not to be helpful in preparing this population for DMT.

5. The young people did not perceive the sessions as helping them in the ways outlined by the therapist.

6. The terminology used and the information given prior to sessions to some extent determined the young people's perceptions. It is recommended that the words "dance" and "therapy" be avoided since these and other aspects were an influence on their perceptions.

7. There is a need for researchers involved in arts therapy fieldwork to separate out their investment in the research and their investment in the therapeutic treatment they are also responsible for; hence, supervision was highly recommended.

Many implications can be drawn from these conclusions. For instance, it seems possible to engage such young people's willing cooperation in the DMT if enjoyment, specifically linked to free-flow with weight or overcoming gravity, is perceived as the main outcome. Their particular needs for sensory weight flow movement experiences were perceived as important for engaging their participation. Group work was less threatening than individual work for this age group, especially with a female therapist. Group work could be helpful in building up a therapeutic relationship prior to working individually or in dyads.

The fact that DMT focuses on the body and on movement influences clients' experience of DMT. How clients feel about their bodies and their movements and thus themselves will determine to some degree their responses to DMT. Therefore, research on self-image, body image, and body concept is valuable, not only in helping to determine the value of DMT but also in the understanding of DMT processes. Clients' perceptions of DMT relate to how they experience it on bodily or sensory levels in addition to intellectual and emotional levels.

It may be that drawing and other projective methods, such as thematic apperception tests, would be better at discovering perceptions from this population. Verbal expression does not reveal enough owing to the limited language abilities of the young people.

Vocalization and verbalization may be a development in the process of DMT or a supportive aspect to the content of DMT for this group. It aided interaction between the therapist and the young people.

In summary, this section introduced DMT from an historical perspective and outlined the principles of DMT as the author understands them together with relevant research. The latter was designed to provide the rationale for using DMT with groups of male adolescents labeled delinquent. Finally, an overview of the author's recent research was presented. This was an evaluation of the young people's experience of DMT, not a measurement of any resulting outcome or benefits.

THE TECHNIQUE

The approach to DMT employed by the author in her work with troubled young people grew out of a firm grounding in Rudolf von Laban's work (1879–1958) in the field of dance in education (Laban, 1978). His methods for teaching dance in schools and colleges were adopted in the United Kingdom after World War II, although Dalcroze's eurhythmics had flourished since the 1920s, as had Margaret Morris movement. Many children in schools had experienced modern educational dance that was child based and stressed creativity and groupwork. Both primary and secondary schools used the approach. Most primary teachers were given at least a basic understanding of Laban's methods and many physical education teachers studied Laban-based dance for specialist secondary school teaching. In addition, early students of Laban adapted his methods to a variety of situations, including special education (North, 1972; Sherborne, 1974; the health services (Wethered, 1973), and management (Lamb, 1965; Ramsden, 1973). As early as 1948, dance and fundamental movement was introduced into a London psychiatric hospital with the aim to coordinate action and thought (BSPP, 1986).

Despite these beginnings, Laban-based DMT remains a newly emerging profession in the United Kingdom, and even now there are few fulltime posts for therapists. There has been evidence of a steady development in the practice, however, in special education (Payne, 1977, 1979, 1980, 1984), hospitals (Holden, 1980), day centers (Pasch, 1985), prisons (Ling, 1983), and voluntary settings (Meekums, 1986). There are also some therapists who see clients privately (Pearmain, 1980).

Dance movement therapy and Laban's modern educational dance share several tools; for example, Laban's categorization of movement into body, effort, and space (Laban, 1978). Dance movement therapy uses Laban Movement Analysis (LMA) for assessment and development of movement range (see pages 83–84). The process of developing insight, interpretation, movement dialogue, relationship building, symbols, and alternative behavioral responses are all aspects of DMT. The client's behavioral or perceptual manifestations are used as thematic material that is then developed within the therapeutic relationship together with an awareness of developmental needs (Leventhal, 1980, 1986). The approach to DMT by the author is founded in humanistic psychology as developed by Rogers (1967), Maslow (1968), and Rowan (1975), together with group psychoanalysis (Bion, 1961).

Southgate's (1980) creative energy cycle is used as a guide to the development of sessions. A warm-up period for nurturing and preparation, an energizing time for a release of theme material and movement range exploration, a core time of the theme being worked with and through, and finally a quiet recovery period in which calming relaxation, closure, and anticipation of the next session is engendered. Techniques and teaching are not important aspects, but acceptance of the preverbal symbols generated by the young people are important, as is the encouragement of nonverbal communication and movement range. It is acknowledged that DMT as delivered by the author may be different from DMT delivered by another practitioner.

Themes from the sessions emerge from tasks and activities designed to facilitate responses in communication and an awareness of self with regard to others and the environment. Movement and creative rhythmic structures often form the basis of the sessions and themes (i.e., hiding, trusting, being stuck, and resistance) are dealth with using time, energy, and spatial dimensions— and, where appropriate, percussion, props, music, and relaxation techniques. Verbal counseling is also used when appropriate.

Both playing and moving are natural media of self-expression, being spontaneous and creative acts; both process and product are revealing and have the important advantage that they provide evidence of feelings and states of mind. The themes that emerge are significant to both client and therapist. A child's feelings and fantasies undergo a process of transformation in the process of DMT. Freedom of self-expression grows with time and trust, and discussion of movement or of therapeutic process is used only if the therapist feels it is appropriate. Sensitivity to the individual is a guiding factor. The therapist is a partner, closely involved, sharing the client's inner world as far as possible. It should not make any difference if the client moves or just sits; it is the client's time and this is made explicit. In line with play therapy, DMT is a method of helping troubled adolescents and adolescents in trouble to help themselves. The dancing, movement structures, and games act as other modes of self-disclosure alongside words and behavior. This gives DMT groups an added dimension not found in verbal groups. The structures are seen as starting points, rather than as finishing points.

Thus the DMT approach employed, while utilizing some psychoanalytic ideas, builds on the humanistic, nondirective method whereby the assumption is that the growth impulse makes mature behavior more satisfying than immature behavior. It grants individuals permission to be themselves; the therapist accepts that self completely, without evaluation or pressure to change. Recognition and clarification of the expressed attitudes is achieved by a reflection of what the client has expressed and by the process of allowing clients the opportunity to be themselves and to learn to know themselves, charting their own courses openly.

Limits are kept to a minimum to make way for smoother progress. Leaving the room, coming back, and leaving again constitute an evasion of the process; therefore, rules are imposed. To emphasize clients' responsibility for the process, it is important that they understand that if they leave it is because they feel bored, angry, or stubborn; however, if they leave they cannot return to that session. Often it expresses a need to meet some sort of anxiety.

There is thus no pressure to bring about change. Any change that is worthwhile is believed to come from within the client if it is to have any lasting effect. Rules are not used as a pressure. For example, swearing could lead to being excluded from the session, but this exclusion is not used in self-directive therapy. The client makes the choice whether to swear or not to swear, although the therapist's position concerning unacceptable behaviors may be clearly stated, for example, disappointment in the client.

The presence of physical aggression does involve the therapist in a rule that calls for authority and judgment. This might appear as partiality to certain members of the group. Axline (1974) recommends that limits be set for physical attacks in group work but that they need only be introduced when the therapist is certain of the imminence of violence.

The author therefore makes four clear rules with these young people: no hurting of themselves, of others, or of property, and remaining in the space for the duration of the session. These are stated at the beginning of the course of sessions and at various times during sessions when they seem necessary.

Change in a client's adherence to rules does not mean conformity through some kind of pressure. The therapist attempts to help the clients realize that if they are responsible for themselves, they achieve self-respect and self-confidence enabling them to make their own choices.

The technique used in DMT sessions with young people will be related to the particular training and experience of the Dance Movement Therapist. The following examples were part of a 20-session program for volunteer male adolescents in Scotland. It was held twice-a-week for one hour each session.

The content of the program was deliberately not predictable in order to respond to the themes and developmental needs of the group, although activities and structures were used when relevant to a theme. The content of the sessions developed out of each session and its processes and interactions, rather than being planned prior to the sessions.

A brief outline of possible content, given in retrospect, follows: functional movement activities; moving spontaneously with music or rhythms; moving in a formed way with musical accompaniment; moving alone or with others in a coordinated manner; learning new movements and using ones already known (using particular clients' movement-dance interests); learning more about the body and how to move; floor work; grounding activities; relaxation techniques; whole body movements; discussion of experiences; verbal exchange; self-disclosure; assertive techniques; exercises and movement games to enhance self awareness and awareness of others; interaction and non-verbal communication structures; tension-release tasks; sensation experiences such as jumping, swinging, and stillness; use of apparatus as a stimulus for movement choices; and cooperation and interaction with others through objects such as ropes, trampette, parachute, and elastic.

The content of the pilot field work included mirroring exercises, relaxation techniques, dancing in the group, improvisation, games involving objects, percussion and music, group movement tasks, role play, nonverbal and verbal exchange structures, and drawing. Themes included "choice versus no choice," arising out of feelings of a lack of control in the subjects' lives; "resistance and motivation," arising from the issue of nonparticipation and participation; "controlled versus controller," which emerged from aspects of power and leadership; and "trust" and "attacker versus defender."

Activities were intended to serve various aims. Some of these were release of energy and tension, expression of preverbal symbols, development of sensitivity toward self and others, peer leadership and sense of autonomy, group cohesion, increase in body awareness, enhanced self-concept, sense of fun and well-being, and development of spontaneity.

Four seemed to be the minimum acceptable number of young people for a group considering the levels of absenteeism found in the pilot study. It was hoped that this number would allow the group to function if one or two members were absent, although it might have caused difficulties for dyads. Any larger a group and the therapist might have found the numbers too great to facilitate a variety of interactions while remaining responsive to both the group and individual needs.

One part of the school's gymnasium was used for final fieldwork sessions, with benches screening off three-quarters of the space where ropes and mats were to be found. Space influences the content of sessions, as do objects in the space, individual goals, and subjects' responses.

Since DMT does not work on a cause-and-effect mechanism, there are no specific activities which are automatically utilized for any specific goal in a one-to-one correspondence. For one young person, with a personal goal of wishing to say "No" to others, gestures and sounds representing "No" to the client were explored symbolically in the sessions. This was developed into a rhythmic "Saying No" dance and finally into words and phrases incorporated within a movement interaction. In this, the client moved as if he were in a situation with his friends stealing something; he nonverbally enacted his withdrawal from them. His feelings about the situation were explored and the movement was repeated with the new awareness.

As a further illustration, one goal was to work with each boy individually in the group during the first stages of the development of the group. However, Gary could not let himself make contact with the therapist in this way; hence a goal for the next session was to engage Gary within a movement structure. Since he enjoyed testing his physical strength against others and there was a need to ground the group in some floor work, a wheelbarrow race was devised with the therapist partnering Gary.

Group sessions began with a warmup using loosening exercises, often to music the subjects chose, to relax bodily tension and to sensitize the boys to personal body sensations. There was group interaction, such as personal introductions using name games, sounds, gestures, or whole body movement. The therapist encouraged easy peripheral movements and then focused on specific areas of the body where there seemed to be tension. Next, there would be a period of more spontaneous free-form responses, sometimes with music, often in a structure. Here the aim was to enable the boys to discover the movement they liked to do—their own form of self-expression. This section merged into live situational themes such as "being closed versus being open" in sculpting each other, "mood postures," forming interactions with the therapist through structures of movement echoing, and others using touch where appropriate, for example, leaning against each other in twos.

Later, a relaxation section was introduced to help relieve long term residual tension and the temporary fatigue built up during movement activities. This usually involved a visualization or muscle tension release work and breathing, followed by a gradual transition from relaxation to movement again, and providing for a closure preparation. Sometimes a verbal feedback period was introduced to reinforce any good feelings and closeness, to provide for sharings of feelings, and to relate events in daily lives that connect with what had been experienced in sessions.

1. time and length of session   Date   Session Number

2. Setting

3. Population

4. Props/music used and reasons

5. Predominant themes (movement and psychodynamic)

    (a) Themes arrived with

    (b) Themes evolving

    (c) Themes clients thought of

6. What was the behavior overall? (Use symbols.)

7. Changes noted

8. Expressive gestures

    (a) Verbal   (b) Nonverbal

9. Goals achieved

10. Goals for next session

11. Any other comments

Figure 3.1. Evaluation sheet for dance movement therapy session.

The form shown in Figure 3.1 was designed by the author to aid observation, recording, and evaluation of sessions. In addition, for individual work in particular, movement observation is valuable when diagnosing and when planning and evaluating DMT programs. The observation sheet shown in Figure 3.2 is one method the author has found useful.

CASE ILLUSTRATION

This section contains a selection of material relating to one boy, called Paul for the purpose of this study, who participated in the fieldwork. The first selection is a process recording made by the therapist after session 17. This was a group session and introduces Paul as a member of the group, the other members being Brian, George, and John. These notes serve as an example both of the content of a DMT session and of therapeutic issues that can arise.

Name: _____

Date: _____

Date of Birth: _____

Contexts

1.

2.

3.

4.

5.

6.

Six 5-minute observations should be made in different contexts, giving a total in each column. From this an indication of the strengths in movement preferences may be derived. The profile is only a guide; it may need to be supported by other observation sheets, for example, behavioral checklists.

Mark 1 when movements are observed in any of the categories

OBSERVATION		1	2	3	4	5	6	TOTAL
Weight	Strong							
	Heavy (no weight)							
	Light							
Space	Direct							
	Meandering							
Time	Vital							
	Sustained							
Flow	Carefree							
	Cautious							
Body	Broad							
Shape	Thin							
Still	Rounded							
or	Twisted							
Moving	Shapeless							

Figure 3.2. Example of movement observation sheet.

Mark 1 when movements are observed in any of the categories

OBSERVATION		1	2	3	4	5	6	TOTAL
	Rise							
Body	Sink							
Shaping	Open							
Movements	Close							
	Advance							
	Retreat							
	Symmetry							
	Asymmetry							
Phases	Long							
	Short							
Personal	Wide							
Space	Close							
Gen. Space	Curved							
Pathways	Angled							

Comments on profile

Figure 3.2. (Continued)

THERAPIST'S NOTES

This was the first time with all four boys together, quite an achievement in itself. I had called the care staff to say that I would be in on Monday at 9:30, asking that a reminder be given to the boys. They were all waiting and when I arrived and entered the room, John remained outside. His teacher said he wanted him to wait there at the end of the session; he had been in trouble again. Brian and George took their shoes off; Paul and John refused. There was some annoyance from Brian about his white socks getting dirty. They all took their coats off eventually too, although George and John worked under them at the beginning, back to front with their hoods up.

We began with reflecting a movement. Brian and Paul chose to work together. A good start was made. George and John sat on chairs and did not move for the first section. I continued to say "change leaders" at intervals. Second section, and I guessed who was the leader. They enjoyed outwitting me. Brian's movement was very limited and close to his body and he refused to reflect Paul's movement as a follower. They were both up and standing on the bench. Paul began using his hips and hands, pretending to hold a microphone and singing to the music (Madness). Brian withdrew. John took his shoes off and he and George began moving their fingers under their coats, with some tickling of each other, too.

Next we sat in the center on cushions and they were asked to give, in a sentence, a thought on how they perceived their partner. Comments ranged from "he's daft" to "he's great"—all good humoured though, smiles on faces. George thought everyone was great after insulting them. Paul said Brian was no fun. They all wanted to do the warm-up again. I asked them to change partners but they didn't want to. John got up and George did a lot of show-off dancing.

During the next talking phase Paul said he wanted me to take my clothes off. George wanted to "do a play on how girls and boys wank together" and John supported this idea. Somehow I made it quite clear that taking my clothes off was not what I was there for. However, I allowed the fantasy to develop, stressing it was fine to fantasize as these feelings were natural, yet also aware that Paul had been arrested once for indecent exposure. I structured this by saying that they had to stop when told. They enjoyed this game, stopping each time as requested, although I did have to address each of them by name before they stopped.

They then moved as much as they could in 10 seconds. John organized a football game for this, using a shoe bag that was in the room on the floor. The next time, someone else organized a cushion fight for 10 seconds. Once they threw me a cushion and pulled me into the middle. I said "stop" and they froze. I explained I was not going to participate with them. For the next 10 seconds John elected that he was not going to join in as a play-fight had developed. George was particularly overactive, trying to pull Paul and Brian down to the floor. John organized them into a game "the first to hit the deck." George had a shield and sword (made from cushions). Lots of activity ensued. On each stop we talked about what had happened. I made a running commentary for the last one. Fears about injury arose from Brian and George. Brian said he wasn't joining in anymore, or coming again: "It's daft," he said. John replied that he came and he was older. John expressed his anger at Brian for not participating anymore. I said it was their group; they could make it as daft or stupid as they liked, but if others didn't like it they could club together to change it. I had an idea for a group lean but they did not want to do this. Finally, George said he would fall towards me if Paul and I caught him (trust game). Paul tended to throw George at me. George was self-directed, making his fall when he chose rather than passively letting us control him. He collapsed in his center, however, and usually caught himself before we caught him; perhaps the gap was too wide or perhaps he needed to be in complete control. George then had an idea to put coats on back-to-front with their hoods up for 10 seconds.

The head coordinator pushed on the door and interrupted us in one of our talking phases. The boys said we couldn't stop him because he was the head. They did not want to complete journals, but apart from a few resistant individuals at times, they cooperated successfully. More autonomy is evident now.

The boys at times made me feel useless, helpless, rejected, abandoned, messed up, and cruelly treated; precisely the experiences and feelings they found intolerable or intolerable to bear. This reversal of the painful experience seems the key to understanding the inner world of these boys whose outward behavior itself is often a vital message.

Much of their communication is through action rather than words.

My responsibility seems to be to protect the groups' integrity from my own ambivalence and maintain it as an internal conception despite disturbing assaults made on it by group members who remained fearful of intimacy and relatedness. My own sense of loneliness and hopelessness was great.

Distressing countertransference feelings were evoked by the group. Judging the effectiveness of these groups by the usual standards of group therapy experience is inappropriate and leads to devaluation of group members, of the therapy, and of the therapist.

CASE HISTORY

This is Paul's case history abstracted from his file and left deliberately in note form.

Age: 14 years
Sexual Offenses indecent assault -11/17 May 1983
Admitted CHE: 7/18/83

Social Work Report: 9/28/83
Benefit from masculine environment. He needs to learn control and respect for others, especially women whom I suspect he thought of no consequence, no doubt modeled on his experience with his mother who covered up for him and denied his excesses.

Social Aspect
Inept attempts to make friends.
—Aim to establish friendships.
Friendships short lived.
—Aim to remove causes of breakdowns.
Imitates peers.
—Aim to eliminate.

His passivity for involving himself in clownish behavior irritates peers, therefore prevents positive social interaction. Gullible and naive, often butt of his peers. Name calling, doesn't realize that he is so ridiculed because of immature behavior. Discussion helped him gain insight into why not particularly popular and encouraged him to think before acts, thus develop his own level of self-control. As yet he shows no real responsibility for self or others.

Problems
10/5/83:   Lots of effort from Paul in house decorating.
1/13/84:   Good behavior most of week. Therefore senior status. Very pleased. Talkative and sensible at Youth Club.

1/14/84 and 1/15/84:   Good behavior over weekend in house.

1/18/84:   Admitted theft of cigarets from office. Sanctioned. Quieter moments says he did not do this but self-reports unreliable.

1/26/84:   Odd behavior, starry eyes, fixed gaze, snatching at food with teeth.

2/1/84:   Banging head off door in toilets. Precipitated by niggling by/to another. Intervention to prevent self-injury.

3/17/84:   Paul making efforts of the order requiring gentle coaxing.

Background

5/5/82:   Admitted to Observation and Assessment Center after care order (place of safety order) by Juvenile Court, where Paul appeared charged with criminal damage.

Stepfather; natural-mother, never married Paul's father—since the father was dominated by his own mother. Paul has one sister. Mother says can discipline Paul and surprised he was taken into care. Developmental milestones normal, occasionally nocturnal enuresis.

Results of Interview

Child's view: Expressed deep feelings for mother and stated they have very close relationship, not to exclusion of sister. Mother never physically punished him but shouts when he displeases her. He said she was very disappointed with him when he was in trouble recently but also cried bitterly when he was taken away from home.

Stepfather's family bond with Paul: was in care himself from 9 years of age. Paul thinks of him as own father—good relationship. Mother and stepfather married when Paul was 5 years old (1974). Paul uses father's surname. Paul spends much time with grandmother. Gifts from grandmother given to him. Visits from parents who want him home. He is in the Army Cadets and goes to discos.

Care order -"Beyond control of his parents."

Educational psychologist (at 13 years) recommended remedial teaching. Paul has had no involvement with child guidance or psychology services.

Paul is easily led and sees his main weakness as the friends he has. When he goes home he will not see them if he can help it. Wants to join the army.

Presents, as anxious and psychometric data suggest, slightly higher-than-average anxiety. Poor social skills, limited self-control and concern for others. Emotionally shallow. Denies problems—only has minor ones. Impulsive.

Functioning at below average ability academically. Not described as established delinquent.

EVALUATIVE SESSION

The young people volunteering for sessions would always attend an evaluative session in which the therapist made an attempt to diagnose and be receptive to material which could be developed during the program. First, the plan, structure, and ground rules for Paul's evaluative session are noted. A summary of his diagnosis goals and possible content, structures, and methods are then presented.

Place: Resource Room, Education Center, Training School, CHE.

Rules and Structure (i.e., rules prepared by the therapist)

1. Arrive on time outside Resource Room (the space made available for DMT). Make contract with each boy, for example, I will . . . . and he will . . . . Shoes and socks removed for sessions.

2. Work for 30 minutes individually for several weeks then in dyads with another boy for a few weeks. Finally we will work in a small group for a short while. The whole program will take place for this term only.

3. Confidentiality issue.

4. Journals. Two minutes at end of session to write down things important to you; for example, what good things/bad things happened to you this week, anything about your family, friends, pets, hobbies, ambitions. Anything felt about session or how you feel. Drawing acceptable. Spelling doesn't matter. This is a message system between us and no one else is to see the journals, only you and I. I will give out and collect at the end of the session then write in a reply comment for next time. We both put our names on the journal.

5. We will aim to work together as a team to try to help you to overcome some of your difficulties.

6. When I say *stop* I expect you to stop and sit down immediately.

SESSION

Equipment: Chairs/tables/crayons/music/large paper/percussion/mats.

Task: Drawing to music on table. Chairs available.

1. Piece of paper each. Add music and give examples of marks.

2. A paper for us to share and repeat.

3. Draw with unusual hand, with mouth, with foot.

Task: Move hand as though drawing to the music on an enormous sheet of paper on whole wall.

Music: Ask for their favorite.

Task: Relaxation: Allow limbs/head to be moved by me—which parts most relaxed?

Aims of Session

1. To establish the beginning of a relationship through contact using a focus outside of self as the transitionary stage.

2. To use what they can do (i.e., the healthy part) as a way of developing confidence.

3. To give some structure within which unusual things are asked of them.

4. To assess any potential areas which could be worked with.

DIAGNOSTIC STATEMENT

The following material summarises the therapist's impressions of Paul from the evaluative session.

CONTENT   Tough versus gentle theme
                  Reinforcing that to have sexual feelings is okay

GOALS   To make contact
                  To develop trusting relationship
                  To use movement experience to draw out difficulties
                  To extend movement range
                  To reinforce sexuality
                  To enhance his expression through movement

PROCEDURES OF THERAPY

Rhythm

Percussion work

Range of feeling—tone music—(Tough and gentle)

Fight and non-fighting theme

PROBLEMS/POSSIBLE CAUSES/AREAS NEEDING CHANGE

1. Sexuality—possible—no girl friend—can't express sexual feelings to anyone—who is it safe for him to show sexual feelings towards?
2. Needs confidence building.

MOVEMENT OBSERVATIONS

Effort: quick/flexible. Alternatives in time factor.

Shaping: saggital, some opening and closing. Long phrases.

Passive escape in situations not to his liking which leads to anxiety.

SUMMARY OF SESSIONS FOLLOWING EVALUATION

This is included in order to illustrate how issues arose and were developed using DMT techniques over the duration of Paul's individual sessions.

For the first couple of sessions Paul was overeager to attend. Despite later ambivalence at coming, once he was in the room, his eyes sparkled and he seemed motivated to participate.

He worked with movements that developed from low to high, and open, often accompanied by his choice of music, a band called "Madness" which had a strong rhythmic beat. I selected some music with an opposite feeling tone: John Williams' guitar music. We moved together in a mirroring technique from sitting to kneeling to standing to walking. He was less inhibited with the lighter music, displaying considerably more free flow with sustained and flexible movements, beginning to move into spaces further from his body.

He was also keen to show his skills of body management in jumps, turning jumps, and strong postures with fists. He described these dances as "fit" and "exciting," made strong eye contact and commented on how good I was and that dance was tiring. He disclosed that he wanted to grab me and kiss me. Discussion focused on who it would be appropriate to show such feelings to, and on my role with him.

In a later session we worked from a rhythmical framework, particularly with stuck, rigid, and bound movement and with relaxation. It was noticed that Paul associated fear with rigidity and verbalized considerably about such situations in his life.

During the following session we worked with bound movement again. The following notes are from that session and describe perhaps the most significant event in his individual program.

I took his rooted, bound movement and asked him to exaggerate it moving his bones inside the skin of his feet, but without being able to move from the spot. I asked him what this felt like: "A struggle," he replied. I then pulled his hips and asked him to try to move to the next space in front. He pulled away, leant his body forwards, keeping his legs straight and remaining very bound and tight. "How does that feel?" "Good," he said, with lots of smiles—he seemed to enjoy the contact and struggle. We then developed onto hands and knees; his objective was to reach another space, mine to arrest his movement by holding his hips. We made a short phrase of this. I asked whether he had felt this struggle before. He avoided responding at first, asking if he could do "that hip thing" to me. I explained that the idea was for me to give him attention but since it was his initiation I decided to reverse roles. I felt that he was enjoying the contact but had struggled in that role enough. (I felt his fingers on my belly although he held my hips as I had demonstrated.) I wondered if this was appropriate and I decided to change to wrist to wrist contact. Paul said, "No, don't go." I replied, "Let me go—I'm going." "Who was he holding back?" I asked. "No one," came the reply; then he continued "When coming to this CHE my mother was holding me tightly, she didn't want me to come here but I had to. She got a bit upset." He made this association and seemed able to share it with me at this later stage, perhaps because he was in the more powerful position (the holder back) or at enough of a distance from himself to allow the feeling and words to emerge.

I suggested he move as though he were himself and I would pretend to move as if I were his mother. He became very involved, eventually breaking away saying "I've got to go," and ran in a free run in the general space. I turned saying, "Come back." "No, I've got to go," he exclaimed. I sank down in the space and sadly said that I was unhappy he had to leave. I felt lonely as though he would never return. I hid my head in a low shape. Silence. He did not answer. He was looking at me, then quickly looked away when I made eye contact. I felt his sadness. I moved into a different shape and said, "We'll finish there, how are you feeling?" "Alright," he answered, his eyes going up and watering. I asked him if there was anything else he'd like to say to his mother, placing a cushion in the space. "Yes—but not to a cushion." "Imagine that is her and speak to her," I encouraged. He was not at all happy with this idea. "I know it's not her—it really cracks you up this place." He seemed angry now. He got up and put his shoes on. I explained that this was a safe place to explore such feelings, that our sessions were about working with these difficulties. I reassured him that it was okay to feel sad and angry here. "Of course I'm angry," he exclaimed. He was definitely very angry. He seemed to be projecting strongly that I was his mother holding onto him—perhaps smothering him. The movement and verbal interaction must have brought back hurt feelings from the past when he was removed from home and brought to the CHE. He may also have resented that and have been feeling a sadness at missing his mother, perhaps seeing for the first time that she was dependent in some way on him.

This illustrates how working with movement, that is, beginning with exaggerating a predominant quality and spatial orientation, and adding physical contact and verbal associations, can lead to working with fear, anger, sadness, and so on.

For Paul the outcome was not only catharsis but more importantly a recognition of his relationship with his mother who was holding him back. His own lack of power (being frozen and rigid) was evident and he was able to experience this at a more conscious level—and particularly at a symbolic level—in his movement. Subsequently, Paul became even more free, quick, and strong in his movement and began to initiate movement in the group. His confidence was evident in other areas of his treatment program and he was promoted to a more senior care facility where peer group responsibility was the main emphasis, each boy being responsible for his own actions in a less authoritarian, controlled environment. It is acknowledged that this was not necessarily a result of his DMT program.

Dance movement therapy thus helped Paul develop a trusting relationship with the therapist in which the "holding environment" was facilitated through the use of rhythm and space. Verbalization and quality of movement were utilized when they emerged as significant material for Paul, enabling him to become more aware of aspects of himself and his relationships.

SUMMARY AND CONCLUSIONS

Techniques of DMT have not been validated, and not enough research has been done in comparable areas to this study to quote any investigations related to adolescents labeled delinquent. Descriptions of work done with a variety of groups show that some benefits may be expected. It is reasonable, therefore, that some value from experience of DMT can also be expected for male adolescents labeled delinquent.

This author supports the description of DMT which was previously presented. In addition, the author regards vocalization, verbalization, and sound as integral to the DMT process and believes that the therapeutic alliance is crucial for effective therapy.

Suggestions for Further Research

Both the pilot and final fieldwork findings found that verbalization and vocalization were important aspects of the participants' experience of DMT. Future research could be concerned with challenging the assumption that DMT is a nonverbal modality. Questions about the amount of verbalization that takes place with different therapists working with a similar population could be studied, with reference to whether verbalization is encouraged, used in particular ways, or stems mainly from therapist to client and vice-versa, or arises between clients. Is verbalization due to the population—its attitudes, values, level of development, disorder, intelligence, personality, or anxiety level? Are vocalizations and verbalizations used as a defense? When do they take place: in combination with movement or without it? Is it used mainly at the beginning, the middle, or the end of sessions and what is its content? Classroom interaction techniques could be used, such as the Flanders Scale (1972), to discover whether speech or vocalization was therapist-or client-initiated, and to determine which activities provoke spontaneous sound. Any links between vocal sounds and verbal expression could be explored together with receptive and expressive language ability in relation to movement interaction. Analysis of a videotaped DMT session could be carried out to discover whether verbalization was used in a supportive role or as a primary activity. Exploration could take place as to whether there is more or less verbalization-vocalization in a group, dyad, or individual session. Spontaneous as opposed to formal language could be compared with the movement processes in use. This kind of research would have important implications for DMT practice and training, and for the theory of nonverbal communication generally.

In the field of perceptions, further study comparing the therapist's perceptions with the client's would yield more information on how DMT is understood, and how the different experiences of therapist and client could be explained. It would be of interest to monitor clients' experiences over a long term program and see what similarities and differences emerged.

The following recommendations are offered. They were developed from the issues arising out of the pilot and final fieldwork findings. Some of these may be of use as guidelines for other practitioners attempting an intervention program with troubled or troublesome young people—in particular a program of DMT or another creative arts therapy.

1. Be clear about your aims and objectives and how you plan to implement them.
2. Spend time forming a liaison with the principal or director of the setting and the educational psychologist first, explaining the project and eliciting their prejudices and biases.
3. Give a presentation to all staff, outlining the project and focusing on the need for their full cooperation and support. Do not promise or guarantee anything: There is a tendency for staff to believe the outsider holds

a magic formula and will change bad behavior into good overnight. However, explain any benefits that have taken place as a result of previous programs.

4. Give a demonstration session to the young people. From this, volunteers may come forward willing to participate in the project. Limit numbers to between 4 and 6 per group.
5. Be careful about what you tell the young people: The words you use and the information given will be determining factors in the attitude they will present about sessions.
6. Be aware of the institution's philosophy, time management, organizational resistance, and so on. Be sure to adapt your program to fit in with these elements in order to avoid conflict and confusion for staff and young people.

This chapter has introduced the history and background of DMT. It focused on the author's research study with male adolescents labeled delinquent, and used this study to illustrate DMT practice. Consequently, a number of questions were touched on: (1) What is the conceptual/theoretical foundation of DMT? (2) How should DMT/therapy/research be conducted to provide understanding? (3) How can DMT help clients? (4) What do dance movement therapists do?

Dance movement therapy is emerging and becoming established as a profession. It needs research in order to enable further understanding of its methods and theoretical foundations. However, it is being found to be a powerful process even by those used to verbal or other arts therapies. Currently, DMT is still underground in the United Kingdom but strong roots are now established; DMT needs to push up into the daylight.

REFERENCES

Anderson, W. (Ed). (1977). *Therapy and the arts*. NY: Harper and Row.

Apter, H., Sharir, I., Tyano, S., & Wijsenbeck, H. (1978). Movement therapy with psychotic adolescents. *British Journal of Medical Psychology, 51* (2), 155–159.

Axline, V. (1974). *Play therapy*. NY: Ballantine Books.

Bainbridge-Cohen, B., & Mills, M. (1979). *Developmental movement therapy*. (Booklet available through Association for Dance Movement Therapy Publications). London.

Bainbridge, G.W. (1953). Dance mime: A contribution to treatment in psychiatry. *Journal of Mental Science, 99,* 308–314.

Bartinieff, I. (1971). *How is the dancing teacher equipped to do dance therapy?* American Dance Therapy Association Monographs 1 and second Annual Proceedings 1967.

Bernstein, P. (1971). *Theory and methods in dance movement therapy*. Iowa: Kendall/Hunt.

Bender, L., & Boas, F. (1941). Creative dance in therapy. *Amercan Journal of Ortho-psychiatry, 235–244.*

Bion, W. (1961). *Experiences in groups.* London: Tavistock Pub.

Bowlby, T. (1982). *Attachment and loss (Vol. 1).* London: Hogarth Press.

Brown, G., McDowell, R. L., & Smith, J. (Eds.). (1981). *Educating adolescents with behavioral disorders.* Columbus, OH: Charles E. Merrill.

Chace, M. (1953). Dance as an adjunct therapy with hospitalized mental patients. *Bulletin of the Menninger Clinic, 17,* 219–221.

Condon, W.S., (1968, October & 1969, November). Linguistic-kinesic research and dance therapy. *Proceedings of the Third and Fourth American Dance Therapy Association Annual Conference* (1968, pp. 21–44; 1969, pp. 21–39). Columbia, MA: ADTA.

Condon, W.S., & Ogston, W. (1966). Sound film analysis of normal and pathological behavior patterns. *Journal of Nervous and Mental Disease, 143,* 338–343.

Cratty, B. (1979). *Perceptual and motor development in infants and young children.* Englewood Cliffs, NJ: Prentice-Hall.

Darwin, C.R. (1955). *The expression of the emotions in man and animals.* New York: Philosophical Library Edition. (Original work published in 1872.)

Davis, M. (1973, February). The potential of non-verbal communication research in dance. *C.O.R.D., 5,* 10–27.

Delaney, W. (1973). Working with children. *Proceedings of the Eighth American Dance Therapy Conference.* (pp. 3–15). Columbia, MA: American Dance Therapy Association.

Dickinson, M. (1957). Music as a tool for psychotherapy for children. *Journal of Music Therapy,* 97–104.

Dunne, C., Brugen, P., & O'Brian, C. (1982). Touch and action in group therapy of younger adolescents. *Journal of Adolescence, 5,* 31–38.

Espenak, L. (1981). *Dance therapy: Theory and application.* Springfield, IL: Charles C Thomas.

Feder, E. & Feder, B. (1981). *The expressive arts therapies.* Englewood Cliffs, NJ: Prentice-Hall.

Flanders, A. (1972). Interaction analysis and in-service training. *Social Psychology of Teaching.* London: Penguin.

Fraenkel, D.L. (1983). The relationship of empathy in movement to synchrony, echoing and empathy in verbal interactions. *American Journal of Dance Therapy, 6,* 37–48.

Frostig, M. (1967). *Pictures and patterns: The Frostig program for the development of visual perception.* Chicago: Follet.

Gendlin, E. (1962a). *Experiencing and the creation of meaning.* New York: Viking Press.

Gendlin, E. (1962b). Focusing. *Journal of Psychotherapy Research and Practice, 6,* 4–15.

Gunter, A. (1984). Body ego identity in humanistic psychiatry, dance therapy. *Dynamische Psychiatrie, 17* (4), 339–356.

Hazelton, T., Price, P., & Brown, G. (1979). Psychodrama, creative movement and remedial activities for children with special needs. *Journal of Association of Educational Psychologists, 5* (1), 32–37.

Hecox, B., Levine, E., & Scott, D. (1976). Dance in physical rehabilitation. *Physical Therapy, 56,* 919–924.

Hilyar, J.C., Wilson, D.G., Dillon, C., Cara, L., Jenkins, C., Spencer, W.A., Meadows, M.E., & Booker, W. (1982). Physical fitness training and counselling as treatment for young offenders. *Journal of Counselling and Psychology 3,* 392–303.

Holden, S. (1980). Art and dance combined in therapy. *Inscape, 4,* 1.

Hunt, V. (1978). Movement behaviour: A model for action. *Quest,* 69–91.

Johnson, D. R. (1984). Movement and dramatherapy as representation of the internal world of an eighteen year old, male, catatonic schizophrenic. *Psychiatry, 47* (4), 299–314.

Johnson, D., & Sandel, S. (1977, Fall/Winter). Structural analysis of group movement sessions: Preliminary research. *American Journal of Dance Therapy,* 32–36.

Jung, C.G. (1966). *Two essays on analytical psychology.* Princeton, NJ: Princetown University Press.

Keleher, C.G. (1956, March). Modern dance as mental therapy. *Dance Observer.*

Kephart, A.I. (1971). *The slow learner in the classroom.* Columbus, OH: Charles E. Merrill.

Kestenberg, J. (1971). Development of young children through bodily movement. *Journal of American Psychoanalytical Association, 1,* 746–764.

Laban, R. (1951). The educational and therapeutic values of Dance. In W. Sorrell (Ed.), *The dance has many faces* (pp. 145–159). New York: World.

Laban, R. (1978). *Modern educational dance.* London: MacDonald and Evans.

Lamb, W. (1965). *Posture and gesture: An introduction to the study of physical behaviour.* London: Duckworth.

Lesté, A., & Rust, J. (1984). Effect of dance on anxiety. *Journal of Perceptual and Motor Skills, 58,* 762–772.

Leventhal, M. (1980). Dance therapy as treatment of choice for emotionally disturbed and learning disabled children. *Journal of Physical Education and Recreation, 51,* 7.

Leventhal, M. (1986). Dance movement therapy: Education or therapy? *Association for Dance Movement Therapy Newsletter, 1,* 15.

Ling, F. (1983). In touch with self: In touch with others. *Prison Services Journal, 51,* 18–20.

Lovell, S.M. (1980). The bodily-felt sense and body image changes in adolescence. In F. Levine (Ed.), *Compendium of presenters* (pp. 34–36). Columbia, MA: American Dance Therapy Association.

Lowen, A. (1975). *Bioenergetics.* London: Conventure.

Mahrabian, M. (1972). *Non-verbal communication.* Chicago: Aldine.

Maslow, A.H. (1968). *Towards a psychology of being.* New York: Van Nostrand.

Mason, K.C. (1974). *Focus on dance VII—Dance therapy.* Washington, DC: American Association of Health, Physical Education and Recreation.

Meekums, B. (1981). Dance your whole being. *Energy and Character,* 45–47.

Meekums, B. (1986, May 12). The light fantastic. *The Guardian,* p. 8.

Meier, W. (1979). Meeting special needs through movement and dance drama. *Therapeutic Education, 7,* 1, 27–33.

Merek, P.A. (1976). Dance therapy with adult day patients. *Dissertation Abstracts International* (University Microfilms No. 76-1/069).

Nicol, A. (1979). Annotation: Psychotherapy in the school. *Journal of Child Psychology and Psychiatry, 28,* 81–86.

North, M. (1972). *Personality assessment through movement.* London: MacDonald and Evans.

Ornstein, R. (1973). *The psychology of consciousness.* New York: Viking.

Parlett, M. (1981). Illuminative evaluation. In P. Reason & J. Rowan (Eds.), *Human inquiry* (pp. 219–225). New York: Wiley.

Pasch, J. (1985). Dance with psychiatric patients. *Association for Dance Movement Therapy Newsletter, 1,* 8.

Payne, H.L. (1977). *To examine the value of movement therapy in improving relationships for a number of emotionally disturbed children.* Unpublished doctoral dissertation, Laban Centre, University of London, Goldsmiths College, London.

Payne, H.L. (1979, April). Movement therapy in a special education setting. In *Current developments in special education* (pp. 44–52). Proceedings of conference held at the Cambridge Institute of Education, England.

Payne, H.L. (1980). *Body boundary, social adjustment and self actualization: Their relationship in a group of learning disabled children.* Unpublished dissertation. Cambridge Institute of Education, England.

Payne, H.L. (1981). Movement therapy for the special child. *British Journal of Dramatherapy, 4,* 3.

Payne, H.L. (1985). Jumping for Joy. *Changes: Journal of Psychology and Psychotherapy, 3,* 5.

Payne, H.L. (1987). *The perceptions of male adolescents labelled delinquent towards a programme of dance movement therapy.* Unpublished masters thesis, University of Manchester, England.

Payne-West, H.L. (1984, Autumn). Responding with dance. *Maladjustment and Therapeutic Education, 2,* (2), 42–57.

Pearman, R. (1980, January). Grounding and movement. *Energy and Character, 2,* 1.

Penfield, K. (1978, October 26). To dance is to learn to live again. *Therapy Magazine,* 5.

Peterson, B., & Cameron, C. (1978). Preparing high anxiety patients for psychotherapy through body therapy. *Journal of Contemporary Psychotherapy, 9* (2), 171–177.

Ramsden, P. (1973). *Top team planning.* London: Carsell/Associated Business Programme.

Reich, W. (1945). *Character analysis.* New York: Simon and Schuster.

Rogers, C. (1967). *On becoming a person.* London: Constable.

Rosen, E. (1954, January). Dance as therapy for the mentally ill. *Teachers College Record, 55,* 215–222.

Rosen, E. (1957). *Dance in psychotherapy.* New York: Columbia University, Teachers College, Bureau of Publications.

Rowan, J. (1975, September 11). Exploring the self. *New Behaviour,* 406–409.

Rutter, M.C., Tizzard, J., & Whitmore, K. (1970). *Education, health and behaviour.* London: Longman.

Sandel, S. (1973). Going down to dance. In E. Fulton (Ed.), Proceedings of the *Eighth Annual Conference of the American Dance Therapy Association.* (pp. 15-24). Columbia, MA: ADTA.

Schilder, P. (1955). *The image and appearance of the human body.* New York: International Universities Press.

Schmais, C., & Felber, D. (1977, Fall). Dance therapy analysis: A method for observing and analyzing a dance therapy group. *American Journal of Dance Therapy,* pp. 18-25.

Serlin, L. (1977). A portrait of Karen: A Gestalt phenomenological approach to movement therapy. *Journal of Contemporary Psychotherapy, 8* (2), 145-153.

Schaefer, C. (1976). *Therapeutic use of child's play.* New York: Jason Aronson.

Sherborne, V. (1974). Building relationships through movement with children with communication problems. *Inscape, 1,* 10.

Shirley, C. (1980). Art therapy linked with movement. *Inscape, 4,* 1.

Siegal, E.V. (1984). *Dance movement therapy: Mirror of ourselves, The psychoanalytical approach.* New York & London: Human Sciences Press.

Silberman, L. (1973). A dance therapist's experience of working with disturbed adolescent boys in a city prison hospital. In E. Fulton (Ed.), *Proceedings of the Eighth Annual Conference of the American Dance Therapy Association.* (pp. 63-76). Columbia, MA: ADTA.

Southgate, J. (1980). *Community and group dynamics.* London: Barefoot Books.

Spencer, P. (Ed.) (1985). *Society and the dance.* Cambridge: Cambridge Press

Torrance, E.P., & Torrance, P. (1972). Combining creative problem solving with creative expressive activity in the education of disadvantaged young people. *Journal of Creative Behavior, 6* (1), 1-10.

Wethered, A. (1973). Drama and movement in therapy. London: MacDonald and Evans.

Whitehouse, M. (1977). The transference in dance therapy. *American Journal of Dance Therapy, 1*(4), 3-7.

Wickes, F. (1968). *The inner world of childhood.* London: Mentor Books.

Wilhelm, R. (Trans.). (1968). *The I Ching or book of changes.* London: Routledge and Kegan Paul.

Wright, B. (1980). Dance as the cure: The arts as metaphors for healing in Kelantanese Malay spirit exorcisms. *C.O.R.D. 12* (2), 3-11.

CHAPTER 4

Serial Drawing: A Jungian Approach with Children

JOHN A.B. ALLAN

Serial drawing is a therapeutic approach whereby the counselor meets on a regular basis with the child and simply asks the child to draw a picture. Over time, a relationship is formed, problems are expressed symbolically in the drawings, and healing and resolution of inner conflicts can occur. This paper provides background information, describes the method, and gives examples of three different ways in which the technique can be used.

BACKGROUND

The theoretical underpinnings of this approach are based on the work of Carl Jung. During the latter days of the First World War, Jung wrote that he

> sketched every morning in a notebook a small circular drawing, a mandala, which seemed to correspond to my inner situation at the time. With the help of these drawings, I could observe my psychic transformations from day to day. . . . I had to abandon the idea of the superordinate position of the ego. . . . I had to let myself be carried along by the current, without a notion of where it would lead me. (1965, pp. 195–196)

Throughout much of his life, Jung continued to draw and paint, write and illustrate his dreams, and carve in wood and stone. He felt that psychological health was a delicate balance between the demands of the outer world and the needs of the inner world. To him, the expressive arts represented an important avenue to the inner world of feelings and images. He came to see the unconscious mind not only as a repository of repressed emotions but also as a source of health and transformation. He felt that in time of stress one could turn inward toward the unconscious for dreams and images that carried within them the potential or seeds for healing. His was not a reductive method of analysis but rather a synthetic, teleological point of view. He was interested in where a person's inner life was leading. From this framework, the psychotherapist does not necessarily analyze the images of the client but rather encourages the client to make the images and to follow them as they unfold. To a certain extent, it is as if the ego moves aside a little to allow unconscious movements and images to have ascendency over the conscious mind.

Jung (1966) believed that the establishment of the therapeutic alliance and rapport activated the healing potential that is embedded in the human psyche. He saw this healing potential as part of the "archetype of the self" which leads a person on the path to individuation or toward the fulfillment of potential. The archetype, when activated by the therapeutic alliance, takes the client where the client needs to go. For example, in play therapy children will often spontaneously work on fantasy themes that have direct relevance to their psychological struggles. This is also true with drawings.

SERIAL DRAWING

In talking about drawings and paintings, Jung (1959) emphasized the importance of viewing them "in series" over time rather than just viewing or analyzing one or two pictures. When a child draws in the presence of the therapist on a regular basis, the healing potential is activated, conflicts are expressed and resolved, and the therapist can gain a clearer and more accurate view of the unconscious at work. Serial drawing refers to drawing week after week in the presence of the counselor. The time and place variables act as a sanctuary space, a time out of ordinary time, that—together with a positive therapeutic alliance—fosters psychological growth and transformation. From a Jungian perspective these conditions activate in the unconscious mind the drive toward healing. Fantasies and images are produced that, if symbolized or concretized (i.e., expressed in tangible form through play enactment, drawing, clay, writing, etc.), facilitate psychological growth. The 8½" x 11" piece of white paper becomes the safe place onto which projections are placed, while the symbols and images become the containers for various emotions, thus allowing feelings to be expressed safely. With this safe expression, movement occurs in the unconscious and new images (feelings) are produced.

Children move at their own pace, depending on the nature of the trauma or the psychological struggle and the child's ego strength. Although general patterns have been observed (Allan, 1978a), some children will start by producing images of pain, others images of reparation and healing, while others show only very stereotyped drawings. Some children spend a long time on painful images, others move directly into images of healing (never seemingly needing to deal with the pain anymore), while others appear to get stuck in powerful ambivalent clashes between the desire to grow and the wish to destroy. These unique patterns only become apparent over time; hence, the serial nature of this treatment approach.

Symbolic Themes

Quite often in serial drawing, a child will pick up on one symbolic theme and use that theme throughout many of the drawings. Seldom is the image used in a perseverative way; rather the image changes in its form or function. Many times there is a movement from damage and violation to repair and healthy functioning. For example, Pam, six years old and sexually abused, constantly drew bedrooms and bathrooms with people enacting sexual intercourse and showing genitalia. At the end of treatment, there were still bedrooms and bathrooms, but people were sleeping each in their own separate bed, the rooms were tidy, and the lights were on. Luci, a psychotic five-year-old, thought she was a seagull. She carried around a seagull feather in her hand and twirled it in front of her eyes. At first she drew seagulls (Figure 4.1), then supergirl with seagull wings and one feather sticking out (Figure 4.2), then herself as a girl with a seagull flying above her (Figure 4.3), and finally herself as an Indian princess with a feather tucked into her headband (Figure 4.4).

In another case, Joey, 11 years old, very quiet, withdrawn, and with facial tics, drew a tiny house surrounded by giant hills. Over the weeks, the house moved from the background to the middle of the page, and the hills diminished in size. The house then became houses, the houses villages and towns,

Figure 4.1. Seagull

Figure 4.2. Girl as seagull (note feather)

Figure 4.3. Girl as person. Seagull above.

Figure 4.4. Indian princess (note feather)

and finally, after six months, he drew Manhattan. The whole sheet of paper was full of skyscrapers. At this point he started to talk. Referring to the drawing he said, "This picture is like my dad. These buildings lean over me. Press down on me just like my dad. They suffocate me. He suffocates me. He kisses me, lies on top of me, squeezes my bum and makes me touch him. I hate it. *I hate him!*" At this point, Joey exploded into a fit of rage and weeping. This led to a disclosure of sexual abuse; after it came major improvements. This vignette showed how one child used this method, and how one particular symbol, a tiny home away in the distance (i.e., deep within the unconscious), slowly surfaced week after week until it was in the forefront of consciousness (Manhattan) and led to a verbal self-disclosure.

Stages in Serial Drawing

When used by counselors with mildly to moderately disturbed children in the public school system, three main stages have been noted: initial, middle, and termination. Each stage seems to be characterized by or to reflect certain typical images or themes. In the initial stage (1 to 4 sessions), the drawings seem to (a) give a view of the child's internal world, often showing images that reflect a cause of the child's problems; (b) reflect loss of internal control and the presence of feelings of despair and hopelessness; and (c) offer a vehicle for establishing the initial rapport with the counselor. The counselor is often incorporated into the actual drawing in symbolic form as a friendly giant, helicopter pilot, doctor, or nurse.

In the middle stage (5 to 8 sessions), the drawing content seems to reflect (a) an expression of an emotion in its pure form; (b) the struggle between opposites (good vs. bad) and the isolation of ambivalent feelings; and (c) the deepening of the relationship between the child and the helper. At the end of this phase, the child often uses the drawing as a bridge to talk directly about a painful issue or to disclose a secret.

In the termination stage (9 to 12 sessions), the child tends to draw (a) images that reflect a sense of mastery, self-control, and worth; (b) scenes reflecting positive imagery (i.e., an absence of war, violence, and damage); (c) a central self symbol (i.e., self-portrait or mandala forms); (d) humorous scenes; and (e) pictures reflecting the removal of the attachment bond from the helper.

Other Media in the Serial Approach

Although this chapter focuses on drawing, the method works equally well with other forms of creative expression. The task facing the counselor is to find the right medium for each child. With some children it is sandplay (Allan & Berry, 1987), with others fantasy enactment (Allan, 1986; Allan & MacDonald, 1975). Some children work best with painting (Thompson & Allan, 1985), others in clay (Allan & Clark, 1985), while others use creative writing (Allan, 1978b; Buttery & Allan, 1981).

Setting

Serial drawing has been used in a variety of settings from residential care to day care (Allan, 1978c) and from private practice to counseling in the schools. In many ways it is ideally suited to the school system, where counselors are often faced with overwhelming caseloads (Allan, Doi, & Reid, 1979; Allan & Barber, 1986) because the method can be conducted in only 20 to 25 minutes per week per child. The methods of serial drawing described next and the case studies mentioned below were all conducted in the public elementary school system where the author works both as a counselor and as a counselor educator.

METHODS

Serial drawing involves seeing a child alone for 20 to 25 minutes once a week and asking the child to draw a picture. Some children, in acute crisis, might need to be seen every day. White paper (8½" x 11"), a table, and a pencil are the only requirements. The counselor can say to the child something like:

> Mary, I'm Dr. Allan, the school counselor. Schools want to help children not only with school work but also with their life, their feelings, and with things that trouble them. That's my job in the school; to help children. Your teacher (parent) told me that life in the classroom (at home) seemed hard for you right now, and she thought that coming to see me would help you. Often children like to draw and talk when they come to see me. Drawing and talking seem to help children feel better, overcome problems, and enjoy life more. Your teacher suggested I

see you every Tuesday from 10:00 to 10:20. You can draw or talk about whatever you wish. What we talk about is private, just between you and me unless something is against the law. I will keep your pictures here in my office in this file. (Show the child the file.) Usually I write your name, date, and title of the picture on the back and keep it safe in here (i.e., the file). When life goes better and when you and I have finished seeing each other, then I will give the file, with all of the pictures, back to you. Do you have any questions? (At this point, I usually slide the paper and pencil across the desk and slightly towards the child.)

The key ingredients here are (a) establishing rapport; (b) identifying the helping role; (c) placing treatment in the context of school life; (d) suggesting that talking and drawing help; (e) identifying time and place variables and the counselor's connection to the teacher; (f) storing the pictures (i.e., containing, protecting, and valuing the products); (g) stating that the drawings will be returned to the child later; and (h) offering the child a chance to talk and question.

Because the treatment time is short, crayons, ruler, and eraser can be kept out of view. Crayons seem to detract from the process because the child will tend to spend a lot of time shading. Coloring and shading both have therapeutic value, but in this brief counseling context they should not be promoted. However, if a child asks for crayons or for an eraser, then provide them. Obviously there must be some flexibility in the use of this approach. Try to use the same office or, if not available, a quiet corner of the classroom or library. A new piece of paper is placed in front of the child each time. Some children may ask for an old drawing and spend five or six sessions reworking it. If children ask to take the picture out of the office with them, reflect their wish but add that it is important to keep it in the file (i.e., boundaries, limits, and protection of the psychological material are important for transformation). Try to discover the importance and meaning of this act (taking the picture out), dialogue about it, and if the impasse is maintained make a photocopy of the picture and try to keep the original for the file.

Counselor's Behavior During the Sessions

During the sessions, the counselor sits near or beside the child. The counselor does not talk much, in the beginning stage, unless the child initiates it. Introverted children will tend to work silently on their pictures, and this silence should be respected. Extroverted children are often full of action sounds and like to talk a lot while drawing. Respond minimally to them so that the focus is placed on the drawing. The counselor does not initiate any conversation or take any notes. The counselor observes the child, how the child approaches the drawing, the placement of the figures and the types of images, symbols, and themes that emerge in the child's pictures.

The counselor needs to be sensitive to the "subtle body" (Schwartz-Salant, 1986), to the invisible feeling-toned space that develops between the counselor and the child. As the child draws, there is movement in the unconscious mind of the child, old feelings are expressed and new ones rise to the surface, the transference-countertransference develops, and the counselor needs to be aware of the subtle feeling changes in the child and in himself. This helps the counselor understand the child's psychological struggles and to make silent hypotheses. This silent understanding and acceptance seem to help the child move forward. Sometimes a child may become stuck with a certain theme that will be repeated time and time again without any apparent movement. When this occurs, the counselor may have to take a more active role in verbalizing or interpreting the conflict. (See the case of Billie below.)

The counselor's verbal and nonverbal behavior are all critically important in the success of the method. Most importantly, the counselor needs to believe that the method will help the child and that the activity has important psychological benefits. The counselor tries to provide an environment that reflects unconditional positive regard, facilitates the establishment of trust, and enables the child to draw and talk. As the children vary so much in their styles of interaction, the counselor will have to be flexible. At first the counselor needs to try to follow the direction of the child. If the child talks while drawing, the counselor responds, sometimes by reflecting feelings and sometimes by answering questions. If the child is involved with the drawing and is very quiet, then remain quiet, attend to the child, the images, and your own feelings.

At the end of each session, the counselor asks the child, "Does the picture tell a story? Can you tell me what's going on in the picture? Does the picture have a title?" Sometimes it is helpful to obtain amplifications by asking, "What went on in the story before this picture? What happens next?" Also, in this termination phase of the session, it is legitimate for the counselor to ask about anything unusual that has been observed during the drawing time. For example, "Mike, while you were drawing the house, I noticed you spent a long time on the doorknob. I wonder if you could tell me what you were thinking while you were drawing and shading it? What does the doorknob do (or mean to you)?" Questions then should be left to the end so that they do not interrupt the flow of the child's drawing activity. The drawing is more than just drawing: It is an opportunity for the child to psychologically work through some inner representations, issues, or conflicts.

Specific Serial Drawing Techniques

There are three main techniques: nondirective, directive, and partially directive. Directiveness in this context refers only to whether or not the counselor suggests a topic or symbol for the child to draw.

Nondirective

Some children come to the sessions, see the paper and pencil, and start drawing before the counselor can talk. These children readily respond to the counselor and the therapeutic environment and seem to know what they want or need to draw. They seem to commence psychological work right away and in the early stages seem to need the counselor only as a witness to their drawings. With these children, it is important to use a very nondirective approach because the children are connected to their own curative process. They intuitively know where they need to go and what they need to draw.

Directive

Some children seem withdrawn, stuck, trapped in stereotyped images, confused, and very uncertain of themselves. Often a suggestion of what to draw helps these children get underway with their own work. With these children, the session can be started with a House-Tree-person test series (Buck, 1948) and continued with other directed drawings until the children seem ready to draw on their own, reject or substitute their own images, or until the counselor feels it is no longer appropriate to direct the process. The direction (for example, with a very angry child: "Could you draw an exploding volcano?") is not made randomly, but is based on the counselor's psychological assessment of a central emotion that the child is currently struggling with or an image and symbol that seems to have special meaning to the child at this moment in the child's life.

Partially Directive

Sometimes one particular symbol has a special relevance to the child. The child attaches to or communicates this image very early on to the counselor. Often the image is broken or damaged or represents a symbol of wholeness or health to the child. This symbol seems to represent a central force in the child's development. It could be anything that has special meaning to the child: a house, a garage, a flower, a tree, a worm, the underground, the sun, a cage, a dog, and so on. In the partially directive technique, every 4 to 6 weeks, the counselor asks the child to draw that particular symbol. The counselor can simply state at the start of the session, "Simon, I've been thinking about the cage today. I wonder if you could draw me a picture of it. I wonder what has been happening to it since the last time you drew it?" Four to six weeks seems to be an optimum time in which the psyche registers change and for a child to develop a slightly new attitude or relationship to a key symbolic theme. Case examples, using these three different approaches, are given next.

CASE EXAMPLES

Nondirective Approach

Some children seem to know what they need to draw and how best to heal themselves. Children like this can make significant improvement in 10 to 12 weeks, and in retrospect their drawings seem to go through three phases: initial, middle, and termination, with each phase being characterized by distinct themes and images. For optimum facilitation, the counselor's responses and actions need to be different in each of these stages. In order to illustrate these stages and themes and the counselor's response patterns, examples from the protocols of two children, Sam (age six years) and Billie (age seven years), both of whom demonstrated severe behavioral problems in their classrooms, will be given. Sam and Billie both came from broken homes. Sam had moved about 14 times in his life, and Billie's mother had deserted the family, breaking off all contact with him.

INITIAL STAGE.   (1 to 4 sessions). These pictures seem to:

Give a view of the child's internal world.
For example, Sam's drawings depicted long-distance moving trucks smashing into little cars, killing people, crossing the lane dividers of freeways, and crashing into houses on the other side (Figure 4.5). Billie's pictures showed "The Whole World on Fire" with volcanoes everywhere, earthquakes cracking and tearing the world apart, houses being blown up, people trapped in them, rockets and bombs exploding. The central themes in both cases were devastation and disaster.

Reflect the feelings of hopelessness.
The themes of the first three drawings often tend to reflect the overwhelming and incapacitating effect of the trauma on the child's sense of competency and mastery. Helplessness is clearly revealed in Billie's drawing as he depicts himself trapped in a mountain during an earthquake (Figure 4.6). There may be some rudimentary attempt on the part of the hero figures to try to escape destruction or to do something positive. However, in this phase, the negative

Figure 4.5. Truck crashing

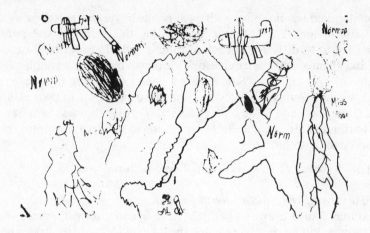

Figure 4.6. Earthquake

or destructive forces always win. With Billie, the trapped figure got out of the mountain but was killed by a rock, and with Sam, crashes always occurred on the freeway.

Represent a vehicle for establishing the initial contact with the helper. Children frequently use the drawings to start to build a relationship with the counselor. Sam began to draw many helicopters and airplanes flying about the freeway. He also drew road maps and mazes and began to challenge the counselor to find his way out: ''Bet you can't get out of that one'' (Figure 4.7).

Figure 4.7. Maze

Billie kept asking his counselor, "Can you guess what I'm drawing?" It seems that underneath the children were asking, "Do you understand me?" "Do you know what has happened to me?" "Are you smart enough to help me?" Billie also always asked his counselor to write her name on the front of his drawing.

MIDDLE STAGE. (5 to 8 sessions). These drawings tend to reflect the following:

An expression of an emotion in its pure form.
In this phase, it is as if certain painful feelings are separated out from other feelings and expressed in pure form. For example, Sam continued to draw freeways, but showed his depression by drawing "the truck disappearing down a great hole in the middle of the road." With Billie, one main focus was that of rage—a giant pouring out of a mass of fury and anger from his mouth (Figure 4.8), while a later picture reflected grief and sadness as "an army of ants carried a huge teardrop off to a safe place so it could break open without hurting anyone" (Figure 4.9).

A struggle with ambivalent feelings.
Other later drawings had both positive and negative forces coexisting as equals: "a log, hurtling towards earth, containing explosives but prevented from crashing by a thousand birds holding it up" (Figure 4.10). In another drawing, Billie showed "a mean tree throwing a spear at Jack Pumpkinhead but a snowman quickly puts a shield over jack's head which protects him" (Figure 4.11).

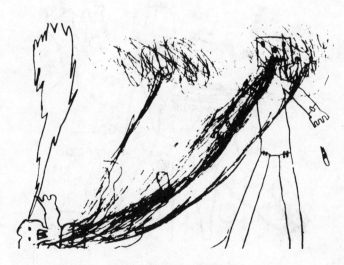

Figure 4.8. Giants fighting

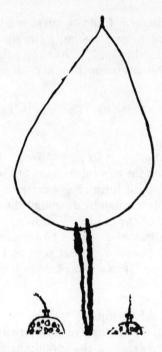

Figure 4.9. Tear drop above ant houses

Figure 4.10. Log (note birds underneath log)

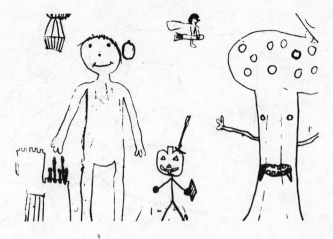

Figure 4.11. Mean tree

Deeper relationship to helper.
The helper now tends to be incorporated into the drawing as a positive helpful image. Sam began drawing "a man flying helicopters with logs and supplies to repair the holes in the roads." Billie drew a "friendly giant rescuing a boy from the floods that came to earth after the fire" (Figure 4.12).

The disclosure of a deep issue.
With the establishment of the therapeutic relationship, the child begins to trust the helper and shares some deep feelings and thoughts. Sam wrote the words

Figure 4.12. Rescuing giant

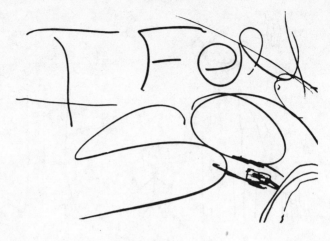

Figure 4.13. I feel sad

"I feel sad" (Figure 4.13) and talked about his grief over moving so many times; how he did not like it, how it hurt to make and lose friends, and how frightening he found his new school. Billie started to draw "help" (five in one picture), and he revealed how the hero in the picture "had wanted to kill himself a year ago" (i.e., when his mother left) and how "he still thought about killing himself sometimes" (Figure 4.14). At this point in the therapeutic relationship, it is important that the counselor begin to relate the content of the drawings directly to the child's life (i.e., to use some interpretation). For example, in the above situation: "I guess when your mother left home it really hurt you and at times you wished you were dead and wouldn't have to be in so much pain. I am glad you are telling me about these feelings."

TERMINATION STAGE. (9 to 12 sessions). Once the deeper feelings and pain have been expressed symbolically and/or shared verbally, there tends to be quite a rapid movement toward a resolution. The drawings now show:

Images of mastery, self-control and worth.
The drawings begin to reflect feelings of competency and coping. For Sam, the freeway traffic was back to normal; all the cars and trucks were running smoothly, the road dividers stood in place, the repairs to the road were finished; and there were even control towers to regulate and keep a watchful eye on the traffic.

Emergence of positive imagery.
There were no wars or explosions and fewer conflicts now. Billie drew Hawaiian scenes—a big bright sun, coconut and pineapple trees, and smiles on everyone's faces (Figure 4.15).

Figure 4.14. Help

Figure 4.15. Hawaii

Figure 4.16. Cutting the log

Humor.

Dangerous forces or imagery are now related to humorously. Billie redrew the dangerous log of session 7 that was going to blow the world up, but this time there was a swordfish cutting it up into tiny pieces, and next to it a pile of used and broken swordfish blades that had been blunted in the process (Figure 4.16).

A central self-symbol.

Sam drew a series of self-portraits: a big smile on his face with a cigar sticking out of the corner of his mouth (Figure 4.17). Often, these drawings are protected by a frame or border. There is also the emergence of mandala forms such as a square, circle, or triangle around the central image. Billie drew his

Figure 4.17. Me

grandmother lying on a towel in Hawaii; she was in a bikini and near her was a dish of pineapple and coconut. The rectangular border of the towel protected her and reflected the sunlight in rays, so that the grandmother was highlighted in the drawing (Figure 4.18).

These drawings reflect the internalization of positive images. That is, Sam now carried a positive image of himself (albeit slightly omnipotent!), and Billie reestablished connection to the mother archetype (Neumann, 1974) in the form of his inner grandmother.

Removal of attachment to the helper.

In this phase, the child now withdraws some libido from the helper. For example, in the picture of Sam's self-portrait, there was a tiny portrait of the helper in the background. The helper no longer had the prominence of the helicopter pilot in the earlier drawings. Billie had always asked the counselor to write her

Figure 4.18. Grandmother

name on every picture he drew, first on the front, then on the back; but in the last drawings this was not requested.

After these types of drawings, the child usually says, "I don't want to come any more," and at this point the counselor, too, becomes aware that there is no need to continue seeing the child. There is the feeling of resolution both internally and externally. Positive inner images (*introjects*) have been restored and behavioral problems in the classroom that led to the referral are often no longer present.

Discussion of the Counselor's Role

The question of the degree of counselor-initiated activity is a difficult one and probably ultimately depends on the counselor's own personality style. At first it is important that the counselor say very little, believing that understanding and meaning occur symbolically on an unconscious level. However, if the child is in great pain and struggling, and if the counselor feels the need to strengthen the attachment bond and the transference, then linkages can be made from the drawings to the therapeutic relationship or to outer world situations. This can be done when the counselor perceives the child to be stuck in repetitious cycles or when there is a need to reduce pain or anxiety through the use of interpretation. Too much questioning, reflection, or interpretation, however, can sometimes block the spontaneous healing process of the child.

Such linkages or interpretations should be left to the end of the session and then used in conjunction with the content of the drawings as the initial bridge into the empathic response. For example, with Sam, one could say:

> I see you have drawn a lot of moving vans crashing into cars, houses and people. . . . I guess you've moved a lot in your life and it's really upset you and left you feeling pretty hurt and angry.

or, at another time:

> I see the helicopter pilot is repairing the hole in the road. . . . I wonder if at times you feel that I'm like that pilot helping you mend some of your hurts.

At certain times this use of interpretations seems to greatly facilitate transference and growth. It becomes particularly important to use when a child becomes stuck in strong ambivalent feelings that cannot be separated alone. In these drawings, the positive images or symbols (babies, young children, flowers, trees) are constantly being destroyed by negative forces (explosions, guns, knives, logs, trucks). It is the repetition of an ambivalent theme over four to five sessions, coupled with the counselor's internal feeling ("this child is stuck") that is the stimulus for the counselor to reflect on and interpret the dynamics of the process. For example, if Billie kept on drawing "mean trees throwing spears at little Jack Pumpkinhead," the counselor could say something like:

Billie, I've noticed this is the fourth time that the mean tree has tried to kill Jack. . . . I guess the tree is very angry at jack and wants to hurt him. . . . Perhaps part of you is still really angry at your Mum for leaving home, and this anger pops up in you every now and again and makes you wreck things. What else does the mean tree want to do? . . . I wonder if there's anything we can do for the tree to make him feel better so he won't need to continually hurt Jack.

In this way, it is possible to dialogue with the images of the drawings and the child's outer reality at the same time. What is occurring in the drawing is a symbolic representation of an inner psychological struggle. Rapport, timing, and accuracy of the interpretation are key variables here if the interpretation is to be accepted and understood by the child. Resolution and behavior change can be initiated and invoked on a symbolic level; hence, the counselor's request to the tree. Here the counselor is acknowledging the angry part of the child (as symbolized by the "mean tree") and offering to help it.

Before using the more advanced techniques, the counselor needs to be well versed in the child's family history and some psychodynamic principles and to be able to consistently respond at level four on the Carkhuff Empathy Scale (Carkhuff, 1969). Whether to reflect and interpret the children's drawings is usually a question relating to the art of counseling.

In the termination stage, the counselor needs to emphasize the positive aspects in the pictures, the ascendency of the hero figures, and the order and calmness that have been restored. For example, with Billie, on his last picture one could say:

The grandmother really looks happy; she has lots of good food near her. . . . The dangerous log is losing its power. . . . You seem to be feeling so much better these days, and the teacher tells me you are enjoying school, making friends, and doing your work.

Another aspect of this stage is for the counselor to review the child's progress with him:

Remember when you first came in to see me, Billie, life was pretty hard for you, wasn't it? But by drawing with me about some of your thoughts and feelings, you have changed a lot.

The counselor needs to leave the child with an awareness of how to ask for help. For example, near the end the counselor could ask, "Billie, if something upsets you in the future, what do you think you would do about it?" Then the counselor works with this response until the child has described a number of possible coping strategies. At the very end, the counselor can lay out all of the pictures on the table or floor in chronological order and have the child review them ("What do you think of when you see all of your drawings?") and add some summative comments ("When you first came in I noticed you drew . . . and then . . . and now your drawings seem to show. . . . ''). The counselor then asks whether the child wants the file with all the pictures, or whether the child's parents, or the counselor, should keep them in a safe place for retrieval later.

Directive Approach*

In this method of serial drawing, the counselor suggests the topics and images for the child to draw, up to the point where the child starts to draw spontaneously or rejects the counselor's topics. Some children seem to need a little help and direction in order to start the process of drawing and self-disclosure. Once again, timing is critical because inevitably one reaches a point where it is no longer appropriate for the counselor to make a suggestion; that is, the child's own psychological drives are ready to take over. Simply stated, the method involves the counselor asking the child to draw or redraw a particular image or symbol that seems to match the child's emotional state or that seems to have symbolic relevance to the child.

There are three main components to this method: (a) use of the House-Tree-Person (H-T-P) test; (b) directed drawings; and (c) free drawings.

Use of House-Tree-Person Test.

Once rapport has been established, the counselor proceeds by administering the H-T-P test (Buck, 1948). After the three drawings have been completed, the counselor places the house drawing back in front of the child and proceeds with a simplified posttest inquiry. For each picture the counselor asks: (a) "Is there a story that goes with the picture?"; (b) "Has anyone ever hurt the house?"; (c) "What does the house need?"; and (d) "Does the house have a wish?" The counselor ends the session by saying, "I've asked you to draw three pictures for me and I wonder if you would like to do a drawing of your own choice now?" (If the child takes a long time over each drawing, spread them out over several sessions.) Based on these four drawings, the counselor assesses whether to intervene with directed art counseling or free choice drawings.

Directed Drawings

Though there are many possible diagnostic indicators in the H-T-P test, it has been my observation that children reveal specific emotional concerns or needs by: (a) spending considerable time on one particular aspect of the drawing; (b) focusing on a particular symbolic component (e.g., a flower, a light fixture, a bedroom, or a smoking chimney); or (c) experiencing considerable affect from one image (e.g., black clouds, a broken tree, or an exploding bomb).

*Copyright 1984 AACD. Adapted with permission from Allan, J., & Clark, M. Directed art counseling. *Elementary School Guidance & Counseling 19,* 116–124. No further reproduction authorized without written permission of AACD.

These three processes tend to reflect either a stuck emotional position (i.e., blocked affect) or an area where new psychological growth is possible. When using the directed art technique, the counselor focuses on either the painful area or the area of new growth and asks the child to draw another picture of that particular image. The counselor takes these drawings as meaningful representations of inner emotional states and, at the start of the next session, asks for further amplification. For example:

> I've been thinking about the drawings you did last week, and I remember that you spent a lot of time on the broken tree. I wonder how the tree is doing this week and whether you could draw me another picture of it.

When working with images and symbols, the counselor talks directly to the symbol as if it were real. In other words, the symbol is used as a focusing device or as a vehicle through which further growth can occur. When the counselor accurately focuses in on the key symbolic area, the child usually goes ahead willingly with the additional drawings. If there are many symbols of pain, the counselor selects the one the child seems most involved in.

In the subsequent sessions, the counselor looks at the new drawings for symbols of either pain (hurt, wounds, damage) or growth (new trees, flowers, babies). In the early sessions, if indicated the focus of the counselor's direction needs to be on the pain areas (i.e., "Could you draw me a closeup of the broken branch in last week's picture?"), whereas once images of growth have ascendency in the pictures, the counselor follows that lead in the next session.

> I remember last week you drew the broken branch on the ground and when that was finished you added flowers and a hummingbird. I wonder what's going on with them this week. Could you draw me a picture of the flowers and the birds?

Though this method is quite directive, it must be remembered that the counselor takes direction from the material the child produces.

Free Drawings

If the directed drawings reveal neither areas of pain nor areas of new growth, then the counselor simply asks the child to do a drawing of the child's own choice. This often happens toward the end of the counseling sessions, for in the beginning phases symbols of pain, emptiness, or fixation frequently occur.

In order to show how the process of direct art counseling can be used, a case study will now be presented. It should be mentioned that throughout the counseling sessions no attempt was made to interpret the drawings to the child. Rather, the focus was placed on the content of the drawings (symbols) and on encouragement of further exploration of the themes.

CASE STUDY

Dennis a seven-year-old boy in second grade, was referred for counseling in September by his teacher because of his failure to adjust to the new class. He was very quiet, withdrawn, looked sad, had no friends, and was very anxious about attempting any new tasks. He became helpless whenever any work was required of him and usually tried to get another child to do it for him. His parents were in the process of a bitter divorce, and he had been placed in his grandmother's home.

Session 1. Dennis was asked to draw the H-T-P series, and immediately his concern with the ground became apparent. His house was drawn with heavy bars over the three windows, and he spent 10 minutes shading the ground under the house (Figure 4.19). The tree had a straight trunk with a few squiggly lines as bare branches near the top. Once again, the ground line was drawn and a very elaborate root system depicted under the tree (Figure 4.20). In the posttest inquiry, he described the tree as "hurting because they tore its skin off." Later, he added, "The roots will help the tree get better."

Session 2. The focus in this session was placed on the underground and on the roots. This was done for two reasons: first, Dennis spent a long time drawing both the ground under the house and the root system of the tree; and, second, he had indicated where the area of healing might occur by stating, "The roots will help the tree get better." At the start of this session, then, the counselor said:

Figure 4.19. House.

Reprinted with permission from Allan, J., & Clark, M. Directed art counseling. *Elementary School Guidance & Counseling, 19,* 120.

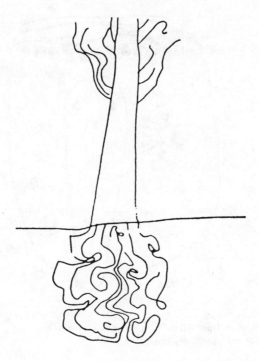

Figure 4.20. Tree.
Reprinted with permission from Allan, J., & Clark, M. (1984). Directed art counseling. *Elementary School Guidance & Counseling, 19,* 120.

Dennis, I've been thinking about the hurt tree and the roots. I remembered what you said about them. It looks like the roots have a lot to offer the tree. I am wondering if you could do another picture of the roots for me.

Once again, Dennis was very involved in the drawing and drew a more elaborate root system but this time added in worms and their homes. He was very careful to ensure that each of the worms had its own home.

Session 3. As a significant new area (worm homes) had been revealed in the last session, the counselor asked Dennis to draw a picture of a worm's home and to show what goes on inside it. Dennis drew a mother worm in her home caring for the baby worms, some of whom had not yet hatched and were still in their eggs. He also drew a large spider that he said was food for the babies. There were 10 worms and 14 worm eggs. Each worm had eyes and a nose but no mouth. The mother was huge in comparison to the babies—at least 12 times as big (Figure 4.21).

This drawing seemed to reflect the activation of the mother archetype (Neumann, 1974), psychological incubation (i.e., the eggs), nourishment (i.e.,

Figure 4.21. Mother and eggs.
Reprinted with permission from Allan, J., & Clark, M. (1984). Directed art counseling. *Elementary School Guidance & Counseling, 19*, 121.

food), and rebirth (i.e., the babies). In other words, the transference to the counselor was beginning to activate the feelings of acceptance and caring which, in turn, generated new psychological life and growth.

Session 4. It seemed that the mother worm and the babies were the key features in the previous drawing, so the counselor asked Dennis to draw the mother worm and one of her babies. His picture showed the very large mother worm, with a big smile and more human face features, beaming down on a just-hatched baby worm surrounded by hearts. The scene depicted an exchange of love between the mother and child. Dennis wrote the words, "I love you," near the mother worm with the baby worm replying, "I love you too" (Figure 4.22).

Session 5. As the previous picture seemed to reflect the start of the internalization of a positive mother-infant attachment bond, the counselor pursued this issue further by asking Dennis to draw another scene of the mother worm and her son. This drawing showed that the baby worm had grown to four times its original size and was now a "child" worm. The mother says to the child worm, "Can you help me?" and he answers, "Okay." The mother then tells the child, "You are good," and the child replies, "You are good too" (Figure 4.23).

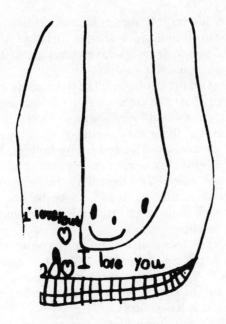

Figure 4.22. I love you

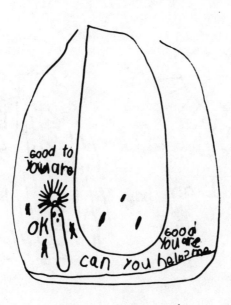

Figure 4.23. You are good

123

Session 6. As certain critical aspects seemed resolved and as the previous drawing did not seem to indicate a definite direction, the counselor said to Dennis, "I've asked you to draw several pictures and today I'm wondering if there is anything you would like to draw."

His picture showed on the left-hand side a boy smiling in the bright sunshine saying, "I am happy." At the right side of the drawing, clouds, rain, and lightning were present but did not impinge on the boy (Figure 4.24). The drawing seemed to reflect that the stormy period of his life was moving away and was being replaced by more positive and happy feelings. The turmoil was still there at the edge of his life, but it was not dominating all of his existence. The teacher at this point commented on the child's dramatic overall improvement. His happiness showed on his face and, in class, he was making friends and doing much more work on his own. He was also becoming more daring and even disobeyed the teacher at times.

Session 7. In order to focus once again on the positive aspects and to help them be internalized, the counselor asked Dennis to draw a picture of "the boy in the sunshine." This drawing showed a happy smiling boy in the sun with no signs of a storm. Dennis wrote next to the boy, "I am happy and I am glad because the rain has gone away."

Sessions 8, 9, 10. Dennis's drawings began to change at this point, and he drew pictures of many situations with his friends. At the start of the ninth session, the counselor announced the termination procedures and Dennis drew a spaceman getting ready for blastoff to the moon. The story that went with it was expansive and positive.

Figure 4.24. I am happy.
Reprinted with permission from Allan, J., & Clark, M. (1984). Directed art counseling. *Elementary School Guidance & Counseling, 19,* 122.

Contact with the teacher and grandmother, with whom he was living, now indicated that he was out of his shell, his academic work was improving, and he was able to concentrate on his school work. Also, his behavior had improved; he was making friends and moving into neighborhood activities.

Follow-up. A follow-up session was held five months later, and Dennis was asked to do four drawings: H-T-P and an underground scene. All the pictures reflected healthy images. The house was open at the front and one could see people eating at a table under the lights (Figure 4.25); the tree was the normal trunk and leafy top of the primary-aged child; and the person was his friend, the next-door neighbor child. When asked to draw a picture of the ground underneath the earth, he reacted with surprise and seemed to have no recollection of drawing the series of underground pictures some months before. The new drawing had no resemblance to the previous ones and showed a busy, interesting place filled with life and activity. There was a good connection between the outside world and the underground through a system of tunnels and roots. Unlike the earlier drawing of the barren tree, the plants appeared healthy both above and below the ground. There were ants, worms, buried money, old and new cents, and even a miner going down one tunnel to find the lost treasure (Figure 4.26). This drawing seemed to reflect continued psychological growth and the establishment of a positive relationship between his conscious and unconscious mind (i.e., easy access to the underground and many positive symbols). Follow-up, three years after the termination of treatment, indicated no problems and continued development.

Figure 4.25. House.
Reprinted with permission from Allan, J., & Clark, M. (1984). Directed art counseling. *Elementary School Guidance & Counseling, 19,* 123.

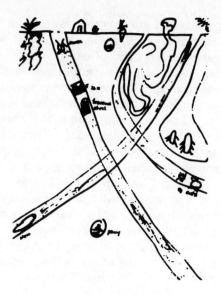

Figure 4.26. Miner

Partially Directed Approach

In this method of serial drawing, the counselor identifies a visual theme that has relevance to the child and every four to six weeks asks the child to draw that image. In the other intervening sessions, the children are free to draw whatever they wish to draw. These partially directed drawings are often useful indicators of the progress that the child is making in treatment and can also offer a focal point for the psychological working through of a particular symbolic issue that the child is struggling with.

At the start of treatment, in the assessment phase, children are asked to do an H-T-P series followed by a picture of their own choice. Following the post-test inquiry and a discussion (from the child's frame of reference) of the child's free drawing, the counselor attempts to assess which picture carries the most symbolic meaning for the child. Usually one image or symbol seems to stand out. The image alone may not look meaningful, but when the child describes the image, the intensity of meaning becomes apparent. For some children it is the house, for some the tree, for some the person, while for others this specific intense meaning is held in their free drawing. It may be anything: a butterfly, a river, a horse, a battlefield, a car, or a dog. The counselor makes an assessment, keeps the image in mind, allows the therapy to progress as the child wishes, but when needing another assessment or review, may ask the child to draw the specific image identified earlier. The case below describes one way to use this method and the results.

CASE BACKGROUND

Carl, a sixth grader who would lose his temper if things were not perfect, was referred to the school counselor on account of acting out behaviors and alienation from friends. Although an excellent student, he often created problems through his own anxiety. His family was going through a separation, and Carl alternated between being either very explosive or very withdrawn.

He talked freely in the first session, said he got into trouble a lot, did not like it but was not sure why it happened. He did an H-T-P, wanted a ruler, and asked, "Do you want me to do it (the house) looking down?" He spent 20 minutes on the house, meticulously drawing the front door and stained glass windows, 4 minutes on the tree, and about 6 minutes on the person: a hockey goalie. During the posttest inquiry, he focused more on the tree, adding the wind ("It's slanting because the wind is blowing") and the fungus ("The tree is growing fungus on it") (Figure 4.27).

During the next four sessions, Carl drew self-portraits and talked about life at school. He did some role playing around being cooperative and noncooper-

Figure 4.27. Fungus

ative and identified feelings connected with each role. At home he was often in tears and refused to talk about the separation. At the start of the sixth session, the counselor said: "Carl, I've been thinking about the windstorm and the tree. I wonder what has happened to the tree, the growth on the trunk and its condition."

Carl immediately started to draw the tree, saying, "It's got more rotten." He then colored it, adding, "Wood bugs and ants are eating away inside where it is rotten" (Figure 4.28).

Over the following three sessions, Carl continued to talk about school and was able to acknowledge that his parents were splitting up, though he added, "It doesn't really bother me." Life in school continued to improve, and after another month the counselor stated at the start of a session, "Carl, I wonder how the tree is doing?" He immediately replied, "It's fallen down" and proceeded to draw it lying on the ground with grass sprouting from it. Later he commented, "There are bugs and ants in the log still" (Figure 4.29).

Figure 4.28. Woodbugs

Figure 4.29. Fallen down

In the next few sessions, he began to talk openly about the divorce and his hurt, sad, and mad feelings. The counselor tied together his feelings about the divorce and getting into trouble. He said at times he tried to pretend the divorce was not happening but then would get really mad when he knew it was. He was having a few more eruptions at school and was feeling embarrassed and mad at himself. He started to cry and to talk about how his life used to be fun and to go smoothly. But now things had changed and would never be the same. He was acutely experiencing the pain over the divorce and the loss of father and family. Toward the end of the session the counselor asked, "I wonder how the tree is doing?" Carl started to draw it and said, "It's decaying" (Figure 4.30).

In the next 5 sessions Carl talked about life at school, his father, and issues that bothered him. He problem-solved and role-played various conflicts. He had a violent outburst at school, damaged some property, and felt very embarrassed and upset. It was a big step for him to be able to talk about his role in it, to accept the fact that he had blown it, and to apologize to the teacher. When this was worked through, the counselor asked him how the tree was doing. He replied, "The tree has decayed into dirt and there's new bushes" (Figure 4.31). There were a few more sessions to the end of the school year in which Carl was able to talk quite freely about his struggles. Counseling was terminated at this point. His last picture he called "New Tree" (Figure 4.32).

Follow-up one year and eight months later with Carl, now an eighth grader, indicated a well-adjusted boy. When asked about the tree he said, "It's deveoped into a new one. It's a strong tree now and there's a waterfall flowing down the hillside beside it" (Figure 4.33).

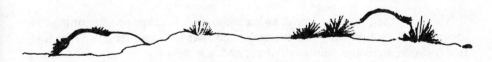

Figure 4.30. Decaying

Figure 4.31. New bush

Figure 4.32. New tree

This whole sequence of tree drawing seems to reflect the process of psychological death and rebirth. The counselor felt that Carl had let go of his childhood, experienced the pain of divorce, and was now on his way to becoming a confident young adolescent. The hurt had been expressed and shared, the wounds healed, and new growth was now possible.

Figure 4.33. Strong tree

SUMMARY

Three ways of using serial drawing are described: nondirective, directive, and partially directive, along with common stages observed in the drawing process and the various counselor skills needed at each stage. When children draw in the presence of the counselor on a regular basis, themes depicting trauma, the transference, the struggle with ambivalent feelings, reparation, and healing are revealed. Many children use one main symbolic theme as the vehicle for change, and with counseling the symbol changes from the initial damaged form to one reflective of healthy functioning. In the middle stages of treatment, children often use the content of the drawing as a bridge to direct verbal self-disclosures. Termination images tend to depict the emergence of self-confidence, restoration of the lost object, humor, the experience of nurturance, removal of attachment to the counselor, and emerging independence.

REFERENCES

Allan, J. (1977). The use of creative drama with acting-out sixth and seventh grade boys and girls. *Canadian Counsellor, 11,* 135–143.

Allan, J. (1978a). Serial drawing: A therapeutic approach with young children. *Canadian Counsellor, 12,* 223–228.

Allan, J. (1978b). Serial storywriting: A therapeutic approach with a young adolescent. *Canadian Counsellor, 121,* 132–137.

Allan, J. (1978c). Facilitating emotional and symbol development in young children. *Journal of Canadian Association for Young Children, 4,* 8–19.

Allan, J. (1986). The body in child psychotherapy. In N. Schwartz-Salant, & M. Stein (Eds.). *The body in analysis* (pp. 145–166). Wilmette, IL: Chiron Press.

Allan, J., & Barber, J. (1986). Teacher needs and counselor response: One example. *Elementary School Guidance and Counseling, 20,* 277–282.

Allan, J., & Berry, P. (1987). Sandplay. *Elementary School Guidance and Counseling, 21,* 300–306.

Allan, J., & Clark, M. (1985). Art counselling in elementary schools and child guidance clinics. *Canadian Journal of Art Therapy, 2,* 23–31.

Allan, J., Doi, K., & Reed, C. (1979). Need assessment: A survey of B.C.'s principals, primary and intermediate teachers' perception of counselling needs. *Canadian Counsellor, 14,* 132–137.

Allan, J., & MacDonald, R. (1975). Fantasy enactment in the treatment of an autistic child. *Journal of Analytical Psychology, 20,* 102–111.

Buck, J. (1948). The H-T-P test. *Journal of Clinical Psychology, 4,* 151–159.

Buttery, J., & Allan, J. (1981). Journal writing as a developmental guidance method. *Canadian Counsellor, 15,* 134–138.

Carkhuff, R. (1969). *Helping and human relationships* (Vol. 1). New York: Holt, Rinehart & Winston.

Jung, C.G. (1959). *Archetypes and the collective unconscious.* Princeton, NJ: Princeton University Press.

Jung, C.G. (1965). *Memories, dreams, reflections.* New York: Random House.

Jung, C.G. (1966). *The practice of psychotherapy.* Princeton, NJ: Princeton University Press.

Neumann, E. (1974). *The great mother.* Princeton, NJ: Princeton University Press.

Schwartz-Salant, N. (1986). On the subtle-body concept in clinical practice. In N. Schwartz-Salant, & M. Stein (Eds.), *The body in analysis* (pp. 19–58). Wilmette, IL: Chiron Publications.

Thompson, F., & Allan, J. (1985). Active art counselling in the elementary schools. *Guidance and Counselling, 1*(2), 63–73.

Acknowledgments

The author gratefully acknowledges the help of his senior graduate students in data collection, especially Doug Lee, Judy Moon, Mary Clark, and Suzanne Elliot.

PART 2

Relaxed State Techniques

Techniques Involving Altered
States of Consciousness

CHAPTER 5

Hypnotic Techniques with Children

PETER TILTON

INTRODUCTION

Learning and using hypnotic techniques with children can bring unexpected and quick, yet longlasting, results. This chapter gives examples of how to use hypnosis with children and how to stimulate hypnotherapists' creativity in helping children. The techniques described offer a great deal of flexibility and a wide range of styles to help therapists feel comfortable with the use of hypnotherapy.

History

Hypnosis has been used since antiquity, in modern times its use began with Franz Mesmer, who practiced his animal magnetism in Vienna and Paris in the late 18th century. Despite success, his theory of a magnetic fluid being passed to his patients to effect a cure during a crisis was repudiated by the Franklin Commission in 1794. However, the controversy continued: Hypnosis was carried on by an English physician, John Elliotson, who agreed with Mesmer's theory and continued to achieve success. It was another Englishman, James Braid, who first understood the psychological aspects of hypnosis and adopted the term *hypnosis* from the Greek word for sleep, *hypnos.*

Two schools of thought developed in France in the late 19th century. One was centered around Jean-Claude Charcot in Salpetriere, who proposed the neurological theory that stated that hypnosis could only occur in a pathological state in predisposed hysterical individuals. It was this theory that, although incorrect, gave scientific credence to hypnosis. The other group was centered in Nancy with Ambroise Auguste Liébeault and Hippolyte Marie Bernheim, who proposed the first psychological theory including the doctrine of suggestibility.

While Pierre Janet and others were investigating hypnosis and recognizing the splitting of consciousness that led to the theory of dissociation, Sigmund Freud greatly influenced the use of hypnosis. His investigations of hypnosis left him disappointed in its use, but had great influence on the development of his charting of the unconscious and his use of free association. However, the popularization of psychoanalysis and Freud's abandonment of hypnosis led to its decline in the early 1900s. The work of Clark Hull, Milton Erickson, and Ernest Hilgard finally brought it back into popularity and respectability.

Most of the above-mentioned pioneers successfully treated children with hypnosis, discovering the ease with which children can be hypnotized.

Theories, Definition, and Characteristics

Even today controversy exists over an accurate definition of hypnosis, as evidenced by the number of theories purported. Most experts believe that hypnosis is characterized by an altered state of consciousness. Hilgard's (1979) research lends credence to his neodissociation theory, stating that there are varying degrees of dissociation ranging from a limited and superficial response of light hypnosis to the deeper states of fugue or multiple personality. Fromm (1979) discusses her ego psychological theory, which is characterized by a state of ego receptivity. Orne (1959) describes an alteration of perception and memory in response to hypnotic suggestion sometimes characterized by what he terms "trance logic." Shor (1979) defines hypnosis as a reduction in general reality orientation (GRO), a nonconscious or involuntary response, an archaic involvement (a temporary displacement of emotive attitudes formed early in life onto the hypnotist), drowsiness, relaxation, vividness of imagery, absorption, and access to the unconscious.

While there are many other theories, one more, by Barber (1979), is worth mentioning. He believes that hypnosis is not characterized by a special state of mind but is in reality a situation in which subjects' responses are determined by their attitudes, expectations, and motivations.

It is easier to say what hypnosis is not than to say what it is. However, in this author's opinion, hypnosis is characterized by an altered state of consciousness in which there is a reduction of the GRO, a focusing or narrowing of attention, and an absorption of the mind with access to unconscious processes characterized by a greater receptivity to ego-syntonic suggestions.

On the other hand, contrary to some popular misconceptions, hypnosis is not a state of sleep or a loss of consciousness. It is also not a state in which a person surrenders control or loses willpower to the hypnotherapist, and hidden secrets are not revealed. Most people are easily hypnotized and dehypnotized, and they usually remember what occurs during the hypnotic state after it is over.

Some characteristics of hypnosis (but not always unique to hypnosis alone) are the following: relaxation, age regression and revivification, hypermnesia, amnesia, positive and negative hallucinations, dissociation, hypnoanalgesia and anesthesia, hyperesthesia, automatic writing, time distortion, catalepsy, ideomotor and ideosensory activity, self-hypnosis, and posthypnotic suggestion and conditioning (Kroger, 1977).

It is universally accepted that children are more easily hypnotized than adults. While most research indicates that children are most easily hypnotized between the ages of 7 and 14, anyone who has worked hypnotically with children recognizes that children as young as 4 (and sometimes earlier) can be hypnotized.

THE HYPNOTIC PROCESS

Before describing hypnotic inductions and how to set up a relaxing and responsive mood for the child, it is important to point out that it is not possible to gain an adequate understanding of how to work hypnotically with children by reading it from a book. For those who are familiar with the techniques, this chapter can serve as a useful guideline with helpful examples to add to an already existing repertiore. However, for those without experience in hypnosis, the chapter is meant to be only an introduction. Readers who develop an interest in the field of hypnosis are urged to get proper professional training before attempting hypnosis with children. Both the American Society of Clinical Hypnosis and the Society for Clinical and Experimental Hypnosis offer excellent workshops and training opportunities.

Preinduction Process

In order to insure a successful outcome in hypnotherapy, some required groundwork must be done. Much of this can occur in the initial interview with the child and the parent(s), usually referred to as the *preinduction talk*. During this interview it is important to determine the parents', as well as the child's, attitude toward hypnosis, and to clarify any misconceptions or negative attitudes.

It is equally important to assess the child's attitude about his problem and motivation for wanting to get better.* This is also the time to establish a rapport with the child and find out about his likes and dislikes, interests, and attitudes, if they have not already been established. This also presents the opportunity to discuss the problem and the rationale for the use of hypnosis.

It is important to stress that a good rapport with the child is essential for a successful therapeutic outcome. It is important to neither talk down to a child nor use words that he cannot understand. Finding out and using the means of expression and communication, language and vocabulary, and the specific words used to describe situations or conditions helps build this rapport. Milton Erickson (Haley, 1967; Beahrs, 1971) has stated how important it is to meet the client where he is: This is even more important with children.

Often it is necessary to ask the child if he knows why he has been brought to the office. Many children will not have this information. It then becomes

---

*In the remainder of this chapter, for simplification, all references to gender will be in the masculine with no slight to the female gender intended.

necessary to bring it out into the open and to help reassure an unwilling or frightened child about the prospects of being helped through the use of hypnosis.

This is also a good time to assess the child's motivation and his feelings about the possibilities of a successful outcome to therapy. If there seems to be a negative or pessimistic attitude, the therapist can match it initially. This helps build rapport, refrains from setting up false expectations, and disallows the patient from making the treatment fail. Then the therapist can add stories about the success of other patients with similar problems, attempting to give the child some hope of success. It is also helpful to have the child talk about how his world and life will be different after the completion of therapy. The child usually becomes more optimistic and more willing to enter into a positive therapeutic relationship, rather than remaining an unwilling participant.

Once a good rapport and proper motivation are established and the child has a relatively accurate idea of what to expect, the next step is hypnotic induction.

Hypnotic Induction Techniques

There are many different inductions or ways to hypnotize a child. It is necessary to feel comfortable with different techniques so that if one induction does not work, the therapist can quickly and easily switch to another with equal confidence. More important than technique is the confidence and familiarity of working with and being with children—with or without hypnosis.

The question of whether to allow parents to stay in the room depends upon the situation. The author's preference is to have the parents leave the room once a good rapport has been established. Too often parents can serve as a distraction and even undermine the process. However, if a child seems too frightened to be alone, which is common in younger children, it is appropriate to request that parents stay in the room but remain seated separately. Actually there are no hard and fast rules, and flexibility is the key to a successful therapeutic outcome.

One technique the author frequently uses involves the use of eye fixation and the coin-drop method (Olness, 1975). A smiling face is painted (a colored marker or felttip pen will do nicely) on the child's thumbnail, and the child is asked to hold a coin (preferably a large, heavy one such as a half-dollar) between the thumb and index finger. The following is an example of this type of induction:

> I would like you to hold the coin like this [therapist then demonstrates holding the coin so the smiling face on the thumbnail faces the child]. . . . Good, now I want you to stare at that funny, smiling face, or you can just stare at the coin. . . . and as you look at it you may notice how heavy it becomes . . . so heavy that it may want to fall. . . . and it's okay to let it fall; you don't have to worry about it because we can pick it up later. . . . And when the coin falls you

can just close your eyes, or you may find that as you drop the coin your eyes will want to close, and that's okay, too. . . . or you may find that you get so tired of holding the coin that you just want to let it go, and you can do that and then close your eyes. . . .

This represents the beginning of the actual hypnotic process. The therapist must pay careful attention to the child and judge the proper timing for use of induction suggestions. Again, it is important to stress the need for professional training in learning how to hypnotize a child. For the remainder of the chapter, the reader's knowledge of hypnosis will be assumed.

Another favorite is the television technique. It is important to inquire about the child's television viewing (i.e., favorite programs, favorite characters, the favorite time for watching, and a good description of the room where the child likes to watch). With all of this information at hand the therapist can then begin. A sample dialogue could be as follows:

How would you like to watch television now? Good. Now I want you to close your eyes and see [or "imagine," or "pretend"] your living room. Perhaps you can feel how soft and comfortable the couch is, and you can see the carpeting and the other chairs. . . . and maybe you can smell the popcorn [or some other food the child likes to eat while watching TV if this is deemed appropriate]. And now you can see the television set. I'm going to turn it on and you can see "the Bugs Bunny Show" [or the child's favorite show, or you can wait and ask the child what show comes on].

Then you can have the child describe what he is watching or you can describe a show while interspersing relaxation or therapeutic suggestions.

There are many different techniques that can be used, limited only by the creativity of the therapist. Other examples include having the child describe (or asking the child to imagine) his favorite place, animal or pet; favorite activity or sport; or—for those children who prefer music—his favorite song or instrument. Active children can be asked to imagine flying in a space ship, riding a horse, playing sports, playing in the playground, or being a bouncing ball. Besides a coin, other eye-fixation techniques include staring at a picture, toy, or stuffed animal. Additional techniques include progressive relaxation and storytelling with either patient, therapist, or both participating in an evolving tale which can then be used for therapeutic purposes. Gardner and Olness (1981) give an excellent overview of many inductions with partial descriptions for their use.

Many of the techniques mentioned here seem to fall into the category of formal inductions, wherein both patient and therapist expect something to be done to the patient to enable him to enter the hypnotic state. However, there is a wide range of informal techniques that simply use a conversational approach. Many times the author has asked a child if he would like to play a game or pretend or use his imagination. If the response is affirmative, the child is asked to close his eyes "because it is so much easier to do this with the eyes closed," and then the game can begin with wonderful descriptions. When the child's interests are utilized, the methods of inducing a hypnotic state are infinite, limited ony by the creativity of the therapist.

Children naturally enter hypnosis easily and frequently by themselves, as evidenced by children playing with an imaginary friend, personifying a favorite stuffed animal, or playing with toys in some imaginary game. The therapist's job is to provide an atmosphere that permits the child to enter this world of make-believe so that successful therapy can begin.

In working with children it is a good idea to avoid the use of the word "sleep" since it can have some negative connotations, for example, a pet being put to sleep, an operation in which they were told that they were going to be put to sleep, or being told to go to sleep when they wanted to stay up later. Instead, words and phrases such as "relaxed," "drowsy," or "loose and floppy like a Raggedy Ann doll" usually work best to help children enter the hypnotic state.

Another caution should be applied in asking the child to close his eyes. Some children, especially the younger ones, may be too afraid to close their eyes; the therapist should be flexible in this regard, letting the child know that it is all right to keep them open and still enter hypnosis. (For the beginning hypnotherapist this may be uncomfortable, but it must be stated that children can enter hypnosis just as easily with their eyes remaining open.) After a time the therapist can suggest that it is easier to imagine things with the eyes closed and perhaps it would now be okay to try it. It is important to avoid getting into an argument or a control battle over this issue.

Fully assessing the child and his needs is most important to determine which induction technique works best. Even if the therapist likes to use the TV method, it might not be effective for a child who rarely watches TV but prefers, instead, to practice music.

Any induction technique can be followed by a different one to ensure a deeper trance, for example, following the coin drop with the TV technique or a story. Since children are easily hypnotized, it is not so important to worry about deepening the trance with a separate technique, rather, it is more important to keep the child absorbed in whatever he is experiencing. That in itself will lead to a successful trance experience.

Therapists must remember that children have short attention spans and they may start to fidget or move about and even open their eyes briefly and close them again. It is important to realize that a child will usually remain hypnotized during this fidgeting or brief eye opening. However, it is equally important to judge when the end of the child's attention span has reached its limit and end the therapeutic session. The author once observed a child swiveling around in a chair ending up facing in the opposite direction from when the hypnosis began. When the trance ended the child remarked that he was surprised by this new position and had no idea that he had been using his feet to turn the chair around and round.

Because they have short attention spans, it is usually sufficient to spend between 15 and 30 minutes with children. Older teenagers, may require longer sessions, but they are also able to tolerate it better.

Hypnotizability varies not only from child to child but also from session to session with each child. For example, the author conducted several successful hypnotic sessions with one 5-year-old girl and then was not able to gain her cooperation in another session. There could be many reasons for this, such as disappointment due to failure in treatment, resistance due to secondary gain, or discomfort with the therapist or therapy process. Sometimes it is necessary to explore the reasons, while at other times it is better to switch to other modalities of treatment.

There is some controversy over the issue of the importance of hypnotizability and therapeutic outcome, with many researchers believing that the highly hypnotizable patients are the ones most likely to benefit. However, since most children are easily hypnotized, it may be the nature of the problem and its underlying dynamics in combination with the treatment method that have a greater impact on the success or failure of therapy.

When it is time to end the hypnotic trance, any number of methods will suffice, again, based upon the child's age and needs. Counting from one to five with the eyes opening and the child being alert and awake at the count of five is one method. Another is simply to tell the child it is time to end the session and turn off the TV (or end whatever he was doing) and bring his attention back into the room and open his eyes. It is important to give the child adequate time to make a smooth transition from the hypnotic state to the waking state. The therapist should know that on occasion the child will enjoy the trance so much that he might resist coming back into the waking state; gentle prodding will usually work.

At the end of the initial hypnotic session, the therapist should spend a few minutes going over the procedure with the child, ensuring that the child knows how to do self-hypnosis and has the desire to do so on his own. Many times the continuation of therapy by self-hypnosis at home is extremely important for the child to gain a sense of mastery that leads to a successful outcome.

Hypnotic Style

Before discussing the application and uses of hypnosis with children, it is necessary to discuss the style and attitude of the therapist in the use of hypnosis. For many years the major approach to giving hypnotic suggestion was direct and authoritative. While this method does work and still has merit, many therapists have adopted a more permissive attitude that allows a great deal more maneuverability between therapist and patient.

According to Diamond (1984), it is the interpersonal relationship between patient and therapist that ensures a successful experience. However, it is the skill and qualities of the therapist that provide this healing milieu. Lazar and Dempster (1984) have identified some characteristics that a therapist should have to ensure a positive outcome. These are the ability to be realistic and objective in goal setting, persistence combined with flexibility, sensitivity, empathy, and confidence in abilities: the same characteristics necessary to be a good therapist. Thus one does not merely hypnotize another person but, rather, hypnosis is an interaction between two people, and trust and rapport need to be developed to ensure a successful hypnotic experience.

Hypnotherapists today are adopting a more naturalistic, permissive, and sometimes indirect approach. This style, first exemplified and encouraged by Milton Erickson (Haley, 1967), has been expressed by others. According to Araoz (1985), an inner transformation occurs through the feeling and experiential state of the patient in hypnosis, facilitated by a therapist who is client-centered and respectful of the patient and who can observe the patient and deal with him on his level of communication.

Hypnotic Techniques

The best-known and perhaps oldest technique is simple, straightforward, direct suggestion. However, it is usually responded to with better results if given in a more permissive style. An example would be ". . . and perhaps your bedwetting can stop soon. . . . maybe you will wake up tomorrow with a dry bed or it could happen in a few days . . . and won't it be nice to eventually wake every morning with a dry bed." This kind of suggestion gives the child a sense of hope that the desired outcome will take place soon, but at the same time relieves the child from any pressure to make it happen right away and avoids creating a sense of failure and hopelessness if the change does not immediately occur. (The older, more authoritative approach was exemplified by "and you will have a dry bed tomorrow.")

A variation of the direct approach, termed "the hypnotic hero," was developed by the author (1984; 1980). In this approach, the suggestions are given as if they were coming from a significant person in the child's world, often a fictional cartoon character, a TV or movie star, a sports figure, or anyone with whom the child positively identifies who seems appropriate for the therapeutic problem. This technique serves to increase self-esteem and create a more secure reality for the child, enabling him to behave more autonomously and face future situations with a better self-image. In some cases it can be diagnostic as well, by allowing the therapist to gauge the areas of improvement while at the same time assessing any failure in terms of the child's ego strength. This offers valuable information pointing as to where more in-depth work needs to occur.

There are many indirect styles of giving hypnotic suggestions that have the advantage of overcoming or sidestepping resistance to change, since the suggestions are given in such a manner that they are not recognized as such by the conscious mind. These styles include storytelling techniques, analogies, metaphors, interspersal technique, (Haley, 1967; Tilton, 1986), and others.

HYPNOTHERAPY WITH CHILDREN

General Considerations

In dealing with any childhood problem, it is important to assess the family situation to determine whether there are any contributing factors that need to be addressed, such as secondary gain, sibling rivalry, and so on. It is important to ascertain, for therapeutic success, whether the parents' hope is for the child to be "fixed" by hypnosis, or they are unwilling to look at the possibilities of family dynamics as a causative factor.

One of the easiest and most important situations to look for is parental involvement in the presenting problem. It is helpful to know whether it is the parent that wants successful therapy or the child or both. Another factor to look at is overenmeshment or underinvolvement on the part of parents. Once these factors are known, they can be dealt with directly by the instructions or statements made to the parents by the therapist, and perhaps without extensive family therapy.

For the overenmeshed parent, the therapist can shift the responsibility for the problem from the parent to the child, reducing any ridicule or scolding and setting up any punishments in the therapist's office so that the child knows exactly what to expect. The parent is also told that the child will do his self-hypnosis on his own and is not to be bothered or nagged about it; if it seems that he is not doing so, it can be dealt with at the next session. On the other hand, the parent who seems uninvolved or too distant from the problem is instructed to help the child with the self-hypnosis by providing the coin and painting the face on the thumbnail each day before the child begins his self-hypnosis practice. The parent is also told to check on the child's progress and report it at the next session. Using these techniques, the home situation and its difficulties can be resolved, and the rest of therapy can proceed.

At other times it is important to point out his uniqueness to a child and to emphasize how wonderful it is to be different from parents in some ways and similar to them in other ways, especially if the presenting problem is one that is also shared by a parent. For example, an enuretic child was told that he could stop bedwetting, even though his father still did it occasionally, because his bladder was different, just as he was different from his father. However, it did not mean that he did not love his father or want to be like him in other ways.

Alternatively, the author has commented directly to a parent about his or her own obesity or tic when the child was brought in to be changed. The author has sided with the child on his anger at being brought in and made to feel bad about a problem that the parent also had, and then sent the parent out to work further with the child (as in the case of the bedwetting). This helps establish immediate rapport with the child by setting up a tacit understanding and alliance.

It should also be stated that hypnosis can be added to any form of therapy because hypnosis is merely an adjunctive tool that provides an atmosphere to create change. Therefore, it can be utilized with many of the other techniques described in this book. Whether the orientation of the therapist is behavioral, analytical, dynamic, or anything else, hypnosis can be a useful, additional technique.

The use of hypnosis and self-hypnosis allows the child to experience a sense of mastery over a problem and also allows the child a way to relieve anxiety in a manner that can be playful and creative. When the child learns to reduce tensions and anxieties through self-hypnosis, the unwanted symptoms or behaviors no longer appear.

One excellent and simple technique is the use of wires and switches. The child is asked to imagine many wires inside the body originating in the head and leading to different parts of the body (the word "nerve" is used if the child is familiar with this concept). He is told that each wire has its own switch or control dial. These wires can have many different uses to control different bodily functions.

For example, if hypnoanesthesia is the desired effect, the patient is asked to find the wire that leads to the back of the hand. He is told that if he turns the switch, it will cause numbness in the hand (the therapist can draw a large, imaginary circle on the back of the child's hand). Then, when the child indicates that the numbness is present (most children can do this easily and quickly), the hand is tested with a sharp object such as the point of a letter opener. The child is asked to watch this with his eyes open. The other hand is then tested for comparison. This type of procedure can have a dramatic effect on the child and gives him a sense of wonderment and awe at his own heretofore unknown abilities. It is then suggested that just as he has the ability to make his hand numb, he has the ability to do other things as well. Additional wires and switches can be utilized or other types of suggestions can be linked to his success at learning to control his body, behavior, and so on. The possibilities are endless. Other examples will follow in specific case studies discussed later in the chapter.

Hypnoanalytical Techniques

There are many useful hypnoanalytical techniques that help a child uncover repressed material or forgotten episodes from the past. These can aid in the resolution of unconscious conflicts. Often this is an important and necessary step for the removal of psychological blocks that have resulted in unwanted behaviors or feelings. Such techniques can be utilized in conjunction with dynamic or analytical work, or can be useful in more short-term work as well.

Techniques such as dream induction, free association, or age regression can bypass conscious resistance and reveal important material. Other techniques that have a dissociative or projective quality include watching scenes on an imaginary television (or the use of movies, theater, crystal balls, or mirrors), automatic writing, play or art therapy, or the affect-bridge (Watkins, 1971). Hartland (1971) gives an excellent review of the use of these techniques.

A good example can be a child who has difficulty going to school and develops physical symptoms severe enough to excuse him from school. He might develop some bad or difficult behavior, a school phobia or avoidance such as getting sick or vomiting on the school bus each day. Many times these situations arise from an embarrassing or emotionally upsetting situation that the child is unable to resolve or talk about that has now been displaced or repressed into unwanted behavior. Using age regression or another uncovering technique in this situation that can allow the child to retrieve and work through a previously related but disavowed unpleasant experience can be a useful and effective method. In working with any psychological problem it is important to understand the dynamics. These techniques can be a quick, effective inroad to the underlying conflicts that might otherwise take longer to see or be less effectively uncovered.

Psychological Problems

In discussing the hypnotherapeutic treatment of children with psychological problems it is the author's view that it is easier to do what works effectively as quickly as possible, especially if time and money are issues with the family (as they usually are). Therefore, when approaching any problem, the author usually proceeds with hypnosis during the first session, giving appropriate suggestions and having the child imagine a successful outcome. The results are then assessed at the beginning of the second session to determine whether the proposed treatment plan should proceed in this direction or a change is required. If after two or three sessions there are no appreciable results, and if the child has been judged to have been hypnotized and cooperative, then the author employs uncovering techniques or abandons hypnosis in favor of family therapy or other forms of individual work.

Phobias and Anxiety

Phobias and anxiety are common problems that can be successfully treated with hypnosis. Hypnotic desensitization and the use of ego-strengthening suggestions, combined with hypnotic imagery of successful mastery of the anxious or phobic situation, work exceedingly well. The addition of suggestions from the hypnotic hero is another tool that can be of great significance in brief therapy for these kinds of problems. Sometimes an age regression to the originating experience and resolving it or desensitizing it can also help. Some case studies will help illustrate this.

CASE 1

A 12-year-old boy was seen by the author because of his fear of being hurt in karate practice. This had extended to his fear of drowning and getting injections from the doctor. He related easily that the problem began a year ago when he was hit on the nose during karate practice, which hurt and caused him to complain and want to sit out for awhile. This behavior caused the instructor to tell the patient's mother that he needed to toughen up.

After the patient was hypnotized he was instructed to imagine himself with the Legion of Superheroes (his favorite characters) and was told that he also had special powers. He was instructed in how to induce hand anesthesia by the method of wires and switches. Upon the successful testing of this hand numbness he was told that he had many other powers that he didn't realize and that these included doing well in karate practice, swimming, and going to see the doctor. He was then asked to imagine himself doing these things to his satisfaction and without fear. He was asked to see himself both hitting and getting hit in karate practice without anything other than normal concern—even though getting hit might hurt. After the session he related to the therapist how he had imagined the instructor congratulating him, an act that made him feel good. He also said he felt no more headache (of which the therapist had been unaware).

The following week he returned stating that he had done self-hypnosis and enjoyed it and that he was no longer afraid. He did, however, mention that he was still afraid to go to bed in the dark. He was hypnotized again and saw himself going upstairs to bed with the superheroes protecting him. He then imagined going up by himself. When he was satisfied, the hypnosis was terminated and the boy left without further problems.

CASE 2

A second case was a 14-year-old boy who had been successfully treated with hypnosis for a medical problem (Tilton, 1984,). The presenting problem was the fears and anxieties resulting from what the patient described as a hyper-imagination. He felt there was always someone lurking in the shadows wherever he walked. He was also concerned about things falling on him and severely injuring him. He hoped hypnosis could help him. He was hypnotized and age-regressed back to when these kind of fears first began. He related being six years old and hitting his thumb with a hammer. He was afraid because of both the bleeding and the pain. He was then told that he was now older and could do things better. He was asked to imagine the scene again, but at his present age. He was reminded of his success with hypnosis and his use of the wire and switch technique (which was again reproduced). He was asked to imagine having more fun and walking around without fear. When the trance was over he talked about some bad dreams and memories. The next week he reported feeling better, no longer checking behind the shower curtain or in the shadows. After the hypnosis he again talked about past memories. The following week he reported feeling normal and again talked about some past frightening experiences, which no longer bothered him.

CASE 3

Multiple problems of a five-year-old child—including fear of being kidnapped or killed, nightmares, and behavioral problems—were successfully treated by hypnotic intervention, by encouraging the mother to exercise more control and discipline, and by the use of storytelling and drawings. These techniques finally revealed a memory of a little girl being killed in an auto accident in front of his house when he was three (Tilton, 1984, case 6).

Social anxiety, test-taking anxiety, fears of going to sleep, and many other childhood fears can be treated similarly. Other techniques that work well with young children include throwing fears away, sending them away in a jet plane or in a balloon, burying them, or being protected from them by a favorite hero.

Behavioral Problems

Behavioral problems can be treated similarly with a willing client.

CASE 1

A five-year-old girl started to refuse to go to school, stating that she preferred to stay at home with her mother and draw. Because she got nauseous and vomited on the school bus frequently, and because the mother had a lifelong history of motion sickness, the mother thought that the two problems were related. The child stated that she liked school but simply preferred to stay at home where she could do what she wanted. However, she did agree that she did not like getting sick on the bus. She was hypnotized and asked to imagine riding in the school bus with Mickey Mouse and Pluto and having a fun ride to school. Then, after having imagined a fun day at school, she was asked to imagine riding home with Pluto and Mickey without any problems. She replied that she wanted to play a little longer at school and then, when she was ready, she rode home in the bus, said goodbye to Mickey and Pluto, opened her eyes, and left with her mother. The next day the child was fine and went to school. A year later the mother reported that the child had not been sick in a bus or car since that one treatment.

CASE 2

A different situation confronted a 14-year-old boy who limited himself to eating only five foods (corn on the cob, macaroni and cheese, pizza, spaghetti, and French toast) and, therefore, prepared his own food. He did not eat with his family and did not go out to eat with his friends, two situations that made him unhappy. He stated that he had begun to be fussy about his eating habits in fifth grade. Hypnotic suggestions in the past had had little effect on his behavior, but a recent newspaper article about the therapist had made the patient's mother hopeful.

In this case a dissociative technique was used in which the patient was asked to see a picture of himself with his eating problem off to the left, but to view it from a position outside his body from over on the right. Then he was asked to view the situation and was told that he could learn everything he needed to know about the situation to help him change. He was told he could do this in silence and did not have to tell the author anything about his problem if he did not want to. After a few minutes in silence, he indicated that he was finished. He was then asked to merge the two parts of himself so that he could feel totally unified and be able to make the changes he desired. This technique was utilized because of the reluctance on the part of the patient to discuss the problem in any detail. At the end of the session the patient stated that he would try a different food each day. He returned the next week stating that he had tried five new foods but that he preferred self-hypnosis over hypnosis with the therapist. The therapist's parting words were, "A new food a day keeps the doctor away." A follow-up years later revealed that the boy continued to eat more foods for a while but stopped doing self-hypnosis and returned to his former eating patterns. One interpretation might be that the underlying conflict was too difficult for the patient to deal with, and that he felt more comfortable in his old habits. His desire to have no more therapy or hypnotic suggestion supported this reversal.

Habit Disorders

Nail biting, thumb sucking, enuresis, tics, stuttering, encopresis, and overeating are just some of the many habits that can be effectively treated with hypnosis by either hypnobehavioral models or, if necessary, by uncovering the underlying dynamics through hypnoanalysis. Many of these habits represent a form of self-induced trance which is the child's way of relieving anxiety. Therefore, it is helpful to encourage the child to use self-hypnosis instead of the habit to relieve the anxiety. Eventually, this will aid in the disappearance of the unwanted habit.

CASE 1

An example of nail biting involves the case of a nine-year-old boy who always bit his nails, although he wanted them to grow like his dad's and then have his father cut them. He stated that he bit them when he was nervous or excited, especially when watching movies or TV. He also seemed very connected to his father, who prided himself on his hygiene, stressed his own beautiful nails, and liked to manicure his son's nails. When asked whether he would like to have long white, juicy, nails to be cut by a nail clipper, the patient responded affirmatively. He was then asked whether he felt he was old enough to cut his own nails. He replied in the affirmative and then mentioned that his grandmother had given him his own nail clipper that he had never used. He seemed happy to feel separate from his father on this issue and seemed excited at the prospect of cutting his own nails. His hero was Lionel of the Supercats, who had a magic sword that was used for good.

The boy was hypnotized and imagined himself watching the Supercats on TV. He was asked to go inside the TV and be with them. He was then given his own magic sword, which he used to make his hand numb. He could use this magic sword to help his nails grow long and juicy so that they could be cut by his nail clipper. He was then asked to imagine himself watching TV or being in a movie theater without biting his nails. Then he saw himself cutting his own long nails and it was stressed how happy and proud of himself he was. The next week he was extremely happy, had enjoyed doing self-hypnosis, and had not bitten his nails all week. He proudly presented his nails with white showing on the end of each one.

Thumb sucking can be treated with the use of wires and switches (to prevent the thumb from going in the mouth) and the added suggestion that if the thumb is sucked the other fingers will feel left out. Therefore, they must also be sucked an equal amount of time. If the sucking continues, it is usually more difficult and less pleasurable to suck them all; the suggestion can then be given that it is probably easier to suck none of them than all of them, but the choice is to be left to the child.

An end to bedwetting can also be initiated with the use of wires and switches. The child is instructed in the use of self-hypnosis so that he can turn the switch every night before going to bed. He is also told that if he has to urinate, his bladder (after the explanation of what a bladder is has been given) will wake him up. He will go to the bathroom while being wide awake and then he will return to his bed and fall asleep easily and happily, knowing that he will wake up with a dry bed and dry pajamas (the words used should be ones that the child clearly understands). The parents are told not to use the word "wet" anymore, but to praise and encourage the child instead by stressing the dry areas on the bed, especially as they increase. Again, if the parents seem too removed from the problem, they are encouraged to help him begin his self-hypnosis; if they are too involved, they are told to leave the child alone to practice on his own. The latter parents are told that it is the child's problem and he has to learn how to handle some things on his own to gain more self-respect. To encourage the child and to increase his motivation for success, it is helpful to have him imagine doing things that he is prevented from doing because of his bedwetting problem, things such as sleeping overnight at a friend's house or going away on a camping trip.

Encopresis can be a difficult problem to treat, but the use of hypnotic suggestion to practice squeezing the muscles for stopping and starting defecation with the use of the hypnotic hero has been successful in the past (Tilton, 1980). Gardner and Olness (1981) give an excellent review on this subject.

Sleep Disorders

Difficulties in falling asleep can usually be dealt with by teaching the child one of two procedures: (1) to do self-hypnosis before going to sleep with the suggestion that he will fall asleep while doing the hypnosis; or (2) imagine walking down 20 steps and being asleep before reaching bottom. If simple techniques do not work, then the use of uncovering techniques is warranted.

Nightmares can be treated by the use of hypnotic storytelling. Either therapist or patient can tell a story and have the child learn to give it a happy ending. Then the suggestion is made that the child can change the ending of any nightmare just like he did during the hypnosis. The child is also taught to suggest pleasant or fun dreams just before bedtime during self-hypnosis. Night terrors are best dealt with by attempting to uncover any precipitating events through the use of hypnosis because often these events may not be remembered or easily talked about by the child.

Medicine and Surgery

The list of hypnotically treatable conditions is endless, but it can be broken down into the following areas: chronic diseases, psychsomatic and psychophysiologic disorders (including somatization disorders such as hysterical conversion), pre-and postsurgical situations, emergency situations, and pain control.

It is imperative before deciding to do hypnosis with a child with a medical problem that a thorough physical examination and diagnosis be obtained and that proper medical treatment and medication be given. Hypnosis, while it is not a substitute for sound medical care, can reduce the need for medication in some disorders or obviate the need in others. However, it can also mask physical signs and symptoms, which if not attended to, can lead to serious and severe repercussions (e.g., using hypnoanesthesia to block the pain of appendicitis, thinking it to be a psychosomatic stomachache).

While many pediatricians seem reluctant or ignorant of the value of hypnosis in this area, it is important to know its uses and limitations; these are often dependent upon the therapist's skill, the child's ability to utilize self-hypnosis, and the rapport and encouragement received from both parents and physician (or hypnotherapist, if different from the physician).

It is not necessary to differentiate between psychosomatic and supposedly purely medical or organic disorders here. No one is quite sure of the exact mechanisms through which effective hypnosis works. This area demonstrates the psychophysiologic nature of most diseases; in other words, there seems to be a psychological component in all disease processes. The fact that hypnotic suggestion works so well clearly demonstrates how the mind is able to effect a positive and curative response. How much of this could be placebo (an extremely powerful healing mechanism), relief of anxiety (which may upset the homeostatic mechanisms in the body), or the effects on the autonomic and voluntary nervous systems or the immune system remains to be elucidated. But as this research continues it becomes important to eliminate the mind-body duality concept and to think of the mind and the body in a more holistic way—to be treated caringly and effectively as one unit, no longer separating the two.

In dealing with medical problems, it is important for the therapist to have good working knowledge about anatomy, physiology, and disease processes. Great harm might be done by not recognizing the severity of symptoms or the effects of the disease. Mistakes with grave consequences can be made because of ignorance on the part of the therapist; while this does not mean that the therapist need be as well informed as a physician, it does mean that he should have adequate knowledge before working in this field.

It is not possible to cover all the areas of medicine in a short chapter, nor is it possible to give examples of the wordings of the suggestions used in all cases. The following examples are the most frequently encountered cases, and the reader will have to extrapolate to situations not covered.

Asthma

Asthma is a disorder that can present many problems for both the child and parents. Depending on the severity of the symptoms and its effect on the child's overall health, it can cause dependency, difficulty in socialization, and poor self-esteem. It is imperative that the child be examined and take the proper medication. During the preinduction talk, and depending upon the child's age, the therapist has a choice of images. The image of a honeycomb full of honey can be likened to the lungs when they are full of mucous making it difficult to breathe. Other times it is extremely helpful to draw a child with lungs deflated, with a narrow trachea, and then inflated, with a wide-open trachea, explaining which is asthmatic breathing and which is normal (open tubes or pipes can also be utilized if the anatomical concepts are difficult for the child to understand). It is then explained that there are circular muscles that control the opening (diameter) of the trachea to the lungs.

In hypnosis, to start, hand anesthesia can be demonstrated with the suggestion that if wires and switches can cause numbness in the hand, they can also work to make breathing easier by opening up the trachea. The child is then asked to imagine turning the switch to open the trachea (or alternatively, to allow the honey or mucous to empty out from the honeycomb or lungs). At this point the child's wheezing usually reduces and the breathing becomes more normal. The child should be praised for this. Linking this relaxed state of breathing to an enjoyable and happy real-life situation enhances the effect. With this success, the child can next imagine himself breathing easily in previous situations when he has wheezed. Then he can imagine himself breathing easily in similar situations in the future. He is then told that he can gain control over his breathing by learning how to do this by himself. He is instructed in self-hypnosis and sent home to practice several times a day.

Following successful practice, any decision to reduce medication should be made in consultation with the child's physician. Any increase in the child's activities, if they have been restricted, should be slow, after careful explanation to the parents about the child's ability to function normally within the limitations of his symptoms. The parents often need careful explanation of the disease and support for allowing the child more autonomy after he has demonstrated success. For children with exercise-induced asthma, the technique should be practiced just before exercising.

Dermatological Problems

Dermatological problems frequently respond to hypnotic suggestions and imagery. Since most skin problems involve itching, burning, and uncomfortable sensations, it is important to utilize the words "cool" and "comfortable." Adding images and suggestions that bring this feeling to mind, such as a cool breeze, playing outdoors in the snow, swimming in nice cool and comfortable water, and so on, can increase the effect. For conditions that are affected or brought about by anxiety, doing self-hypnosis may cause the relaxation and relief of anxiety necessary to break the cycle and create a healing milieu.

For acne, suggestions such as using wires and switches to heal the face and imagining the face clear, along with the feelings of coolness and comfort, are helpful. Imagining using medication and feeling or seeing it work more efficiently will increase the enthusiasm as well as the proper use of medication.

For neurodermatitis (eczema) or rashes, adding the image of the rash disappearing by itself or by use of the switch along with feelings of coolness and comfort can decrease healing time and help the rash to fade.

CASE 1

An 8-year-old girl was seen twice because of chronic dermatitis behind her ears which caused embarrassment, preventing her from putting her hair in a ponytail. In hypnosis she was told that the rash probably would not disappear right away, but that it would disappear soon. She was then asked to imagine the rash fading away and had Tom and Jerry (her favorite cartoon characters) help her. She was also told to use her medicine (steroid cream) as she was instructed by her doctor (which she had not been doing). She was seen intermittently during the next year in the therapist's waiting room whenever she accompanied her mother (who was in treatment with the therapist). The rash receded remarkably—which enabled her to put her hair in a ponytail.

Hyperhidrosis, or excess sweating, is usually caused by anxiety or fear. If the cause is known, hypnotic imagery of successful outcomes may eliminate the feared situations, creating a sense of mastery for the child resulting in decreased symptoms. Hypnoanalysis may be used if the cause is not known; at times simply using self-hypnotic imagery and relaxation can succeed.

CASE 2

A case example involves a teenage girl of 15 who complained of excess sweating of her palms (described by her as cold and clammy) and underarms. She was shy and complained of lack of confidence when talking to her peers or adults. It was precisely in these situations that the symptoms occurred, embarrassing her even further. She was desensitized by imagining herself talking successfully with a few friends. This was extended to a group of friends and then finally to a crowd of people. The same thing was repeated with adults. She was also instructed in the use of wires and switches and taught self-hypnosis. During the therapy her strengths were stressed and she was told that "no one can get under your skin." She rated her problem as a 10 when she first came in, a 6 at the second session, a 4 the next week, and a 2 at the end of seven weeks, when she concluded therapy. A follow-up phone call four years later revealed that she was fine and no longer had the problem. She feels that she was greatly helped by the sessions and by her use of self-hypnosis.

Warts also respond well to hypnotic suggestion. The imagery utilized can be of seeing the warts grow smaller and smaller until they disappear. The suggestion can be given to imagine cutting off the food and blood supply by constricting or narrowing the blood vessel that feeds the wart by turning the proper switch; this would leave it feeling cold and tingling.

CASE 3

One 11-year-old girl who was seen by the author for dental phobia had a forehead covered by a multitude of flat warts. At the end of the session the author remarked casually that self-hypnosis could also be used to eliminate the warts by simply imagining them disappearing. At a second visit the image of disappearing warts was suggested during the hypnosis, and several weeks later the author was informed by the patient's mother that while the patient still feared going to the dentist, she no longer had any warts on her face, which pleased her even more.

Gastrointestinal Problems

Gastrointestinal problems are quite common in childhood and often have no organic findings. Many times they are thought to be of emotional cause. Stomachaches, nausea and vomiting, excess gas and flatulence, and diarrhea fall into this category, along with irritable bowel syndrome (which may occur in older teenagers). Much of this can be alleviated by hypnosis even if the cause or secondary gain is not always clearly uncovered or resolved. Ulcers can also be treated with hypnotic imagery and relaxation, with the addition of resolution of any area of conflict. Prevention of future ulcers may require long-term therapy. Acute episodes of ulcerative colitis may be treated in the same manner, but again, long-term therapy may be required for a resolution of the disease process.

CASE 1

An eight-year-old boy was seen by the therapist for headaches and abdominal pain, fatigue, difficulty sleeping, and poor attention at school, No organic basis was found for his problems, and his mother believed it was all emotional. He was taught self-hypnosis and techniques to control his symptoms, which he successfully did during the first session. He returned the second week with the same symptoms and said he had not done any self-hypnosis but did not know why. The process was repeated, and again he ended the trance feeling better. The therapist stated that if he wanted to keep his symptoms, he should not do any self-hypnosis. He returned the next week without symptoms. In a follow-up phone call several years later, the mother stated that he still got an occasional headache or stomachache that he relieved by going off by himself (and perhaps doing self-hypnosis). She stated that the important thing he had gained from the hypnotic sessions was that he no longer felt out of control.

Neurological Problems

Neurological problems such as headaches, seizure disorders, pseudoseizures, tics, and speech disorders respond well to the relaxation and anxiety-reduction of self-hypnosis, especially if practiced regularly. In the case of seizures or migraine headaches, if the patient can learn to identify the prodromal phase, self-hypnosis can be instituted immediately to abort or reduce the severity of the attack. Here, the use of successful imagery can increase the child's self-esteem and reduce the shame or embarrassment of having a neurological disorder. The relief of pain will be discussed under the heading "Pain Control."

Speech and learning disorders can be helped through relaxation by self-hypnosis along with suggestions for increasing motivation and increasing the abilities of the mind to function in a better way. Suggestions to forget about past failures, praise for having the courage to strive for success and the ability to face problems, and use of positive and successful imagery help to achieve good results.

CASE 1

An 11-year-old girl was brought in because of making a strange noise in her throat that her mother thought might be Tourette's syndrome. She also had occasional stomachaches, nocturnal teeth grinding (bruxism), and difficulty concentrating at school, with resultant poor grades. Her explanation that she made noises in her throat because it felt like there was something in it, and the fact that this occurred when she was nervous was consistent with a nervous tic or habit disorder. During the next three sessions she was taught how to use the switches to stop grinding her teeth at night as well as to reduce her noise-making. All went well until six months later when, under the stress of taking gymnastics and the anxiety of her horse giving birth, the noisemaking returned. She was reinstructed in the switches, and while she was hypnotized, given the analogy of her problems to Rubick's cube (which she enjoyed playing). She was shown many possible ways to work her problems out. A year and a half later she was no longer making noises, but was still having emotional problems and difficulties at school.

Pain Control

Pain control, or hypnoanalgesia and hypnoanesthesia, play an important part in treating children in the hospital, in the office, and in the emergency room. Gardner and Olness (1981) give an extensive review of considerations, rationale, and use of hypnosis in this area, Therefore, only a few useful techniques and their rationale will be recounted here.

Acute pain in an emergency situation generally lends itself to rapid and successful treatment. The switch can be used to turn off pain or make the area numb. Direct suggestion can also be utilized to make the area numb. Imagining the application of a topical anesthetic or a protective barrier often can suffice. Dissociative techniques, for instance, suggesting that the pain is leaving, reducing, or moving to another area, or that the painful area feels like it is not attached to the body, can be useful. Alternatively, telling stories, distracting the child, the use of laughter, imagining being somewhere else with a favorite person or hero can also be effective. These techniques can be used for chronic pain as well.

Chronic or intermittent pain such as arthritis or headaches should be approached differently. The distinction between organic and psychogenic origins must be made to ensure proper treatment. Besides using the wire-and-switch technique, the child can be told to imagine that there is a control dial inside his head with 10 numbers (10 being the most pain and 0 being no pain at all). The dial points to the amount of pain he is having. The child is then told that he can turn that dial toward zero to reduce the discomfort (the word "discomfort" is always used euphemistically to lessen the pain's intensity and to get the child to think about pain in different terms). He is told that he can imagine anything or anyone to help him turn the dial. He is also told that he can get close to zero but not all the way to it. This is done to ensure that organic pain is not masked. Some pain may be necessary so that an important physical finding is not missed or so that an injured body part is not used as if it were not injured. It is also important to leave a little discomfort in those situations wherein secondary gain or psychogenic pain exists. This leaves the child in much less discomfort but with his dignity intact until the underlying cause can be dealt with.

Surgery

Surgery can be a very frightening experience for a child. Hypnosis can help allay a lot of the accompanying fears. Posthypnotic suggestions can also be used to help a child recover faster and have more rapid wound healing, less pain, a quicker return of bowel and bladder function, less nausea, and better appetite. Much emotional and physical trauma can be avoided by having the child imagine a successful operation, rehearse it on his own, and give himself similar suggestions for postoperative success. It is also important to tell the child that before the operation he will be given medication to make him take a nap (saying "nap" is preferable to saying "sleep"). This also serves to reduce any preoperative anxiety.

Similarly, this can be done with a child before going to the dentist, with the additional use of hypnoanesthesia as an adjunct or in place of chemical anesthesia.

Conversion

Conversion or medical symptoms entirely of psychogenic origin, must be dealt with by respecting the patient's need to have the symptoms. It is important to get an understanding of the psychogenic and underlying causes, if possible. It is also best to avoid using direct suggestions for the symptoms to disappear. There is often a combination of physical (or organic) problems and psychogenic ones, making both the diagnosis and the treatment difficult. The two cases presented will exemplify the difficulties in treating this type of patient.

CASE 1

An eight-year-old girl was brought to the therapist because of a possible neurological problem. The child suffered from confusion and memory lapses, exemplified by finding herself in a closet without knowing how she got there. An EEG was consistent with a seizure disorder with generalized cerebral dysfunction. Based on this, plus the history of headaches and recent behavioral changes, the child was placed on medication by the consulting neurologist. After several visits and one hospitalization, her medication was adjusted and the seizures controlled. Five months later she developed daytime and nocturnal enuresis and was seen by a urologist. Her abnormal cystometrogram was consistent with a hyper-reflexive, uninhibited, neurogenic bladder. Medication controlled the daytime enuresis: The therapist was again consulted by the mother, this time for hypnosis to control the nocturnal enuresis.

For the six weeks following that consultation, and without informing the therapist, neurologist, or urologist, the mother had her daughter practice self-hypnosis to control all her problems. The child stopped all medication and was asymptomatic until her father ended his recent visit. Hypnosis was again utilized to help eliminate the enuretic symptoms, and the mother was encouraged to give the child her antiseizure medication. At this time another cystometrogram was performed, again showing a hyperreflexive, uninhibited, neurogenic bladder, but when the test was repeated under hypnosis it was normal. While this surprised the urologist, the therapist was familiar with a report by Godec (1980) of successful treatment of an adult with this same disorder by hypnosis.

Five months later the child was brought in because of three recent bedwetting episodes but had, otherwise remained asymptomatic without the aid of any medication. There were difficulties in this case because the mother was inconsistent in bringing the child to her appointments and was a poor historian. The mother had been abused and molested as a child, and there was evidence that the child herself had been beaten and neglected at different times. She was lost to follow-up soon after. As the reader can see, it is difficult to determine the boundaries of organic causes from psychogenic causes in this case, making diagnosis and treatment difficult and confusing.

CASE 2

A 17-year-old female was referred by her urologist because of the persistence of flank pain. She had been hospitalized and treated for a urinary tract infection that was no longer evident. No organic cause could be found for her pain despite a rather extensive workup. The patient revealed that the pain had begun several weeks after she had left her father's house to live with her mother. Hypnotic suggestion for pain control during the first session was effective, but self-hypnosis proved unsuccessful.

Over the next few sessions, there was gradual improvement as she talked about problems in trying to please her father and feelings that he did not love her. However, she denied any connection between her emotional pain, which was present throughout her treatment, and her physical pain. In hypnosis she was asked to go back to the time when her pain began. She regressed to Christmas (just after her parents' separation) and revealed that the pain had begun the next day. The patient had complete and spontaneous amnesia of the entire trance experience upon awakening. Following this session she was able to do self-hypnosis and reduce the pain by utilizing some healing images. In hypnosis at the next session, she said that she would be better by Easter (two weeks away). She was. Interestingly, she imagined her painful kidney as a large black spot that she was able to reduce. At the last session it was removed and changed into a bug. When asked about the image, she responded by saying that occasionally things bug her—like her father.

Three years later the patient underwent an abortion and a dilation and curettage. The pain persisted and was not relieved by the use of antibiotics for any possible infection. Since no organic basis could be found for her pain, the patient was put on tranquilizers as a last resort. After having the pain for nine more days, she called the therapist. When she came in she complained of severe pain and threatened that at any moment the pain could get so bad that she might have to lie on the floor. She was told that this would be okay. After giving a history of her treatments she developed acute pain and curled up into a fetal position on the floor. She was hypnotized and was able to reduce the pain by hypnoanesthesia. When she was asked to imagine looking inside her body, she said she wanted her baby and began crying. Her loss was discussed for a while, and she was helped to realize that her decision had been the best one. When she imagined her body all torn up inside, she was asked to sew it up and help it heal. She was told to continue both the grieving process and the sewing and healing process at home with self-hypnosis. She then remarked that she would be all better by Mother's Day, just three days away. She was given an appointment for the day after Mother's Day, but told to cancel it on Monday morning if she was all better. She cancelled. Here again was an interesting mixture of an organic beginning with a conversion overlay.

In these two cases hypnosis rather than psychotherapy was requested to help remove unwanted physical symptoms. One could speculate about the psychodynamics and underlying causes, which could be treated in many other ways, but the important aspect is how the use of hypnosis can be utilized with some brief and indirect approaches.

CONCLUSION

There are many ways to hypnotize a child and there are many reasons to do so. It is important to take into account the variability of each child in planning the best ways of working hypnotically. Proper training, experience, and creativity can help make hypnosis a useful and valuable technique for any professional who works with children.

REFERENCES

Araoz, D. (1985). *The new hypnosis.* New York: Brunner/Mazel.

Barber, T.X. (1979). Suggested ("hypnotic") behavior: The trance paradigm versus an alternative paradigm. In E. Fromm & R.E. Shor (Eds.), *Hypnosis: Developments in research and new perspectives* (2nd ed., pp. 217–271). New York: Aldine.

Beahrs, J.O. (1971). The hypnotic psychotherapy of Milton H. Erickson. *American Journal of Clinical Hypnosis, 14,* 73–90.

Diamond, M.J. (1984). It takes two to tango: Some thoughts on the neglected importance of the hypnotist in an interactive hypnotherapeutic relationship. *American Journal of Clinical Hypnosis, 27,* 3–13.

Fromm, E. (1979). The nature of hypnosis and other altered states of consciousness: An ego psycholocical theory. In E. Fromm & R.E. Shor (Eds.), *Hypnosis: developments in research and new perspectives* (2nd ed., pp. 81–103). New York: Aldine.

Gardner, G.G., & Olness, K. (1981). *Hypnosis and hypnotherapy with children.* New York: Grune & Stratton.

Godec, C.J. (1980). Inihibition of hyperreflexic bladder during hypnosis: A case report. *American Journal of Clinical Hypnosis, 22,* 170–172.

Haley, J. (Ed.). (1967). *Advanced techniques of hypnosis and therapy: Selected papers of Milton H. Erickson, M.D.* New York: Grune & Stratton.

Hartland, J. (1971). *Medical and dental hypnosis and its clinical application* (2nd ed.). London: Bailliere Tindal.

Hilgard, E. (1979). Divided consciousness in hypnosis: The implications of the hidden observer. In E. Fromm & R.E. Shor (Eds.), *Hypnosis: Developments in research and new perspectives* (2nd ed., pp. 45–79). New York: Aldine.

Kroger, W. (1977). *Clinical and experimental hypnosis.* Philadelphia: Lippincott.

Lazar B., & Dempster, C.R. (1984). Operator variables in successful hypnotherapy. *International Journal of Clinical and Experimental Hypnosis, 32,* 28–40.

Olness, K. (1975). The use of self-hypnosis in the treatment of childhood nocturnal enuresis. *Clinical Pediatrics, 14,* 273–279.

Orne, M.T. (1959). The nature of hypnosis: Artifact and essence. *Journal of Abnormal and Social psychology 58,* 277–299.

Shor, R.E. (1979). A phenomenological method for the measurement of variables important to an understanding of the nature of hypnosis. In E. Fromm & R.E. Shor (Eds.), *Hypnosis: Developments in research and new perspectives* (2nd ed., pp. 105–135). New York: Aldine.

Tilton, P. (1980). Hypnotic treatment of a child with thumbsucking, enuresis and encopresis. *American Journal of Clinical Hypnosis, 22,* 238–240.

Tilton, P. (1984). The hypnotic hero: a technique for hypnosis with children. *International Journal of Clinical and Experimental Hypnosis, 32,* 366–375.

Tilton P. (1986). Effective use of Erickson's interspersal technique. In B. Zilbergeld, G.M. Edelstein, & D.L. Araoz (Eds.), *Hypnosis: Questions and answers* (pp. 225–260). New York: Norton.

Watkins, J.G. (1971). The affect bridge: A hypnoanalytic technique. *International Journal of Clinical and Experimental Hypnosis, 19,* 21–27.

CHAPTER 6

Relaxation Training for Childhood Disorders

MARIAN C. FISH

Relaxation training is a behavioral treatment approach that seeks to develop a person's ability to consciously relax the muscles of the body at will (Walker, 1979). The purpose of this training is to identify and then lessen tension during normal daily activities, and prior to or during stressful environmental situations (Borkovec & Sides, 1979). Reduced muscle tension is most often accomplished by using progressive muscle relaxation procedures, but may also be achieved through a number of other techniques and procedures, such as meditation, imagery, biofeedback, and autogenic training, all of which are described below.

Treatments designed to enhance voluntary control and lower the level of muscle tension have been in existence for centuries. Benson, Beary, and Carol (1974) describe practices from many of the world's religions which seem to lead to a relaxed condition. The similarities between relaxation training and such practices as yoga, Zen, and transcendental meditation are also noted by Walker (1979).

It was Jacobson's pioneering work on the role of rest and relaxation in the treatment of stress-related disorders in the 1920s and 1930s, however, that provided the first scientific study of the effects of relaxation training (Tarler-Benlolo, 1978). Jacobson (1938), using progressive muscle relaxation, showed that a reduction of muscle tension resulted in reduced autonomic nervous system activity, such as decreased pulse rate and blood pressure. Benson, Beary, and Carol (1974) used the term "relaxation response" and described its physiology as "an integrated hypothalamic response which results in generalized decreased sympathetic nervous system activity, and perhaps also increased parasympathetic activity" (p. 37). The major physiological characteristics of this relaxation response are decreases in oxygen consumption, respiratory rate, heart rate, carbon dioxide elimination, blood pressure, and muscle tension, as well as pupil constriction. These changes are opposite to those during the fight-or-flight response that occurs when we are faced with a threat from the environment and brace ourselves for action. Wolpe (1958), noting that the physiological correlates of relaxation are incompatible with those of anxiety, and, in fact, diminish anxiety responses, incorporated this information into his procedures for the systematic desensitization of fears and phobias.

Relaxation training as a treatment strategy alone or as a component in systematic desensitization procedures has been widely used with adults (e.g., Beiman, Graham, & Ciminero, 1978; Goldfried & Trier, 1974); studies employing this procedure in the treatment of anxiety and stress disorders have generally resulted in positive effects (Hillenberg & Collins, 1982). These successes have led clinicians to broaden their application of relaxation to such an extent that the approach has been labeled the "behavioral aspirin" of behavior therapy (Russo, Bird, & Masek, 1980).

RELAXATION WITH CHILDREN

A natural extension of adult relaxation training has been relaxation training with children. In the past 15 years there has been considerable growth in the research literature as well as increased use of relaxation training with children as a therapeutic intervention in both clinical and school settings. For example, relaxation training has been used to improve classroom attention span (Lupin, Braud, Braud, & Duer, 1976; Omizo & Williams, 1982; Redfering & Bowman, 1981), handwriting (Jackson & Hughes, 1978), academic achievement (Carter & Russell, 1985), and self-concept (Omizo, 1980a, 1980b). It has been used with youngsters who are hyperactive (Braud, 1978; Dunn & Howell, 1982; Klein & Deffenbacher, 1977), learning disabled (Carter & Russell, 1985), autistic (Marholin, Steinman, Luiselli, Schwartz & Townsend, 1979), and gifted (Roome & Romney, 1985). It has also been used in dental settings (Winer, 1982), for insomnia (Anderson, 1979), and for managing anxiety (Piggott, 1985; Rubenzer, 1984).

The burgeoning use of relaxation training with children has resulted from the recent emphasis on both research and practice of the self-regulation of behavior. Traditionally, behavioral interventions have relied on external agents, for example, teachers, therapists, and parents, and/or drug treatment to effect change (Zipkin, 1985). Currently there is considerable interest in teaching children methods to alter their own behavior (Karoly & Kanfer, 1982). A number of researchers have reviewed the use of self-control procedures with children (e.g., O'Leary & Dubey, 1979; Rosenbaum & Drabman, 1979). They suggest that children's self-management fosters independent growth and development in academic and social skills. When relaxation is taught as a self-control procedure, it can be applied voluntarily whenever a situation is creating problems for the child. Matthews (1983) sees relaxation as a stopping technique. It allows children to take a deep breath and to relax instead of plunging into a difficult situation. It is hoped that relaxation will generalize to new situations and will result in stronger maintenance effects than when under external controls (O'Leary & Dubey, 1979). The child can continue to use relaxation after training or therapy is completed. In addition,

Severson (1976) suggested that voluntary self-regulation through relaxation and/or biofeedback training could serve a preventative mental health function and enhance human potential.

RELAXATION TRAINING PROCEDURES

In their review of relaxation methodologies, Hillenberg and Collins (1982) discuss the variety of treatment modalities that have been labeled relaxation training. They identified 26 distinct referenced relaxation approaches that have been reported in the adult literature. In the current review of the children's relaxation literature, there are five discrete procedures that are reported and used either alone or, more often, in combination to promote relaxation: progressive muscle relaxation, autogenic training, biofeedback, meditation, and mental imagery. Although not generally considered a distinct procedure, deep, slow breathing is a technique that is often incorporated with these other relaxation approaches. In addition, relaxation is a component of systematic desensitization. Preparation for relaxation training is generally similar for all these procedures.

Preparation for Relaxation

The recommended setting for relaxation training is a quiet, softly lit room which minimizes outside noises (Morris & Kratochwill, 1983). The child should be quite comfortable; Morris and Kratochwill (Ibid.) suggest seating the child in a reclining chair or couch, while Cautela and Groden (1978), when working with young and with special needs children, use a low chair so the child can sit with feet touching the floor. What is most important is that there is minimal muscular tension in the child's position. Clothes should be loose, and shoes can be removed. An age-appropriate explanation about relaxation is presented to the child emphasizing that people learn to be tense and they can also learn to relax. As with any new skill, the child is told that it will be necessary to practice relaxation. Some children do not know what relaxation means or when it would be appropriate to use it (Wielkiewicz, 1986). A simple rationale for its use might include its helpfulness in reducing tension and anxiety and a discussion about when these feelings arise. It is important to stress that control of relaxation remains with the child. It is generally recommended that the therapist have experience with relaxation prior to using it with a child. Also, when using relaxation training with a group, it is important to make sure that all the children in the group have enough space.

When working with younger or with special needs children, Cautela and Groden (1978) use a readiness pretest to ensure that the basic skills necessary for relaxation are acquired before the relaxation procedures are taught. These skills include sitting still for five seconds, maintaining eye contact for three seconds, imitating an adult's movements, and following instructions (see Figure 6.1).

Progressive Muscle Relaxation

In progressive muscle relaxation the child systematically tenses and releases muscle groups throughout the body; this leads to greater awareness of tension and relaxation (Borkovec & Sides, 1979). This procedure was developed by Jacobson (1938), whose original technique involved having the person lie in a supine position, alternately tensing and relaxing major muscle groups, then slowly eliminating the tensing until the person practiced only the passive relaxation (Tarler-Benlolo, 1978). Modified versions of Jacobson's techniques are now used by most clinicians. An example of instructions to the child derived from several sources (Cautela & Groden, 1978; Lupin, 1977; Morris & Kratochwill, 1983) follows:

> Make a fist with your right hand and tighten your whole arm. Hold it tight. Notice how it feels to have tension; it's stiff, hard (have the child feel tight parts with the other hand). Now, let's relax, let all the tension (stiffness) go. Focus on the muscles as they relax completely. Notice what it feels like as your muscle becomes more and more relaxed. Enjoy the feeling. Notice how good it feels.

This instruction is repeated for the left fist, both arms, both feet, both legs, and stomach muscles. Then, the shoulders can be tensed by shrugging, the mouth by opening wide or pulling back the corners, the tongue by pressing hard on the roof of the mouth, and the eyes and forehead by clenching the muscles in the upper face. Cautela and Groden (1978) recommend initially tensing for 2 seconds and relaxing for 10 seconds. After the child has alternately tensed and relaxed, each muscle group is relaxed without tensing. Morris and Kratochwill (1983) estimate about 20 to 25 minutes for the entire procedure, but, of course, this will vary with the age, receptivity, and ability of the child. Some children will need considerable guidance and prompting. Cautela and Groden (1978) provide some novel ideas for special needs children; for example, they suggest using bulb-type toys which emit sounds as they are squeezed for those children who have trouble tensing hand and/or arms. It is usually helpful, at least in the beginning, for the clinician to demonstrate the correct procedures by practicing along with the child.

Autogenic Training

Autogenic training is a system of self-regulation which was developed by Schultz and Luthe (cited in Tarler-Benlolo, 1978, p. 730). It consists of a series of exercises that promote "heaviness and warmth in the extremities, regulation of cardiac activity and respiration, abdominal warmth and cooling of the fore-

Pretest—Readiness Procedures

The following pretest should be administered to the child. Give three trials for each response.

Name of Child: _____   CODE: ✔ = Correct

Date: _____   X = Incorrect

Teacher/Parent: _____   NR = No Response

	Trial 1	Trial 2	Trial 3
A. BASIC SKILLS 1. Ask the child to sit quietly in a chair for 5 seconds, feet still, back straight, head up, without moving or vocalizing. Repeat 2 more times.			
2. Say "Look at me," and ask the child to maintain eye contact for 3 seconds. Child must respond within 5 seconds. Repeat 2 more times.			
B. IMITATIVE SKILLS 3. Say "Do this," and raise your hand above your head. Child should imitate this response correctly within 5 seconds. Repeat 2 more times.			
4. Say "Do this," and you tap the table. Child should be able to imitate this response correctly by tapping the table. Repeat 2 more times.			
5. Say "Do this," and you tap your chest. Child should be able to imitate correctly by tapping his chest. Repeat 2 more times.			
C. FOLLOWING SIMPLE INSTRUCTIONS 6. Say "Stand up." Child should stand up in front of his chair within 5 seconds. Repeat this instruction 2 more times.			
7. Say "Sit down." Child should sit down in his chair within 5 seconds. Repeat this instruction 2 more times.			
8. Stand 6 feet from the child and say "Come here." Child should stand up and walk toward you without inappropriate movements or vocalizations. Repeat 2 more times.			

Figure 6.1. Procedures to determine relaxation readiness.
Reprinted with permission from Cautela, J.R., & Groden, J. (1978). *Relaxation: A Comprehensive Manual for Adults, Children, and Children with Special Needs.* Champaign, IL: Research Press.

head" (Schultz & Luthe, 1969, p. 6). This type of training is typified by the following phrases:

I feel quite quiet.
I am beginning to feel quite relaxed.
My feet feel heavy and relaxed.
My ankles, my knees and my hips feel heavy, relaxed and comfortable.
I am quite relaxed.
My arms and hands are heavy and warm.
I feel serene and still.

Unlike progressive muscle relaxation where the child is initially expected to be an active participant in the training, autogenic training requires only passive concentration and is more covert.

Biofeedback

Biofeedback is a procedure in which the child is provided with immediate and continuous feedback of physiological activity (Linkenhoker, 1983). The feedback signal may be delivered through any of the senses, for example, audio stimuli or visual stimuli (such as a graph, meter, or blinking lights). Graphics and animation can now be added to biofeedback through computer hookups. The rate of delivery and intensity can be determined by the clinician (Tarler-Benlolo, 1978). Early work in this area was done by Budzynski and Stoyva (1969) who developed the first instrumentation in the field. The sensitive electronic equipment continuously monitors the physiological response (e.g., muscle tension, blood pressure, galvanic skin response, temperature) and helps the child to self-regulate or to consciously control physiologic functioning.

There are two types of biofeedback which are most often used with children. First, for electromyographic (EMG) biofeedback, electrodes are placed on the frontalis muscle (on the forehead) to detect and amplify the muscle activity. Changes in tension of facial musculature can then be controlled. Electromyographic biofeedback can also be used at other muscle sites. Second, temperature feedback is frequently used with children. Skin temperature is measured on the fingers (or wrist) and information is usually fed back through a visual signal such as a meter. Recent technological advances have resulted in compact easy-to-use biofeedback equipment. Still, the clinician using biofeedback will need more training and equipment than the clinician using other relaxation procedures. Also, the child will need additional explanation about the equipment.

Meditation

Meditation is a procedure where the child focuses attention, thoughts, and feelings on a particular object, thought, or theme (Zipkin, 1985). While there are many forms of meditation, such as yoga and Zen, that have been practiced in the East, transcendental meditation (TM) is the most widely practiced form of meditation in the West (Tarler-Benlolo, 1978). Transcendental meditation with children involves the repetition of a special word, phrase, or sound that has been provided by the clinician. Usually, this procedure is practiced for 15 to 20 minute periods several times a day.

Mental Imagery

Mental imagery involves the use of pleasant scenes of peaceful situations to promote relaxation (Zipkin, 1985). It refers to the child's visualization of soothing, restful images. Guided fantasy trips are one component in the series of relaxation tapes developed by Lupin (1977). In one story, the narrator (clinician) describes a visit to the woods detailing the tall pine trees, the light shining through the branches, the stillness of the forest, and a bird singing. Images of beds of pine needles are described, and their softness and fresh smell are conveyed. Soft music is played in the background. Endemic images for relaxation include the following examples:

> Imagine that you are sitting on a balcony on a sunny winter afternoon and that all the surroundings are covered with snow. In the distance you can see a mountain peak partially covered with snow.

> Imagine that you are sitting under a tree by a lake and that you can see a boy throwing pebbles into the water. Concentrate on the ripples that the pebbles are making. (Saigh & Antoun, 1984, pp. 182–183)

Once trained in imagery, the child must learn to shift from unpleasant images to those that induce relaxation.

Deep Breathing

Deep breathing exercises are often incorporated by clinicians into the relaxation approaches described above. Deep breathing plays an important part in yoga and in other Eastern relaxation systems. Frequently, breathing exercises lead off the progressive muscle relaxation training. For example, Morris and Kratochwill (1983) state their first step in relaxation: "Take a deep breath and hold it (for about 10 seconds). Hold it; Okay, let it out." Omizo, Loffredo, and Hammett (1982) use a variation of these instructions during an initial session for deep breathing:

1. Relax muscles in the diaphragm (demonstrate) and stomach area. Draw air in through the nose, allowing the stomach area to balloon out and fill completely.
2. As you inhale again, direct your attention to the rib cage. Let your ribs expand

sideways. Close your eyes and imagine an accordian expanding. Begin with your lower ribs, but keep the chest and shoulders motionless. Exhale, relax the rib cage, and let the air flow out. Repeat two or three times.

3. Now inhale as you would with a normal breath. The air now fills only the upper chest area. Exhale. (p. 603)

Systematic Desensitization

Systematic desensitization is a procedure that includes relaxation training as an essential component. It involves having the child imagine various aspects of an anxiety producing situation while in a relaxed state. It is based on the notion that pairing fear with an incompatible response will reduce the fear. Wolpe (1958) observed that the physiological characteristics of relaxation and anxiety are antagonistic. He then hypothesized that an anxiety or fear response could be inhibited by a relaxation response. Systematic desensitization is employed similarly in adult and child treatment.

The steps in systematic desensitization involve providing relaxation training for the child first. While this is being mastered, the therapist and child construct a hierarchy of anxiety provoking events or scenes where the top of the hierarchy is the most fearful event or object (to the child). During the actual desensitization procedure, the child is gradually exposed to the anxiety provoking events in the hierarchy. The child is initially asked to relax and then to visualize the scenes in the hierarchy starting with those that are least upsetting. Once a relaxed state has been achieved and no fear is signaled, the child moves on to the next level. As the scenes are visualized, the child uses the relaxation response to counter the anxiety. The hierarchy may be presented through verbal description (imaging) or *in vivo* (i.e., where a series of graded real life situations are used).

Additional Procedural Considerations

While relaxation training is a relatively straightforward and simple procedure, individual client differences must be considered in treatment planning. First, physical health factors and capabilities should be ascertained prior to treatment. Physical handicaps may restrict muscle control as may one or more medications (Cautela & Groden, 1978). If the child is having problems with breathing exercises, Cautela and Groden suggest such toys as whistles, harmonicas, horns, and party blowers to facilitate air flow.

Second, motivation for relaxation will vary among children. In addition to social reinforcers (e.g., smiling, nodding, or patting), concrete reinforcers such as food, tokens, or activities can be used with young and special needs children when encouragement is necessary (Cautela & Groden, 1978). Parental consent should be obtained. With biofeedback, novel methods of alternating the feedback signal can be used to maintain interest and motivation (Linkenhoker, 1983).

Third, the age and cognitive skills of the child are important considerations in treatment (Wielkiewicz, 1986). With younger children who have a shorter attention span, the sessions may be briefer and spread over a longer period of time. The actual pacing of the sessions may be modified and instructions may be simplified. With regard to the ability to visualize images, some research has shown that 7- and 8-year-old children can produce and manipulate images (Wielkiewicz, 1986). Morris and Kratochwill (1983) summarize other evidence that suggests that by age 9, children can form visual images. Obviously, both mental imagery and systematic desensitization procedures will be affected by this skill. It may be necessary to informally substantiate that the child is able to visualize images. One way this can be done is by showing the child a picture that is then removed, and asking the child to describe it and to point out on a blank paper where various items in the picture were placed (Morris & Kratochwill, 1983). Another alternative is to have children draw pictures depicting themselves doing something relaxing or enjoyable (Wielkiewicz, 1986). This can then be incorporated into the relaxation procedure.

Finally, Morris, and Kratochwill (1983) listed a number of behaviors that indicate that a child is not relaxing: giggling or smiling, frequent yawning, rapid movement of the eyelids, rapid and uneven breathing, searching for a comfortable position, and so on. These serve to warn the therapist that procedural modifications or temporary discontinuation of training is warranted.

RESEARCH FINDINGS

In order to make knowledgeable clinical judgments about when to use relaxation training, it is necessary to examine the literature on the effectiveness of relaxation training for different childhood problems. This section reviews 45 studies conducted since 1975, that have contributed to understanding the use of this procedure. The outcomes are summarized in Table 6.1.

Areas of Application

Hyperactivity

Much of the research has focused on the use of relaxation training procedures with hyperactive children. The rationale for using relaxation to treat hyperactive youngsters is based in part on the suggestion that such children manifest abnormalities in physiological arousal (Colassano, 1986). This has led to the exploration of alternate means (e.g., relaxation) for affecting physiological parameters (Walker, 1979). In a seminal case study, Braud, Lupin, and Braud (1975) administered 11 sessions of EMG biofeedback training (frontalis muscle) to a six-and-a-half-year-old hyperactive boy. Results indicated that muscle tension decreased both within and between sessions and at a seven-month follow-up. Improved scores on the Metropolitan Readiness Test and the Stan-

TABLE 6.1. Summary of Relaxation Training Study Outcomes for Childhood Disorders

Study	Subjects (No./Age)	Sessions	Experimental & Control Conditions	Outcomes			
				Physiological	Behavioral	Cognitive	Affective/ Self-Concept
Hyperactivity							
Braud, Lupin, & Braud (1975)	$N = 1$ 6.5 years	11	E: BF C: None	Decreased muscle tension	Improved behavior	Improved 4 ITPA scores and achievement test	NM
Klein & Deffenbacher (1977)	$N = 24$ 3rd grade	5	E: PMR C: Exercise Attention-control No treatment Nonhyperactive	NM	NM	Increased MFFT accuracy for PMR, exercise, nonhyperactive, no differences on CPT	NM
Putre, Loffio, Chorost, & Gilbert (1977)	$N = 20$ 7–13 yrs	10	E: Taped PMR C: Adventure stories	Decreased muscle tension for both groups	NM	NM	NM
Brown (1977)	$N = 40$	12	E: Relaxation Relaxation with task motivational instructions (TMI)	NM	Improved for relaxation with TMI	NSD	Improved for relaxation with TMI
Watson & Hall (1977)	$N = 36$ 4th–6th grade	12	E: PMR + Auto. PMR + Auto. + BF BF (All + "Think Aloud")	Decreased muscle tension in all E groups	Increase in Conners scale; no difference in behavioral observation. BF had lowest hyperactivity	Improved PIAT reading, MFFT latency. No difference WISC-R, PIAT math. BF had lowest MFFT errors.	NM

169

TABLE 6.1. *Continued*

Study	Subjects (No./Age)	Sessions	Experimental & Control Conditions	Outcomes			
				Physiological	Behavioral	Cognitive	Affective/ Self-Concept
Braud (1978)	$N = 30$ 6–13 years	12	C: Placebo control No treatment			Improved Bender Gestalt, ITPA, Visual Sequent., WISC digit span & coding	NM
			E: BF Taped PMR C: Control Nonhyperactive	Decreased muscle tension for both E groups	Improved Conners, David, Lupin & Cogwill parent scales		
Flemings (1979)	$N = 10$	10	E: BF C: None	Decreased muscle tension	NSD	NM	NM
Bhatara, Arnold, Lorance & Gupta (1979)	$N = 9$ 6–10 yrs.	8	E: BF + PMR C: None	Decreased muscle tension	NSD	NM	NM
Omizo (1980a)	$N = 56$ 13–16 yrs.	3	E: BF + taped PMR C: No treatment	NM	NM	NM	DOSC level of aspiration increased; LOC more internal
Omizo (1980b)	$N = 52$ 9–11 yrs.	3	E: BF + taped PMR C: No treatment	Decreased muscle tension	NM	NM	DOSC improved; LOC did not change
Omizo (1981)	$N = 30$ 8–11 yrs.	4	E: BF + taped PMR C: No treatment	NM	Improved parent & teacher ratings	NM	No change in LOC
Omizo & Michael (1982)	$N = 32$ 10–12 yrs.	4	E: BF + taped PMR C: No treatment	NM	NM	Increased MFFT latency and accuracy	No change in LOC

Study	Sessions	Treatment	Physiological	Behavioral	Cognitive	Self-concept/Mood
Menking (1980) N = 36	—	E: BF + PMR C: Attention-placebo No treatment	Decreased muscle tension	Improved Conners Scale for E and attention-placebo	NM	No difference on Piers-Harris Self-Concept
Potashkin (1981) N = 18 10-13 yrs.	10	E: BF C: Ritalin No treatment	Decreased muscle tension	Increased teacher ratings for E and no treatment; No difference on parent ratings	NM	Improved on Piers-Harris Self-Concept
Dunn & Howell (1982) N = 10 6-12 yrs.	10	E: BF PMR	Decreased muscle tension BF-deeper, PMR-faster	Increased time on task, improved self-control & parent ratings for both groups	Improved cognitive performance	NM
Christie, Dewitt, Kaltenbach & Read (1984) N = 12 3rd-4th grade	—	E: BF (neck) C: None	Decreased muscle tension	NM	NM	NM
Loffredo, Omizo, & Hammett (1984) N = 32 5-7 yrs.	3	E: Group PMR	NM	NM	NM	Improved on Primary Self-Concept Inventory

Other behavioral difficulties

Study	Sessions	Treatment	Physiological	Behavioral	Cognitive	Self-concept/Mood
Elitzur (1976) N = 22 12-16 yrs.	1-5	E: Taped group PMR C: None	NM	Self-reported improved behavior	NM	Positive mood change

TABLE 6.1. *Continued*

Study	Subjects (No./Age)	Sessions	Experimental & Control Conditions	Outcomes			
				Physiological	Behavioral	Cognitive	Affective/Self-Concept
Lupin, Braud, Braud, & Duer (1976)	N = 13 6–10 yrs.	@90	E: 6 tapes for parents & children: PMR behavior mod., visual imagery, etc. C: None	NM	Improved parental ratings on 2 of 9 measures; improved classroom behavior on 3 of 5 measures.	Improved WISC-R digit span, coding; No change in object assembly, or visual sequential memory	NM
Walton (1979)	N = 5 5th–6th grade	64	E: BF + PMR + Auto. + mental imagery C: None	Decreased muscle tension	NSD, but 4 of 5 children inappropriate behavior reduced by 50%	NM	NM
Redfering & Bowman (1981)	N = 18 8–11 yrs.	5	E: Taped meditative-relaxation C: Rest instructions	NM	Decrease in nonattending behavior	NM	NM
Marino (1983)	N = 56 10th–12th grade	—	E: BF + PMR C: None	Decreased muscle tension, increased finger temperature	NM	Improved Gates-MacGinite Reading Comp.; No change in vocabulary.	Change to more internal LOC; No change state/trait anxiety
Oldfield (1986)	N = 21 4th–6th grade	80	E: Relaxation response C: Behavioral charting	NM	76% decrease in acting out incidents	NM	Improved on Piers-Harris Self-concept

Learning Disabilities

Study	Sample		Treatment				
Omizo & Williams (1982)	$N = 32$ 8–11 yrs.	3	E: BF + taped PMR C: No treatment	NM	NM	Improved MFFT latency and accuracy	No change in LOC
Chaumier (1983)	$N = 56$ adolescents	4	E: BF + taped PMR C: Old radio shows	NM	NM	NM	Improved on 2 of 5 DOSC measures
Palmeri (1980)	$N = 64$ LD & ED with learning problems	10	E: Cue controlled relaxation (CCR), i.e., PMR + cue training C: Verbal training (VT) CCR + VT No treatment	NM	CCR group improved on Conners scale LD: attentiveness ED: attentiveness and aggressiveness	Improved PIAT for ED group; No change in Porteus Maze or coding	NM
Carter & Russell (1985)	(a) $N = 32$ elementary boys	25	E: BF + PMR + visual imagery C: No treatment	Decreased muscle tension	Improved parent ratings	Improved WRAT reading, spelling, Gray-Oral Reading Test, Slosson IQ, Bender Gestalt, Slosson drawing, auditory memory, handwriting	Improved self-concept
	(b) $N = 30$ elementary boys		E: BF C: No treatment	Decreased muscle tension	Improved parent ratings	Same as above except for Slosson IQ & auditory memory	Improved self-concept

TABLE 6.1. *Continued*

Study	Subjects (No./Age)	Sessions	Experimental & Control Conditions	Outcomes			
				Physiological	Behavioral	Cognitive	Affective/ Self-Concept
Anxiety							
Proeger (1978)	$N = 135$ 4th graders	10	E: Taped deep muscle relaxation C: Placebo No treatment	NM	NSD in teacher ratings	NSD in MAT reading test	NSD on Children's Manifest Anxiety Scale
Scardapane (1983)	$N = 80$ 8–14 yrs.	—	E: PMR Meditation Benson's relaxation C: Sitting quietly	NSD in heart rate	NM	NSD WISC-R coding	NSD on 2 anxiety scales
Laird (1981)	$N = 102$ 12th graders	6	E: PMR PMR + BF C: Counseling No treatment	Decreased heart rate for both E groups; NSD in finger temperature	NM	NM	Decreased state anxiety for both E groups; NSD on self-report
Day & Sadek (1982)	$N = 62$ 5th grade	30	E: Meditation C: Reading	NM	NM	NM	Decreased anxiety on TASC & GASC
Autism							
Marholin, Steinman, Luiselli, Schwartz, & Townsend (1979)	$N = 5$ 11–19 yrs.	—	E: PMR C: "Simon Says"	NM	NSD on 3 behaviors: on-task, disruptive, stereotypic behavior	NM	NM

Giftedness

Study	Sample	Sessions	Treatment			
Rubenzer (1984)	N = 30 5th–6th grade	10	E: BF + PMR C: No treatment	Decreased muscle tension	Improved on WISC-R sim., arithmetic, digit span, WAIS vocab., divergent product test, verbal flexibility	NM
Roome & Romney (1985)	N = 30 11–14 yrs.	6	E: BF + taped PMR C: No treatment	NM	NM	Decreased state anxiety, no change trait anxiety; Shift toward internal LOC.

Insomnia

Study	Sample	Sessions	Treatment			
Anderson (1979)	N = 1 13 yrs.	3	E: PMR + decreased parental attention C: None	Insomnia eliminated	NM	NM

Other

Study	Sample	Sessions	Treatment			
Mead (1976)	9th grade potential dropouts	20	E: Taped PMR C: No treatment	NM	NM	NSD on school attitudes or on IPAT Anxiety Scale
Meanor (1979)	N = 31 H.S. students	—	E: Relaxation C: No treatment	NSD on number of discipline problems or absences	NM	NSD on IPAT Anxiety Scale

TABLE 6.1. *Continued*

Study	Subjects (No./Age)	Sessions	Experimental & Control Conditions	Outcomes			
				Physiological	Behavioral	Cognitive	Affective/Self-Concept
Abelson (1985)	N = 88 H.S. chemistry students	—	E: Live autogenic + finger temperature + taped autogenic C: No treatment	NM	NM	NSD on Gates MacGinitie Reading Comprehension	NM
Hutchison (1983)	N = 3 classes 3rd grade	30	E: Stress Management Program (PMR + Breathing + guided fantasy + tension awareness) C: No treatment	NM	Decreased blaming behavior and externally reliant behavior	NM	Increased positive attitude and generalized relaxation
Matthews (1983)	N = 532 7th grade	@270 (daily for 9 mos.)	E: Taped PMR + autogenic + thermal BF, etc. C: None	Increased wrist temperature	Decrease in class cutting, fighting; No change in absence or tardiness	No change in CTBS	Improved self-concept
Colassano & Fish (1984)	N = 2 2nd grade	8	E: PMR C: None	No change in muscle tension	Increase in on-task behavior and teacher ratings	No change in math performance	NM

176

Study	Sample		Treatment		Outcome		
Jackson & Hughes (1978)	$N = 30$ 4th graders (poor cursive handwriting)	9	E: Taped relaxation + posture; Poor handwriting C: No treatment Normal no treatment	NM	Improved handwriting	NM	NM
Jackson, Jolly, & Hamilton (1980)	$N = 114$ 4th graders	8	E: Taped relaxation-suggestion (TRS) C: Taped traditional (TT) TRS + TT Plain relaxation	NM	Most improvement with TRS + TT	NM	NM
Zenker, Fava, & Slaughter (1976)	$N = 36$ 7th–8th grade	5	E: PMR C: None	NM	Improved handwriting	NM	NM

Note. E = experimental group; C = control group; NM = not measured; NSD = no significant difference; PMR = progressive muscle relaxation; BF = biofeedback; LOC = locus of control.

ford Achievement Test, as well as on four subtests of the Illinois Test of Psy-cholinguistic Abilities (ITPA), were reported. Also, the authors indicated posi-tive behavioral change based on informal observation. Klein and Deffenbacher (1977) compared brief (five-session) progressive muscle relaxation and exercise programs with attention-placebo, no-treatment, and nonhyperactive controls. The study participants were 24 third graders diagnosed as hyperactive-impulsive, and they used two cognitive measures as dependent variables. They found that accuracy on the Matching Familiar Figures Test (MFFT) (measured by mean error rates) was significantly higher for the relaxation, exercise, and nonhyperactive controls as compared to the untreated control. However, there were no significant differences on an abbreviated version of the Continous Performance Test. The authors noted that shortening the latter test seemed to bias their results.

A comparison of the effectiveness of taped progressive muscle relaxation and taped adventure stories for boys in reducing muscle tension was made by Putre, Loffio, Chorost, Marx, and Gilbert (1977). While both groups of these 7- to 13-year-old hyperactive children decreased muscle tension over the 10 sessions, no significant difference was found between the experimental and the control groups.

Brown (1977) looked at behavior, self-concept, and performance on three Wechsler Intelligence Scale for Children-Revised (WISC-R) subtests of 40 hy-peractive children. The treatment groups were systematic relaxation, and sys-tematic relaxation with task motivational instructions (TMI) designed to en-courage participation. Following the 12 treatment sessions, the relaxation with the TMI group did significantly better than the relaxation group on behavioral ratings and self-concept measures. There were no differences on the WISC-R subtests. In a comprehensive study, Watson and Hall (1977) treated 86 fourth through sixth graders in one of three experimental groups: progressive muscle relaxation and autogenic phrases; progressive muscle relaxation, autogenic phrases and EMG biofeedback; and EMG biofeedback. All experimental sub-jects also participated in a cognitive behavior modification program called "Think Aloud" at the same time. In addition, there was a placebo-control group which received sensorimotor training and a no-treatment control group. Following 12 sessions, the children were measured on seven general factors (Watson & Hall, 1977, p. 15): hyperactive behavior, muscle tension level, at-tention span, cognitive integration, social dimensions, sensorimotor function, and academic functioning. Significant differences were found between the ex-perimental and the control groups on the Conners Behavioral Rating Scale, the Peabody Individual Achievement Test (PIAT), a reading comprehension subtest, and the MFFT latency measures, but none were found on the WISC-R subtest, on the PIAT math subtest, or in behavioral observation measures. Comparison within the experimental group showed the biofeedback condition resulted in the lowest hyperactivity ratings possible and in fewer errors on the MFFT. However, the three groups did not differ on the EMG scores.

In another comprehensive study, Braud (1978) was interested in investigating whether high tension levels aggravated the symptomatology of hyperactivity. Fifteen hyperactive 6- to 13-year-olds were placed in one of three groups for 12 sessions: EMG biofeedback, progressive muscle relaxation (taped), or hyperactive control; there was also a nonhyperactive control group. Physiological, cognitive, and behavior dependent measures were used. Braud found that, indeed, these hyperactive children had significantly higher muscle tension levels, more behavioral problems, and lower test scores. After treatment, the biofeedback and relaxation groups showed significant improvement in muscle relaxation, parent behavioral ratings, performance on the Bender-Gestalt Test, WISC-R Digit Span and Coding subtest, and an ITPA subtest; they were not significantly different from each other except that the biofeedback group had greater reduction in muscle tension than the relaxation group had. Flemings (1979) gave 10 hyperactive children EMG biofeedback over 10 sessions. At posttesting there was decreased muscle tension, but there were no changes on a behavioral rating scale.

Bhatara, Arnold, Lorance, and Gupta (1979) report conflicting evidence for effectiveness of relaxation with hyperactive children in their review of eight studies using tension reduction procedures. In their own study, they worked with nine hyperactive 6- to 10-year-olds. The treatment group received both EMG biofeedback and muscle relaxation tapes, and showed significantly reduced muscle tension levels compared to the control group. However, there was no change in teacher or parent ratings.

Omizo (1980a, 1980b, 1981) and colleagues (Omizo & Michael, 1982; Loffredo, Omizo, & Hammett, 1984) conducted a series of studies in which significant experimental group improvement was effected with combined EMG biofeedback training and progressive muscle relaxation tapes. Consistent improvement in self-concept following treatment was found through studies using three or four training sessions and hyperactive youngsters ranging in age from 8 to 16 (Omizo, 1980a, 1980b; Loffredo, Omizo, & Hammett, 1984). They found improvements in behavioral ratings by parents and teachers (Omizo, 1981) and in the area of decreased impulsivity (Omizo & Michael, 1982); one study reported improved (more internal) locus of control (Omizo, 1980b), although two other studies found no significant differences in this area (Omizo, 1981; Omizo & Michael, 1982). In a similarly designed study, Menking (1980) compared a combined biofeedback and relaxation training group with an attention placebo and no-treatment control group. He found no differences in self-concept, but found improved ratings on the Conners Behavioral Rating Scale for the experimental and attention control groups. Muscle tension was reduced in the experimental group. Potashkin (1981) compared biofeedback with Ritalin and control conditions over 10 sessions. The dependent variables included muscle tension, teacher behavioral ratings, parent ratings, and a self-concept scale. Results showed reduced muscle tension for the biofeedback group and improved teacher ratings for both the biofeedback and control groups. There were no differences in parent ratings; there was significant improvement in self-concept for the biofeedback group, a finding similar to that of Omizo (1980a, 1980b).

In a study to assess the differential effectiveness of EMG biofeedback and relaxation training, Dunn and Howell (1982) found both treatments to be equally effective in increasing time on task, improving self-control, improving parental ratings, and raising cognitive performance of ten 6- to 12-year-olds. They report that the relaxation tapes produced faster reduction of muscle tension, but that the biofeedback produced deeper muscle tension reduction. Finally, Christie, DeWitt, Kaltenbach, and Reed (1984) found that EMG biofeedback using the neck muscle led to decreased muscle tension levels for 12 third and fourth graders.

Thus, these 17 studies provide inconsistent but promising evidence of the effectiveness of relaxation training with hyperactive children. In 11 of the studies, muscle tension was reduced by some form of relaxation training. Using parent and teacher behavioral ratings as dependent measures, six studies reported improved behavior, two showed no differences, and two showed mixed results. Cognitive performance measures were improved in four studies, not improved in one study, with mixed results in two other studies. Finally, four studies report improvements in self-concept, and one reports no change.

Other Behavioral Difficulties

Children described as having behavioral difficulties often display actions in the classroom that are inappropriate (they are said to "act out"), or that hinder their educational and/or social performance in some way. Excluded from this definition are those youngsters who have been diagnosed as hyperactive. The use of relaxation training for these youngsters is as a mechanism for coping with strong emotions, such as anger, by diffusing them without engaging in disruptive behavior (Redfering & Bowman, 1981).

Elitzur (1976), in an anecdotal report, treated 22 acting out adolescents in a residential facility attached to Family Court. Treatments were group administered, taped, progressive muscle relaxation. The participants received from one to five sessions, averaging three each. Posttreatment informal interviews disclosed positive mood change in all adolescents; half claimed behavior change as well. Lupin, Braud, Braud, and Duer (1976) treated thirteen 6- to 10-year-olds "who had behavior problems severe enough to hinder their classroom performance, and who met minimal brain-injured classification requirements" (p. 106). Both parents and children were instructed to use the six relaxation tapes daily for three months. The tapes included behavior modification principles, adult relaxation exercises, and visual imagery in stories. At posttreatment there was significant behavioral improvement in two of nine parent ratings (i.e., children were happier and had improved in their interpersonal relationships). Three of five classroom behaviors improved significantly: working on assigned tasks, communicating with another child, and fidgeting or nervous behavior. WISC-R Digit Span and Coding subtests were significant whereas Object Assembly was not. Visual sequential memory was not significant.

Five severely emotionally handicapped youngsters in the fifth and sixth grades participated in a treatment program to reduce their inappropriate behaviors (Walton, 1979). They received EMG biofeedback and relaxation procedures including progressive muscle relaxation, isometric exercises, autogenic training and mental imagery. Each child attended 64 sessions. Muscle tension was significantly reduced and inappropriate behavior (operationally defined as six clusters of behavior) was reduced, on the average, by more than 50 percent in four of the five children. Statistically this was not significant. Redfering and Bowman (1981) examined nonattending behavior in eighteen 8- to 11-year-olds. The experimental group had five sessions of taped meditative-relaxation. Rest instructions were provided for the control group. The experimental group significantly decreased nonattending behavior as compared to the control group. Marino (1983) treated 56 tenth through twelfth graders with biofeedback thermal training (fingertip) and relaxation. Improvement on the Gates-MacGinitie Reading Comprehension test, EMG readings, finger temperature, and locus of control orientation were related to the training. There were no significant changes in vocabulary scores or in state and trait anxiety scores. Oldfield (1986) assigned 21 disruptive fourth through sixth graders to either a relaxation response or a behavioral charting condition. Following 80 treatment sessions, the number of acting out incidents decreased significantly (by 76 percent) for the relaxation group; also, self-concept as measured on the Piers-Harris Self-Concept Test was significantly improved.

While the trends in these studies with behaviorally disordered youngsters are toward improvement following relaxation training, the record is sparse and further evidence is needed.

Learning Disability

Children with learning disabilities are often described as distractible and impulsive (Omizo & Williams, 1982). It has been reported that learning disabled children show more autonomic liability and inability to focus attention than do normal children (Carter & Russell, 1985). Thus a number of researchers have reasoned that relaxation, particularly using biofeedback training, can be useful in treating learning disabled youngsters. Omizo and Williams (1982) randomly assigned thirty-two 8- to 11-year-old learning disabled youngsters to experimental and control groups. The experimental group treatment was a combination of EMG biofeedback training and relaxation tapes from *Peace, Harmony, Awareness* (Lupin, 1977) and lasted for three sessions. Dependent variables for this study were attention to task and impulsivity as measured by the number of errors and by the latency score on the MFFT. The Nowicki-Strickland Scale was used to measure locus of control. Significant differences were found between the experimental and control groups on MFFT measures, but there were no changes in locus of control. Chaumier (1983) studied 56 learning disabled adolescents under two conditions: a combined biofeedback and relaxation tape treatment, and a control condition where they listened to old radio shows. Following four sessions, students were given the Dimension of Self-Concept (DOSC) which is a self-report instrument with five factor dimensions. Results indicate that two of the five dimensions, level of aspiration and identification versus alienation, were valid discriminators between the two groups. Palmeri (1980) compared verbal training with cue-controlled relaxation (CCR) to see if they would increase the effectiveness of remediation with children having learning problems. The 64 treated children were diagnosed as either learning disabled or as having emotionally related learning problems. In CCR, youngsters are first trained in progressive relaxation. Then, when they are in a deeply relaxed state, they focus on their breathing and subvocally present a cue word or phrase such as "calm" or "relax" as they exhale. This pairs the cue with the relaxed state (Deffenbacher & Suinn, 1982). Results showed that the CCR group with the emotionally related learning problems made greater gains on the PIAT and improved on the attentiveness and aggressiveness factor of the Conners Teacher Rating Scale. The learning disabled children receiving CCR improved on the attentiveness factor of the Conners scale.

Most recently, Carter and Russell (1985) conducted two investigations with elementary age learning disabled boys. In the first study, in a clinic setting, the experimental group received EMG biofeedback (flexor muscle) for 10 sessions and then 15 sessions of taped relaxation and visual imagery. There were very significant differences between the experimental and control groups on WRAT reading and spelling scores, the Gray Oral Reading Test, the Slosson Intelligence Test, the Bender Gestalt Test, Slosson drawing, auditory memory, handwriting, and EMG levels. Also, parent behavior ratings and self-concept scales were significant. The second study attempted to replicate the findings from the clinic study in a school setting. However, there were only 18 sessions of EMG relaxation. Still, children in the experimental group made significantly greater gains over the controls on all the dependent measures except the Slosson IQ and the auditory memory. Carter and Russell concluded that when children relax, they have more efficient access to previously learned material.

These five studies are fairly consistent in their support for relaxation intervention with learning disabled youngsters as they resulted in improved physiological, behavioral, cognitive, and self-concept measures.

Anxiety

There is little consensus in the professional literature on the definition of fears, phobias, and anxiety (Morris & Kratochwill, 1983). However, relaxation training has been used alone and as a component of systematic desensitization to treat these problems. First, let us look at the studies that have attempted to treat more general anxiety or stress where there is no specific object of fear. Proeger (1978) assigned 135 anxious fourth graders to a taped deep muscle relaxation condition, a placebo, or a control condition. Following 10 treatment sessions, there were no significant differences between the groups on any of the dependent measures, including the Children's Manifest Anxiety Scale, the Feelings Checklist, the Metropolitan Achievement Test Reading subtest, and a teacher scale. Similarly, 80 anxious youngsters, ages 8 to 14, received training in progressive muscle relaxation, meditation, Benson's relax, or sitting quietly (Scardapane, 1983). No differences between groups were found in heart rate, the WISC-R Coding subtest, or on two anxiety scales. Laird (1981) placed 102 anxious high school seniors in one of four treatment groups: progressive muscle relaxation, progressive muscle relaxation combined with biofeedback, counseling, or control. Following six treatment sessions, there was decreased anxiety in both the progressive muscle relaxation and the combined progressive muscle relaxation and biofeedback groups as measured by the State scale of the State-Trait Anxiety Inventory (STAI) and by heart rate, but not for self-report or finger temperature measures. The author suggests that the addition of biofeedback training to the progressive muscle relaxation may provide greater reductions in anxiety.

In a highly stressful natural environment, Day and Sadek (1982) examined the effect of meditation on 62 fifth grade Lebanese children living in a climate of war. While no pretest was given, following thirty 10-minute treatment sessions, the experimental group had significantly lower scores on the Test Anxiety Scale for Children (TASC) and on the General Anxiety Scale for Children (GASC). Girls were reportedly more highly stressed than boys as measured on the GASC. At a three week follow-up, the effects had disappeared.

Autistic

A preliminary study using a multielement design with five autistic adolescents (ages 11 to 19) comparing progressive muscle relaxation and a game activity was reported by Marholin, Steinman, Luiselli, Schwartz and Townsend (1979). They found no differences on three behavioral dependent measures: task oriented, disruptive, and stereotypic behavior.

Asthmatic

A comprehensive review by Erskine-Milliss and Schonell (1981) reports three studies that investigate the use of biofeedback and the treatment of asthma. They conclude that biofeedback assisted relaxation procedures lead to improvement in ventilatory function and to a decrease in asthma attacks, infirmary visits, and steroid usage in asthmatic children.

Giftedness

Rubenzer (1984) studied fifth- and sixth-grade gifted students experiencing test and math anxiety. The 30 youngsters were assigned to 10 sessions in a combined biofeedback-progressive muscle relaxation group or in a control group. The experimental group performed significantly better than the control group on all cognitive measures including the WISC-R Similarities, Arithmetic and Digit Span subtests, WAIS vocabulary, Divergent Product Test, and Verbal

Flexibility. In addition, their muscle tension was significantly reduced. Roome and Romney (1985) assigned 30 gifted youngsters, ages 11 to 14, to biofeedback, taped progressive muscle relaxation, or control conditions for six sessions. The dependent measures were locus of control and the STAI. They report that state anxiety decreased in the biofeedback condition, while there were no changes in trait anxiety. A shift toward an internal locus of control was seen in both the biofeedback and the progressive muscle relaxation groups.

Insomnia

Anderson (1979), in a case study report, describes a two-part treatment plan for insomnia for a 13-year-old boy. It included both progressive muscle relaxation and decreased parental attention. Three one-hour relaxation training sessions were held, and the insomnia was eliminated. However, it is not clear which part of the treatment was responsible for the result.

Other

Relaxation training has been used with youngsters in the mainstream who do not have classifiable psychological or physiological disorders. For example, Mead (1976) used relaxation tapes with ninth-grade potential dropouts for 20 sessions. No significant differences were found between the experimental and the control groups on school attitude or on the IPAT Anxiety Scale Questionnaire following treatment. Similarly, Meanor (1979) assigned 31 normal high school students to relaxation or control conditions and found no significant differences on the IPAT Anxiety Scale, the number of discipline problems, or the number of absences. Abelson (1985) used live and taped autogenic phrases and finger temperature with a group of 88 normal high school chemistry students over eight weeks. There was no significant difference on the dependent measure, the Gates-MacGinitie Reading Comprehension Test, between experimental and control conditions.

Hutchison (1983) investigated the effectiveness of a teacher-taught stress management program for third graders. The program participants met daily for six weeks, and were given muscle relaxation, breathing, guided fantasy, self-talk, and tension awareness. Dependent measures were teacher ratings of achievement related behavior, student self-reports of anxiety, child and teacher attitudes toward the program, and ability to relax. Results showed that external blaming behavior and externally reliant behavior decreased in the experimental group, though it was not possible to separate out the effect of the relaxation component in the stress management program.

Matthews (1983), in a schoolwide study, examined the effect of a relaxation program on 532 seventh graders. The experimental group received 15 minutes of taped relaxation for nine months. The treatment included quiet reflex, autogenic phrases, visual imagery and thermal biofeedback using the wrist. Results at the year's end showed significant decreases in class cutting and in fighting, improved self-concepts, and increased wrist temperature for the experimental group. No changes in absences, tardiness, or the CTBS were found. Colassano and Fish (1984) investigated whether progressive muscle relaxation using the first two Lupin (1977) tapes would affect behavioral ratings on task behavior, EMG muscle tension, or math computations of two second grade youngsters. There were eight training sessions. Increases in on-task behavior and teacher ratings were noted, but there were no changes in EMG or math performance.

Jackson and Hughes (1978) and Jackson, Jolly, and Hamilton (1980) looked at the effect of relaxation on students with poor cursive handwriting. In the first study, 30 fourth graders in the experimental group received taped relaxation. Results indicated that after nine sessions, the experimental group improved more than the control group with poor handwriting and more than normal controls. In the second study 114 fourth graders received either taped relaxation-suggestion, traditional handwriting instruction, a combination of relaxation and the traditional approach, or plain relaxation without mention of writing. For poor writers the least effective method was the relaxation without any handwriting instruction, and the most effective was the combined relaxation and traditional instruction group. Zenker, Fava, and Slaughter (1986), in an anecdotal report, used five minutes of relaxation training at the beginning of seventh- and eighth-grade classes for five sessions with the goal of improving handwriting. They report that informal observations reveal improvement following treatment. Handwriting seems to be a motoric behavior which is responsive to relaxation training, but a cognitive instructional component was still necessary.

Systematic Desensitization Research

Systematic desensitization is probably the most widely used behavior therapy procedure for reducing children's fears (Morris & Kratochwill, 1983). While the adult literature on systematic desensitization is rather extensive, the research with children is much more limited (Morris & Kratochwill, 1983). Saigh and Antoun (1984) worked with test-anxious high school students. They report reduced levels of anxiety (as measured on the Suinn Test Anxiety Behavior Scale) and improved grade point average (GPA) both following systematic desensitization treatment and after imagining a series of pleasant, relaxing images that were counterposed with the items from a test anxiety hierarchy. Both treatment groups were significantly different from the control group. In addition to the seven treatment sessions, three sessions of study skills were conducted.

Forman and O'Malley (1984) reviewed a number of studies that show systematic desensitization as an effective treatment for student test anxiety. They conclude that its effectiveness in reducing test anxiety is supported by self-report and physiological measures, but concomitant evidence on academic and/or test performance is not consistently found. Reviews by Morris and Kratochwill (1983, 1985) report mainly uncontrolled and descriptive case studies on systematic desensitization. They tentatively conclude that systematic desensitization " . . . is a potentially effective treatment for reducing a variety of fears and phobias in children from 9 to 17 years of age" (1985, p. 86).

Methodological Considerations

It is evident from the research review that, as with the adult relaxation literature, numerous methodological weaknesses warrant caution when drawing conclusions from these studies. Richter (1984), in a comprehensive review, presents a discussion of many of the methodological concerns. It is apparent that many of the research reports are anecdotal in nature and/or not well controlled. Often, the treatment groups have very small sample sizes (e.g., five subjects). Further, the studies are hard to compare because they differ along a number of dimensions, for example, age of subjects, length of treatment sessions, number of treatment sessions, the type of relaxation procedure used, live versus taped presentation, and group versus individual treatment. More significantly, the dependent measures that vary include self-report and physiological and behavioral indices.

One of the more serious problems is the "imprecise definition of subject populations" (Richter, 1984, p. 319). Hyperactivity, for example, is defined in a variety of ways using direct behavioral observation, teacher rating scales, and/or medical diagnosis. With the exception of two studies in this review, no follow-up was described; in one of the two follow-ups, treatment effects disappeared. One of the important considerations in using relaxation for self-regulation has been to encourage long term maintenance, yet it is not routinely measured. Support from parents and teachers and compliance with practice are also inconsistently reported. It is frequently difficult to separate out the effects of relaxation alone from the effects of the rest of the treatment. Finally, it is interesting to note that the degrees of baseline tension present in the studies is quite varied. For example, Dunn and Howell's (1982) successful treatment was applied to a sample whose mean level of muscle tension was 44 microvolts. In contrast, the mean muscle tension in the Putre, et al. (1977) study, where relaxation tapes were no more effective than adventure stories, was 2.75 microvolts. This issue of preexperimental muscle tension baseline is made more complex by the fact that most studies employing relaxation training fail to assess these levels at all (Luiselli, Marholin, Steinman, & Steinman, 1979).

IMPLICATIONS FOR TREATMENT

Despite the methodological concerns discussed, the potential of relaxation training to effect specific outcome variables under certain conditions is apparent. Let us consider the evidence. The first trend from the research is that physiological outcomes (i.e., decreased muscle tension and increased finger or wrist temperature) were improved in all but three of the studies in which they were measured. Of these three studies, one found no significant change in heart rate, one no significant change in muscle tension and one no significant change in finger temperature. Virtually all the studies that used biofeedback had positive physiological results. It seems that the expected physical correlates of relaxation are present, and that the children in these studies had successfully learned to relax.

A second concern is to what degree physiological outcomes result in concomitant behavioral, cognitive, and affective change. Of 14 studies that had both physiological and behavioral dependent variables, seven, or 50 percent, reported improved behavioral outcomes measured either by observational instruments or by parent/teacher rating scales. There were three with mixed results, three with no behavioral changes despite relaxation, and one study with behavioral change without relaxation. Similarly, looking at physiological and cognitive outcomes, we see that of 11 studies measuring both, five report improvements in both areas, three have mixed results on cognitive measures, and one found no cognitive improvement; for two studies neither outcome was significant. Finally, the relationship between physiological and affective variables follows the same pattern; five of nine studies report improvement in both areas, one found neither improved, two found mixed affective outcomes, and one resulted in no significant differences. Generally, in about half the cases, physiological change was accompanied by other more ecologically valid outcomes.

When various relaxation procedures were compared within studies (e.g., biofeedback vs. progressive muscle relaxation), there were no clear indications of the superiority of any one procedure. This suggests that all procedures described were effective ones for use with children. Further, looking at live versus taped presentations, about 40 percent of each type of treatment resulted in positive outcomes, another 40 percent resulted in mixed outcomes, and the remaining studies reported no significant results. This is hard to interpret because of the enormous variations in study characteristics, but it suggests that taped progressive muscle relaxation, for example, can be a useful alternative when using relaxation training, not only for group work, but also to encourage home practice.

In this review there is no discernible relationship between number of sessions and treatment success. Borkovec and Sides (1979) in their conclusion from the adult literature review have indicated that multisession treatment increases the likelihood of significant physiological improvement with progressive muscle relaxation. Richter (1984) arrives at a similar conclusion in his review of the children's relaxation literature.

With regard to the effect of relaxation training on specific types of disorders, it appears that there is consistent improvement in studies with learning disabled youngsters. Physiological disorders, such as asthma, also respond well to relaxation training. For hyperactive and behaviorally disordered children, relaxation training was moderately successful. Surprisingly, the results with anxious students were rather poor and quite opposite to the consistently positive results with systematic desensitization. Perhaps this points to the insufficiency of just learning relaxation, and to the need for practice of the skill in coping situations for anxious youngsters. For children who did not have behavioral, affective, or cognitive deficits, relaxation training provided limited benefit.

It appears from this review and others that the relaxation response is a skill that requires practice and that can be successfully learned by children with behavioral, cognitive, and affective disorders. While training procedures may vary, 10 or more sessions may be necessary for changes to occur that are environmentally meaningful. Additionally, the relaxation training is enhanced when accompanied by appropriate skill training. Combining relaxation with cognitive and/or role playing experiences increases the functional utility of the procedure for the child. It allows the child to practice coping with the troublesome situation. Further, the support of the family, and perhaps their participation in relaxation training, is usually reinforcing to the child.

In conclusion, relaxation training is a viable component of a treatment package for childhood disorders. It is a straightforward, easy to administer procedure that can be used to help children develop control of their own behavior.

REFERENCES

Abelson, R.M. (1985). Effect of biofeedback techniques on reading comprehension in a high school chemistry class. *Dissertation Abstracts International, 46,* 926A.

Anderson, D.R. (1979). Treatment of insomnia in a 13 year old boy by relaxation training and reduction of parental attention. *Journal of Behavior Therapy and Experimental Psychiatry, 10,* 263–265.

Beiman, I., Graham, L.E., & Ciminero, A.R. (1978). Self-control progressive muscle relaxation training as an alternative nonpharmacological treatment for essential hypertension: Therapeutic effects in the natural environment. *Behavior Research and Therapy, 16,* 371–375.

Benson, H., Beary, J.F., & Carol, M.P. (1974). The relaxation response. *Psychiatry, 37,* 37–45.

Bhatara, V., Arnold, L.E., Lorance, T., & Gupta, D. (1979). Muscle relaxation therapy in hyperkinesis: Is it effective? *Journal of Learning Disabilities, 12,* 182–186.

Borkovec, T.D., & Sides, J.K. (1979). Critical procedural variables related to the physiological effects of progressive relaxation: A review. *Behavior Research and Therapy, 17,* 119–125.

Braud, L.W. (1978). The effects of frontal EMG biofeedback and progressive relaxation upon hyperactivity and its behavioral concomitants. *Biofeedback and Self-Regulation, 3,* 69–89.

Braud, L.W., Lupin, M.N., & Braud, W.G. (1975). The use of electromyographic biofeedback in the control of hyperactivity. *Journal of Learning Disabilities, 8,* 21–26.

Brown, R.H. (1977). An evaluation of the effectiveness of relaxation training as a treatment modality for the hyperkinetic child. *Dissertation Abstracts International, 38,* 2847B.

Budzynski, T.H., & Stoyva, J.M. (1969). An instrument for producing deep muscle relaxation by means of analog information feedback. *Journal of Applied Behavior Analysis, 2,* 231–237.

Carter, J.L., & Russell, H.L. (1985). Use of EMG biofeedback procedures with learning disabled children in a clinical and an educational setting. *Journal of Learning Disabilities, 18,* 213–216.

Cautela, J.R., & Groden, J. (1978). *Relaxation: A comprehensive manual for adults, children and children with special needs.* Champaign, IL: Research Press.

Chaumier, R.E. (1983). The efficacy of biofeedback/relaxation training on dimensions of self-concept among learning disabled adolescents. *Dissertation Abstracts International, 43,* 3540A.

Christie, D.J., DeWitt, R.A., Kaltenbach, P., & Reed, D. (1984). Using EMG biofeedback to signal hyperactive children when to relax. *Exceptional Children, 50,* 547–548.

Colassano, F. (1986). *The relative effectiveness of cognitive self-instruction and progressive muscle relaxation for treating the deficits found in hyperactive youngsters.* Unpublished manuscript, Graduate Center, City University of New York.

Colassano, F., & Fish, M.C. (1984, August). The effect of relaxation training on children's attention to task, activity level, and computational ability. Paper presented at the American Psychological Association Annual Convention, Toronto, Canada.

Day, R.C., & Sadek, S.N. (1982). The effect of Benson's relaxation response on the anxiety levels of Lebanese children under stress. *Journal of Experimental Child Psychology, 34,* 350–356.

Deffenbacher, J.L., & Suinn, R.M. (1982). The self-control of anxiety. In P. Karoly & F.H. Kanfer (Eds.), *Self-management and behavior change* (pp. 393–442). New York: Pergamon Press.

Dunn, F.M., & Howell, R.J. (1982). Relaxation training and its relationship to hyperactivity in boys. *Journal of Clinical Psychology, 38,* 92–100.

Elitzur, B. (1976). Self-relaxation program for acting-out adolescents. *Adolescence, 11,* 569–572.

Erskine-Millis, J., & Schonell, M. (1981). Relaxation therapy in Asthma: A critical review. *Psychosomatic Medicine, 43,* 365–372.

Flemings, D.G. (1979). A study of electromyographic biofeedback as a method to teach hyperactive children how to relax within a public school setting. *Dissertation Abstracts International, 39,* 6693A.

Forman, S.G., & O'Malley, P.L. (1984). School stress and anxiety interventions. *School Psychology Review, 13,* 162–170.

Goldfried, M.R., & Trier, C.S. (1974). Effectiveness of relaxation as an active coping skill. *Journal of Abnormal Psychology, 83,* 348–355.

Hillenberg, J.B., & Collins, F.L. (1982). A procedural analysis and review of relaxation training research. *Behavior Research and Therapy, 20,* 251–260.

Hutchison, S.M. (1984). Effectiveness and feasibility of a stress management program for third grade children. *Dissertation Abstracts International, 45,* 80A.

Jackson, K.A., & Hughes, H. (1978). Effects of relaxation training on cursive handwriting of fourth grade students. *Perceptual and Motor Skills, 47,* 707-712.

Jackson, K.A., Jolly, V., & Hamilton, B. (1980). Comparison of remedial treatments for cursive handwriting of fourth grade students. *Perceptual and Motor Skills, 51,* 1215-1221.

Jacobson, E. (1938). *Progressive relaxation.* Chicago: University of Chicago Press.

Karoly, P., & Kanfer, F.H. (1982) *Self-management and behavior change.* New York: Pergamon Press.

Klein, S.A., & Deffenbacher, J.L. (1977). Relaxation and exercise for hyperactive children. *Perceptual Motor Skills, 45,* 1159-1162.

Laird, G.S. (1981). The effects of progressive relaxation on anxiety among high school students. *Dissertation Abstracts International, 42,* 1552-1553A.

Linkenhoker, D. (1983). Tools of behavioral medicine: Applications of biofeedback treatment for children and adolescents. *Developmental and Behavioral Pediatrics, 4,* 16-20.

Loffredo, D.A., Omizo, M., & Hammett, V.L. (1984). Group relaxation training and parental involvement with hyperactive boys. *Journal of Learning Disabilities, 4,* 210-213.

Luiselli, J.K., Marholin, D., Steinman, D.L., & Steinman, W.M. (1979). Assessing the effects of relaxation training. *Behavior Therapy, 10,* 663-668.

Lupin, M. (1977). *Peace, harmony, awareness: A relaxation program for children.* Hingham, MA: Teaching Resources Corporation.

Lupin, M., Braud, L.W., Braud, W., & Duer, W.F. (1976). Children, parents, and relaxation tapes. *Academic Therapy, 12,* 105-113.

Marholin, II, D., Steinman, W.M., Luiselli, J.K., Schwartz, C.S., & Townsend, N.M. (1979). The effects of progressive muscle relaxation on the behavior of autistic adolescents: A preliminary analysis. *Child Behavior Therapy, 1,* 75-85.

Marino, M.D. (1983). The effects of biofeedback thermal training and relaxation training on reading scores, locus of control, state and trait anxiety, EMG readings, and fingertip temperatures of behavior disordered students. *Dissertation Abstracts International, 44,* 1033A.

Matthews, D.B. (1983, November). *Relaxation training: Its usefulness in the middle school curriculum.* Paper presented at the Annual Meeting of the National Middle Schools, Chicago, IL. (ERIC Document Reproduction Service No. ED 236 150).

Mead, R.J. (1976). The effects of relaxation training on the attitudes and anxiety level of 9th grade potential dropouts. *Dissertation Abstracts International, 37,* 5612A.

Meanor, G.C. (1979). A study of the effects of a short, daily relaxation period on some important behaviors of secondary school students. *Dissertation Abstracts International, 39,* 7213A.

Menking, S.M.R. (1980). The effects of electromyographic biofeedback and relaxation on the behavior of hyperactive children. *Dissertation Abstracts International, 41,* 1894B.

Morris, R.J., & Kratochwill, T.R. (1983). *Treating children's fears and phobias: A behavioral approach.* New York: Pergamon Press.

Morris, R.J., & Kratochwill, T.R. (1985). Behavioral treatment of children's fears and phobias: A review. *School Psychology Review, 14,* 84-93.

Oldfield, D. (1986). The effects of the relaxation response on self-concept and acting out behaviors. *Elementary School Guidance and Counseling, 20,* 255–260.

O'Leary, S.G., & Dubey, D.R. (1979). Applications of self-control procedures by children: A review. *Journal of Applied Behavior Analysis, 12,* 449–465.

Omizo, M.M. (1980a). The effects of biofeedback induced relaxation training in hyperactive adolescent boys. *Journal of Psychology, 105,* 131–138.

Omizo, M.M. (1980b). The effects of relaxation and biofeedback training on Dimensions of Self-Concept (DOSC) among hyperactive male children. *Educational Research Quarterly, 5,* 22–30.

Omizo, M.M. (1981). Relaxation training and biofeedback with hyperactive elementary school children. *Elementary School Guidance and Counseling, 15,* 329–332.

Omizo, M.M., Loffredo, D.A., & Hammett, V.L. (1982). Relaxation exercises for the LD and family. *Academic Therapy, 17,* 603–608.

Omizo, M.M., & Michael, W.B. (1982). Biofeedback induced relaxation training and impulsitivity, attention to task, and locus of control among hyperative boys. *Journal of Learning Disabilities, 15,* 414–416.

Omizo, M.M., & Williams, R.E. (1982). Biofeedback-induced relaxation training as an alternative for the elementary school learning disabled child. *Biofeedback and Self-Regulation, 7,* 139–148.

Palmeri, J.J. (1980). Relaxation and cognitive coping statements as supplemental remedial interventions for learning problems in children. *Dissertation Abstracts International, 40,* 5796–5797B.

Piggott, D.C. (1985). A relaxation and visualization program for mathematics anxiety. *Dissertation Abstracts International, 45,* 2021A.

Potashkin, B.D. (1981). Relative efficacy of ritalin and biofeedback treatments on hyperactivity. *Dissertation Abstracts International, 42,* 1617B.

Proeger, C.G. (1979). Relaxation training with children. *Dissertation Abstracts International, 39,* 7166–7167A.

Putre, W., Loffio, K., Chorost, S., Marx, V., & Gilbert, C. (1977). An effectiveness study of a relaxation training tape with hyperactive children. *Behavior Therapy, 8,* 355–359.

Redfering, D.L., & Bowman, M.J. (1981). Effects of a meditative-relaxation exercise on non-attending behaviors of behaviorally disturbed children. *Journal of Clinical Child Psychology, 10,* 126–127.

Richter, N.C. (1984). The efficacy of relaxation training with children. *Journal of Abnormal Child Psychology, 12,* 319–344.

Roome, J.R., & Romney, D.M. (1985). Reducing anxiety in gifted children by inducing relaxation. *Roeper Review, 7,* 177–179.

Rosenbaum, M.S., & Drabman, R.S. (1979). Self-control training in the classroom: A review and critique. *Journal of Applied Behavior Analysis, 12,* 467–485.

Rubenzer, R.L. (1984). The effects of biofeedback-induced relaxation on test/math anxiety and related test performance for children in a special elementary school for the gifted. *Dissertation Abstracts International, 45,* 1042B.

Russo, D.C., Bird, B.L., & Masek, B.J. (1980). Assessment issues in behavioral medicine. *Behavioral Assessment, 2,* 1–18.

Saigh, P.A., & Antoun, F.T. (1984). Endemic images and the desensitization process. *Journal of School Psychology, 22,* 177–183.

Scardapane, J.R. (1983). A developmental study of the effects of progressive muscle relaxation and mediation on state anxiety in children and adolescents. *Dissertation Abstracts International, 46,* 969B.

Schultz, J.H., & Luthe, W. (1969). *Autogenic therapy. Vol. I Autogenic methods.* New York: Grune & Stratton.

Severson, H.H. (1976, March). *The use of biofeedback and relaxation training by school psychologists.* Paper presented at the Annual Meeting of the National Association of Student Personnel Administrators, Dallas, TX. (ERIC Document Reproduction Service No. 143 945).

Tarler-Benlolo, L. (1978). The role of relaxation in biofeedback training. A critical review of the literature. *Psychological Bulletin, 85,* 727–755.

Walker, C.E. (1979). Treatment of children's disorders by relaxation training: The poor man's biofeedback. *Journal of Clinical Child Psychology, 81,* 22–25.

Walton, W.T. (1979). The use of a relaxation curriculum and biofeedback training in the classroom to reduce inappropriate behaviors of emotionally handicapped children. *Behavioral Disorders, 5,* 10–18.

Watson, D.L., & Hall, D.L. (1977). *Self-control of hyperactivity.* Sacramento, CA: California State Department of Education. (ERIC Document Reproduction Service No. Ed 148 093).

Wielkiewicz, R.M. (1986). *Behavior management in the schools.* New York: Pergamon Press.

Winer, G.A. (1982). A review and analysis of children's fearful behavior in dental settings. *Child Development, 53,* 1111–1133.

Wolpe, J. (1958). *Psychotherapy by reciprocal inhibition.* Stanford, CA: Stanford University Press.

Zenker, E., Fava, S., & Slaughter, K. (1986). Improving writing skills through relaxation training. *Academic Therapy, 21,* 427–432.

Zipkin, D. (1985). Relaxation techniques for handicapped children: A review of literature. *Journal of Special Education, 19,* 283–289.

CHAPTER 7

Biofeedback Training with Children

RONALD H. ROZENSKY

Luke, a 12-year-old male with a six-month history of headaches, is described by his parents as a good student. He is brought to a psychotherapist's office after the headaches and his accompanying nausea and vomiting have caused him to miss two weeks of school. He has seen both his pediatrician and a pediatric neurologist, both of whom have carried out an extensive series of diagnostic medical tests. They have attempted to manage his migraines with muscle relaxant, analgesic, and abortive medications. Initial mental status and history indicate a highly motivated, intelligent young man who wants to do well in school. No signs of anxiety or depression are noted. His hobbies are computers and stamp collecting. He had been the pitcher on the Little League team the previous summer. There have been no major changes in the family and his parents can provide no description of antecedents to the onset of any of the headache episodes. Since there was no successful medical management of his migraines, the therapist is asked to treat this young man. Both Luke and his parents deny any stress-related issues contributing to his headaches. Normally the therapist would proceed psychotherapeutically to form a relationship with Luke and would begin to explore the emotional and intellectual experiences of his world in a manner consistent with the therapist's theoretical philosophy.

BIOFEEDBACK DEFINED

A central feature of all psychotherapies is the use of some type of corrective feedback offered by the therapist to the patient. The patient may then utilize this feedback in developing new awareness of his motivations or behaviors.

The author wishes to thank Drs. James Downey, Joseph Pasternak and Barbara Trommer for their clinical support of our biofeedback work with children. Gratitude is also extended to the Women's Auxiliary of Evanston Hospital for their financial support of the Biofeedback Center. Drs. Sloan, Sweet, and Tovian provided much needed editorial assistance in the development of this manuscript.

He, in turn, may use these insights to learn new ways of experiencing or of coping with the environment (Schwartz, 1973). In the case of Luke—described above—we see an individual and his family with little present awareness of his antecedent stressors or of his reactions to those stressors. Psychotherapy may well be a long and winding road for this patient who is in immediate physical pain and who has dropped out of his social sphere.

Biofeedback can be seen as a very specialized set of techniques for offering therapeutic feedback to patients. Herein, biofeedback will be referred to as a variety of procedures and techniques used to learn about the voluntary control of autonomic or reflexive psychophysiological functions utilizing the continuous feedback of information about those functions (Brown, 1977). Fuller (1977) offers a more specific definition of biofeedback as the "use of instrumentation to mirror psychophysiological processes of which the individual is not normally aware and which may be brought under voluntary control" (p. 2). Such physiological functions as muscle tension, heart rate, skin surface temperature, galvanic skin response, blood pressure, and brain wave activity have been identified as among the processes that biofeedback training can influence.

The experience of biofeedback is not new to any of us. If you have learned to walk, lift a glass of water to your mouth, ride a bicycle, thread a needle, or throw a ball through a hoop, you have experienced feedback from your body and your environment telling you how successful you have been in learning those skills each step of the way. As Miller points out, "imagine trying to take a coin out of your pocket without sensory information telling you what your hand is doing" (1985, p. 54). What is new about clinical biofeedback is the experience of receiving precise feedback concerning physiological functions that are usually not within awareness (i.e., skin temperature to the 100th of a degree, heart rate in beats per minute, or microvolts of tension in your frontalis muscle, to name a few). The patient's awareness of and use of those physiological parameters to voluntarily make changes in physiological functioning is the basis of biofeedback.

The mind/body interface in this biocybernetic loop—that is, the actual mechanisms controlling the interplay between cognitive/affect events and physiological changes—is discussed in depth by Green and Green (1977) and by Olton and Noonberg (1980). Sargent (1977) offers a graphic adaptation of Green and Green's model (see Figure 7.1). In this model one can see that the individual's perception of events external to the body (a) bring about both cognitive and affective responses via simultaneous stimulation of the cortical and limbic systems (b). Somatic responses (e) occur as a result of hypothalamic stimulation (c) that is carried through by the pituitary-hormonal axis and the autonomic nervous system (d). These internal somatic activities are normally not within our conscious awareness. Electrophysiological monitoring of these internal events (f) offers the patient a window onto these activities in the unconscious involuntary domain. The monitoring of these events (f) allows the patient to relate the internal events with objective data. With this new aware-

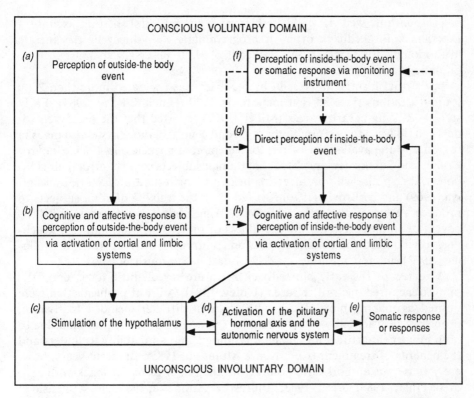

CONSCIOUS VOLUNTARY DOMAIN

(a) Perception of outside-the body event

(f) Perception of inside-the-body event or somatic response via monitoring instrument

(g) Direct perception of inside-the-body event

(b) Cognitive and affective response to perception of outside-the-body event
via activation of cortial and limbic systems

(h) Cognitive and affective response to perception of inside-the-body event
via activation of cortial and limbic systems

(c) Stimulation of the hypothalamus

(d) Activation of the pituitary hormonal axis and the autonomic nervous system

(e) Somatic response or responses

UNCONSCIOUS INVOLUNTARY DOMAIN

Figure 7.1. Sargent's adaptation of Green and Green's model of the mechanisms underlying biofeedback.
Reprinted with permission from Sargent, J.D. (1977). Biofeedback and biocybernetics. In E.D. Wittokower & H. Warnes (Eds.), *Psychosomatic medicine: Its clinical applications* (pp. 166–170). New York: Harper & Row.

ness of physiological changes (g) there also occurs cognitive and affect events (h) that, in turn, effect hypothalamic stimulation. Green (1985) states that the crucial link in the development of stress and psychosomatic illnesses is the limbic system and the cognitive and affective interface. "This same link is used to promote psychophysiological health through biofeedback training and therapeutic techniques which promote a pro-homeostatic interaction of mind and body" (Green, 1983, p. 124). As Figure 7.1 suggests, it is the biofeedback equipment that carries the unconscious internal events into the patient's conscious awareness. Self-regulatory activities can then be trained and mastered using that information. There is nothing inherently useful or relaxing in feedback of information. Biofeedback information is an aid in learning to relax (Shellenberger & Green, 1986).

The image of a child watching *Frankenstein* for the first time is a convincing oversimplification that illustrates that external experiences can, indeed, influence cognitive, affective, and physiological reactions in an excitatory direction. The focusing of that same child upon relaxing images and offering feedback upon how well the child is relaxing is the antithesis of that excitatory experience. Biofeedback offers a programmatic, (physiopsycho)therapeutic methodology for teaching the self control skills necessary to master those physiological phenomena.

In its brief history, interest in biofeedback has generated more than 2000 journal citations since its first mention in 1970 (Hatch & Riley, 1985). Early studies utilizing curarized rats (Miller, 1969) reported that the paralyzed rodents could learn to perform autonomic and central nervous system changes in response to the availability of reinforcement contingencies. In 1964, Shapiro, Crider, and Tursky demonstrated that human subjects could control their skin-potential response without affecting heart rate or respiration. Work by Kamiya (1969) and by Brown (1970) focused upon the training of adult subjects to produce a state of alert relaxation by altering brain wave patterns. With the advent of studies assessing the usefulness of biofeedback techniques in teaching individuals to control muscle tension (Budzynski, Stoyva, Adler, & Mullaney, 1973), interest in biofeedback's clinical utility mushroomed.

A review of the early biofeedback literature reveals little focus upon the biofeedback treatment of children (Finley, 1983). A list of problems that were posited as making biofeedback with children difficult included motivation problems, distractibility, short attention span, poor physiological data due to both movement artifact and labile physiology, and an inability to understand the benefits of treatment (Andrasik & Attanasio, 1985). In recent years, however, numerous authors have pointed out the utility of biofeedback with children (Finley, 1983; Green, 1983; Andrasik & Attanasia, 1985; and Attanasio et al., 1985). Among those looking at the facility with which children can master biofeedback skills were Suter and Loughry-Machado (1981). They found that children were more able than their parents to learn peripheral skin temperature control during two training sessions. It has even been noted that younger children were found to perform better at skin temperature control than older children (Hunter, Russell, Russell, & Zimmerman, 1976). Finally, Attanasio et al. (1985) stated, after reviewing a series of 110 children who were treated in their clinic (where they specialized in stress-related disorders), that children exhibit greater self-regulatory abilities, quicker acquisition of response, and better overall symptomatic improvement than adults. They note that while adults typically take 8 to 12 sessions (Taub & Emurian, 1976) to learn peripheral temperature control, most children in their sample learned this skill in 3 to 4 sessions.

Biofeedback may well be a way to proceed with Luke, and might be the initial treatment of choice in addressing the psychophysiological aspects of his problems.

LITERATURE REVIEW

A review of the existing literature on the use of biofeedback with children helps emphasize its growing acceptance as a clinical tool with that population. There have been a wide range of disorders that have been focused upon in the literature, some of which are headache, asthma, fecal incontinence, disorders of movement, epilepsy, cerebral palsy, learning disabilities, chronic vomiting, insomnia, nose bleeds, temper tantrums, anxiety (Green, 1983; Andrasik & Attanasio, 1985; Finley, 1983); functional diarrhea (Furman, 1973); stuttering (Craig & Cleary, 1982); scoliosis and kyphosis (Miller, 1985); and facial expression training (Marshall & Peck, 1986).

A brief review of the headache, epilepsy, asthma, and learning disability (including hyperactivity) literatures is useful in supporting clinicians' decisions to incorporate biofeedback into their practices.

Headache is among the most prevalent medical complaints in the pediatric population (Waranch & Keenan, 1985; Gascon, 1984). It has been noted as such a common symptom in children that as many as 40 percent of all children experience some form of the problem. Between 4 to 6 percent of those experiencing headaches can be expected to report symptoms once or more per month. As children get older, the reported incidence of headache symptoms rises to include up to 70 percent of all those between 14 and 19 years of age (Bille, 1967a, 1967b; Sillanpaa, 1983; Andrasik & Attanasio, 1985; Finley, 1983). For childhood migraine, males report symptoms 3 years earlier than females with onset ranging between 6 and 10 years of age (Congdon & Forsythe, 1979). Longitudinal studies reported by Bille (1981) and by Sillanpaa (1983) suggest that children with severe migraines continue their symptoms into adulthood.

The etiology of migraine headache is vascular in nature. Vasoconstriction of extra- and intracranial arteries occurs during the prodromal phase prior to headache pain onset. During this prodrome, visual disturbances or muscle weakness can be reported. This constriction is then followed by a compensatory vasodilation rebound that accounts for the pain (Ad Hoc Committee on the Classification of Headache, 1962; Raskin & Appenzeller, 1980). While younger children sometimes report attacks that are incomplete, with all the typical migraine symptoms but with no heachache (Finley, 1983), older children describe attacks characterized by intense, unilateral, throbbing pain of rapid onset with associated symptoms of anorexia, nausea, and vomiting.

Tension or muscle contraction headaches are the result of sustained contractions of the musculature of the head, neck, and/or shoulders. Stress is believed to be the chief precipitant to these headaches (Ad Hoc Committee on the Classification of Headache, 1962). The stimulation of local pain receptors and ischemia are the casual factors (Haynes, 1980). Andrasik and Attanasio (1985) note that muscle contraction headaches in children closely parallel the adult tension headache pattern with a slow, steady, bilateral onset of pain.

The majority of literature that is available on the biofeedback treatment approaches of children with headaches is of a case report nature. Only recently have controlled studies been undertaken with this population.

A series of multiple treatment studies with children with headaches offers encouragement as to the overall utility of biofeedback. The inability to partial out the differential effectiveness of the various treatment components, however, limits the scientific strength of the results while offering a picture of clinically useful shotgun approaches (Diamond & Franklin, 1975; Waranch & Keenan, 1985; Houts, 1982). Similarly, in such studies as Werder and Sargent (1984), a mixing of patient types (migraineurs and tension headache sufferers) makes interpretation of successful results equally as difficult. With that in mind, several representative studies can be presented.

Using a combination of thermal biofeedback and electromyographic (EMG) frontalis feedback, Diamond and Franklin (1975) reported on the treatment of 32 migraineurs between the ages of 9 and 18 who were resistant to medical management. Autogenic training and relaxation exercises were used. Decreases in frequency and in severity of migraine symptoms were noted in 81 percent of the subjects over a 30-month period. Other studies reporting combined treatment techniques, such as autogenic phrases, relaxation training, and thermal biofeedback (Werder, 1978); self-hypnosis and thermal biofeedback (Olness & MacDonald, 1981); and relaxation training plus thermal biofeedback (Houts, 1982) also reported decreases in headache symptoms. Werder and Sargent (1984) used a combination of techniques, progressive relaxation, autogenic phrases, self-awareness, guided imagery, and EMG and thermal biofeedback with 31 children suffering from tension, migraine, or a combination of tension and migraine headaches. They noted an 87 percent decrease in medication used, a 39 percent decrease in mean tension headache hours reported per week, and a 71 percent decrease in mean migraine headache hours reported per week. Twenty-eight of the 31 children were able to control 51 percent or more of their headaches after a two-month training period. A one to three-year follow-up suggested continued reductions in headaches.

In a study using a controlled group outcome design, Labbe and Williamson (1984) assigned 28 childhood migraineurs (age 7 to 16) to either a waiting list or an autogenic thermal biofeedback treatment group in a two group by four phases repeated measures design. The results of this study suggest that children learned to increase their skin temperature only during those phases that presented the biofeedback data. Their data also suggests that the continued use of either biofeedback based home practice or in-office booster sessions were more useful in maintaining gains than simple autogenic practice without machine feedback.

A case study that looked at the EMG biofeedback treatment of an 11-year-old girl, who had been suffering with muscle tension headaches since she was 8-years-old, was presented by Andrasik, Blanchard, Edlund, and Attanasio (1983). After a nine-week baseline period, 12 sessions of EMG frontalis feedback over another 9 weeks was offered. Although the patient was described as "slow to respond to treatment," significant improvement in all headache measures were noted at termination of treatment and at a one year follow-up. The patient was reported to have practiced relaxation at home an average of 13.9 times per week during treatment, and 4.3 times per week at follow-up. Andrasik, Burke, Attanasio, and Rosenblum (1985) studied the headache reports of 53 children, only 5 of whom were reported as muscle contraction sufferers; the rest were migraineurs. Similarly, in the studies by Waranch and Keenan (1985) and by Werder and Sargent (1984), the majority of the children studied presented with migraines. Werder and Sargent, in comparing the migraine with tension headache sufferers, found that prior to treatment the tension headache subjects reported more headache hours a week than the migraineurs. The literature offers little else regarding either muscle contraction headache data or treatment studies with children.

Continued research with childhood headaches must focus upon controlled studies that look toward homogeneous patient samples and design techniques that can sequentially review the relative effectiveness of available treatment techniques. While anecdotal and case study material offer hopeful clinical techniques, continued controlled studies will make the office practice of biofeedback with childhood headache sufferers more sound. This is especially true because of the suggested negative side effects of the pharmacological management of headaches in children (Congdon & Forsythe, 1979) and the increasing referrals for biofeedback treatment from those who value the objective data upon which it is based (Andrasik & Attanasio, 1985).

Epilepsy has been a focus of biofeedback work since Sterman, LoPresti, and Fairchild (1969) were able to show that the production of sensorimotor rhythm (SMR) could delay the onset of drug induced seizure activity in cats. Work with adults in producing the 12 to 14 cycles per second rhythm over the sensorimotor cortex began with the training of a 23-year-old female epileptic who, with increased production of SMR, showed a dramatic decrease in seizures. As part of a series of case studies, Sterman, Macdonald, and Stone (1974) discussed the use of electroencephalographic (EEG) biofeedback in the treatment of a 6-year-old male epileptic who had various types of seizures and who was poorly controlled on medication. The training of SMR activity resulted in a gradual normalization of the child's EEG. Once training stopped, however, seizures returned until the SMR biofeedback was reinstated.

Finley, Smith, and Etherton (1975) reported the case of a 13-year-old male with a seizure disorder of 11 years' duration. He was experiencing up to 70 seizures per day according to his by parents' report. Biofeedback training of EEG was initially restricted to 12 HZ activity signaled to the patient by the illumination of a blue light and a tone. In order to motivate this mildly retarded and learning disabled child, he was able to earn a point for every 5 seconds of blue light and tone he produced. If he could accumulate a predetermined number of points during a session he was able to earn between one and three dollars. After a few sessions he was able to alter his 12 HZ EEG showing a sixfold increase. After three months of biofeedback training, his seizure rate was down to one per hour. At month three the procedure was changed so that a red light would turn on when serious epileptiform EEG activity was measured. This red light overrode the blue light, thus reducing the patient's chances to earn money. The patient quickly learned to suppress these EEG abnormalities with a resultant marked improvement in his EEG (reduction in amplitude of slow wave abnormalities, reduction of paroxysms). Introduction of a 7 week period of noncontingent feedback led to an increase in seizure activity. In a follow-up study, Finley (1976) reported an improvement in seizure activity with a return to biofeedback based reinforcement of a normalized EEG.

Additional studies of SMR biofeedback with various subjects report decreases in seizure activity after training. Six epileptic adolescents (12 to 19 years of age), refractory to medical management, were trained in SMR production with five of the six showing improvement (Seifert & Lubar, 1975). In a population of retarded adolescents with refractory seizures, Lubar and Bahler (1976) used both SMR production and epileptiform feedback (of abnormal EEG activity) to increase normalization of EEG activity and to decrease seizures.

As with the headache literature, and although the treatment of epilepsy with biofeedback is bioelectronically the most sophisticated, the majority of the studies published are no more than a series of single-case studies lacking in scientific rigor (Finley, 1983). Regarding children, Andrasik and Attanasio (1985) note that it is often the youngest child in a given sample reported that has the most difficulty with the EEG training. This raises the issue of motivational problems in EEG training per se. Additionally, although SMR training has anecdotally been found to decrease reported seizures, it is possible that the inadvertent training of decreases in epileptiform activity might account for improvement. Finley (1983) focuses upon the normalization of the EEG as a constant feature found in those patients who respond well to biofeedback training for seizures. The results of power spectral analysis of the EEG, continues Finley, deemphasizes SMR and emphasizes EEG normalization as a focus of treatment. Such training of the suppression of abnormal high voltage, slow wave frequencies, and the augmentation of all fast frequencies for which the untrained epileptic EEG is abnormally deficient, says Finley, may be particularly suitable for children given the view that the central nervous system of the young is particularly plastic and malleable. Although further controlled research is needed in this area to better describe the clinical protocols for the biofeedback treatment of epileptic children, it is useful to note that the ability to control one's EEG and to suppress seizures may contribute to the improvement of self-esteem and to an increase in independence in those whose disability often results in poor emotional adjustment (Andrasik & Attanasio, 1985).

Asthma is one of the most widespread and potentially devastating disorders of childhood, with estimates of prevalence upwards of 23 percent of all children (Finley, 1983). The treatment of asthma has received more attention than any other psychophysiological disorder (Andrasik & Attanasio, 1985). Asthma can be defined as the intermittent, variable, and reversible obstruction of the airway (Scadding, 1966). While the exact etiology of the disorder is unknown, a group of possible causal factors include unsuspected bronchial infection, inhaled allergens, psychological phenomena (personality or character disturbances, normal excitement, anger, or fear), parasympathetic overactivity, hypothalamic depression, decreased adrenal cortex response, epileptic foci, both classical and operant conditioning to various stimuli, or a combination of all of the above (Finley, 1983; Andrasik & Attanasio, 1985).

Medical management continues to be the treatment of choice for the asthmatic child. Most physicians, however, advise the child to remain calm during an attack. It is commonly known that emotional factors are often the precipitants of an attack and the fear/anxiety experienced during an episode can exacerbate the bronchial muscle constriction, thus making already labored respiration more difficult. The use of biofeedback training for asthma relief is based upon the clinical observations that have shown that relaxation will alleviate wheezing and other respiratory symptoms. Training has focused upon either frontalis EMG training to bring about generalized relaxation or specific airway resistance feedback training to improve airflow into and out of the lungs.

Davis, Saunders, Creer, and Chai (1973) placed 24 children into one of three treatment groups: Jacobsonian relaxation training with frontal EMG biofeedback, relaxation training alone, or no treatment control group wherein subjects were given reading material and asked to relax. Peak expiratory air flow was measured before and after each training session. For the less severe asthmatics, airflow measures were significantly improved with the combined relaxation and biofeedback experience. The other groups showed no significant changes. The changes that were noted were not sustained at follow-up. Because of the confounding of treatments, the differential effectiveness of the EMG training alone could not be ascertained in this study. A study by Scherr, Crawford, Sergent, and Scherr (1975) replicated the Davis et al. (1973) study and found that such additional measures as medication taken and the actual number of asthma attacks experienced by the treatment group subjects decreased while positive changes in airflow increased. Methodological problems, however, restrict the generalizability of that study.

Similar experimental control problems soften the results of Miklich et al. (1977) who combined a systematic desensitization approach with EMG biofeedback. First, children constructed a hierarchy of items focusing upon the anxiety experience associated with asthma. They were then taught Jacobsonian relaxation skills. Some clinicians chose to use frontalis biofeedback to reinforce relaxation. Once the child learned relaxation as reflected by a predetermined EMG criterion, desensitization was begun by having the child imagine the hierarchy items on a graduated basis while remaining relaxed. This was designed to replace the anxiety response to the imagined asthma experience with physiological relaxation. Nineteen asthmatic children received this treatment while seven others continued in their regular medical regimes, serving as a control. Dependent measures included medication use, need for hospitalization, frequency of asthma attacks, and forced expiratory volume. Only this last variable differed at the conclusion of treatment and at follow-up. This was due, in most part, to the control group becoming sicker rather than to an improvement per se in the experimental group. Further review of individual cases, however, showed some improvement in some of those who actually received biofeedback as part of their relaxation training. The lack of controls in this study precludes any understanding of the relative import of the biofeedback training to these children.

Two studies designed to measure the effects of EMG directly on pulmonary functioning offer more support for the frontalis EMG work with asthmatic children. Kotses, Glaus, Crawford, Edwards, and Scherr (1976) assigned 36 asthmatic children to a contingent feedback, noncontingent feedback, or control group. Using a yoking procedure, the contingent subjects received veridical feedback based upon their actual facial EMG levels while the noncontingent subjects were fed the data from a yoked contingent subject, thus receiving no actual data on their own musculature. This design permits the study of any placebo factors due to participation in a biofeedback experience. Only the contingent feedback group showed significant decreases in forehead tension; they were the only ones to show improvement in their peak expiratory flow ratings. In a subsequent study (Kotses, Glaus, Bricel, Edwards, & Crawford, 1978), subjects were assigned to four groups: contingent or noncontingent forehead EMG (as above), or contingent or noncontingent feedback from another muscle, the brachioradialis. Similar yoking procedures between the contingent and noncontingent groups were used as in the 1976 study. Only veridical feedback from the forehead muscles led to significant improvement in pulmonary functioning. Andrasik and Attanasio (1985) suggest that the results of the frontalis EMG studies with asthmatics find that EMG training has considerable promise. Questions remain as to the long term carryover of this training and as to whether EMG training is helpful for patients other than the less severely impaired.

Actual biofeedback information measuring airway parameters has also been used in treatment of asthmatic children. Herein, children were given feedback on actual forced expirator volume (Khan, Staerk, & Bonk, 1973; Khan, 1977). Actual bronchial dilatation or constriction was reflected in the amount of air exhaled during a 1-second period. A light came on (the feedback) when a criterion of forced expiratory volume was reached. Once the child used this feedback successfully to self-induce relaxation of the bronchial tubes, bronchoconstriction was induced and the child had to abort the bronchospasms associated with the wheezing of an attack. Pre- and postdifferences on all clinical variables (emergency room visits, hospitalizations, medication amounts) showed significant improvement for those subjects receiving the forced expiratory volume biofeedback training program.

Feldman (1976) studied the training of lower respiratory resistance in the treatment of asthmatic children. By lowering a tone, four severely asthmatic children were given feedback on "breathing better." After 3 to 10 training sessions of lowering total respiratory resistance, each lasting between 5 and 10 minutes, the children showed significantly improved total respiratory resistance and maximum midexpiratory air flow. These observed improvements were approximately equal to pulmonary function increases due to a therapeutic dose of Isoproterenol. Feldman concluded that severe asthmatics can learn to lower airway resistance in a brief biofeedback training program.

While continued controlled research is necessary, Finley (1983) and Andrasik and Attanasio (1985) believe that clinical biofeedback will become a primary tool in the treatment of childhood asthma.

Learning problems and hyperactivity have been the primary focus of remedial biofeedback in the educational setting (Andrasik & Attanasio, 1985). While comparing the ability of 30 learning disabled (LD) and 30 normal children to learn thermal biofeedback skills, Hunter, Russell, Russell, and Zimmerman (1976) found that the LD children were able to learn the skill better and were more successful overall than the normal children. The major difference was that the LD children showed a slower response acquisition than the normal children. However, no changes in standardized tests measuring learning were noted. A conclusion reached was that given the difficulties that many learning disabled children have in concentrating, biofeedback may offer a focus and may decrease interference. In a pilot study and then in a larger experimental study, Russell and Carter (1978) report that forearm EMG training was used successfully to teach relaxation to learning disabled children. Posttraining achievement test scores indicated increases related to increased concentration and increases in the ability to learn. Parents and teachers were described as reporting improvements in self-control, distractibility, and conscientiousness. Andrasik and Attanasio (1985) report that in two additional reports, Carter and Russell found that EMG training of learning disabled children improved their academic performance. Additionally, at a 1 year follow-up, those children who received biofeedback training maintained or improved their academic performance, while those who did not receive the training showed no change across time.

Electroencephalographic (EEG) feedback has also been utilized in working with learning disabled children. Cunningham and Murphy (1981) and O'Malley and Connors (1972) found minimal academic effects of having learning disabled adolescents learn to differentially influence cortical hemisphere EEG patterns. In contrast, Gracenin and Cook (1977) taught alpha-enhancement biofeedback skills to learning disabled children and found that they all improved in reading comprehension and in maladaptive behaviors. Andrasik and Attanasio (1985) report two studies using EEG feedback conducted by Carter and Russell. Given that verbal tasks enhance alpha production on the right hemisphere and that spatial tasks produce the opposite effect (Ornstein, 1973), Carter and Russell proposed that the verbal and performance discrepancy of learning disabled children, often seen on the Wechsler Intelligence Scale for Children (Revised), might reflect discrepancies in hemispheric activity. Individuals with low verbal scores given left hemisphere training showed increases in verbal scores and no performance score increases. Those with low verbal scores given right hemisphere training were found to show no increases in performance or verbal scores. On the other hand, those with low performance scores given right hemisphere training showed performance score increases and no verbal changes. Those with low performance scores given the left hemisphere training showed no changes on either measure. Andrasik and Attanasio (1985) conclude that this relationship between hemisphere specificity and learning has either potential treatment or educational remediation implications for learning disabled children.

Hyperactivity, hyperkinesis, or attention deficit disorder with hyperactivity has received much attention in the biofeedback literature (Finley, 1983; Andrasik & Attanasio, 1985). Characterized in the DSM III (American Psychiatric Association, 1980), the hyperactivity dimension of attention deficit disorder includes two of the following: excessive running or climbing about, difficulty sitting still or fidgeting, difficulty staying seated, excessive movement during sleep, and always being on the go. Three theories of the etiology of hyperkinesis, overarousal, underarousal, and hypoinhibitory are reviewed by Finley (1983). Research concerning and treatment of the hyperactive child has focused upon EMG and EEG biofeedback training.

Braud, Lupin, and Braud (1975) present the case study of a six-and-a-half-year-old hyperactive boy. After 11 training sessions of frontalis EMG, increases in learning ability test scores, self-concept, and frustration tolerance were noted along with decreases in somatic complaints and disruptive behavior. Similarly, Hampstead (1979), Omizo (1980), and Omizo and Williams (1981) report equally successful academic and behavioral improvements of hyperactive children receiving EMG training. In a study by Haight, Jampolsky, and Irvine (1976), children receiving EMG feedback showed a decrease in their hyperactivity despite no significant decrease in EMG frontalis measures.

In comparing the relative effectiveness of biofeedback training to relaxation training without feedback, Jeffrey and Hayes (1978) concluded that at follow-up the biofeedback group showed significant decreases in amphetamine usage while Braud (1978) concluded that progressive relaxation was equally as useful as biofeedback in working with hyperactive children.

The EEG training of sensorimotor rhythm (SMR) to control the motor activity of hyperactive children was presented in a series of case studies by Lubar and Shouse (1976, 1977) and by Shouse and Lubar (1979). In their earliest study of an 11-year-old hyperactive child, they found that SMR training was correlated with increments of cooperativeness and schoolwork and with decrements in time out-of-seat and undirected behaviors. In the 1979 study, four severely hyperactive children were studied. Again, those able to learn the SMR skills showed classroom behavior improvement. The combination of SMR training and medication (Ritalin) was more effective in producing changes than medication alone. A 10-year-old hyperactive boy was treated with a combination of SMR and EMG biofeedback by Tansey and Bruner (1983). Academic skills improved and overactivity and distractibility decreased after the training.

Andrasik and Attanasio (1985) conclude that the use of biofeedback training as part of treatment programs for children with learning problems seems warranted. Both the increases in attention or concentration skills and the increases in self-efficacy that biofeedback training engenders are useful to the learning disabled and/or hyperactive child.

Shellenberger and Green caution the reader when critically reviewing biofeedback research. They suggest that " . . . biofeedback research has lacked clear and appropriate conceptualizations and has lacked appropriate experimental design" (1986, p. 1). In short, before one can conclude that a research protocol's results or that a case study's outcome are supportive or damaging to biofeedback's credibility, the actual biofeedback training reported must have been shown to have taught the subject(s) mastery of the physiological parameter(s) in question. Without such training to mastery, little can be said of the effectiveness of the procedures used. This caution is useful both for the researcher and for the clinician who are planning to use biofeedback in routine practice.

TECHNIQUE

The application of biofeedback principles involves the "constant monitoring of one or more physiological processes via electronic instrumentation, and . . . external feedback of these processes and subsequent changes in them, which permits the person to learn strategies that enable control of these processes" (Andrasik & Attanasio, 1985, p. 242). It is the mastery of physiology, cognitions, and behavior (transfer of training) that are the goals of successful biofeedback training (Shellenberger & Green, 1986).

Before the therapeutic monitoring and training to mastery can begin, a complete understanding of each patient's presenting complaints and history must be established. Biofeedback is clearly a treatment included under the general field of behavioral medicine and the majority of disorders treated by biofeedback are medical in nature (Olton & Noonberg, 1980). As such, initiation of biofeedback treatment should begin only after the patient has been seen by the primary care physician. While this is obviously true for such complaints as headaches, epilepsy, stomach disorders, or respiratory problems, even anxiety disorders should be reviewed by a physician to rule out possible endocrinological or other physical causes. With a (relatively) clean bill of physical health, biofeedback treatment can proceed.

Several things can be done to smooth the transition into treatment, prior to the child's and parents' arrival for biofeedback training. It can be beneficial to offer referral sources a brief description of the biofeedback process. Such a description serves to educate these sources about the utility of biofeedback. This can help them offer information about the nature of biofeedback to children and their parents. It can alleviate potential negative anticipation of the treatment. Green (1983) suggests referring to the therapist as the biofeedback teacher. An attempt to demedicalize the procedure by referral agents, minimal reference to machines, and assurance that no needles are involved helps to reduce potential anxiety. This reassurance is especially useful if the biofeedback therapist happens to be located in a hospital setting where the negative anticipation often runs high.

Biofeedback therapy can be thought of as occurring in four phases: intake, treatment, termination, and follow-up (Fuller, 1977).

Intake

During the initial intake session Olton and Noonberg (1980) suggest the following goals:

1. Description of the client's problems
2. Medical and psychological history
3. Discussion of the rationale and procedure used for biofeedback treatment
4. Demonstration and/or practice of the biofeedback techniques to be used
5. Psychophysiological profile of the client when stressed
6. Psychophysiological profile of the client when relaxed
7. Establishment of procedures for recording symptoms and other data
8. Specification of a treatment program for the client, the procedures to be followed, and an outline of the results sought

With children as the focus of the treatment, it becomes necessary to collect the relevant symptomatological and historical data from both the child and the parent. Initially, this should be done separately in order to avoid the possibility of each respondent influencing the other. Given the nature of the etiology of some psychophysiological disorders, this separate history taking followed by a shared time to compare stories can often elucidate material lost in denial by either parents or child of any psychological or environmental stressors.

Data that help the clinician understand the exact nature of the complaint are a primary goal. Subjective descriptions of site in the body, frequency, intensity, and duration of each episode are of prime importance. At this point, some authors suggest the use of standardized psychological testing or adjective checklists to further enhance the diagnostic overview (Olton & Noonberg, 1980; Fuller, 1977).

A clear picture of trigger events including environmental or interpersonal stressors is necessary. This can be elicited by utilizing the following outline, remembering that historic data are subject to censoring and memory loss that can distort information. The use of separate and joint histories presented by child, parents, and parents with child can enhance data collection.

1. What do the child and parents understand about why they have come to you? Questioning should elicit their understanding of biofeedback, psychotherapy, the mind/body interplay, and their goals and wishes about their up-

coming treatment. If the referral comes from another health care professional, you can often learn how that professional perceives your work and what expectations were imparted to your new patient(s).

2. When did the symptoms first appear? This question should include specific information regarding life changes for the child, parent(s), or family. Does the initial symptom differ from the present complaints? Do changes in symptom reflect any direct or indirect attempts of the child to manipulate his environment?

3. During the average day or week (depending on the form, the complaint, or the history-taking ability of the respondent):

   a. How often does the symptom occur?

   b. How long does each episode last?

   c. How severe were the symptoms on the average? Families often have formulated their own rating systems of severity, say 0 to 5, with 0 meaning no headache and 5 meaning most severe headache. If they have not constructed such a system, then asking them to use a 0 to 5 schedule helps concretize the subjective complaints. Again, the separate history taking can often raise issues to be discussed around perception of severity of symptoms.

   d. What is usually done about the symptoms? This includes routine medical management or home remedies including self- or family-taught relaxation skills. Some children have been told to use Lamaze relaxation exercises. Knowing what has worked and what has not is useful in treatment planning. Similarly, how quick parents are to seek medical intervention or to give prescribed or over-the-counter medication may offer some indication as to how supportive they may be of the biofeedback regime.

   e. Specific antecedents? What are the circumstances at the onset of symptoms? This includes a review of the week leading up to each episode, as well as the immediate circumstances. Who is around and what has the child been doing for the days preceding the problem? This should include behavioral, affective, interpersonal, and dietary influences.

   f. Consequences? Who responds and how do they respond to each episode? Are there consistent operant reinforcers noted? Are there any functional or secondary gain dimensions that are detectable? Does the child consistently fail to carry out some activity as a result of the symptoms?

   g. Are any patterns noted? Are there time, event, or people interaction patterns that can usually (retrospectively at this point) predict symptom occurrence?

This type of detailed history taking is useful in a number of ways. First, it provides a baseline against which the treatment can be compared. Second, it is hoped that trigger events can be noted and further historical or psychotherapeutic exploration of those events can take place if necessary. Finally, this detailed eliciting of information actually trains the patient and the family to look for the type of data that, until this point, they may have ignored, not thought relevant, or found to be too psychologically uncomfortable to note.

A technique useful in formulating biofeedback treatment is that of the BASIC ID as described by Lazarus (1981, p. 15). A shorthand structure for organizing both diagnostic and treatment planning data, the BASIC ID reminds the therapist that the patient presents with a broad spectrum of issues surrounding the presenting complaint. The multimodal foci are: B—behavior; A—affect; S—sensation; I—imagery; C—cognitions; I—interpersonal issues; and D—drugs and biology. The following profile offers a summary of the data describing Luke (see the beginning of this chapter) after the initial intake:

Behavior:	Behaving in sick role
	Withdrawal
	Works very hard in school
Affect:	Frustrated with headaches
	Happy
	Fears failure
Sensation:	Unable to relax
	Tense
	Headache pain with nausea
	Fatigue
Imagery:	Images of days before headaches
	Images of being Cy Young Award winner
	Images of attending Ivy League college
Cognitions:	Worries about not doing well in school
	Very intelligent
	Recent problems concentrating in math
	Thoughts of disappointing dad
Interpersonal:	Describes good homelife
	Many friends at school (class officer)
	Recent withdrawal socially
	Missing school often (recently)
Drugs/biological:	Migraine headache diagnosis
	No other physical problems at this time
	Medication:
	Receiving Fiorinal, p.r.n.
	Recent d/c of Dilantin

Once a detailed diagnostic understanding of the child and his presenting symptoms is obtained, demonstration of biofeedback treatment per se can begin.

Preparation for Biofeedback Training

It is clear that relationship variables inherent in any therapeutic activity also hold for biofeedback (Taub, 1977; Suter, Fredericson, & Portuesi, 1983). While the content of the biofeedback sessions may be perceived by some as cut-and-dried physiological measurements, there is still the process of the interpersonal relationship between therapist and patient to foster. Additionally, the therapist should continue to be aware of the psychological processes occurring within the patient and within other family members (Shellenberger & Green, 1986).

The initial rationale offered to the child and the family for the biofeedback treatment can set the tone for the duration of the relationship. The initial demonstration to the child of the biofeedback equipment should be done with the parents out of the consulting room—if the child permits this. The normal physiological arousal of meeting the biofeedback equipment for the first time, plus the stress of performing the biofeedback exercises in front of one's parents can often cause the child to do poorly. Once children have learned some skills they are usually excited to show their parents the new accomplishment. Care must be taken to tell both child and parent that performance is usually not very good at first in front of an audience in order to minimize disappointment or skepticism.

Attanasio et al. (1985) list several strategies for ameliorating children's possible apprehension of biofeedback treatment. These include a careful explanation of procedures and a demonstration of equipment. They suggest limiting any humorous references to the electric chair or to electric shock. All electrodes should be referred to as sensors or pickups. Finally, they have found it useful to show a videotaped biofeedback session to child and parents to acquaint them with procedures.

Children seem to have few, if any, doubts about the biofeedback equipment or about the possibility that it will help them. Attanasio et al. (1985) suggest that this may be the function of children's exposure to the media that shows them both the science fiction and science fact of physiological self-control. Additionally, children, as a function of their age, present with less chronic problems and with a shorter history of treatment failures than adults. As with Attanasio et al. (1985), our experience has found that biofeedback is often offered to children earlier in the natural history of their problems than it has been to adults. This is a function of the sensitivity of physician referral sources to the clinical utility of biofeedback and parents' and physicians' reluctance to engage in more extensive medical or pharmacological treatments of children until something more conservative has been tried.

A clear discussion with the child at the child's intellectual or developmental level concerning how the biofeedback experience will affect their body and how that effect will transfer outside the consulting room and help them control their symptoms is of utmost importance. It is this understanding that helps motivate the child to learn and to practice the exercises. Working with the child alone and then having the child explain to the parents how biofeedback will help is useful in several ways. First, it reinforces the knowledge through verbal practice. Second, it helps the therapist assess the child's level of understanding. Third, it helps the therapist to see the parent-child interaction around the issue and to look for ways to assist the parents in supporting the treatment. Finally, and perhaps most importantly, it helps the child begin to develop that initial sense of self-control or mastery of his body that is sought through the biofeedback training itself.

Green (1983), in the clinical role of the biofeedback teacher, introduces biofeedback to children through seven basic ideas: the mind-body team, stress response, "your symptom," blood flow and stress, relaxation, information feedback and learning, and practice and learning new habits. In a research protocol, Labbe and Williamson (1984) followed a similar series of introductory remarks to teach biofeedback concepts to children. The following introductory statements are based upon the techniques I have found useful for both adolescents and children. These are modified, of course, based upon the individual's level of intellectual maturity:

Things that you think about can have an affect on the way your body feels and works. For example, how would you feel if (softly) after we sat here calmly for a while, talking quietly like we have been talking, [loudly] I told you that a bear had just walked into the office? That's right, you'd jump. Notice anything else about your body? Is your stomach jumping, has your breathing gotten faster? I bet your heart is even beating faster. See how your thinking, your imagination, made you jump.

I'll show you another example of how powerful your mind is. Up until right now you haven't noticed that you can hear the sound of the air conditioning vent humming. Now that I point it out, you hear it. It has always been there but your mind, your thoughts, were on something else. Up until now you haven't noticed the feeling of the chair you are sitting on pressing on your body. Now that I point it out, you can notice it. Up until now your thinking, your mind, was busy with something else so you haven't felt the chair until I reminded you of it.

Biofeedback can work in a similar manner. We can help to train your mind in a way to help your body relax [reduce your headaches, help your breathing, etc.]. When your body is stressed, your symptoms get worse. [The physiology and psychophysiology of the symptom is briefly described. Using a cartoon [see Figure 7.2], for example, is useful in working with children. The example shown is the migraine headache explanation.] For example, when you are going to do something you have never done before, you might get "cold feet." Have you ever heard that term? Well, when we are under stress our blood vessels tighten up. When they close down like that there is less blood flowing near the surface of our body and we feel cooler. Uptight equals cooler. Look at the little man in the cartoon when he is stressed out. He runs over and closes the blood vessel. When he has been uptight too long he becomes exhausted and he crashes. When that happens the blood vessel control valve is unattended and it pops too wide

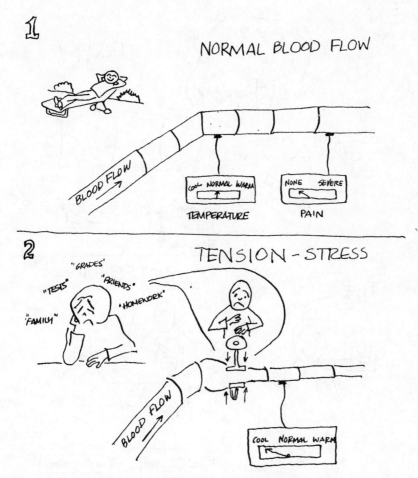

Figure 7.2. A cartoon used in teaching children about the vascular constriction-dilatation cycle in migraines. (From an idea by R.H. Rozensky, as drawn by S.M. Tovian.)

open. Bang, you get a migraine with that throbbing feeling and pain as the blood flows through the too wide open blood pipe.

What we are going to learn to do with our biofeedback is to teach that little person inside you how to keep that blood vessel open when he is stressed out. In that way, by staying relaxed, the blood pipes stay normally open during stress and don't slam shut. Keeping them normally open will keep the next day's headaches away because we will help that little person inside of you from tensing up too much, closing the blood vessels down, and tiring himself out. That way, you will learn to control your blood flow and keep the blood vessels from popping open and causing pain.

The biofeedback machine will act like a very fancy thermometer. It will tell you your skin temperature. It will tell you your temperature so accurately that you will learn to raise your temperature and keep the blood vessels normally open under stressful times. After learning to relax using some of the special skills I will

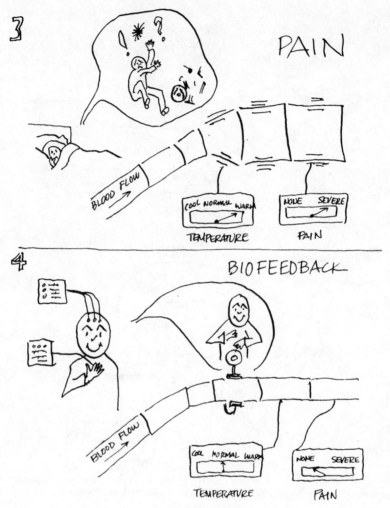

Figure 7.2 (*Continued*)

teach you, you will accomplish this. [Explain briefly the relaxation techniques to be taught.] The biofeedback machine will be your window to how well you are learning your relaxation skills. It will take time to learn these new skills, but you will be surprised how quickly you will learn to warm yourself. Many of your friends won't even believe that you have learned to open up your blood vessels to keep tomorrow's headache away. This is like learning anything new, the more you practice this new skill, the quicker you will be able to succeed in keeping your headache away. The more you practice, the better you will be at doing your relaxation.

After this introduction, questions can be answered and the introduction to the relaxation exercises can occur.

During the introductory phase of treatment, parents often ask how long the treatment program will take. Sharing with them both the data from the research literature and your own clinical experiences with children presenting with the same problems is useful. Use of graphs that display symptom intensity changes across weeks for the modal patient is helpful to both the child and the parent in understanding the expected course and duration of the treatment (see Figure 7.4, p. 222, for example). It is important at this time to explain to both the parents and the child that the understanding of any possible psychological aspects of the situation may be part of the treatment and that, if necessary, treatment may segue into a psychotherapeutic interaction without equipment. This must be presented to all concerned in a manner that they can understand and that will not attack individual or familial defenses that the somatic problems may have grown to support.

Treatment

The choice of a specific treatment regime should be based upon the specific problem presented. As the patient is helped to gain control over that specific physiological function, the patient is also being taught to achieve, maintain, and produce a general state of relaxation at will (Fuller, 1977). The choice of the biofeedback instrumentation to monitor and feed back the physiological data should be made so that it measures the disordered function as closely as possible. Fuller (1977, p. 31) suggests the following physiological measures and the problems they reflect or help manage:

EMG (electromyograph):	General relaxation
	Tension headache/neck and back pain
	Bruxism/temporomandibular join syndrome
	Cerebral Palsy
	Essential hypertension
	Anxiety reduction
	Phobic desensitization
	Neuromuscular reeducation/stroke
Peripheral skin temperature:	Migraine headaches
	Raynaud's disease/peripheral vascular
	Asthma/hypertension
	Resistance (in psychotherapy)
GSR (Galvanic skin response):	Asthma
	Stuttering
	Systematic desensitization
	Guided imagery/exploration
EEG (electroencephalography):	Epilepsy
	Insomnia
	Pain reduction
	Concentration/reading disorders

Once the proper measurement tool is chosen, the child is connected to the biofeedback equipment. Attanasio et al. (1985) point out that standard adult placement of electrodes do not always yield clear signals from children. Placement of EMG electrodes, for example, may need to be positioned more closely for children. The advantage of thermal feedback is the ease of placement of the thermistor on the distal portion of the child's finger. Valid and reliable measurement across sessions is assured with accurate and consistent placement of sensors. Within-session validity is enhanced with attention paid to encouraging the child to remain calm, thus decreasing movement artifacts (Attanasio et al., 1985).

The child's initial experiences with the biofeedback equipment chosen should be successful. Such perception of success should facilitate the learning of biofeedback skills (Holroyd et al., 1984). It is often easier to show a child how to increase physiological arousal than how to decrease it. Raising EMG frontalis measurement can be accomplished simply by having the child raise the eyebrows. The child can quickly see that this increase in tension is reflected in the changes displayed by the biofeedback equipment. Similarly, having the child image that the bear, or the Frankenstein monster, has just walked into the office can quickly produce noticeable GSR or skin temperature changes. Once the child understands that tension or imagination can produce changes in the body, as reflected by the machine, training of relaxation responses can begin.

The mode of feedback should be reinforcing to the child. The saliency of both the presentation of relaxation techniques and the actual data fed back to the child has been focused upon by several authors (Attanasio et al., 1985; Rozensky & Pasternak, 1985). The use of concrete and interesting images was shown to enhance biofeedback responses in six children with headaches who were initially resistant to treatment (Rozensky & Pasternak, 1985). It is common practice to have the patient adjust the pitch, tone, repetition rate, and volume of auditory feedback and the hue, brightness, or intensity of visual feedback. However, Attanasio et al. (1985) suggest that the typical feedback displays (i.e., voltmeter, digital readout, or light bars) most often used with adults are not inherently reinforcing or useful in maintaining children's attention. They suggest the use of computer graphics displays that can be varied across trials as helpful in maintaining interest and motivation as an alternative. They also offer the use of concrete reinforcers (trinkets, toys, money) as a possible additional technique to augment the feedback signal. However, after a series of over 151 children and adolescents treated by three different psychologists at the Evanston Hospital, the use of typical visual and auditory feedback was found to maintain interest and motivation. What does seem to need to be addressed when formulating the child's individual treatment plan is the child's idiosyncratic response to the feedback stimuli available. Flexibility of feedback modalities is of obvious usefulness.

Introduction to Relaxation Techniques

Once the proper equipment is chosen, the feedback stimuli specified and the excitatory responses demonstrated, relaxation techniques can be taught. As with the immediate success of the excitatory response mentioned above, care should be taken to help the child find some immediate success in seeing the relaxation responses reflected on the equipment. No research exists to date to specify the best technique to use in beginning to teach biofeedback relaxation skills to children. The approach should be chosen from the wide range of techniques available and should be tailored by the therapist's skills and the child's response style.

Olton and Noonberg (1980) list autogenic training, progressive relaxation and the relaxation response approaches as variants of biofeedback training methods.

Autogenic training begins with a series of six statement groups wherein the patient concentrates upon verbal cues that are repeated out loud or silently. The exercises begin with muscle relaxation and go on to focus upon increasing peripheral blood flow, lowering heart rate and respiration, relaxing the upper abdominal cavity, and general sedation and drowsiness. The statements are initially repeated by the therapist or patient, held mentally for 30 to 60 seconds and practiced thrice daily for five minutes. Such statements as "my right arm is heavy . . . my left arm is heavy . . . " induce heaviness in the extremities and muscular relaxation. Warmth in the extremities is enhanced with a series of statements beginning with "my right arm is warm" and ending with "my arms and legs are heavy and warm." Cardiac and respiratory rates are controlled with statements such as "heartbeat calm and regular," "breathing calm and regular." Concentrating on "my solar plexus is warm" fosters abdominal warmth while "my forehead is cool" enhances drowsiness and calming (Schultz & Luthe, 1969).

Progressive relaxation utilizes a series of instructions to first contract and hold tense a muscle group, followed by a period of relaxation of that muscle. A patient is trained to progressively relax a series of 16 muscle groups by following this procedure. Bernstein and Borkovec (1973) suggest a sequence when focusing upon each muscle group: attention is focused upon the muscle group, at a predetermined signal from the therapist the muscle is contracted, tension is maintained for five to seven seconds, tension is released at a predetermined cue while the patient's attention is focused upon the muscle group as it relaxes. Their suggested sequence of muscle groups is: dominant hand and forearm, dominant biceps, nondominant hand and forearm, nondominant biceps, forehead, upper cheeks and nose, lower cheeks and jaws, neck and throat, chest, shoulders and upper back, abdominal or stomach region, dominant thigh, dominant calf, dominant foot, nondominant thigh, nondominant calf, and nondominant foot. This type of relaxation training is useful in providing a very guided and controlled introduction to relaxation to a child who has difficulty in concentrating on less structured techniques.

The relaxation response technique involves having the patient repeat a word silently while concentrating on it (Benson, 1975). This variant of yoga is designed to block any distracting thoughts as the cue word captures the person's consciousness (Olton & Noonberg, 1980). While seated (not lying down), the patient repeats the word on each exhalation. With practice, the person should be able to decrease all metabolic activity (Beary & Benson, 1974). Breathing should be relaxed, quiet, and regular. Benson suggests that the word "one" is a sufficient focus given a quiet environment, comfortable position, and a passive attitude. As in most relaxation techniques, this quiet attitude must be reinforced by the therapist as the child is told that he can take his time to learn the skills.

Cautela and Groden (1978) offer an illustrated manual with specific instructions for various relaxation techniques for both adults and children. Green (1983) offers a range of child-oriented relaxation techniques to specifically facilitate biofeedback training. One technique called "Guess your tension," uses the placement of EMG electrodes on the forearm while asking the child to guess when their flexed muscle registers 10 microvolts. Herein, after six to eight trials, children learn that their own bodies are good biofeedback machines that, if paid attention to, can accurately tell them how tense they are.

Breathing instructions (Green, 1983) involve having the child lying on the floor, one hand on the chest, one on the abdomen. These instructions ask children to imagine that they are breathing into the lower hand while the lungs fill like balloon. In relaxed breathing, the lower hand should move while the upper hand remains quiet.

Body scan instructions tell the child "with the power of your mind, put your attention into the bottoms of your feet" (Green, 1983, p. 131). The child is then instructed to progressively move upward, feeling each body area and pausing at tension areas to breathe slowly and to relax that area.

The "limp rag doll" technique involves asking children to pretend to be limp dolls. They are to pretend that they have no bones, no muscles. You can see how relaxed they are by picking up their limbs (Green, 1983).

Green (1983) also suggests that the use of imagery techniques as imagination is the child's forte. If you ask children about their favorite spot in the world, their quietest place, or their most relaxing image, they can often spontaneously imagine themselves there and begin relaxing. If necessary, guiding their imagery can help them recreate for themselves their most comfortable place (real or imagined). I have found the warm bath, floating on a raft in a warm pool, sitting on the beach, or in "your bedroom" as very common and useful relaxation cues. Several children have been able to reference their blanket or favorite stuffed animal when all else has failed.

Rather than use any single technique suggested, I have found that children seem to do best with a combination of techniques. Suggesting that they focus upon counting backwards or saying the alphabet is often useful in maintaining attention initially. Stressing the breathing instructions with the addition of visual imagery has been very successful.

> I want you to breathe slowly, like this (with demonstration). Each time you
> breathe in I want you to see a number. Let's start with 100. As you breathe out,
> the 100 will disappear. As you breathe in again, you will see the next number,

99. Decorate the number with designs or colors. Tell me which colors you see and what the design looks like (let child respond). Then, as you slowly breathe out, that number will disappear. As you breathe in again the next number will appear. I want you to repeat this slowly as you go from 100 down to zero.

Children seem to learn this technique quickly and have relatively immediate reinforcement via the biofeedback machine. "As you do this breathing and counting, the biofeedback machine will tell you that you are becoming more and more relaxed. Each time it beeps (for thermal; or as the beeping slows for EMG) you will know that your body is becoming more relaxed." If the equipment can be set so that no feedback is received if the child shows arousal and so that feedback is received upon relaxation, negative feedback and discouragement are minimized.

Homework and Expectations at Home

During the entire course of treatment, homework is assigned to each child. This includes thrice-daily relaxation practice. Midmorning, midafternoon, and midevening (not at bedtime) are suggested practice times. Often a note to the school nurse can provide a needed haven to which the child may go for a quiet practice session midday. Shellenberger and Green (1986) suggest that the failure to use homework practice of biofeedback relaxation skills (with or without a machine) accounts for many of the failures in biofeedback therapies and research. Children can easily understand that, as in school or on the sports field, practice builds mastery.

Formally reviewing progress with parents once every five weeks seems useful in assuring that they support the ongoing treatment and that they are comfortable with the treatment plan. Each week (or session), a brief discussion with the parents regarding progress is helpful especially if there is some concern about the veridicality of the child's self-report data.

Charting of symptom intensity, as well as practice sessions, is a necessity for monitoring progress across time. A typical homework chart for headaches is shown in Figure 7.3 (adapted from Stoelting-Cyborg, 1983). Use of the simple rating scale and x's for each five minutes of home practice seems to be easy enough to allow most children to keep their own records. I usually ask parents only to remind the child to practice relaxation and not to prompt symptom ratings or practice recordings at first. This gives children a sense that this is their own special activity. It also helps in assessing any resistance the child might have to treatment. If recordkeeping or relaxation practice flags, or if the child is too young to comply, parents are, of course, encouraged to help. The graphic presentation of the change in average symptom intensity across time is useful visual feedback both to parents and to children. According to Fordyce (1976), graphs have a direct reinforcing function, as well as offering a rapid and precise means of monitoring progress.

I remind parents and children that while biofeedback is new and different,

Home Record: Biofeedback Training for Headache

Name _____ Week of _____

HEADACHE INTENSITY		Mon	Tues	Wed	Thur	Fri	Sat	Sun
0. No headache								
1. Slight headache	Morning	___	___	___	___	___	___	___
2. Moderate head- ache								
3. Fairly severe headache	Afternoon	___	___	___	___	___	___	___
4. Very severe headache								
5. Most severe headache	Evening	___	___	___	___	___	___	___

AURA								
0. No signs that headache is coming	Morning	___	___	___	___	___	___	___
	Afternoon	___	___	___	___	___	___	___
1. Some sign that headache is coming	Evening	___	___	___	___	___	___	___

MEDICATION TAKEN								
Type 1 _____ __								
Name mg	Morning	___	___	___	___	___	___	___
	Afternoon	___	___	___	___	___	___	___
Type 2 _____ __								
Type 3 _____ __	Evening	___	___	___	___	___	___	___

PRACTICE								
(x = 5 minutes)	Morning	___	___	___	___	___	___	___
	Afternoon	___	___	___	___	___	___	___
	Evening	___	___	___	___	___	___	___

Figure 7.3. A sample "homework" chart for recording symptom intensity, medication usage, and relaxation practice.

it is not magical. They should not expect any major changes for the first few weeks although the more they practice at home the better skilled they will become. I especially ask parents not to encourage use of relaxation skills during symptom episodes in the early phases of treatment. I have found that it is difficult for children to be successful with distracting themselves from pain or discomfort until they become more skilled at their relaxation techniques. By avoiding this early potential failure with the techniques, both the child's and the parent's motivation are maintained.

Waranch and Keenan (1985) offered behavioral counseling as part of a treatment protocol for children with recurrent headaches. Children were encouraged to minimize complaints about symptoms, get their own medications, and practice relaxing. Parents were instructed to minimize attention given to the child's symptoms and to encourage follow-through with scheduled activities. Parents were also asked to minimize their own complaints of somatic symptoms (i.e., headaches) thus modeling coping behaviors to the child. This protocol, and others offered by Fordyce (1976), are useful in helping shape new, adaptive behaviors around symptoms.

Termination and Follow-Up

Criteria for terminating treatment should be established early on. This includes a decrease in presenting symptoms so that both child and parent are satisfied. Following symptom intensity graphically, based upon the child's self-report, is useful in monitoring progress and in evaluating outcome. Other variables such as medication usage, hospitalization, school and social activity attendance, and mood should be monitored. Possible psychological issues should be addressed prior to the decision to discontinue treatment. Again, this will assure that the biofeedback treatment will be successful (Shellenberger & Green, 1986).

There are no studies that specify the dosage of biofeedback training necessary to assure maximum treatment in general (Shellenberger & Green, 1986), let alone specifically for children. Termination should be based upon a clinically sound number of trials or sessions wherein the child can produce rapidly and consistently the physiological changes measured. It is the evidence of this continued self-regulatory skill at termination and at follow-up that we should witness as a measure of mastery. Treatment should be terminated only when such mastery is seen (Shellenberger & Green, 1986).

Treatment should be spaced out towards its end. Biweekly sessions, followed by a couple of once-a-month appointments, are useful. This allows the child to receive some booster sessions while assessing the strength of the transfer of learning.

It is important to explain to both the child and the parent the concept of spontaneous recovery. I usually state that:

As we decrease treatment it is not uncommon that the symptom will increase slightly. Don't panic. This is often a meaningful sign that the treatment has been effective and that decreasing biofeedback contact permits the symptom to reappear. Continue practicing as usual and the slight increase will go away quickly.

This is reassuring to child, parent, and therapist. Children will often come to a session and say, pointing to their record sheet, "See, here's where it (i.e., the headache) came back just like you said it would." This preparation serves as an inoculation that helps the family continue with the home practice while assuring them that they can overcome increases in symptoms on their own.

Both parents and children often ask if home relaxation practice should continue once office visits cease. I suggest continuing to practice on a once-a-day or on an as-needed basis. This becomes a lifestyle change—I point out that stress management will serve them well throughout their lives. Practicing relaxation briefly while the teacher is passing out an examination is a useful example of how continued practice will help them in stressful situations throughout life. Like piano playing, skating, reading, or math, continued relaxation practice keeps the skills sharpened.

CASE STUDIES

The Resistant Child

Treatment began with Luke (Rozensky & Pasternak, 1985) utilizing standard visual and tonal feedback using thermal biofeedback training. The Cyborg Thermal P642 unit with the thermistor attached to the distal portion of his right index finger was employed. Degrees Fahrenheit to the 100th place were displayed with a tone and a sequence of 10 lights indicating progress. No feedback was given when temperature fell. During baseline training, as digits on the machine reached 88.98, for example, progress would slow, stop, and temperature would fall. Luke began to ask, "How am I doing," "What's the highest you can get," and "can you get 100?" Attempts to distract Luke from watching his performance by using only auditory feedback, eyes closed, or machine turned away, was unsuccessful in helping with the relaxation training. Luke would count beeps, peek, or stop the proceedings and ask his score. "In order to defocus the subject from his achievement oriented, stress inducing, biofeedback resistant approach to hand warming, a technique was necessary that focused upon success through relaxation" (Rozensky & Pasternak, 1985, p. 11).

The *Star Wars* trilogy created by George Lucas is one of today's youths most well seen, read, and played out sagas. . . . In this story a young lad, Luke Skywalker, discovers his roots as a Jedi Knight and is first taught by Obi-Wan Kenobi the principles of The Force. In the movie *Star Wars* (Kurtz & Lucas, 1977), Obi-Wan Kenobi begins Luke's education in The Force by telling him:

"Get on with your exercises."

"Remember a Jedi can feel The Force flowing through him."

"Let go your conscious self and act on instinct."

"Stretch out with your feelings."

"You see, you can do it."

Later, when Luke must destroy the Death Star, but is obviously anxious and trying too hard, Obi-Wan says:

"Use The Force, Luke,"

"Let go, Luke."

"Luke, trust me."

"Remember, The Force will be with you always."

(Rozensky & Pasternak, 1985, p. 11)

Star Wars images in setting a scene and then using the above lines worked immediately and remarkably well to defocus Luke from his achievement orientation. Besides the lines listed above, other embellishments of story, cadence, and relaxation instructions were used. Once the scene was set, hand warming began immediately and he could relax with little interference. Luke's self-report of headaches reached zero within 3 weeks and remained there at a 7 month follow-up. Figure 7.4 shows Luke's (Subject #4) rapid course of treatment, as well as demographic information.

He returned to school and was without medication by the fourth week of treatment. During the last two sessions of biofeedback training, time was set aside to talk with Luke and his parents regarding his high need to achieve and the effects that his fear of failing had upon his physiology. This family was fast to see these connections and Luke's parents were helpful in encouraging his continued relaxation practice after termination of treatment. Five other overachieving young boys, initially resistant to biofeedback training, responded similarly to this technique by simply using their names in the place of Luke's.

This series of case examples illustrates that the use of biofeedback machines without an understanding of the child involved will lead to a stalemate. The machines and the feedback alone are not the curative agents.

In the case where an overachieving child is working too hard to overcome his score, using a metaphor can be helpful in overcoming the resistance to change. Gordon notes that stories through the ages " . . . all have as a constit-

TABLE I
HEADACHE HISTORY AND DEMOGRAPHIC & TREATMENT DATA

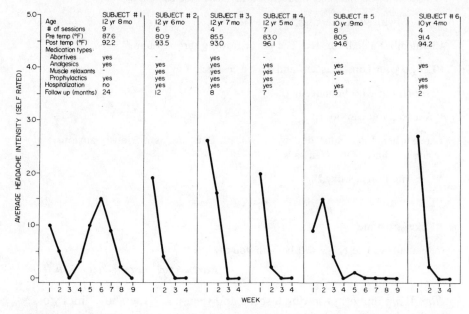

Figure 7.4. Headache rating reports for six children initially resistant to biofeedback training. Luke is subject #4.
Reprinted with permission from Rozensky, R.H., & Pasternak, J.F. (1985). Obi-Wan Kenobi, "the force," and the art of biofeedback: A headache treatment for overachieving young boys. *Clinical Biofeedback and Health, 8,* 9–13.

uent part the ability to convey a message or learning about a particular problem" (1978, p. 7). In utilizing the metaphor therapeutically, according to Gordon, the therapist can reframe the unwanted behavior and recast it as a potentially useful solution. In the *Star Wars* metaphor, the benevolent teacher shows the young knight how to use his own inner strength (self-regulation) to achieve a goal by not struggling with either internal or external resistance.

Three issues inherent in biofeedback training are illustrated by the resistant child. First, Franks (1982) suggests that biofeedback and psychotherapy are most effective when the patient's sense of mastery of self-efficacy is enhanced. This mastery is the core of the metaphor presented. Second, the person factor of the biofeedback therapist may be at work here (Taub, 1977; Suter, Fredericson, and Portuesi, 1983) as both the therapist's trustworthiness and enthusiasm were stressed and enhanced by identification with The Force. Finally, the use of concrete and interesting imagery (Kelton & Belar, 1983) may have been most important in helping these overachievers find something relaxing upon which to focus. The ability of biofeedback therapists to successfully use their understanding of the psychology of the patient as well as incorporating other therapeutic techniques can assure successful treatment.

The Case Where Biofeedback Is Not Enough

Beth was a 10-year-old girl with headache complaints that began after a successful hospitalization treatment of meningitis. Complaints included nausea, restlessness, and an inability to concentrate, necessitating a readmission that again ruled out any ongoing medical problems. Beth was seen for two sessions of biofeedback while in the hospital the second time, and then followed with outpatient treatment. Although her self-reports of headache intensity did not show any decreases, she returned to school after a three-week absence. She was the oldest of two children and her parents had been divorced since she was four. Mother had remarried shortly thereafter and Beth had not seen her biological father since. She was a good student, had many friends, and complained of little other than her headaches.

After three rather unsuccessful weeks of biofeedback training with little response to either EMG or thermal training, Beth began to talk about two different kinds of headaches. She spoke of "pain headaches" and "feeling headaches." Pain headaches were sharp, unilateral aches often accompanied with nausea and light sensitivities. Feeling headaches were "dull and fuzzy" experiences. She was able to differentiate these two experiences when record-keeping. When asked to further describe the "dull fuzzies," she said, "It is just there." She was asked to imagine that "It" was sitting in the chair across the office and to describe "It." At first she was unable to address the representation in the chair but it quickly took the shape of the "Purple Grimace." She said this was an angry character although she denied at first that she had any angry feelings to speak of. She was asked to chart on her homework record any angry feelings that preceded any of the fuzzy headaches and to continue her home relaxation practice. During the next session she was able to describe a couple of arguments with her stepfather and some displeasure about a contemplated family move out of the state.

Biofeedback training continued, as did the psychotherapeutic discussions of her anger. The use of some assertive training techniques gave Beth a new repertoire in confronting her parents with her frustrations. Headaches diminished over the next few weeks. Failure to incorporate the emotional aspects of her life (Shellenberger & Green, 1986) into the biofeedback treatment would have limited the success of the treatment.

A Child with Asthma

This case study is reported in detail by Green (1983). E., a 10-year-old girl who had been suffering with asthma since the first month of life, was referred by her pediatrician. E. was on several medications, received weekly allergy shots (she was allergic to pollens, molds, dust, animal hair, and feathers), and carried on continual struggles with her mother over medication usage. She was an adopted child who "held some anger towards her parents and younger siblings (Green, 1983, p. 137).

E. was described as bright and verbal, and she easily understood the purpose of biofeedback training. Specific goals of treatment included the reduction of medication, the ability to play longer and harder, and the ability to stop the asthma.

Training included both thermal and frontalis EMG feedback, breathing, and imagery. With asthmatic children, Green uses slow deep breathing with images of an enlarged section of lung tissue. The child is instructed to visualize relaxed bronchiole muscles with air sacs expanding perfectly during breathing exercises.

Home training included temperature feedback assisted relaxation, imagery, peak flow feedback before and after relaxation, and autogenic phrases before falling asleep.

When E. demonstrated sufficient relaxation skills, desensitization was carried out to eliminate her feather allergy response. Imagery was used that involved E. sitting relaxed in the therapist's office and a bird being brought into the room. After sufficient practice, a bird was brought into the office and E. was able to breath in a relaxed manner. The exercise was repeated with a feather pillow, and she again had no allergic reaction.

Imagery training for the mold allergy included having E. visualize herself in a meadow teaming with particles of pollen, mold, and dust. She imagined breathing these "harmless particles of nature" in and out. She was able to continue to remain relaxed and asymptomatic with the introduction of real moldy bread and cheese. Green states that "theoretically, relaxation in the presence of the allergen counteracted the reaction of the immune system" (p. 139). (Obviously, controlled research needs to take place before such a technique becomes commonplace.)

At one year following termination E. had taken over her own medication administration and had reduced it to zero after having her jaw wired shut after a car accident. Although she had had a few setbacks during that year, she remained symptom-free and acquired a bird as a pet.

EMG Treatment of an Adolescent with Back Pain

Karen was a 16-year-old high school sophomore described as "an average student" "too socially active" by her parents. She was the oldest of two children and had been argumentative for as long as she and her parents could recall. Her lower back pain began at the end of summer just prior to the beginning of school. She had dated a boy for eight months; the relationship had ended just prior to the onset of her complaints. Although she began school, she was soon unable to attend. She was initially managed by her physician as an outpatient using muscle relaxants. As her complaints escalated she was hospitalized for a complete neurological workup. No pathology was noted after numerous medical tests. She was referred for EMG treatment to help relax the back spasms she reported. After initial interviews in the hospital, it was determined in concert with her physician that she should be discharged from the hospital and that outpatient biofeedback treatment would begin. It was clear that her sick role was an attempt to avoid schoolwork and parental confrontation and that *in vivo* treatment would be beneficial.

She quickly mastered the relaxation techniques using frontalis EMG to mirror overall body relaxation. She practiced relaxation several times daily during the first few weeks of treatment. Her spasms quickly subsided and she returned to school. In discussion with Karen and her parents it became clear that Karen needed a neutral party with whom she could discuss her adolescent issues. Individual and family treatments were begun. The speed with which Karen mastered her back pains was often used in treatment to help her with her lagging confidence in mastering everything from driving a car to leaving for college some day. Back pains returned briefly during examination periods or during fights with her boyfriend.

CONCLUSIONS

Given the growing literature highlighting the efficacy of biofeedback training with children, it seems that its use in clinical practice is warranted. Not only does it appear to be a tool that children can rapidly learn, but it may be cost effective as well. Blanchard, Jaccard, Andrasik, Guarnieri, and Jurish (1985) showed that, for adult headache sufferers, medical costs averaged $995 for the two years prior to receiving a combination of various relaxation and biofeedback treatments. For the two years after treatment, costs averaged only $52. Although children enter into biofeedback treatment earlier than adults, both parents and insurance companies should take note of these findings.

Shellenberger and Green conclude that the patient's ability to demonstrate mastery of learned psychophysiological changes under stress is the "sine qua non for successful biofeedback training." Clinically, they continue, this mastery is shown when the patient successfully handles "stressful life events in new ways without exacerbation of symptoms" (1986, p. 52). Successful biofeedback training is the result of clinician variables, treatment planning, and outcome goals. A clinician should be trained in individual assessment and have the requisite skill to effectively work with patients. The clinician should have certification or licensure and be required to demonstrate biofeedback skill training. Treatment should be creatively designed to meet the needs of each patient. Treatment protocols should have multiple components maximizing treatment for each patient while remaining flexible enough to meet each patient's changing needs during treatment. Finally, the goals of biofeedback should include stress management techniques and enhancement of quality of life as goals. Using the mastery model of biofeedback training helps assure these goals (Shellenberger & Green, 1986).

Although existing studies illustrate the general clinical utility of the biofeedback techniques with children, what is needed are studies that focus upon the specifics of treatment. Answers to such questions as, What characteristics best predict the child who will be successful with biofeedback training? and What are the criteria that define mastery of self-regulation for a given symptom complex? will be of great help to the practicing clinician. Given that most biofeedback techniques for children are directly translated from the adult literature, future research should focus on the specific clinical needs of children.

The future use of biofeedback training with children seems limited only by the answers to the empirical questions raised above, the clinician's knowledge of biofeedback training, and by the clinician's creativity in applying biofeedback techniques as a natural adjunct to treatment. Children seem to naturally accept, enjoy, and master the challenges of psychophysiological self-regulation. The clinician's responsibility is to provide an environment that reinforces the child's natural curiosity and adaptability.

REFERENCES

Ad Hoc Committee on Classification of Headache. (1962). Classification of headache. *Journal of the American Medical Association, 179,* 127–128.

American Psychiatric Association. (1980). *Diagnostic and statistical manual of mental disorders* (3rd ed.).

Andrasik, F., & Attanasio, V. (1985). Biofeedback in pediatrics; current status and appraisal. In M. Wolraich & D.K. Routh, (Eds.), *Advances in developmental and behavioral pediatrics* (pp. 241–286). Greenwich, CT: JAI Press.

Andrasik, F., Blanchard, E.B., Edlund, S.R., & Attanasio, V. (1983). EMG biofeedback treatment of a child with muscle contraction headache. *American Journal of Clinical Biofeedback, 6,* 96–102.

Andrasik, F., Burke, E.J., Attanasio, V., & Rosenblum, E.L. (1985). Child, parent, and physician reports of a child's headache pain: Relationships prior to and following treatment. *Headache, 25,* 421–425.

Attanasio, V., Andrasik, F., Burke, E.J., Blake, D.D., Kabela, E., & McCarran, M.S. (1985). Clinical issues in utilizing biofeedback with children. *Clinical Biofeedback and Health, 8,* 134–141.

Beary, F., & Benson, H. (1974). A simple psychophysiologic technique which elicits the hypometabolic changes of the relaxation response. *Psychosomatic Medicine, 36,* 115–120.

Benson, H. (1975). *The relaxation response.* New York: Morrow.

Bernstein, D.A., & Borkovec, T.D. (1973). *Progressive relaxation training: A manual for the helping professions.* Champaign, IL: Research Press.

Bille, B. (1967a). Migraine in school children. *Acta Paediatrica Scandinavia 51,* 1–151.

Bille, B. (1967b). Juvenile headache: The natural history of headaches in children. In A.P. Friedman & E. Harms (Eds.), *Headaches in children.* Springfield, IL.: Charles C Thomas.

Bille, B. (1981). Migraine in childhood and its prognosis. *Cephalalgia, 1,* 71–75.

Blanchard, E.B., Jaccard, J., Andrasik, F., Guarnieri, P., & Jurish, S.E. (1985). Reduction in headache patients' medical expenses associated with biofeedback and relaxation treatments. *Biofeedback and Self-Regulation, 10,* 63-68.

Braud, L.W. (1978). The effects of frontal EMG biofeedback and progressive relaxation upon hyperactivity and its behavioral concomitants. *Biofeedback and Self-Regulation, 3,* 69-87.

Braud, L.W., Lupin, M.N., & Braud, W.G. (1975). The use of electromyographic biofeedback in the control of hyperactivity. *Journal of Learning Disability, 8,* 420-425.

Brown, B. (1970). Recognition of aspects of consciousness through association with EEG alpha activity represented by a light signal. *Psychophysiology, 6,* 442-452.

Brown, B. (1977). *Stress and the art of biofeedback.* New York: Harper & Row.

Budzynski, T., Stoyva, J.M., Adler, C.S., & Mullaney, D.J. (1973). EMG biofeedback and tension headache: A controlled outcome study. *Seminars in Psychiatry, 5*(4), 397-410.

Cautela, J.R., & Groden, J. (1978). *Relaxation: A comprehensive manual for adults, children, and children with special needs.* Champaign, IL: Research Press.

Congdon, P.J., & Forsythe, W.I. (1979). Migraine in childhood: A study of 300 children. *Developmental Medicine & Child Neurology, 21,* 190-192.

Craig, A., & Cleary, P. (1982). Reduction of stuttering by young stutterers using EMG feedback. *Biofeedback and Self-Regulation, 7,* 241-254.

Cunningham, M.D., & Murphy, P.J. (1981). The effects of bilateral EEG biofeedback on verbal, visual-spatial, and creative skills in learning disabled male adolescents. *Journal of Learning Disabilities, 14,* 204-208.

Davis, M.H., Saunders, D.R., Creer, T.L., & Chai, H. (1973). Relaxation training facilitated by biofeedback apparatus as a supplemental treatment in bronchial asthma. *Journal of Psychosomatic Research, 17,* 121-128.

Diamond, S., & Franklin, M. (1975). Autogenic training with biofeedback in the treatment of children with migraine. *Therapy in Psychosomatic Medicine, 37,* 190-192.

Feldman, G.M. (1976). The effects of biofeedback training on respiratory resistance of asthmatic children. *Psychosomatic Medicine, 38,* 27-34.

Finley, W.W. (1976). Effects of sham feedback following successful SMR training in an epileptic: Follow up study. *Biofeedback and Self-Regulation, 1,* 227-235.

Finley, W.W. (1983). Biofeedback with children. In C.E. Walker & M.C. Roberts (Eds.), *Handbook of clinical child psychology* (pp. 1050-1068). New York: Wiley.

Finley, W.W., Smith, H.A., & Etherton, M.D. (1975). Reduction of seizures and normalization of the EEG in a severe epileptic following sensorimotor biofeedback training: Preliminary study. *Biological Psychology, 2,* 189-203.

Fordyce, W.E. (1976). *Behavioral methods for chronic pain and illness.* Saint Louis: Mosby.

Franks, J.D. (1982). Biofeedback and the placebo effect. *Biofeedback and Self-Regulation, 7,* 449-460.

Fuller, G.D. (1977). *Biofeedback: Methods and procedures in clinical practice.* San Francisco: Biofeedback Press.

Furman, S. (1973). Intestinal biofeedback in functional diarrhea: A preliminary report. *Journal of Behavior Therapy and Experimental Psychiatry, 4,* 317-321.

Gascon, G.G. (1984). Chronic and recurrent headaches in children and adolescents. *Pediatric Clinics of North America, 31,* 1027–1051.

Gordon, D. (1978). *Therapeutic metaphor.* Cupertino, CA: META Publications.

Gracenin, C.T., & Cook, J.E. (1977). Alpha biofeedback and LD children. *Academic Therapy, 12,* 275–279.

Green, J.A. (1983). Biofeedback therapy with children. In W.H. Rickles, J.H. Sandweis, D. Jacobs, & R.N. Grove (Eds.), *Biofeedback and family practice medicine* (pp. 121–144) New York: Plenum Press.

Green, E., and Green, A. (1977). *Beyond biofeedback.* New York: Delcorte Press/Seymore Lawrence.

Haight, M., Jampolsky, G., & Irvine, A. (1976). The response of hyperkinesis to EMG biofeedback. *Biofeedback and Self-Regulation, 1,* 326.

Hampstead, W.J. (1979). The effects of EMG-assisted relaxation training with hyperkinetic children: A behavioral alternative. *Biofeedback and Self-Regulation, 4,* 113–125.

Hatch, J.P., & Riley, R. (1985). Growth and development of biofeedback: a bibliographic analysis. *Biofeedback and Self-Regulation, 10,* 289–299.

Haynes, S.N. (1980). Muscle contraction headache: A psychophysiological perspective of etiology and treatment. In S.N. Haynes & L.R. Gannon (Eds.), *Psychosomatic disorders: A psychophysiological approach to etiology and treatment* (pp. xx-xx). New York: Cardner.

Holroyd, K.A., Penzien, D.B., Hursey, K.G., Tobin, D.L., Rogers, L., Holm, J.E., Marcille, P.J., Hall, J.R., & Chila, A.G. (1984). Change mechanisms in EMG biofeedback training: Cognitive changes underlying improvements in tension headache. *Journal of Consulting and Clinical Psychology, 52,* 1039–1053.

Houts, A.C. (1982). Relaxation and thermal feedback treatment of child migraine headache: A case study. *American Journal of Clinical Biofeedback, 5,* 154–157.

Hunter, S.H., Russell, H.L., Russell, E.D., & Zimmerman, R.L. (1976). Control of fingertip temperature increases via biofeedback in learning disabled and normal children. *Perceptual and Motor Skills, 43,* 743–755.

Jeffrey, T.B., & Hayes, S.B. (1978). The effects of operant conditioning and electromyographic biofeedback on the relaxed behavior of hyperkinetic children. *Biofeedback and Self-Regulation, 3,* 205.

Kamiya, J. (1969) Operant control of the EEG alpha rhythm and some of its reported effects on consciousness. In C. Tart (Ed.), *Altered states of consciousness* (pp. 507–517). New York: Wiley.

Kelton, A., & Belar, C.D. (1983). The relative efficacy of autogenic phrases and autogenic feedback training in teaching hand warming to children. *Biofeedback and Self-Regulation, 8,* 461–475.

Khan, A.U. (1977). Effectiveness of biofeedback and counter-conditioning in the treatment of bronchial asthma. *Journal of Psychosomatic Research, 21,* 97–104.

Khan, A.U., Staerk, M., & Bonk, C. (1973). Role of counter-conditioning in the treatment of asthma. *Journal of Psychosomatic Research, 17,* 389–392.

Kotses, H., Glaus, K.D., Bricel, S.K., Edwards, J.E., Crawford, P.L. (1978). Operant muscular relaxation and peak expiratory flow rate in asthmatic children. *Journal of Psychosomatic Research, 22,* 17–23.

Kotses, H., Glaus, K.D., Crawford, P.L., Edwards, J.E., & Scherr, M.S. (1976). Operant reduction of frontalis EMG activity in the treatment of asthma in children. *Journal of Psychosomatic Research, 20,* 453–459.

Kurz, G. (Producer) and Lucas, G. (Director). (1977). *Star Wars* [Film]. Hollywood: Twentieth-Century Fox.

Labbe, E.L., & Williamson, D.A. (1984). Treatment of childhood migraine using autogenic feedback training. *Journal of Consulting and Clinical Psychology, 52,* 968–976.

Lazarus, A.A. (1981). *The practice of multimodal therapy.* New York: McGraw-Hill.

Lubar, J., & Bahler, W.W. (1976). Behavioral management of epileptic seizures following EEG biofeedback training of the sensorimotor rhythm. *Biofeedback and Self-Regulation, 1,* 77–104.

Lubar, J., & Shouse, M. (1976). EEG and behavioral changes in a hyperkinetic child concurrent with training of the sensorimotor rhythm (SMR): A preliminary report. *Biofeedback and Self-Regulation, 1,* 293–306.

Lubar, J., & Shouse, M. (1977). Use of biofeedback in the treatment of seizure disorders and hyperactivity. In B. Lahey & A. Kazdin (Eds.), *Advances in clinical child psychology* (Vol. 1, pp. 204–265). New York: Plenum.

Marshall, M.J., & Peck, D.F. (1986). Facial expression training in blind adolescents using EMG feedback: A multiple baseline study. *Behavior Research and Therapy, 24,* 429–435.

Miklich, D.R., Renne, C.M., Creer, T.L., Alexander, A.B., Chai, H., Davis, M., Hoffman, A., & Danker-Brown, P. (1977). The clinical utility of behavior therapy as an adjunctive treatment for asthma. *The Journal of Allergy and Clinical Immunology, 60,* 285–294.

Miller, N.E. (1969). Learning of visceral and glandular responses. *Science, 163,* 434–445.

Miller, N.E. (1985, February). Rx: Biofeedback. *Psychology Today,* pp. 2, 54–59.

Olness, K. & MacDonald, J. (1981). Self-hypnosis and biofeedback in the management of juvenile migraine. *Developmental and Behavioral Pediatrics, 2,* 168–170.

Olton, D.S., & Noonberg, A.R. (1980). *Biofeedback, clinical applications in behavioral medicine.* Englewood Cliffs, NJ: Prentice-Hall.

O'Malley, J., & Connors, C.K. (1972). The effect of unilateral alpha training on visual evoked response in a dyslexic adolescent. *Psychophysiology, 9,* 467–470.

Omizo, M.M. (1980). The effects of biofeedback-induced relaxation training in hyperactive adolescent boys. *The Journal of Psychology, 105,* 131–138.

Omizo, M.M., & Williams, R.E. (1981). Biofeedback training can calm the hyperactive child. *Academic Therapy, 17,* 43–46.

Ornstein, R.L. (1973, May). The right and left thinking. *Psychology Today* pp. 87–92.

Raskin, N.H., & Appenzeller, O. (1980). *Headache.* Philadelphia: Saunders.

Rozensky, R.H., & Pasternak, J.F. (1985). Obi-Wan Kenobi, "The Force," and the art of biofeedback: A headache treatment for overachieving young boys. *Clinical Biofeedback and Health, 8,* 9–13.

Russell, H.L., & Carter, J.L. (1978). Biofeedback training with children: Consultation, questions, applications and alternatives. *Journal of Clinical Child Psychology, 7,* 23–25.

Sargent, J.D. (1977). Biofeedback and biocybernetics. In Wittkower, E.D., & Warnes, H., *Psychosomatic medicine: Its clinical applications,* (pp. 166–171). New York: Harper & Row.

Scadding, J.G. (1966). Patterns of respiratory insufficiency. *Lancet, 1,* 701–704.

Scherr, M.S., Crawford, P.L., Sergent, C.B., & Scherr, C.A. (1975). Effects of biofeedback techniques on chronic asthma in a summer camp environment. *Annals of Allergy, 35,* 289–295.

Schultz, J.H., & Luthe, W. (1969). *Autogenic therapy: Vol. 1. Autogenic methods.* New York: Grune & Stratton.

Schwartz, G.E. (1973). Biofeedback as therapy: Some theoretical and practical issues. *American Psychologist, 28*(8), 666–673.

Seifert, A.R., & Lubar, J.F. (1975). Reduction of epileptic seizures through EEG biofeedback training. *Biological Psychology, 3,* 157–184.

Shapiro, D., Crider, A.B., & Tursky, B. (1964). Differentiation of an autonomic response through operant reinforcement. *Psychonomic Science, 1,* 147–148.

Shellenberger, R., & Green, J.A. (1986). *From the ghost in the box to successful biofeedback training.* Greeley, CO.: Health Psychology Press.

Shouse, M.N., & Lubar, J.F. (1979). Operant conditioning of EEG rhythms and Ritalin in the treatment of hyperkinesis. *Biofeedback and Self-Regulation, 4,* 299–312.

Sillanpaa, M. (1983). Changes in headache prevalence of migraine and other headaches during the first seven school years. *Headache, 23,* 15–19.

Sterman, M.D., LoPresti, R.W., & Fairchild, M.D. (1969). *Electroencephalographic and behavioral studies of monomethydrazine toxicity in the cat.* Technical Report AMRL-TR-69-3, Air Force Systems Command, Wright-Patterson Air Force Base, Ohio.

Sterman, M.B., MacDonald, L.R., & Stone, R.K. (1974). Biofeedback training of the sensorimotor electroencephalogram rhythm in man: Effects on epilepsy. *Epilepsia, 15,* 395–416.

Stoelting-Cyborg. (1983). *J42 feedback thermometer handbook.* (Available from Stoelting-Cyborg, 1350 S. Kostner Ave., Chicago, IL 60623).

Suter, S., Fredericson, M., & Portuesi, L. (1983). Mediation of skin temperature biofeedback effects in children. *Biofeedback and Self-Regulation, 8,* 567–584.

Suter, S., & Loughry-Machado, G. (1981). Skin temperature biofeedback in children and adults. *Journal of Experimental Child Psychology, 32,* 77–87.

Tansey, M., & Bruner, R. (1983). EMG and EEG biofeedback training in the treatment of a 10-year-old hyperactive boy with a developmental reading disorder. *Biofeedback and Self-Regulation, 8,* 25–37.

Taub, E. (1977). Self-regulation of human tissue temperature. In G.E. Schwartz & J. Beatty (Eds.), *Biofeedback: Theory and Practice* (pp. 265–300). New York: Academic Press.

Taub, E., & Emurian, C.S. (1976). Feedback-aided self-regulation of skin temperature with a single feedback focus: 1. Acquisition and reversal of training. *Biofeedback and Self-Regulation, 1,* 147–168.

Waranch, H.R., & Keenan, D.M. (1985). Behavioral treatment of children with recurrent headaches. *Journal of Behavior Therapy and Experimental Psychiatry, 16,* 31–38.

Werder, D.S. (1978). An exploratory study of childhood migraine using thermal biofeedback as a treatment alternative. *Biofeedback and Self-Regulation, 3,* 242–243.

Werder, D.S., & Sargent, J.D. (1984). A study of childhood headache using biofeedback as a treatment alternative. *Headache, 24,* 122–126.

CHAPTER 8

Hakomi Therapy with Seriously Emotionally Disturbed Adolescents

GREG JOHANSON AND CAROL R. TAYLOR

INTRODUCTION

Hakomi is a form of therapy developed by Ronald S. Kurtz and taught by the Hakomi Institute throughout the United States and Europe. It is a therapy that has pioneered new techniques within the context of five organizing principles (unity, organicity, mind/body holism, mindfulness, and nonviolence), as well as integrated elements from other therapies that have gone before it. The main sources for the therapy are the book *Hakomi Therapy* by Ron Kurtz (1983), and the journal of the Institute, the *Hakomi Forum*, both available through the Institute's main office.

What is and is not considered Hakomi is judged by a method's or technique's congruence with the principles. Since the principles are drawn from contemporary philosophy of science as well as from major religious traditions, they are quite broad and allow for the inclusion and integration of a wide variety of methods.

The unity and organicity principles are especially important to note when applying Hakomi to work with adolescents. Following Bateson (1979), unity includes the notions that a living organic system is a whole made up of parts and that there is a force in life, negentrophy (Prigogine & Stengers, 1984), that persuades elements in the direction of greater complexity and wholeness. An adolescent can be thought of as made up of many organic subsystems, and as participating in larger suprasystems (Skynner, 1976). Hakomi therapists consider it rowing against the stream to not take seriously as many parts of the system as possible. This would include evaluating an adolescent's diet and metabolic dispositions as well as including as many people as possible from the family, school, church, neighborhood, juvenile department, and so on in the treatment.

Another implication of unity is that everything is connected to everything else. Bateson's principle of organicity is that the parts must be communicating within the whole for a system to retain its organic ability to be self-directing and self-correcting. The liver and pancreas must talk with each other through the nervous system and bloodstream. The parts of the mind must be available to each other as well as to the body. The family must communicate. The football team must huddle. One way of thinking of therapy is that of removing barriers to communication, of healing splits in consciousness (Wilber, 1979), eventuating in people regaining the organic wisdom to know what is needful for themselves.

In practice, therefore, Hakomi therapists feel both the freedom and the necessity of participating in a multitherapy approach in working with adolescents (Johanson, 1984b, 1986b) so that the facilitation of communication within all levels of the system is maximized. One way to conceptualize the interplay of therapies is through the S-O-R schema of experimental psychology.

A lot of psychological research toward the beginning and middle of the century went into investigating how the environment molded behavior. This was termed S-R psychology. Stimulus one (S1) led predictably to response one (R1). The system was modified when it became apparent that S1 did not always lead to R1. Sometimes, in another subject, it would lead to R2. For whatever reason, the presence of the same white German Shepherd dog (S1) would lead to fright in one person (R1) and to attraction in another (R2). Without biasing how it happens or how best to deal with it, it becomes necessary to posit an organismic variable (O) between the S and the R, thus creating an S-O-R psychology. The 'O' signifies the program, filters, imagination, mindset, or whatever one calls that which functions within persons leading them to interpret a stimulus in such a way that disposes them toward one behavior instead of another.

Various schools of therapy have grown up around emphasizing the importance of the S, the O, or the R. In the early days, and still today in some cases, the schools were imperialistic in claiming that their emphasis was indeed the most important, crucial, deserving of study, funding and so on. It is hard to back up such claims (Johanson, 1986a). The conclusion of most research surveys of effectiveness studies in therapy is that of the dodo bird judging the race in *Alice's Adventures in Wonderland:* "Everyone has won and all must have prizes."

For Hakomi therapists, the dodo bird's verdict is confirmation of the bias embedded in the principles of unity and organicity, and gives them licence to be responsibly eclectic in valuing the relative merits of a wide variety of approaches. If the S-O-R schema is taken out of a linear progression and placed spatially as a triangle, a graphic representation (see Figure 8.1) emerges of how the environment, the mindset of the person, and the person's behavior are all in a mutually reciprocal relationship of interdependence, implying that the various therapies aimed at each variable can all be of value.

For example, a 14-year-old adolescent boy sees someone he doesn't know coming down the sidewalk toward him (S). He automatically mobilizes around

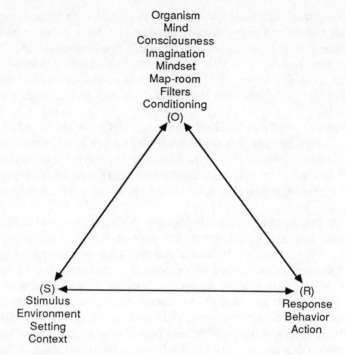

Figure 8.1. Triangular representation of the interdependent relationship among the person's mindset, behavior, and the environment.

thinking the person will not like him (O). He directs his gaze toward the lawn or the bird in the tree (R), as if he is preoccupied, so that he can avert the other's gaze in a socially acceptable manner.

A number of things can affect this scenario. If the other person (S) begins to look away first, looks at the adolescent harshly, or begins to smile graciously in anticipation of a friendly greeting, the gazer's own disposition to respond in a particular way will be affected.

It is also possible that the gazer could catch himself mobilizing around avoiding eye contact and, in a brief moment of awareness, confirm to himself, "Yes, you are a nerd nobody would want to pay any attention to," or "Wait a minute. We are all in this together. Noboby is better than anybody else," or "I'm not going to let anybody intimidate me!" All of these O possibilities could change what happens.

Different behavioral responses could also affect things. He could decide to smile at the other, even though he is scared. He could self-consciously go with looking mean and staring the person down. If he decided to smile, it is possible that this would evoke a smile in the other and change the gazer's mindset to a degree: "Oh, some people do smile back. Maybe other people are anxious too, or maybe I'm more appealing than I think." This change in mindset could change the way he views the next person he meets. Instead of mobilizing around the notion that this person will not like him, he might have a more open, though still cautious, mobilization around the possibility that this person might or might not like him: "I wonder which way it will be?" His ability to make or initiate eye contact will have possibly shifted to include more freedom and choice in behaviors.

In its pure form (Barstow, 1985), Hakomi emphasizes the O variable. Hakomi facilitates characterological change by inviting people to turn their awareness inward toward present, concrete experience and to explore that experience in what is termed a *mindful* state of consciousness. Here Hakomi is in agreement with the research findings of Eugene Gendlin (1978, 1979) who has shown that failure in psychotherapy happens when a therapist gets nonexperiential responses from clients (rationalizations, justifications, stories, etc.) that simply rehash what clients already know, precluding any new learning.

When working with adults, it is common Hakomi practice to facilitate mindfulness for the bulk of a standard therapy session. Friends and family might be included in the session, evaluations by appropriate other practitioners sought, and various kinds of homework given to deepen integration processes. Normally, however, the emphasis of the session is on self-exploration. When working with adolescents, the relative balance is reversed. The environment, what is done in relation to structuring school and/or family time, is crucial and is a first agenda. Many therapies might be included in the overall treatment plan. Hakomi techniques, aimed at facilitating mindfulness and mining an adolescent's inner wisdom, are placed farther in the background, and held in readiness for every appropriate moment when fostering self-exploration is what is needed and possible. It is often used in between the lines of other therapies, though it can also take the forefront during some individual and group sesisons.

In the following section, basic Hakomi methodology will be outlined, especially as it is applicable in work with adolescents. This technique section will give some detail in relation to microprocesses of the method as well as illustrations. It is necessarily incomplete, however, and the reader is referred to the primary sources for additional information, or to the main Institute office in Boulder for information of introductory as well as 390-hour advanced trainings. The section on case illustrations will take focus from a wider lens, providing a more general account of how Hakomi was used in specific instances in a multitherapy approach.

THE TECHNIQUE

States of Consciousness

Hakomi, as Figures 8.2 and 8.3 show, manages states of consciousness in a way that makes specific stages of a process predictable.

STATES OF CONSCIOUSNESS

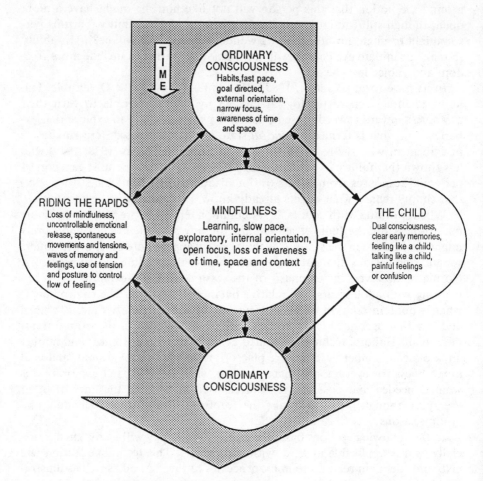

Figure 8.2. States of consciousness.
Reprinted with permission of Hakomi of Ashland.

Ordinary Consciousness

In therapy with adolescents, a lot of time is necessarily spent in ordinary conversation in ordinary consciousness, time that can be quite valuable (Meeks, 1971). Ordinary consciousness, that in which people normally talk and go to the store with, has identifiable characteristics. It is governed, for the most part, by habits and patterns that are operating on automatic, just as our heart rate and breathing operate. It normally has an external orientation, is goal directed, and, therefore, has a narrow focus and fast past. Ordinary consciousness provides an awareness of space and time.

When therapists experience adolescents in ordinary consciousness they are experiencing them as they are, the adolescents using what they have, working out of whatever information is already programmed in their personal com-

STAGES OF THE PROCESS

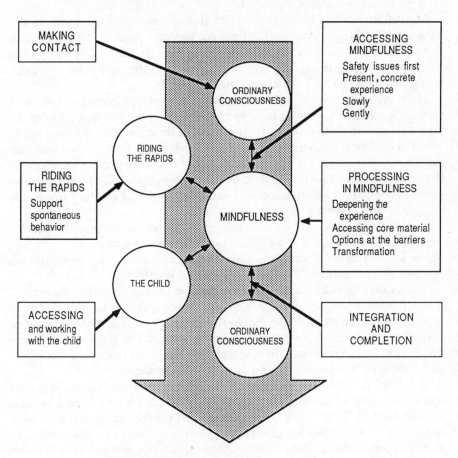

Figure 8.3. Stages of the process.
Reprinted with permission of Hakomi of Ashland.

puters, their O variable. Their behavior is largely automatic and reflexive, which makes it ideal for diagnostic purposes. How the teenagers dress, how they sit; how they carry their bodies (Kurtz & Prestera, 1976); what they say and don't say as well as how they do either; how they interact in relationships with friends, strangers, teachers, and counselors, all give clues to how they are organizing both their experience and their expression in life.

Hakomi therapists are particularly interested in experiencing the person's organization in such a way that clues begin to come together as to the organizing principles at work. Experience and expression are organized. Nothing gets to awareness without going through the filters of the imagination that take incoming stimuli and make them available to consciousness (Horner, 1979; Kopp, 1972; Lowen, 1958, 1975; MacKinnon & Michels, 1971; Missildine, 1963; Loevinger, 1976; Shapiro, 1965.) These organizing principles can be called imaginative filters, scripts, tapes, or whatever. In Hakomi they are often referred to as *core organizing beliefs*.

For instance, what belief is in effect that would make sense out of this adolescent's presentation of self: "I am not welcome here"? "Nobody is ever here for me"? "You have to get them before they get you"? "I'm only liked if I jump through the right hoops"? "I have to perform well or be very interesting before people will notice and include me"?

However unconscious, unaware, miserable, unhappy teenagers are, how they are organizing their lives is viewed by Hakomi therapists as a creative act. This does not imply that the early formation of beliefs was a conscious willful act or that they are conscious of having done so now. It does not mean that the construction of beliefs was anything short of necessary, given the situation they were confronted with. It does imply, however, that the formation of a certain belief, from experiencing and sizing up the world and how one has to survive in it, is a creative human act.

The hopeful aspect of this assumption is that the same creative capacity that formed the belief can be called upon for reexamination of the belief, in the light of new information, and for the exploration of possibilities for reorganizing around more realistic, nourishing beliefs.

The assumption also implies that the creative capacity is within the person. There the inner wisdom lies that will lead to both what is painful and what is possible. Many of us in the therapy field have been far more superior as diagnosticians than we have been as change agents. The issue is how to empower people, old or young, to discover how they have organized themselves and what creative possibilities are open to them in the future.

It is hard to access the core organizing level of character in ordinary consciousness. That is because it is characteristically ruled by habits and patterns already formed. In ordinary consciousness, people rehash variations of what is already known. They are doing what their computers can do, given their present programming. That is why much therapeutic conversation becomes boring. It is dealing with old, stale, dated material.

Mindful Consciousness

The experience of Hakomi is that learning and growth happen most easily in another state of consciousness termed *mindful*, or *witnessing consciousness*. Mindfulness, in contrast to ordinary consciousness, has a slow pace. It is hard to learn a new play in the middle of a game, or a new way of fingering the piano in the middle of a recital. The engine is not rebuilt while it is running, nor is the computer reprogrammed while it is working. Down time, quiet, relaxed, reflective, meditative time is best for curiosity and new learning.

In mindfulness, the orientation is internal as opposed to external. The hallmark of Hakomi therapy is being able to take what someone is presenting—creating—and turn that person's awareness inward toward the immediate, felt, concrete experience of this creation. It then becomes possible to track the contours and outlines of the creation back to the level of the creator.

To do this tracking it is necessary that the focus be open, open to whatever might be; exploratory, curious, experimental, like a young child at play (Johanson, 1987a). Immediate agendas, normal ways of reacting, labeling, and judging need to be suspended. There needs to be faith that preverbal experience can be learned from, that it does contain wisdom. Indeed, mystery is a prerequisite for learning. By definition, nobody learns from what they already know, but from what is not yet clear, understood, or labeled. When people concentrate on live, present experience, the process itself takes on a quality of aliveness, exploration, and a sense of new possibilities. Often, awareness of space and time is lost.

A mindful state of consciousness is sharply distinguished from a hypnotic state, however. In hypnosis the conscious mind with all its habitual patterns and frameworks is distracted; this then allows the hypnotist to engage the unconscious mind (Erickson & Rossi, 1979). In Hakomi, mindfulness allows the conscious mind to suspend its routine functions, but to stay completely aware, even while exploring a deeper level of experience for normally unconscious meanings (Johanson, 1984a).

Riding the Rapids Consciousness

When one mindfully explores present experience, two other states of consciousness with their own attributes become possible. One is called riding the rapids. For instance, an adolescent might come for an individual session and appear a bit uneasy. If the patient is motivated to explore the uneasiness in a mindful way, it is possible that the uneasiness might become clarified in sadness, which has a quality of grief, whose meaning is rooted in something about being left out. At this point the youngster might get so close to the underlying pain that riding the rapids occurs: a spontaneous, uncontrollable, emotional release of feelings and movements, with simultaneous attempts to control the release through tensing and holding back. Though the witnessing part of consciousness is always present, according the Hilgard (1965) in his research at Stanford, mindfulness is basically lost when riding the rapids. The therapist makes no attempt to utilize it at this point.

The Child Consciousness

In riding the rapids, spontaneous waves of memory will often arise that are tied to the feelings and meanings present. Here, and through other circumstances, a state of consciousness with the quality of the child can emerge. In the child state of consciousness there are clear, often early memories present that bring people back to the times and places where they created some of their core orgainizing beliefs about the world.

In the example we are following, the adolescent girl might have a memory wash over her of the time she was at the seashore and her brothers and father laughed at her for being afraid to go into the waves without holding hands with her brothers, who refused to do so; a time they called her a sissy, told her she would never grow up, and left her with profound feelings of humiliation and rejection. This could be a scene in which it becomes quite clear to her that she made a decision never to try new things in a way that made her look like a fool, a time when she decided it would be better to act disinterested than to risk being left out or put down.

The child state of consciousness is a dual state. As in mindfulness, the current-age observer is always present and knows exactly what is happening. At the same time, the memories can be so strong and vivid that persons begin experiencing them again as if they were there. They experience the pain and confusion and begin feeling, talking, and looking like the child of yesterday. In other cases, the memories are quite vivid, but the person remains outside the actual scene, viewing what is happening in an involved way that moves them deeply.

The child state is a highly valuable place to be, therapeutically speaking. Not only can persons come to understand the pain behind their present beliefs and constructions of reality, but at this level where the beliefs became viable, they can come to explore the possibility of new beliefs. The experiences that emerge in the child state can be addressed in a way that did not happen the first time around, giving the child-client new information and support, not available at the time, information that updates the files for both inner child and contemporary person.

In our example, the young girl could entertain the possibility that in addition to the people she grew up with, who she experienced as nonsupportive of her fear and excitement in relation to new endeavors, there are others who would be supportive and understanding. There are those who understand that fear as well as excitement are natural when facing new situations, and that wanting support and reassurance is in no way cause for shame, hiding, or ridicule. The world is big enough to include many responses, some hurtful, some helpful. In the child state and in mindfulness, the girl has the opportunity to examine the barriers she has to letting this expanded possibility in. She has the opportunity to find out what she needs in order to let down her defenses to this more realistic, nourishing option. If, indeed, she begins to organize herself in the world in a way that does not automatically assume that she will be excluded or put down when trying new things, but begins to size up reality according to multiple possibilities, a transformation has taken place.

Stages of the Process

To facilitate transformation through managing states of consciousness, there are particular operations that the therapist can employ at identifiable stages of the process. In the following discussion, these operations and stages are described in a linear fashion. In actual practice, the process depends on the therapist always keying off the spontaneous. The various states of consciousness might be entered into at unpredictable times, in ways neither therapist nor client expected or controlled. The therapeutic ability to key off the spontaneous, to work without preferences for an immediate goal, to be willing to do what is needful in the moment, as well as to have a general map for where the process is at any particular point, are the hallmarks of good Hakomi therapy.

Safety Issues First—Nonviolence

For people to turn their awareness inward toward immediate, felt, present, concrete experience, there is a prerequisite. They must feel safe. People cannot close their eyes and pay attention to their inner world if they sense any form of danger, if they feel the necessity of keeping aware of what is going on in the external world. As Kurtz has commented, "It is like asking someone to fall asleep standing up."

While the adolescent has a good capacity for mindfulness, the rate of achieving this state is at the mercy of the trust level held for the therapist by the adolescent. Here is an immediate problem. Children who legitimately qualify under state guidelines as seriously emotionally disturbed have learned to be highly defended. They assume that finding a trustworthy adult is highly unlikely. This is especially so, given that they rarely seek out a therapist for help. They are normally referred to professional help by people who want them fixed, who cannot tolerate dealing with them anymore. Seldom do they make their own choice of therapists. Who they are referred to is, in most cases, chosen for them by a parent, school official, juvenile court counselor, or some other adult authority. Moreover, they feel labeled as crazy, sick, troublemaker, misfit, or weak. Seldom does their social sense allow them to own that time spent with a concerned, well-trained therapist could make a difference in their lives. Not unlike adults, they would rather solve their own problems and not have others tell them what to do or tell them what is best for them. Some of the previous help they have experienced might have had the quality of helping the helper by finding ways to shape up the helpee.

On the other hand, unless they are actively suicidal, adolescents cling to the belief that anything is possible, that there is hope. Their strong need to feel in control is moderated by their yearning for the safety of a responsible adult exercising positive, loving control on their behalf. In addition, there is the principle of unity at work, seeking to make a more comprehensive, satisfying whole out of all the confused, painful, contradictory elements of the youngster's life.

There is, therefore, an opportunity for therapists to join with disturbed adolescents, who often have keen intuitive senses. If the therapists's genuine regard is perceived through the adolescent's sensitive screening, the therapist will be given the needed access (Taylor, 1985). Safety is the key tool when working with adolescents. As with a new sprout, one must relate to them with care, firmness, honesty, integrity, and regard. They know if these conditions prevail. Their experiential sense of safety will allow them to grow and blossom. If they feel unsafe, they will withdraw, strike out, wither, and refuse the growth possibility.

Therapists grounded personally and professionally in principles of unity, organicity, mindfulness, and nonviolence will have the requisite attitude and being to bring to the therapeutic encounter. No therapist, of course, thinks of himself as violent. Confrontational methods are used with integrity by many therapists, with the adolescent's own good in view.

Nonviolence in the context of Hakomi refers to a high degree of faith in the client's organic ability to be self-directing and self-correcting. This means a high degree of trust in their inner wisdom, in their being able to find the inner meaning of their pain, and to discern what is needed for them to deal with their pain and grow toward a more open future. Hakomi therapists do not major in solving problems or in giving advice. The emphasis is on empowering people through helping them get in touch with their own organic sense of direction. This is no small gift or task. Adolescents respond well when they sense that the therapist is truly on their side, wants to help empower them for their own benefit, and is not making judgments, or setting up agendas that are only self-serving to the therapist or the therapists's institution.

Making Contact

The general goal in Hakomi, beginning with the first meeting with an adolescent, and continuing throughout the process, is that of establishing safety and trust. No therapeutic alliance is possible without it. The main tool is that of making contact. The process of making contact takes much insight from all that Harry Stack Sullivan (1953, 1954, 1956), Carl Rogers (1942, 1951, 1961), and Virginia Satir (1972; et al., 1975) have taught about interpersonal relationships and helpful human interactions.

Therapy with adolescents is a wonderful dance, a dance matched to the tempo of the young person's heartbeat (Bandler & Grinder, 1975a). It is a dance where the moves are often quick and surprising. It is often a masked ball. As the dancers whirl and twirl to the tunes of their own inner music, one waits in anticipation for the masks to be gently, willingly removed, and for the real people to unfold in the safety of a specially chosen and constructed space.

Contact is what makes the dance a mutual, creative enterprise. It is what lets the adolescent know that the therapist is dancing to the same music. It is what helps change the tempo so that, even if for a brief moment, the dance goes from the isolated, unpredictable movements of adolescent hard rock to the more synchronous movements of a waltz, a two-person movement where the therapist is allowed the privilege of becoming the responsible partner, leading and guiding in a way that helps the young person experience unaccessed potential.

Contact statements in Hakomi come from tracking the signs of immediate, present experience in the other, as well as the internal state of the therapist. Contact statements are normally best when short. They attempt to acknowledge the jist, the core, the overall meaning of what might have been a long communication on the part of the other: "Sad, huh?" "So, pretty disappointing, huh?" "A really happy time, huh?" "So, pretty suspicious right now. Checking me out pretty closely, huh?"

If the therapist's contact statement is on target, it lets adolescents know that the therapist is paying attention, is keyed in to their reality, and is acknowledging their reality without judgment. A good contact statement does not call attention to itself and often passes without notice. It does not have the quality of analysis, of the therapist piling up knowledge, like a doctor who is then going to fix something. It is a simple acknowledgment of what is most presently and spontaneously real, voiced in a manner that implies both therapist and adolescent are joined in paying respectful attention to the adolescent's reality.

When the contact is sharp, catching the nuances of change from one moment to another ("Now a little anxiety imagining that, huh?"), the adolescent will feel engaged. If they do not experience the contact conveying an ulterior motive other than understanding and respect, they will welcome it on some level.

The "huh?" at the end of the statement (or some equivalent) is important. It conveys the message that the therapist is not invested in an interpretation, is not invested in *telling* the adolescent how he is feeling, and is willing to be corrected. The main agenda is simply exploring with the adolescent the current reality, whatever that might be.

If the therapist is right on with a particular word, that's good. If something is happening that the therapist is not clear on, general words can be used: "Some emotion comes up around that, huh?" If the therapist is wrong, and tracks a reaction in the adolescent that says so, then that can be contacted: "No, sadness isn't quite right. What's a better word for what you are experiencing?"

The sequence of (1) doing or saying something, (2) tracking the response, and (3) contacting it, is considered a ball bearing in Hakomi that keeps the wheels of the process turning smoothly.

Again, the adolescent is a creative being. Every word, every action an adolescent experiences sets off ripples in the consciousness. It is like dropping a pebble into a pond. The ripples happen automatically, spontaneously. The person can watch them but does not have to self-consciously create them. They are produced automatically. These sensations, feelings, thoughts, and memories that arise by themselves reflect the primary organizing done by the core organizing beliefs. The secondary explanations or justifications that come a second later are an overlay. Hakomi is interested in the characterological issues that flow from the core organizing beliefs. By paying exquisite attention to the little unconscious reactions that go across an adolescent's face in a quarter of a second, clues to primary process can be picked up. By contacting these clues, the therapist assists the adolescent in making the unconscious conscious. Contact draws attention to something, gives it significance, and invites further exploration that can empower the person with more self-knowledge.

TH: Roy, have you considered talking to your dad about that next time you see him?

AD: Naw.

TH: I notice some moisture comes into your eyes when you think about that ((?))

AD: Oh, I don't know. It's like we don't talk so easy.

TH: Is that like, sadness, you have about that?

AD: Not exactly. It's more like . . . uh, . . . I don't know, like something I lost somehow.

TH: Oh, like a quality of grief maybe?

AD: Yah.

TH: Well, maybe that would be worthwhile exploring some more. Maybe you can just hang out with the grief and it will tell you more about itself, what the quality of it is . . . grief like you lost something, or something died, or . . . whatever((?))

In this little example, the moisture in the eyes reflects some important underlying feelings. Contacting the moisture focuses the session on something alive, present, and real to both therapist and adolsecent. The symbol ((?)), at the end of the therapist's acknowledgment of the moisture, reflects a connotation in the therapist's voice that, "this is not something I'm just curious about, but maybe it is something you are curious about?" The voice invites the adolescent to be curious about himself (Johanson, 1987a). It hopes to hook the adolescent's own motivation for exploring, and for providing the energy to carry the process.

When Roy responds here with a "naw" and an "Oh, I don't know. It's like we don't talk so easily," he is saying he is ready and willing to brush off this little matter. The therapist continues to respect the wisdom of Roy's experience more than Roy does by keeping the focus there: "Is that like some sadness you have about that?" Roy directs his awareness inside and comes up with a modification of the word "sadness." It is more like he has lost something. This demonstrates that the therapist does not have to be totally accurate. The process is self-correcting when there is the proper trust. The therapist's attempt at understanding functions to invite Roy to find a more precise understanding. By accepting the invitation to explore the sadness, Roy also demonstrates that he is actually willing and wanting to go deeper into this issue of his relationship to his father. He accepts the therapist's lead in the dance.

Though it is active, the therapist's intervention is also nonviolent in that it goes in a direction Roy wants to go. The therapist was dancing to a deeper, more unconscious part of the melody, a part that Roy's unconscious confirmed through continuing to cooperate. If the therapist had been simply ego-involved and forcefully communicating, "Well, I think exploring your relationship to your father is important, even if you don't," the process would not have gone anywhere. (It is important to note, though, that a therapist can get away with all kinds of outrageous, provocative, confrontive responses, if there is the underlying trust relationship present to support it.)

Notice that the deepening that occurred was a result of a ball-bearing interaction: (1) The therapist mentions Roy's father, which goes through Roy's creative processing, visibly influencing both his experience and expression; (2)

tracks the results; and (3) contacts part of it. The process develops a thread of meaning that leads to a deepening of the process. This would not have happened if both the therapist and Roy had simply agreed to go on to some new topic.

In focusing on the eyes, the therapist made a choice out of all the material the adolescent presented. He felt he had enough contact and trust to invite Roy into a deepening process. He also had the faith that all roads lead home. There was something about Roy that the therapist read as a grief theme. He chose to access through the eyes. Accessing the grief could have happened through other avenues at other times, as well, like through how Roy felt about an upcoming date. If the theory is correct that people are creative beings, then following the thread of any particular part of their creation should lead back to the level of the creator. If someone is deeply involved in unresolved grief, it is reasonable that subtle signs of it would show on the way to the grocery store, at the ballgame, working on homework, thinking about a date, or whatever. (But, if someone wipes his nose, it might just be that it was itchy.)

Accessing

The last few paragraphs demonstrate the move from the contact stage to the accessing stage. Making contact properly, which can take a few seconds or a few years, depending on the situation, functions to establish a number of things: Safety is demonstrated and communicated. The therapist demonstrates that the client's experience is being followed. The client is enabled to come into self-contact, to come into present experience, and to be ready to move on.

To move on means to go into a mindful state of consciousness and to explore whatever is of present concern. Assuming safety issues are taken care of, and the client feels the therapist is both a safe being and is operating in a safe setting, there are many ways to induce mindfulness. They all function by asking for present, concrete experience. They all function by going slowly and gently, with an open, exploratory attitude. They all invite people to suspend habitual ways of judging, labeling, or categorizing their experience. They invite people to savor their experience, to linger longer with an experience so that something more can be learned from it. They all function to turn the process from an interpersonal discussion about something in ordinary consciousness, to a mindful intrapersonal dialogue within the person, that the therapist overhears from the sidelines. Clients are encouraged to comment on their experience while remaining in immediate contact with it, as opposed to contacting their experience and then popping out of it to repeat it conversationally to the therapist.

Methods of inducing mindfulness all invite the person to study the organization of their experience. Hakomi is not interested in just talking about a person's experience, or in having the person emote for the sake of drama, for the sake of drumming up an experience. Persons are experiencing at every moment. As human beings, we all have the gift of reflective reason, at least by age 7 or so. Unlike a 2-year-old who might simply strike out when a child takes his toy, a 7-year-old has the capacity to witness anger rising within, and to make a choice about whether to hit or do something else. The Hakomi method strives to help people focus on their present, concrete experience so that it is live, as opposed to academic history, and to then stand back from it enough in a passive witnessing posture, to study how they have organized it; to be in their experience but not at the mercy of it (Kurtz, 1985).

It is important that the therapist model the behavior wanted from the client. The therapist's own voice and manner should slow down and express creative curiosity. To ask a client to openly, leisurely, and curiously explore their anxiety, using a hurryup, urgent, overly concerned voice, induces a contradictory bind.

One way to help someone access their deeper wisdom is to ask a series of right brain questions, questions that force a person to mindfully check their inner experience to find an answer. Notice where awareness has to go to deal with a question like, "Is your right ear or left ear the warmer right now?" Awareness takes a different route in relation to analytic questions such as, "Why do you think one ear is warmer than the other?" The right brain questions honor present experience as a teacher, and do not presume to know everything ahead of time.

If a contact statement is confirmed, such as "A little anxious, huh?" there are many options to follow. The contact statement itself can lead to deepening, if there is that ((?)) connotation at the end that invites them to be curious about their own experience. Such right brain questions as, "Where is the anxiety in your body((?)) . . . Is it just in the stomach or does it go up into your chest((?)) . . . What is the quality of the anxiety((?)) . . . What does the anxiety seem to be saying((?)) . . . Anxious about what((?))" (Bandler & Grinder, 1975b) all invite awareness to turn inward.

Sometimes direct instructions can be given: "Why don't you just hang out with your sense of anxiety and check if it will tell you more about itself((?))" Following Gendlin, an entire situation can become the focus of awareness. "Let this whole situation with your homeroom teacher be the focus of your awareness. Notice how you sense it in your body and see if any words come up that make sense out of it."

There are a number of ways to access through the body outlined by Kurtz in *Hakomi Therapy* (1983). The example of Roy in the last section called attention to moisture in the eyes. Bodily movements and postures can be contacted. "When you talk about your anxiety, the right corner of your mouth extends to the side a little. Can you do that again and study it((?)) Maybe the meaning of it will emerge if we just hang out with it for awhile."

Encouraging mindfulness in a seriously emotionally disturbed child can be a great challenge. Why should this population be mindful of anything—least of all themselves? Mindfulness has meant to them much pain and futility. They know pain, and they do not need a vehicle to provide more of it (Taylor, 1985). Indeed, the very noisy lifestyle of youth can be highly purposeful. The noisier life is, through literal noise from blasting music, from constant movement, activity, watching TV, and so forth, the less youngsters must experience their own pain and the frustrated sense of their future. To induce adolescents to become mindful, thereby lowering the noise level so that the internal signals that are within to guide them may become conscious, some straight teaching often needs to be done. Some bridge thoughts need to be offered that help adolescents know that mindfulness is a powerful tool they have available to themselves that can lead them to positive growth, and to a way out of their pain.

There are many approaches to this kind of teaching. Sometimes a simple chalk talk like the following does it:

> Collier, I do very little in the way of advice-giving or problem-solving, though I'm willing to explore whatever you want. One thing I can do, that some people have found helpful, is to help you mine the wisdom of your own experience. It's like we all run on programming inside, like computers. Well, we can be experimenters together and check out what programs are running and which ones you might want to update, if they are no longer serving you well. We do that by setting up little experiments. For instance, if you are a little confused about whether to go to your dad's this summer or not, we can explore that. I can invite you to just hang out with that situation, to close your eyes so you can pay better attention to yourself instead of focusing on the room here and me, and to just notice how you experience the possibility of going or not going in your body; to check out what words come up that seem to fit the experience; and to learn from what comes up. It's a kind of process you can do by yourself too, but its nice to do together. Sometimes I can be helpful by your allowing me to listen in on your internal dialogue and ask some questions that help you clarify aspects that might be confusing to begin with. When we do this kind of stuff, we both know exactly what is happening, and nothing happens that you don't want to happen. You come to your own conclusions for what needs to happen next.

That kind of paragraph becomes a pebble in Collier's pond of consciousness. Again, the therapist would track Collier's reaction, make contact with it, and continue the process from whatever is spontaneous in Collier's response. "A little suspicious, huh? What does your experience tell you is out of whack with what I just said? Let's listen real closely to the objections you experience."

Here again, even if Collier wants to make an interpersonal confrontation out of it, the therapist's first choice is to make the process intrapsychic, turning Collier's awareness inward toward his own experience. The therapist acts out his faith in Collier's organismic integrity, as opposed to defending his methods or to confronting him with ultimatums.

If Collier is willing to get mindful about his objections, instead of automatically acting out of an assumption of their unquestioned validity, the process if off and running. If not, as is true whenever a process bogs down, the therapist goes back to making contact with what is present, concrete experience.

TH: So, it's like we are a little stuck here, huh? Like you're not sure you can trust me enough to not lie about what day it is.

AD: Something like that, man.

TH: Do you have a sense of what seems most untrustworthy between you and me right now? Maybe it would be good if you checked me out some more, asked me any questions you have about what I'm up to.

AD: Like what?

TH: You have to check your own curiosity for the what. But, like maybe, who gets to know what about what we talk about?

AD: Yah. Tell me more about that.

In some settings and situations it is not possible to think in terms of the extended use of mindfulness. Sometimes the focus is on some other kind of work, like family therapy, and Hakomi methodology can only be used in brief, timely moments. Sometimes, as in the two examples offered immediately below, it is a group setting with younger adolescents working on behavioral contracts for change. It is very difficult to cultivate mindfulness in this setting because of the safety issue. It is so easy for hurting youngsters to defensively foster further hurt with each other, putting each other down, being sarcastic and brutal when any member offers the slightest opportunity. If groups must be set up this way, it is best to do some kind of special trust-building retreat to form group rapport, and norms of respect and support. That was not possible with the groups these examples came out of, and miniversions of mindfulness were used instead, that hopefully still fostered the general aims of the method.

TH: So, what do you think is going on with you when you don't hand in your reading assignments, Ron?

AD: I don't know.

TH: Think about it for a minute. You must be trying to accomplish something. What could it be?

AD: I can't think.

TH: Uh huh, and Babe Ruth can't hit. You have used all kinds of smarts to get this far. Let's struggle with it a bit. We are not trying to find out stuff to throw you in jail with, you know. You think we are up to something funny here?

AD: Not really.

TH: Okay. Like with everyone else, we are trying to help you find out more about yourself, so you have more freedom to make choices. Are you buying that? Do you think this group wants the best for you, even though folks get kind of ornery and mean once in awhile?

AD: Yah, I suppose.

TH: All right. Let me give you a choice, and you figure out which one seems to fit best. You can think by just listening to your inner voice and which choice it says "yes" or "no" to the loudest. You are the world's expert on what's going on inside you. So, when you don't hand in reading assignments, are you being more self-destructive, or more self-protective?

AD: What do you mean?

TH: I mean is it more like you are screwing yourself, saying to yourself, "I'm no good anyway. Everybody knows it. I might as well prove it, since that's what he thinks anyway." That would be self-destructive. Or is it more like, "I'm not going to let anybody push me around. He can't have control over my life. I'll show him by not turning in this stuff he wants." That would be self-protective. You are trying to protect your spirit, your self-image.

AD: It is more like self-protective, I guess.

TH: Oh, so it's more like you are trying to get him, and not have him get you, huh?

AD: Yah. He's a bum! He doesn't care about me, and I don't care if does! He can just stick it.

TH: Some real anger, huh? . . . Well, I like you wanting to protect yourself and not get trampled on.

AD: For all the good it does.

TH: Yah, there does seem to be a problem here, of you sticking yourself in the process. You'll never get into the Navy or be a diesel mechanic, either one, if you don't get to reading better.

AD: Well, who does he think he is anyway, God Almighty?

TH: You do seem to have given him some power, but he isn't here to deal with right now, and I'm more concerned about you at the moment. Let me toss out another thought and possibility to you, and you check inside yourself to see if it fits for you or not. Is that okay?

AD: Go ahead. Why not?

TH: This is a little hard for anybody as young as you to consider, but if you know what you want, like graduating and doing mechanical work in the Navy, you might consider sizing people up in terms of whether they are helping you or getting in your way. If you don't think your reading teacher is for you, you might want to be sure you did well in his class in particular, just to show him you are not going to let anybody get in your way. Does that make any sense?

AD: Yah. You mean like don't let him have the power by throwing the class down the tubes; like he keeps his fat job whether I graduate or not!

TH: Quick thinking. What do you think, group? Could he be strong enough with some support from us to hang in there and go for what he wants despite other people who don't seem to be supportive? And where do you think Ron will need the most support? How is he most likely to get in his own way on this one? Is it okay if we talk about that as a group, Ron?

AD: Go for it. These idiots know me pretty well.

In this case, as in others, the therapist has to decide when to bring up reality questions, as in whether, in fact, this teacher is against the student or not, and when to simply use what the student presents. Notice that the therapist also uses the student's present beliefs about power as leverage, as opposed to exploring them mindfully, which didn't seem like a viable choice in this particular group. The therapist also frames what the student is doing in positive terms, so there can be a discussion of better ways to achieve the desired outcome. Finally, in terms of mindfulness, it is common to need to suggest choices to adolescents to get them started. They have to get mindful to evaluate the choices, and they will often come up with a third choice closer to the mark, which is good (Johanson, 1987b).

In the next miniversion example, the therapist was discussing with a student how he got in the way of his own progress with grades. The student mentioned that sometimes he would just blank out in class and stare out the window looking nowhere.

TH: Do you understand the blanking out? Do you know when it most commonly occurs?

AD: No.

TH: Well, let me give you two possibilities and you check inside yourself with your own experience to check which one seems to fit most right. Okay?

AD: Okay.

TH: All right. Does your inner wisdom tell you it is a better hunch that you blank out when things get simpler and boring, or harder and more complex?

AD: Harder and more complex.

TH: Pretty quick with the answer, huh? That is real clear to you?

AD: Yah. That's when it happens. I get nervous about getting it, and nervous about guys passing notes and talking, and then I end up getting yelled at to wake up when I'm spaced out.

TH: Okay. And in the same way, does your inner sense tell you that it is okay with you to do as well as you're able in school, or is there a part of you that thinks you should be doing real well?

AD: I should be doing real well.

TH: Uh huh. Have any hunches about that? Where is that voice coming from((?))

AD: I don't know. I'm not sure.

TH: Okay. One more decision. Check whether you think your dad would be more likely to say to you (1) "It's okay with me for you to simply do as well as is right for you," or (2) "You have to do better than I did even."

AD: Better than me even.

All this confirmed for the therapist the observation that while this was a child who looked laid back and disinterested on the surface, underneath there was a lot of tension and drive. He had been talking previously of how high-powered and successful both his father and grandfather were, and how much he admired them. But the student's hunch about what the father would say seemed distorted. The therapist encouraged him to have an actual conversation with his father and mother about the subject. He did, and reported back that yes, his father did want him to do better than he himself had done. The reason, however, was not that dad had done well and had wanted his son to do even better. It turned out that dad had been a flake in school, even though he was successful later, and he wanted his son to get on board from the start and do it the easy way. The student was able to relax more and blank out less.

That is an example of accessing some O variable material (feeling driven to meet high expectations), encouraging some new R behavior (talking directly with father as opposed to assuming what he thought), and changing the S environment (parents now being more aware of the pressure the son was feeling that was getting in his way.)

Processing—Deepening

Once someone is accessing, exploring something in a mindful state of consciousness, the next stage is to keep them doing it. Unless someone has an unusual background, mindfulness is not a common state to be in. There is a temptation to go into it and discover something, and then to pop out of it quickly to discuss the something in ordinary consciousness. The process issue becomes that of deepening, that of keeping someone hanging out with their experience long enough for it to teach them something, to lead them where they need to go.

When people begin accessing, they can report a wide variety of responses in terms of what comes into consciousness next: feelings, words, thoughts, memories, images; physical changes such as tensions, sensations, facial expressions, or altered breathing patterns; spontaneous movements or impulses; or signs of the inner child. Ogden (1983) has developed a chart with about 50 of the myriad ways of responding to these various reports. They all promote deepening by asking questions or by giving instructions that keep persons studying their experience for more information. The answer to any specific therapeutic question is secondary and unimportant. The therapist is not collecting information to feed into a computer. The questions serve their function if they invite people to explore the wisdom of their own experience further. The following questions serve as examples:

"What kind of sadness is that((?))"

"How does your body participate in the sadness((?))"

"What is the quality of that voice you hear that says its no use((?))"

"What color are the walls in the memory? Who's there with you((?))"

"How old are you feeling inside((?))"

"What other muscles participate when you tighten your neck((?))"

"Notice what it is like to repeat that gesture in slow motion((?))"

"What would make it safe for that impulse to emerge((?))"

"What does the child want or need in this memory that it didn't get((?))"

There is often a progression through a hierarchy of experience. A thought becomes grounded in a bodily sensation, which when attended to leads to a feeling, which develops into a more specific meaning, which can open up corresponding memories. In the example back in the contact section, the thought of Roy talking with his father brings moisture to the eyes; it then deepens into a confused sadness or grief that has the quality of having lost something.

Processing—Probes

Following the thread of someone's experience can often lead into core material by itself. It is also possible to set up more structured experiments in awareness. Kurtz (1983) has pioneered the use of probes, which are experiments in awareness that can take many forms, but that normally have the following three-part structure: (1) an invitation into mindfulness; "Notice what happens within you, spontaneously, automatically—thoughts, feelings, sensations, memories, or whatever—when I say (or do, or when you focus your awareness on saying, doing, or experiencing)", (2) a pause to allow the person to be centered in a witnessing state of mind; (3) the experimental words, touch, or whatever. A probe allows the therapist to check a hunch and to direct the process along a specific track that might lead the process more quickly toward the core. A probe is always experimental, with both therapist and client open to whatever ripples it might produce. The therapist picks the probe for good reason, but is willing to work without preferences, is willing to have the probe be mistaken or to lead in a different direction than the original hunch.

Probes can be used for accessing. Students could study how they organize around such a probe as "The history paper is due Friday," or "the date with Terri on Saturday." When in the processing stage, the therapist is often interested in, and getting clearer about, core organizing beliefs that are running the client's life.

In the example of Roy again, the therapist was reading from Roy's way of relating to him and to Roy's peers, from the quality of Roy's voice and the way he carried his body, and from reports of past interactions that Roy was operating out of some kind of core organizing belief that was both pessimistic and angry about Roy's worth in the world. When he asked Roy to hang out

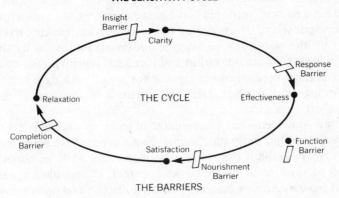

Figure 8.4. The sensitivity cycle.
Reprinted with permission of Hakomi of Ashland.

with his sense of grief to get more information about its quality, nothing emerged very clearly. There seemed to be an overall sense of emptiness, bitterness, and hopelessness. Therefore, the therapist decided to experiment with a probe.

Probes are normally put in what is theoretically a positive form. Probes designed to access the core level of organization are often constructed around words that reflect precisely what the person does not believe at a core level, the opposite of what they believe. Since the probe is designed this way, it is predictable that a correct probe will evoke an automatic, spontaneous rejection of some sort. For instance, to use a probe such as "You are welcome here," with someone with schizoid tendencies will predictably evoke a physical shudder and tightening, along with a corresponding voice in the head that says, "Oh no I'm not!" in no uncertain terms. Thus, though the probe is theoretically positive (and will have a pleasant or neutral effect on someone who has no problem believing it), it can evoke considerable emotion and distress as people get in touch with the pain they have with that issue in their lives.

When this pain and negativity is accessed, people are at what is termed "the barrier" in Hakomi. This is a highly creative place to be, therapeutically speaking. If the therapist can nonviolently assume that there is much good reason and wisdom in the negativity, pain, and resistance, the client can be led to explore it in a way that leads to what is needed for satisfaction and nourishment. The possibility of reorganizing around more realistic, helpful beliefs emerges.

Hakomi has many methods for working with barriers and a theory of the sensitivity cycle that deals with predictable barriers (see Figure 8.4). There are some simple yet necessary functions in life that guide people in an organically satisfying way to increasing levels of sensitivity and efficiency. *Relaxation* allows quietness and sensitivity for the signals of organic needs to emerge (i.e., being hungry). Relaxation then leads to the possibility of *clarity* about what can fill the need (a nice green salad with some cheese). Clarity promotes *effectiveness* of response and action (going to the kitchen and making it). Effective action sets up the possibility of *satisfaction* (being nourished by the meal). Satisfaction leads to more relaxation and increased sensitivity for being aware of the next organic need to emerge (going for a walk, taking a rest, calling a friend, working on a project). Here the system is in fine tune directing and correcting itself as needed.

Adults and adolescents can be evaluated in terms of what barriers arise that keep the cycle from properly functioning. Some people have an *insight* barrier to getting clarity. Perhaps they have experienced the world as harsh and it is too painful to want to be aware of what is real. Others have a measure of insight, but have a *response* barrier to moving directly and openly toward getting what they need. They might have experienced a lot of guilt from independent actions that seemed to hurt or incur the displeasure of meaningful others, so they operate passive-aggressively to get what they want. Different persons might act more manipulatively, and seductively to engineer situations where people give them what they want without them having to ask. They have experienced shame and manipulation in relation to the vulnerability of their needs. A *nourishment* barrier prevents the taking in of satisfaction, even when it is realistically present. People with this barrier might have been raised to be insecure in their needing. They are suspicious, even when emotional support and feeding are available, thinking it cannot be counted on, or is not genuine, or might go away at any moment. Some people experience a *completion* barrier to letting go and surrendering to a state of relaxation. Perhaps they think their self-worth is dependent on achievement, so there is always the next goal to accomplish. There is not time to savor what just happened. Their underlying anxiety about their acceptance arises whenever they begin to relax, and so they take refuge in action.

When barriers to the sensitivity functions arise, the cycle can become a dumb cycle. Roy had an insight barrier to facing some painful issues about his sense of worth that resulted in much underlying anger. The actions he took in relation to his peers did not effectively touch his need at all. They aggravated things. He would assault others verbally, hurl insults, declare disinterest, withdraw from joining activities. The negative responses he got in return did not satisfy anything, or course. He became tighter, more confused, and the cycle spiraled downward.

The probe the therapist used deepened the process and opened Roy's issues up. The therapist said, "Let's do a little word experiment. I'll say a sentence to you and you simply notice what reaction it stirs up inside you. I'm not trying to talk you into anything with the words. I'm not asking you to believe them or not to believe them. Just be open to noticing whatever comes up by itself, automatically. It will tell you something about how you have yourself wired. Okay?" When he was ready, the therapist delivered the probe, "Roy, you are a worthwhile, lovable person."

The barrier was struck instantly. There was an immediate response of strong hurt and pain that Roy tightened against with all the strength of his body. His head became so red it looked like it could blow off like a cork. The therapist contacted the response with a simple:

TH: A lot of pain and hurt comes up around that possibility, huh((?))

AD: It's not true! I'm trash!

TH: Trash((?)) Where does that come from? Is that a voice you hear in your head((?))

AD: I just know it.

Processing—Taking Over

At this point Roy is on the verge of riding the rapids. He is half in, half out because of the tremendous muscle control he is exerting against the spontaneous flood of rising emotion. There is no special virtue in Hakomi of getting into emotional release for the sake of drama. In this situation, though, the muscle tension throughout Roy's body is creating so much noise that there is no room for sensitivity, for learning from the signals trying to be heard.

Kurtz has also pioneered a number of taking-over techniques useful in similar situations to that of Roy's. When people physically tighten against knowledge or expression, when they cover their eyes saying nonverbally that they don't want to see, it could be viewed as resistance. Kurtz views it as an organic expression of the overall process; resistance against the pain certainly, but not resistance to the therapeutic flow. If the resistances are confronted, it would likely heighten the noise level, entrench the resistances, and produce a power struggle between therapist and client.

Kurtz's taking-over techniques are an application of the nonviolence principle, the principle that values going with the flow of experience, as opposed to against it. If people cover their eyes when things get painful, Kurtz would charcteristically help them cover their eyes and say to them, "You don't have to see anything you are not ready to see." If they tighten their shoulders against some inner impulse, he physcially takes over the tightening for them. If they hear a voice in their head saying, "You have to do it yourself, you can't count on others," he or an assistant would take over the voice and say it for them.

There are many variations and possibilities for actively or passively taking over defenses. They all serve to join someone's process by doing for them what they are already doing for themselves. Nothing new is added. What, in effect, is happening, is that the defenses are being maintained, supported, and heightened, as opposed to confronted or torn down. The paradoxical result is that when people know their defenses are safely in place, they can release the energy and investment they have in them to continue the process. The person who did not want to see, develops awareness. The person who was busy imprisoning impulses with tight shoulders begins to identify with the prisoner within. The person who heard, "You have to do it yourself," hears another thought arise, "Well, maybe some people can be there." Again, safety is the key throughout the Hakomi method.

With adolescents, one cannot always use the full spectrum of body oriented techniques developed in Hakomi. One of the hallmarks of Hakomi is the mindful exploration of the mind-body interface. *Hakomi Therapy* (Kurtz, 1983) and Hakomi workshops contain a great deal of material on ways to use the body as an access route to core organizing beliefs, as another royal road to the unconscious. Some body oriented interventions can be used with discretion with youth, though it is often necessary to employ a wider variety of imagery techniques than would be the case in adult settings (Gallegos, 1985; Gallegos & Rennick, 1984; Lazarus, 1977).

With Roy, the therapist noted that he had his forearm resting on his notebook with a clenched fist looking like he would like to smash the notebook with heavy blows, but was holding the impulse back.

TH: Roy, it looks like you are holding back a lot of energy in your arm. How would it be if I did that for you? I'll take over holding the arm in check and you can notice whatever else wants to happen.

Roy agrees with a nonverbal look and gesture. He and the therapist have the kind of relationship that makes this technique possible. The therapist reaches over and puts a powerful hold with both hands on Roy's forearm just as it is resting on the notebook. Roy moves the forearm hesitantly for a moment, and then when he feels secure of the therapist's hold, he begins trying to smash the notebook against the resistance of the hold. Tears begin to flow. Roy's breath starts to come out in gasps and then in a few moments he screams through clenched teeth:

AD: I hate him! I hate him!
TH: Him? Your dad?
AD: Yes, the S.O.B.! He lied to me! He didn't care! He never cared! He's trash!

Processing—The Child

With people riding the rapids, the main task of the therapist becomes simply supporting spontaneous behavior and being aware of openings to move things back to mindfulness or into the child state.

With Roy, transformation around a new belief of being a more worthwhile, lovable person could have taken many possible routes while processing in mindfulness. Most routes take the form of studying and respecting the barriers to new beliefs, and noting what the elements of the barrier need to be willing to let it down. Again, one of the most powerful routes to transformation is through the child state.

Roy got into to a quasi child state of consciousness when the therapist asked him if some particular memories were coming back about times his dad lied to him. Roy bounced back and forth between two memories. Roy was presently 14 years old. When he calmed down enough to just sit with the therapist's supporting hand on his back (not a pitying or condescending hand), he told the therapist of memories from age 10 and age $11\frac{1}{2}$.

At age 10 he had visited his father, the summer after his parents had divorced. During and after the divorce, Roy had heard talk of his father being trash and a no-good alcoholic. When he visited his father he talked with him about how much that bothered him. His father responded by saying people might make mistakes, but they were never trash as long as they cared for other people. He promised Roy that he cared for him, and that if he were ever sick or in trouble, that he would come to him.

Roy returned home a staunch defender of his father, ready to take on anybody who said differently. Then, when he was $11\frac{1}{2}$, he became so seriously ill with pneumonia that he had to be hospitalized. He knew his father would come to him, and he waited expectantly. The father never showed up. Roy was devastated. He decided his father was trash. He had lied; he had never cared. He also decided that he himself was trash. He didn't care either. He hated his father—when he had the energy. Normally, he felt that he could not care less. The world sucked. Nobody cared.

As Roy recounted all this, the therapist functioned as what Hakomi terms "a magical stranger." Children do not need therapists. They only need compassionate adults who will talk with them honestly and truthfully. Children can tolerate an incredible range of pain if they are supported and understood in the process. The long term effect of sexual abuse, for instance, does not come from the physical acts themselves. It comes from the denial, discounting, and blaming that happens afterward when the child tries to talk about it.

The child state of consciousness is such that it allows the therapist to enter into the memory of yesteryear as a new factor, as a stranger, as the compassionate adult who was not there the first round. When allowed access to Roy's memory, the therapist was able to talk to both the younger Roy, with the contemporary Roy present, letting him/them know things about alcoholism and troubles parents get into, letting him know how understandable it now appeared that Roy came up with negative beliefs about himself, recounting the historical effects those beliefs led to, and talking about how different the world and Roy really were from the way younger Roy had decided. Throughout the whole process of talking to Roy in this special state, which makes the common words being used accessible to a normally nonreceptive consciousness, the therapist was constantly tracking how Roy was taking in the information, stopping when there were questions, and making contact as appropriate.

Processing—Integration

Once transformation around a new belief has been explored in mindfulness, the process moves toward integration. The belief must be stabilized and supported. Ways of carrying it home and nurturing it need to be strategized. Indeed, if the old belief is one that goes deep, it will take another 5 years of cultivating the new belief before the client turns around and notices that the old issue is no longer an active force in his life.

There are many techniques for helping to integrate. Reliving one's past life or projecting one's future life in terms of the new belief is one way (Cameron-Bandler, 1978). Storytelling can be an effective tool with children, adolescents, and adults, though junior high students are sometimes put off by anything that smacks of being childish.

With Roy, the therapist asked if he could tell him a little story that reflected something of Roy's experience. Roy agreed. The therapist knew that one satisfying thing Roy had to cling to in his life was working in the garden with his mother. There they could cooperate and feel good about each other, though they didn't say much verbally. The therapist told this story:

A wildflower grew high in the mountains. It was especially hardy and beautiful with bright blue, purple, and yellow colors. But it was growing on a steep bank by an especially treacherous, curving, climbing trial, so that nobody ever noticed the flower and its beauty, because all the hikers were looking down worrying about the trail ahead. The flower didn't understand that, and thought it was being ignored and snubbed. It became angry and tried to dislodge and roll down pebbles and gravel with its roots, to make the trail worse for the hikers. This, of course, made it even more unlikely that anyone would ever discover the flower and its hardy beauty. One day, however, a group of kids were climbing. The boy leading in front was getting so tired that he decided to call a rest right in front of the flower, even though it wasn't a great place to rest. Then he saw the flower and was so excited he called everybody else over to see it. They all were happy and thankful for the flower's beauty, and the flower was so happy it almost cried for the joy of finding out it wasn't an outcast after all. After that the flower went to work concentrating on spreading over the bank as much as possible, filling the bare places, and securing the ground with its roots, so things wouldn't fall on the trail for climbers to worry about. Many other climbers went by. Some were still so concerned with their own balance that they never saw the flower. The flower understood that they had their own things to think about. A number of the climbers did see the flower, and marveled at their good fortune. And the flower was happy for the joy it could give.

Hakomi values keeping consciousness on board throughout a process. Here the story is used at the integration phase. The analogy of the flower to Roy is close enough that Roy understands what is being said and that he is being offered a metaphor with another dimension to help him (Weiss, 1987). This is a different approach than others take who try to work on the unconscious, by making the analogy far enough removed so that the person's consciousness does not pick up that he is being addressed by the story (Gordon, 1978).

For homework, the therapist invited Roy to report back after sizing-up the people around him in terms of what kind of flower they seemed to be and what would cause that in a person. Why were some people undiscovered wild flowers; some pretty, but with thorns that said not to come close; some growing wildly, overgrowing everyone else like they felt they wouldn't be recognized otherwise; some dependable, coming to bloom every year; some happy to be in the garden with everybody else; and so on? Roy also agreed to talk to the guidance counselor about the possibility of getting into a junior college course on landscaping, which would give him additional motivation for learning reading, writing, accounting, drafting, and other skills.

CASE ILLUSTRATIONS

JAKE

Jake was a 15-year-old boy who was a student in an adolescent treatment program. He was an only child. His mother, Sherill, was a protective, overweight woman who had devoted her life to being the family caretaker. His father, Ralph, was seriously physically disabled and had been unemployed and home most of Jake's growing up years.

Reading Jake's school history was like reading a very long and gross description of a child out of control throughout his recorded school life. Hyperactivity was only one of many terms used to describe Jake. Disobedient, out of control, dangerous, abusive, self-destructive, and disrespectful were only a few of the terms of endearment.

Jake came to the treament center frustrated, angry with the system, angry with himself, and—most of all—angry with his parents. He came totally out of control. In studying Jake's history, the therapist discovered that he, too, suffered from the same debilitating disease that his father suffered from, myatonic dystrophy. Jake's mood swings and unpredictable rage proved to him conclusively that the world was truly out to get him. His actions demonstrated a "Why me?" attitude. Jake shouted his unwillingness to accept this fate by acting as aggressive and out of control as one could imagine.

In beginning to work with Jake, many things had to occur. First of all, he was classified as dangerous. He had earned his way out of the public school by wielding a knife at a group of students at a football game. On many occasions he had also threatened both students and faculty on the school grounds. The first step the therapist took with Jake was to establish herself as safe to be with. This meant it was essential to communicate to Jake that (1) she was not afraid of him, and (2) she believed in him and his possibility for hope and change.

Together, they agreed to a three step program. The first step was to enroll him in a classroom that had a strong behavior management system built around assuring success. The class made it extraordinarily safe for Jake by describing exactly what he could and could not do. It took over a lot of his need for structure and security.

Second, they developed an individual therapy proposal directed toward helping him deal with both his rage and his pain around simply existing.

Third, the family was involved in weekly therapy sessions in which the goals were to strengthen the parental subsystem and to give some new parenting skills more relevant to the issues they were now confronting with their teenage son. Overall, it was an ambitious undertaking.

Jake expressed his rage through movement: hitting, running, striking, and kicking; movement so intense that it often resulted in losing his conscious self to what he described as some outside monster. As he talked, it became clear that at these times Jake experienced what might be termed an out-of-the-body experience. He would experience two selves, a stronger self bent on destruction, and a weaker self, an observer watching from a safe distance in awe and surprise of the destruction wrought by the stronger self. Jake also spoke of the quiet times, the times when, after he finished running, he was quiet. He chose to spend this time walking; walking in the woods close to his home was his favorite thing to do.

The therapist and Jake spent their first sessions walking and talking; always moving, sometimes just being quiet together; in that way, trust was formed. Ron was the initial guide. The therapist became the careful, observant listener, tracking carefully, contacting, hoping for Jake to teach her an access route to unlocking the demons within.

In addition to this supportive time with the therapist, Jake learned that he was safely supported within the school environment. He bought the system of earning points and positive reinforcers. He liked earning what he got. He liked the fact that the system guaranteed a specific outcome, providing he played the game. Power struggles were eliminated.

His parents also began to join in the change. For the first time in many years, the phone was quiet. The school no longer called their home reporting their son's most recent hassle. For the first time they stopped and had time to discover and contemplate their own relationship. This was both good and bad, because as they had more time for themselves, it became increasingly clear that their son's outrageous behavior had truly been the focus of their existence. Family therapy became critical in this developmental process.

One day when Jake and the therapist had returned from a walk, and were sitting together, the therapist asked him to close his eyes and to report to her what he would like more than anything in all the world to hear someone say to him. With little or no waiting he responded by saying how he wished to hear that "everything would be okay."

The therapist asked him to imagine that he was floating in space, being the observer he often reported himself to be in one of his rages. When she observed his eyelids beginning to flutter, she knew he had gone into a mindful state. Immediately after posing the probe, "What do you notice happening inside you when you hear me say . . . everything will be okay?" Jake began to weep. Tears came out of his inner depths, unshed tears, tears stopped and choked off by years of rage. Within the safety of the room and the therapist's presence, Jake gave into the painful experience of his frustrated existence. He reported to the therapist how that existence was for him and had it acknowledged. Jake and the therapist rode the rapids of painful awareness.

As Jake refocused his energies back into the room, into ordinary consciousness, he looked at the therapist, smiled, and reached out for a giant but quick hug. For both of them it was a beautiful sharing, and then, quickly, a time to move on. It was a good struggle. It "hurt good," as Jake reported.

Jake illustrates how working with young people requires essential timing. The dance is a fast one. Just a moment for waltzing in mindfulness appears. The therapist enters the moment promoting the young person's self-discovery and empowerment, and the moment is gone. Jake has an "ah-ha" experience and the therapist escorts him back to the safety of his most predictable classroom, and more math and English. It was important that Jake's integrity was maintained, that he not feel that displaying emotion did anything to prostitute himself. The therapist helped Jake to walk out of the therapy session with a sense that his was a dance that even his friends could learn. It was natural, understandable, real, and something they could do again.

ROBERT

Robert walked into the therapist's office for the first time. He was referred by his school counselor. He was described as being extraordinarily complicated, bright, but totally passive resistant. His teachers viewed him as a class nuisance. They had long ago given up on the fact that this young man had an IQ of over 120. According to one teacher, she was simply relieved when Robert sat quietly in class and spaced out, which he continuously did.

The first moment when client and therapist view one another can contain a magical energy exchange in which joining occurs. The therapist can help orchestrate this joining with an element of surprise. In Robert's case, the therapist said, "Please look at me, check me out and decide whether I am trustworthy or not." Robert, who was so used to resisting, was empowered by that question.

"Yah, you're alright," he said.

Within seconds, Robert and the therapist made a contract to begin work in an area that up to that point Robert strongly resisted. In the early seconds of greeting, the therapist's goals had been two fold: (1) to say to Robert that she trusted him to know certain things about himself in relation to his safety needs, and, (2) to say she believed he had the power to do work for himself, if given the opportunity. She trusted Robert's ability to depend on his own intuitive knowing. Few words were necessary. With the trust established, work was ready to begin.

The therapist had been given the assignment by Robert's school counselor to shape up this resistive kid. He was capable of being successful in school and something was obviously infuencing him to be unsuccessful.

Robert's home environment was complicated. He was the oldest of two children. He lived with his natural mom, stepdad, and stepbrother, dad's son from a previous marriage. The natural father had always been out of the picture, living in another state. Both boys were considered problem children by school and parents alike. The whole family was experiencing a great deal of stress and pain at the time of Robert's referral. Robert described dad as "too strict," mom as "cool, but," and brother James as a "total jerk," a description seconded by educational authorities previously involved with the family.

As they talked, it became clear to the therapist that Robert could and would, if given a chance, know exactly what he needed and wanted to do with his life. He could be guided through whatever rapids were necessary and set loose. Robert put it this way to the therapist: "I want to get rid of this crap."

Without even asking him to be particularly mindful, the therapist responded by asking, "What do you experience when you hear me say to you . . . You can get rid of the crap. Everything will be fine((?))" Robert was ready for things to get better. He just needed permission for them to be that way. He became animated with the probe, though it was suggesting what he had previously ruled out as impossible, that things could be all right. The power of the probe came from the agreement of Robert's unconscious, and from the therapist's willingness to go with the flow of Robert's process as it was emerging. She was repeating the lines he was feeding her.

To begin with, the therapist and Robert worked out a plan for school to give him more of sense of empowerment. Home complications were bracketed and put on the shelf for the time being. She asked him to simply hang out in his classes for a week, step back in his mind, and just passively observe what went on in class that disposed him to be unsuccessful. Was it too hard, too easy, too noisy, or what? Here she was supporting a defensive behavior he had been using for years, as opposed to pushing for its removal.

Operating with a sense of freedom and support, Robert returned in a week with a highly creative plan. It involved working in the computer lab with a teacher willing to help him create a self-teaching program for the two classes he was currently failing. He also had clarified some of the reasons behind his poor academic performance, boredom being high on the list. Robert and the computer teacher worked on his plan, and Robert passed those two classes.

Home issues were the next issue to be tackled together. The therapist began exploring this dimension with Robert using the same probe, "Everything will be fine." The barrier arose immediately in Robert, saying this could never be true. The therapist explored the barrier further by asking Robert to check inside and find out what he would like to hear that would open the door for change at home. He quickly responded by saying that he wished his dad (stepdad) would say "You're okay," that all he ever did was yell and send him to his room, and compare him to his little brother who was a creep.

Robert was trusting the therapist at a deep level, a level that it was crucial not to betray. One can never say anything to client that is not true. The therapist talked to Robert a little about mindfulness and how it could help bring up the programming of our personal computers. She invited him to sit back and to be both relaxed and alert. When he was ready she asked him, "What happens, Robert, what do you become aware of, whatever that might be, when you hear *me* say to you, I think you are really okay((?))"

The gate was open, and the tears flowed. The tears went to his natural father and whether he knew Robert was okay. They went to stepdad and the loneliness and need that Robert had about wanting him to provide something he needed from his natural dad, and his expecting him to know this somehow. The tears brought with them a new kind of dawn. Robert moved quickly into another mode and suggested they talk with his mom. Perhaps she could help. An appointment was set for the next week to meet with Robert and his mother. The whole session had taken only 30 minutes.

The report the following week from school was that a miracle had occurred. Robert's school behavior had drastically changed. The meeting with Robert and his mom was likewise miraculous. She had no idea what her son had been experiencing. Once allowed into his inner world in the safety of the therapeutic setting, she was able, with the willing help of her husband, to make some changes at home that reassured Robert that he was okay. Robert was able to provide guidance about what he needed. The expectations of the parents did not change. Their understanding of him was markedly altered, and their approach to him, because of their new understanding, became far different.

SUMMARY AND CONCLUSION

Hakomi operates out of principles of unity and organicity which nonviolently honor the wisdom of an adolescent's experience. Mindfulness is the major means for promoting the study of one's organization of experience and what is needed to foster the communication of all the parts within the whole. Hakomi majors in accessing core levels of belief within a person, at the same time that it acknowledges the interrelationships and interdependence of environmental and behavior variables, cooperating with therapies aimed at these factors.

In terms of research, Eugene Gendlin (1986) has many helpful suggestions that are consistent with Hakomi principles, of which only a few can be mentioned here. One is giving up attempts to pit entire therapies against each other in terms of effectiveness. They are too large, global, diffuse, and contaminated with elements held in common. Do assume the unity of cognition, feeling, imagery, and behavior, and assume they will react with and change each other if tested together. Do a lot of informal experimenting and testing of hypotheses in the field and share the results. Keep live cassette and videotapes of clearly successful cases when possible. Define microprocesses of a therapy and check to see if they are properly carried out in experiments. Don't assume they are. Get research, training, and practice closer together by using the same outlines and definitions of processes in each setting. Employ, teach, use, and study microprocesses of a therapy in larger social settings, not restricting them to therapy settings. Study how to change the process of a therapy to make it more regularly successful for more people. Certainly, give up loyalty to strict party lines, and be willing to incorporate what seems to work.

REFERENCES

Bandler, R., & Grinder, J. (1975a). *Patterns of the hypnotic techniques of Milton H. Erickson, M.D.*, (Vol. 1). Cupertino, CA: Meta Publications.

Bandler, R., & Grinder, J. (1975b). *The structure of magic* (Vol. 1). Palo Alto: Science and Behavior Books.

Barstow, C. (1985, Winter). An overview of the Hakomi method of psychotherapy. *Hakomi Forum*, pp. 8–18.

Bateson, G. (1979). *Mind and nature: A necessary unity.* New York: E.P. Dutton.

Cameron-Bandler, L. (1978). *They lived happily ever after.* Cupertino, CA: Meta Publications.

Erickson, M., & Rossi, E. (1979). *Hypnotherapy: An exploratory casebook.* New York: Irvington.

Gallegos, E. (1985, Winter). Animal imagery, the chakra system and psychotherapy. *Hakomi Forum,* pp. 19–25.

Gallegos, E., & Rennick, T. (1984). *Inner journeys.* Wellingborough, England: Turnstone Press.

Gendlin, E. (1978). *Focusing.* New York: Everest House.

Gendlin, E. (1979). Experiential psychotherapy. In R. Corsini (Ed.), *Current psychotherapies* (pp. 340–373). Itasca, IL: F.E. Peacock.

Gendlin, E. (1986). What comes after traditional psychotherapy research? *American Psychologist, 41*,(2), 131–136.

Gordon, D. (1978). *Therapeutic metaphors.* Cupertino, CA: Meta Publications.

Hilgard, E. (1965). *Hypnotic susceptibility.* New York: Harcourt.

Horner, A. (1979). *Object relations and the developing ego in therapy.* New York: Jason Aronson.

Johanson, G. (1984a, Summer). Watzlawick, Wilbur, and the work (Editorial). *Hakomi Forum,* pp. 1–5.

Johanson, G. (1984b, Summer). Intensive family services. *Hakomi Forum*, pp. 39–53.

Johanson, G. (1986a, Summer). Taking it home with you (Editorial). *Hakomi Forum,* pp. 1–6.

Johanson, G. (1986b, Summer) Hakomi in the trenches. *Hakomi Forum*, pp. 7–17.

Johanson, G. (1987a). *A curious form of therapy: Hakomi.* Unpublished manuscript, The Hakomi Institute, Boulder, CO.

Johanson, G. (1987b). *Theoretical and practical considerations for the conducting of behavioral-contact groups in schools.* Unpublished manuscript.

Kopp, S. (1972). *If you meet the Buddha on the road, kill him!* Ben Lomond: Science and Behavior Books.

Kurtz, R. (1983). *Hakomi therapy.* Boulder, CO: Hakomi Institute.

Kurtz, R. (1985a). *Koerperzentrierte psychotherapie: Die Hakomi methode.* Essen: Synthesis Verlag.

Kurtz, R. (1985b, Summer). The organization of experience in Hakomi therapy. *Hakomi Forum,* pp. 3–9.

Kurtz, R., & Prestera, H. (1976). *The body reveals.* New York: Harper and Row/ Quicksilver Books.

Lazarus, A. (1977). *In the mind's eye.* New York: Rawson Associates.

Loevinger, J. (1976). *Ego development.* San Francisco: Jossey-Bass.

Lowen, A. (1958). *The physical dynamics of character structure.* New York: Grune & Stratton.

Lowen, A. (1975). *Bioenergetics.* New York: Penguin.

MacKinnon, R., & Michels, R. (1971). *The psychiatric interview in clinical practice.* Philadelphia: W.B. Saunders.

Meeks, J. (1971). *The fragile alliance: An orientation to the outpatient psychotherapy of the adolescent.* Baltimore: Williams and Wilkins.

Missildine, W. (1963). *Your inner child of the past.* New York: Simon and Schuster.

Ogden, P. (1983). The options chart. In R. Kurtz (Ed.), *Hakomi therapy* (pp. 133–137). Boulder: Hakomi Institute.

Prigogine, I., & Stengers, I. (1984). *Order out of chaos.* New York: Bantam.

Rogers, C. (1942). *Counseling and psychotherapy.* Boston: Houghton Mifflin.

Rogers, C. (1951). *Client-centered therapy.* Boston: Houghton Mifflin.

Rogers, C. (1961). *On becoming a person.* Boston: Houghton Mifflin.

Satir, V. (1972). *Peoplemaking.* Palo Alto: Science and Behavior books.

Satir, V., Stachowiak, J., & Taschman, H. (1975). *Helping families to change.* New York: Jason Aronson.

Savicki, V., & Brown, R. (1981). *Working with troubled children.* New York: Human Sciences Press.

Shapiro, D. (1965). *Neurotic styles.* New York: Basic Books.

Skynner, A. (1976). *Systems of family and marital psychotherapy.* New York: Brunner/ Mazel.

Sullivan, H. (1953). *The interpersonal theory of psychiatry.* New York: W.W. Norton.

Sullivan, H. (1954). *The psychiatric interview.* New York: W.W. Norton.

Sullivan, H. (1956). *Clinical studies in psychiatry.* New York: W.W. Norton.

Taylor, C. (1985, Winter). Use of elemetns of Hakomi therapy with seriously emotionally disturbed adolescents. *Hakomi Forum,* pp. 35–36.

Weiss, H. (1987, Summer). The use of story telling in Hakomi therapy. *Hakomi Forum,* pp. 31–37.

Weiss, H. & Benz, D. (1986). *Einfuhrung in die Hakomi-Methode.* Koesel Verlag.

Wilber, K. (1979). *No boundary.* Los Angeles: Center Publications.

CHAPTER 9

The Focusing Technique with Children and Adolescents

GEORGE V. NEAGU

Focusing is a new way of therapeutically living with a child or adolescent in a play therapy setting or, for that matter, at school or in the home. Only recently has focusing been adapted to children. For about 15 years, following research findings from psychotherapy that clarified the self-referential processes that distinguish successful adult clients from unsuccessful ones, focusing has been a welcome new addition to the armamentarium of therapeutic procedures.

Despite its effectiveness with adults, this experiential therapeutic procedure has been largely untried with children and adolescents. Can the steps involved in focusing be adapted to children? At what age levels? Can children be taught to focus? Is the crucial determinant for successful therapy with children the same as with adults? Literature regarding the use of focusing in play therapy is limited, and it is too soon to answer these questions. However, this chapter is intended to fill this void and, it is hoped, stimulate others to explore the possibilities of using focusing in working with children.

The growing significance of focusing with children is reflected in the reports by educators in Austria, Japan, and Canada; they are included in this chapter. Also included is the description of a mother who has been using focusing with her three children for the past three years. It needs to be emphasized that focusing is not just another new therapeutic modality; it is, rather, a skill that can be taught in the context of any modality used or that the therapist is trained in. A fundamental assertion of focusing theory, which has its historical roots in the work of Carl Rogers and his colleagues, is that genuine personality change does not occur unless the special internal processing called focusing takes place. Another way of putting it is that no change takes place unless the client engages in a series of experienced, definable, self-referential steps. The fact that successful therapy outcomes have been reported from varying modalities means that the steps described in the focusing procedure have occurred. That these steps, or movements, can be taught to persons who do not possess this skill naturally is a unique and valuable contribution.

This chapter will describe research from which focusing theory and procedures evolved. It will provide a comprehensive overview of focusing work done with children and adolescents and will give case illustrations to demonstrate how children are brought to live their problems differently, and then to separate themselves from whatever troubles them.

FOCUSING—RESEARCH, THEORY, AND PROCEDURES

The focusing theory and procedures were developed by Eugene T. Gendlin (1981a) at the University of Chicago. For many years, Gendlin was a close associate of Carl Rogers and played an important part in the continued development of client-centered therapy. However, his interest in the experiencing process that goes on below the level of awareness, and the way symbolization carries the person's experiencing forward, led eventually to his development of experiential psychology. (In 1970, for his development of experiential psychology, he was chosen by the Psychotherapy Division of the American Psychological Association for their first Distinguished Professional Psychologist of the Year Award.) This was catalyzed by his research with Carl Rogers using client-centered therapy with psychotic patients in Wisconsin. It was also based on a sequence of studies (van der Veen & Stoler, 1965; Tomlinson & Hart, 1962; Rogers, et al., 1967; Gendlin, et al., 1968) with adult patients from whom Gendlin and his colleagues at the University of Chicago discovered what successful patients do and what unsuccessful patients do not do. They discovered that patients who frequently refer, or attend, to their bodily feeling process, the holistic quality of their organismic experiencing (which prompts new images and fresh words to surface), have a different self-reference process than unsuccessful patients. People who link concept-to-concept-to-concept and do not take time to refer to their whole bodily sensing of what they are saying usually intellectualize or engage in what a gestalt therapist would call aboutism or, simply, emoting.

The successful patient (client and patient are used interchangeably in this chapter) makes room for the felt sense. The patient states the problem and then becomes a good listener to what it all feels like inside, the whole quality of it. The patient links concept-to-bodily process-to-concept-to-bodily process, and so on. It is a nonlinear, nonlogical process, but the interaction between the implicit bodily felt sense and the symbolic processing that occurs is crucial to change-steps.

Theory

Central to focusing is its emphasis on bodily experiencing, what Gendlin has termed a felt sense. Felt sense does not refer to mere physical sensations, nor does it refer to emotions, such as sadness, anger, fear, and so on. It is less vivid, not as intense, and usually unclear. One of the distinctive aspects of focusing is that it cherishes those moments of experiencing that are confusing, unfamiliar, marginally there, and fuzzy. It is an assumption of focusing theory that change does not happen if a person stays only with reactions that are known and familiar. Perhaps the reader has experienced using a self-developing film. At first there is no image at all on the film. Very shortly, there is a murky quality to the film and it seems as if nothing is going to appear. However, allowing the time for the chemicals to interact produces a sense, still indefinite, of an image. Finally the person's attention to the film is rewarded with a meaningful image. Now one interacts with a completed picture rather than with something unformed. Suppose the picture were thrown away while still unformed and murky. This would be analogous to being too anxious to attend to any uncomfortable, confused, unformed place within in order to stay with the safety of familiar words and reactions; too impatient to allow the time and attention for something new and different to develop.

Thus, the quality of bodily sensing and knowing is basic in focusing and is of primary concern. A major effort of the therapist is to help clients attend to how they are being with their problematic situations, not just what they are addressing. The view of people is that they are bodily interactions, with others and with their environment. This bodily sense of the complexity of our situations and interactions can be expressed in more than one way. For instance, when hunger is experienced, the words "I am hungry" do not reflect all that being hungry implies (e.g., the extent hunger is experienced, the implicit actions one must take to satisfy one's hunger, etc.). It has already been mentioned that the felt sense is unclear at first (i.e., preverbal, preconceptual). When one receives an image or word that seems to adequately reflect what the feeling-intricacy is communicating, there is an experiential effect. Gendlin has termed this movement a carrying forward, to signify a further bodily living. Most of us have had the experience of sensing that we know a name that cannot be recalled. Our body experiences—felt sense—this knowing. We also know those names that do not fit our bodily sense of what is right. Finally, great relief occurs as the correct symbol is remembered. Our living goes forward in a released, unblocked way. One must constantly refer to the bodily feeling as the energizing source to new words, responses, and images. (Gendlin, 1981a; 1984).

Procedure

It may be useful to contrast the way focusing is done with children as illustrated in this chapter with the six steps taught to adults. Adults can learn to do focusing alone or with someone else. It is important that the adult be comfortable and relaxed, but not relaxed to the point of sleepiness. When first teaching focusing to adults as a skill, the procedure may take longer and appear more mechanical than a naturally flowing process until it is learned. In actuality, the steps may not follow sequentially inwardly; there is nothing mechanical about this approach; in fact, it is sometimes exquisitely subtle. The sense of how the person is experiencing a problem is more important than what the problem is. The experience must feel good to the client or it is not being done right.

The six steps, as outlined by Gendlin, are:

(1) Clearing a space.

This step involves listing all the problems that tense a person, stressors that stand between the person and a sense of well-being. There is no attempt to solve these problems; it is rather like taking groceries out of a grocery bag and looking at each item before placing it aside. In doing this step it is important that the person's attention be on his body. It is valuable at this point for a person to assert to himself that he feels totally fine and then wait to see what uneasiness, problem, or trouble comes up to say, in effect, "No, I'm here. You would be fine if it weren't for me." It is vital that each problem gets a friendly hearing without any compulsion to immediately work on it; that will come later. After each problem it is useful to ask: "Except for this, would I be okay?" Allowing time for each uneasiness to surface is imperative. The goal here is to get the problems out and to experience, if possible, living in one's body as if that uneasiness or problem were not there.

(2) Getting a felt sense.

The person is asked which problem hurts the most, or is the most difficult. The client may be instructed in advance not to analyze or talk to himself about the problem (the client has already done this before coming to therapy and is still stuck), but to distance himself or stand back from the problem and determine how, in a bodily way, it all feels. In the instruction to this step the person may be told directly not to go into the problem but to see a sense of well-being with the problem at a distance. At this point a subtlety may occur. The person may reject the idea of feeling fine about the problem categorically. However, this categorical rejection may be a knowing that is not bodily based at the moment. This can be turned to advantage by asking the person to keep his attention on whatever it is in the body that finds the problem unacceptable. This step promotes bodily sensing of the whole problem while remaining separate from it. One can interact with oneself and the problem but one is not the problem.

(3) Finding a handle.

What is the quality of the felt sense? The person finds a word or image that best describes the way one senses the problem. Sometimes it is helpful to give examples of quality words (i.e., heavy, sticky, shaky, etc).

(4) Resonating the handle.

The handle is useful in the event that the person moves away from the felt sense or gets distracted. By repeating the word, the person may evoke the felt sense again. When a person repeats the word or image, or whatever symbolism best describes the bodily experience, the person is in effect testing whether the symbol and felt sense are congruent.

(5) Asking.

Usually, Gendlin points out, the fourth step may offer a little shift or relief, but not enough to change the problem. This step involves staying with the unclear sense by using the handle. For example, one may state that one feels jumpy inside. Then the therapist may ask the client to ask, "What is there about this problem that makes me feel jumpy?" One does this more than once, allowing sufficient time for the felt sense to shift. It is essential that enough time be allowed for this.

(6) Receiving.

Welcome whatever comes in a friendly way, at a little distance. Gendlin advises one to allow a space for this felt sense, to sense it, and to just be with it. If the person finds himself talking answers to himself (mind-wording) then this step is not happening correctly. The response should have come from the felt sense by now. This step usually feels good; it is like an act of appreciation assuming all has gone well up to this point. When a person receives a sincerely given gift, the act of receiving it involves showing appreciation and savoring the gift, and time must be allowed for this process.

THE SIX STEPS WITH CHILDREN

In doing the six steps with children it is important to underscore that the relationship is more significant than the technique. This also means that the therapist should readily allow the child to break from the game. The goal is to reach the inner felt sense and the strategies used to achieve this must not come to dominate the process. As Schaefer (1976) has shown, there are many different avenues leading to change in play therapy; this technique is not all that occurs during the hour. The following examples of the ways children have been engaged in focusing assume that sufficient rapport has been established and that the child's needs to do something else do not compete.

Step 1

The therapist might say, "Let's play complaint department. You tell me all the things you don't like, that make you mad, things that bother you. Each time you come, if you would like, we'll tape your complaints." After the client exhausts all his complaints, the tapes are played back to him. The pause button is used after each complaint as the child is gently encouraged to refer inward, "See how that feels." No other comments or interpretations are given. The goal here is two-fold: (1) To teach children to allow space for listening to their feelings, and (2) To gradually teach children not to be afraid of their feelings and to value them. One educator in Japan has children put each problem in a separate box that they have drawn. Another has the child draw a picture of how each problem feels. A mother who has been doing focusing with her children introduced this step through a storytelling technique. With an older child, an adolescent, the therapist might say, "Pretend you are emptying your pockets of all the problems, just as if they were things or objects. Put anything that stands in the way of your feeling great on my desk."

Step 2

Step 2 is completed by asking the child to pick the complaint that is most bothersome. The important point is that it is a here-and-now sensing.

Alternatively, the therapist could list all the complaints, read them back, and have the child make clay balls or cut out paper circles that are placed next to each problem to indicate the size of that complaint. How the relationship is, the age of the child, and the type of child determines the way these steps are presented. Obviously flexibility and considerable ingenuity are required.

Step 3

In Step 3 the therapist might ask directly, "How does all that (the complaint that feels worst) feel inside you?" or, "How does your body feel inside when you think of that?" (Focusing questions are usually open-ended.) A variation would be to invite the child to draw or paint a picture of how he feels inside when he thinks of that complaint. Sometimes painting both a picture of the problem and a picture of how the problem makes him feel helps the child gain some distance. It also implicitly gives the child a measure of control of the problem. In addition, the child can be asked, "Does the picture match how you feel inside right now?" If the child says, "Not exactly," he is asked how he needs to change it so that it will match. If there is no need for changing the picture, encourage the child to use words to describe the feelings represented in the picture. (If the child is very young, he may be encouraged to tell a story about the picture and encouraged to tell how he feels about it. Then he may be encouraged to tell a story about his feeling about the story, thus helping the child to learn that behind every feeling there is a story.)

Step 4

In Step 4 the child conveys the way he experiences the problem. For example, the child says he feels "a lot of wavy, very wavy" inside. The therapist invites the child to sit quietly and to say to himself, "a lot of wavy," or the therapist might just quietly repeat the words. The child might be asked just to sit and draw what "a lot of wavy" means to him and then to tell a story about it. If the words match the feeling, then movement to Step 5 occurs.

Step 5

The child is asked what it is that makes it feel wavy. This step, like the others, cannot be hurried. The child is encouraged to listen to the "lots of wavy" inside as if he were at a play and "a lot of wavy" was on the stage performing and he was in the audience. This creates a sense of how it all feels. The child, in fact, may be encouraged to see what comes with "a lot of wavy" on the stage, how that makes him feel, and so on.

Step 6

Finally, the child is encouraged to continue being with the performance. He might even be asked how it would feel to let himself enjoy the performance. After awhile the therapist may ask the child if he would feel like closing the curtain or if there still something going on with "a lot of wavy." Perhaps, following up on the example where the child drew paper circles or made clay balls, the therapist may ask the child how far away he can put the paper circle cutouts or clay balls representing the problem. The writer urges children to be literal about this and to move the circles or balls as far across the room as possible.

The sixth step with the child, as with the adult, is a new biointegrative way of living with the problem. The child is not caught by it but can close the curtain on it. He has the problem but he learns he is not synonomous with the problem. He gains a sense of separateness from it while still relating to it until he can let go of it.

It must be reemphasized that the above steps are not mechanically done, and that they vary according to the ages and personalities of the children as well as the therapist's relationship with them. The introduction to focusing as a skill with younger children is not formally done, as it might be with an adolescent or an adult. (One might say, for example, to a teenager, "I know you've tried many ways of looking at and solving these problems, but I wonder if I could interest you in a different way of going at it?" and then proceed with the steps.) In the writer's practice, the child leads the way and focusing is not imposed; therefore, the above steps may not happen sequentially. The steps are a useful criterion whenever the opportunities arise to help the client be more helpful to himself. The therapist does much listening and reflecting, especially when the child's behavior, verbal or otherwise, is clearly symbolic of important experiential biomeanings inside.

As the reader will see from the literature described below on focusing with children and from the case illustrations, there are many ways of approaching children with the focusing steps.

LITERATURE ON FOCUSING WITH CHILDREN
AND ADOLESCENTS

The research described and the method of experiential focusing developed by
Gendlin has been applied in widely varying contexts: school, business, creative
writing, religion, work with cancer patients, and dream work, as well as psychotherapy. All of these efforts, however, involved working with adults, and
the literature reflects this. Literature reporting work with children and adolescents is very limited. Child therapists who are using focusing have not written
much. Levant and Shlien (1984) lamented that so few child therapists have
taken the time to write; Virginia Axline is one of the notable exceptions.

The first article in this country on focusing and play therapy appeared in
the *Association For Play Therapy Newsletter* in March, 1986, and was reprinted later that year in the *Focusing Folio* published by The Focusing Institute (Neagu, 1986). The first article on the use of focusing with borderline
adolescents was published in 1984 in this country, a reprint of an article from
Holland (Santen, 1984). This was followed by another study using focusing
with a teenage firesetter (Barba, 1985). Exciting projects still underway have
been reported teaching focusing to entire school districts in Schruns, Austria
(Rüdisser, 1986) and in Fukuoka, Japan (Murayama, 1986). In addition, two
Catholic priests, the Reverend Peter A. Campbell and the Reverend Edwin M.
McMahon, both of whom hold Ph.Ds, teach focusing to promote spiritual
growth. Their organization, The Institute for Research in Spirituality, trains
people in focusing and has published pamphlets of the way a California
mother, Marianne Thompson, has taught her own children to use focusing in
their development (McMahon & Campbell, 1985).

FOCUSING IN SCHOOLS AND AT HOME

Dr. Shoji Murayama, a professor of education at Kyushu University in Fukuoka, Japan, and editor of the Japanese *Journal of Humanistic Psychology,*
has been working with a group of schoolteachers in Fukuoka, Japan, developing a research project on teaching clearing-a-space, the first focusing step, to
elementary school students in the classroom (Murayama, 1986). The students
are taught focusing in the classroom for one school year, three to four days
per week, 5 to 20 minutes per day.

His project is built on two years of preliminary work that indicates that
second and third grade students can do clearing-a-space very well after three
months' training of only a few minutes each day. He reported that the students
showed a marked improvement in their personal integration and achievement,
as well as improvement in the class atmosphere.

He first teaches focusing individually to the elementary school teachers, 10
sessions each. Then the teachers are taught to use focusing instructions that

he and his colleagues developed for the children. They ask the students to imagine boxes, or they hand out a sheet on which six open boxes are shown. When the students practice clearing-a-space, they put their felt problems into the boxes in imagery, or write each problem or situation into a box. Follow-up sessions are conducted with the teachers. The goal in their research is to determine whether learning focusing, especially clearing-a-space, has a significant effect on elementary school students' personal integration, achievement, and class atmosphere.

Mary McGuire (1986) of the Focusing Institute in Chicago described how she helped children clear-a-space in a pilot project in a school in Ontario, Canada. She chose to work with two grades. Grade one consisted of 32 children, aged 6 years, and grade six consisted of 28 children, ages 10 to 11 years (McGuire, personal correspondence).

She chose these grades because she wanted to see the differences between 6-year-olds and 10-year-olds. With the first graders she needed something concrete; she had them bring their favorite stuffed animals to the classroom. She began by asking them, "When you feel happy where do you feel that?" They said, "In here!" pointing to their chests. She went through different feelings (e.g., sadness, excitement, anger, etc.). The children always felt inside (stomach, chest, etc.)—throughout the body. McGuire reported that the first graders were able to directly sense their feelings, including positive feelings like loving, through this use of their favorite stuffed animals. She had the children hold their stuffed animals and invited them to cuddle the animals and feel their loving inside, and to let the loving go through their whole bodies. After 2 minutes or so, she had them close their eyes and asked them to remain with the feeling of loving their animals. Then she invited them to see if there was something that worried them, and to see how that felt inside. This was followed by asking the children to take the worry and put it in a secret hiding place. Again, she had them hug the animals to get the loving feeling, in contrast to the worried feeling. She did this alternately, with each worry for brief periods of time (McGuire, 1986). The technique was found useful in helping to sensitize children toward being with their feelings in a body-based way.

The sixth graders were able to clear a space, most of them using vivid imagery. Some imagined the problem to be a hockey puck, shot it into a goalie, and skated away—a beautiful example of letting go and separating oneself from what the problem is and even, from the problem itself. It is clear from McGuire's observations and follow-up work that children can experience a shift in the way they release themselves from problems similar to the shift adults experience.

Frans Rüdisser is a director of an elementary school in Schruns, Austria, where he has been teaching focusing in his school system. His emphasis is on focusing as it is done in the context of a helpful, trustworthy, facilitative relationship, and he provides moving examples of the imagery children produce during group focusing sessions (Rüdisser, 1986).

For example, nine-year-old Swetlana was often rejected by other children.

She had only attended school in Schruns for six years and would return to Yugoslavia in another year. In order to ingratiate herself with other children, she exaggerated her importance in order to impress them; this, of course, defeated her purpose. After group focusing, she explained:

> I arrived on a meadow. Because I was tired I laid down and fell asleep. Then I heard a lot of other children. I didn't know them but they came to me and we played cat and mouse together. When we were done they took their backpacks and left. Then I was alone—not totally alone—but just a little. I was sad. Then I left in a different direction than the others. It was summer and a large, large sun was in the sky. She smiles. Svetlana is sad and smiles.

(Rüdisser, 1986, p. 3; author's translation)

All of the quality of her felt sense of the relationships with her peers, her sadness in leaving, and in letting go of the problem at the end of her imagery were reflected clearly.

Rüdisser observes that children do not need interpretation as much as they need people who will take them seriously and listen to them. He admits that educational systems are designed poorly in regard to having enough flexibility to allow children to relate to their feelings. For him, liking children and the quality of the relationship he maintains with them each day as a facilitator and helper is extremely important and enhances the focusing he does with the children. He does not find it helpful to plan a time each day for a set period of time in school to do focusing; he prefers to do focusing in the context of daily relationships as opportunities or needs occur. He stresses individuation. He laments the pressure lesson plans place upon teachers to insure that children know more; he believes such plans do not insure that children understand more.

Much of his procedure relates to the first step, which is to help children learn to clear-a-space. After the person or group focuses, he has them draw a picture of how their imagery made them feel; this continues the processing of feelings.

Focusing in the Home

Marianne Thompson is a trained focusing facilitator and a mother of three children, ages six, eight, and ten. She is an active member of the California based Institute for Research in Spirituality and assists at focusing and at spirituality workshops. When her children were ages three, five, and seven, she began to introduce them to focusing. Although her work did not take place in a play therapy setting, her approach is instructive to play therapists as she outlines how she did each focusing step.

Because they were so young, she talked to them about stories and how they felt when they were totally involved with a story. She found, without formally mentioning focusing to her children, that the whole idea of stories behind all their feelings was fascinating to the children. She found that the movement of an ongoing story captured and held their attention. As she puts it:

> Stories seem to be important even to adults that I have worked with; it's the more behind what they already know about a situation that unfolds and surprises. And it's the surprise of something happening that they don't plan for that intrigues children (personal communication).

She gradually went further with her children as she sensed in them a certain uncomfortableness around a situation, or noticed some negative behavior that stood out. She found that her children cleared a space (step one of Gendlin's procedure) quite natually and that their number one issue, or most troubling problem, is very clear. She believes that in doing focusing with a child it is very important to stay with the problem that is of most immediate concern, that it helps to ground a child in what is real now.

The second and third steps are moved into simultaneously as they learn to "just be quiet with how it feels inside." Thompson does not do Gendlin's fourth step, which is resonating a handle. She believes it is very important to check with the child to ensure that it is agreeable to be with whatever feeling is there. She shows her respect for the child by always "asking them to check inside to see if it's okay to be with this scary feeling" (or sad feeling, etc.). Thompson stresses that it is importance to the whole process that children learn to respect how they feel inside and to know that sometimes it may be too frightening to be with what they are feeling; therefore, the way she puts it to the child, is important also. If it is scary to the child, she asks, "Would it be okay to stay with how scary it feels?" This often gives the needed distance in order for them to continue, and teaches them that there is never anything too frightening that cannot be sat with in this way. (To this writer, who also works with ambulatory schizophrenic adults who are chronically ill, this point is of immense relevance as many of the patients seen cannot support the inner person and seem so fragmented as to lack an inner core that can be trusted by them. Had they learned to bear their scary feelings in childhood, they may not have had to suffer so much later in their lives.)

For the letting go step, Gendlin's sixth step, Thompson finds that the key element that helps all three of her children is when she asks them if they can be friendly with their hurting place. She nearly always sees a visible release in them as they relax, take a deep breath, and go deeper into themselves. Before they stop, she calls their attention to the difference between how their bodies felt when they first began and how they feel now. She allows a considerable amount of time for this step so that the children can assimilate the difference in how it feels. She stresses to them the importance of appreciating any steps taken in focusing, even if they appear to be very small ones. Thompson's observations and conclusions after three years of implementing focusing with her own children are: (1) She did not find any of the steps to be impossible in teaching focusing to children, although she does not do the fourth step with them. (2) She found it was easier for them to let go when they were very young. As they have gotten older it has become a less spontaneous movement. She states that now it takes a longer, "more gentle, friendly presence within themselves" to accomplish this step. (3) She notes with satisfaction that trust has deepened in them, which she finds exciting. It is becoming more and more natural for them to quietly go inside and wait when they are uneasy or have problems. (4) The oldest child, age 12, is less prone to share details in the initial stage of a focusing situation, although Thompson assures him that she does not need to know any of the details for her to be with him while he is focusing. She has found that the what (the details) loses its importance whenever how he carries an issue changes. (5) Finally, the most visible change she has noticed in them after focusing is a difference in their behavior. There seems to be an inner strenth that appears in the way in which they manage themselves. She states:

> A freedom comes to them as they become more confident in themselves and in their ability to handle difficult situations. There is an ease with which they go inside themselves for answers, so as to become more inner directed rather than always looking to me or outside of themselves for answers (Thompson, personal correspondence).

CASE ILLUSTRATIONS

Focusing with Drawing in Play Therapy

The following is a case illustration prepared by Murayama and Nanae Yuba, who conducted the play therapy session. It illustrates how sensitively and creatively the use of drawing is made as part of the focusing procedure. It shows how drawing can be used in helping a child with clearing a space, the first step in focusing (Murayama, personal correspondence).

The child was 12 years old, and had difficulty in attending to herself and in concentrating. The play therapy session was very unsettled as a result of her lack of a meaningful inner world. The goal was to provide the girl with an experience of learning to be with her felt sense of her difficulties while experiencing herself as being separate from her problems. Murayama and Yuba described three phases that the child went through to get a sense of herself, a biosense of her own identity. In phase one the child seemed to be uneasy and was experiencing difficulties. She had an inadequate sense of her own identity; even a sense of what her problems were is vague. She was a problem to herself.

As the therapist helped the child to develop a more sensitive referential process inwardly through therapist responses, (e.g., "How do you feel now?"), the child became gradually more aware of how she experienced her problem. The distinction between her being, who she is, and the problem, was clarified. In this phase, the child was not the problem anymore. There is now an I-It relation between the child and the problem instead of an I-I relation-ship. It was a subtle change-step but an all important one. While the child received a feeling of the problem, she also had a felt sense of herself managing her feeling of the problem. The sense of herself was evoked and a clearer knowledge and self-identity emerged.

In the second phase, owing to the newly developed and heightened self-identity, she could not only express her feeling of the problem but put it aside and be aware of her separateness from the problem.

In the third phase, the child in effect went through a process that can be verbalized as, "I had such a feeling of the problem but how do I feel now that I've put it aside?" At this point she was in touch with herself, not the problem. The person was in biocontact with herself unimpeded by how the problem made her feel. She achieved a clearer sense of self. She had accomplished a bodily release of the problem and gained confidence in herself. Another effect of focusing is that it not only helps children to learn to pay attention to their experiences but it also helps them maintain a lively sense of how they live their therapy.

As previously mentioned, the client was a 12-year-old girl, who was referred for therapy because of difficulties in her relationships with other children. She had been teased by boys since she was in the third grade. She was very reluc-tant to go to school, and her dread of it was obvious in the slow way she walked to school each day. Additionally, her school record was poor and she was virtually friendless.

Her father had been an alcoholic who frequently displayed a violent temper. There was a great deal of instability in her home. In fact, her mother divorced her father when the client was in the fifth grade. Since then her mother had been overworked attempting to make ends meet. She lived with her mother and older brother.

In her description of the first seven sessions, Yuba gives this account:

> The expression of the girl when I met her at our first session was completely shrunk from overstrain. Clumsy walking, timid eyes, and obscure talking showed it.

> In sessions two, three, and four, the girl began to bring presents for me. Grad-ually she tried to come closer to me but it was like beating the air. She kept chattering restlessly and could not calm down. Through sessions one through five, although the relationship between the girl and I was getting closer, she could not keep calm and her play and speech seemed superficial, emotionally shallow. I thought it was necessary to "put" something down which moving about in her annoyed her (writer's interpretation of this is that Yuba wanted to help the child concretize her problem in some external way), in order that she could be calm and feel herself. So when she drew something unexpectedly, I took advantage of this. I carried on this method at sessions six and seven.

The play therapist continues to describe the sixth session:

In the playroom, the girl and I chatted while strolling and fingering toys. The girl kept on chattering in a monotone about cats and Fuch, who was her only friend, and her classroom teacher, all in a mixed up way. . . . Her eyes were not fixed on anything and she chattered restlessly. I was looking for a chance to settle her. I could do nothing but chime in with the girl. "Do you want to draw something?" I said, when she was fingering crayons and a piece of paper. Then she scattered many crayons and sheets of paper on the floor. In the middle of these we both lay side by side, and did a little drawing together. I thought the state was right for introducing focusing so I suggested that she should clear her mind by drawing. (We continued laying on the floor during the entire session).

CL: How can I do it?

TH: Well, then, how do you feel now?

CL: Er . . . I feel enjoyable. (Her voice was flat.)

TH: Then draw your feelings, won't you?

CL: (She draws flowers quickly, then lies down.)

TH: Say, do you have any troubles or problems these days?

CL: (She lies down on her back and closes her eyes.) Yes, Fuch (her only friend) always watches TV when I go to see her. Even when I speak to her, she reads comics.

TH: When you think about Fuch, how do you feel?

CL: I get angry. (She draws an angry face and a crying face next to it).

TH: Well, when you get angry, how do your stomach and your bosom feel?

CL: Er . . . I feel nauseated. (She chooses a black crayon slowly and carefully, then she colors around so the faces say "nausea" in an outraged manner.)

TH: Okay. You feel nauseated. (I point to the drawing.) Then why don't you put it into something, say a box? Do you know a good container for it? Please tell me when you find it?

CL: (She seems to be thinking about it for awhile.) A dustbin. I'll throw it into a dustbin.

TH: All right. In your mind put the nausea into the dustbin.

CL: (eyes are closed) Okay, I put it in.

TH: Put it in? Then draw it.

CL: (She draws a dustbin with a top and puts her nausea into it by drawing with a black crayon. She looks at it for awhile and adds the words "you are defeated" in writing onto the picture).

TH: As you have just put your nausea into the dustbin, ask if there are any other feelings?

CL: Ummm . . . (She remains still quite a long time on her back.)

TH: You can say anything. Please tell me when something comes up.

CL: Say, Fuch phones me when she comes home from school.

TH: To you. How do you feel when she phones you?

CL: I feel happy. (She draws a smiling girl.)

TH: So, you feel happy. What is it like?

CL: Let me see. (She chooses a pink crayon) "Like this, (she draws waves) and I'm fluttered. (She writes "fluttered" on the picture.)

TH: Um,m, . . . that's it. You are fluttered. Then let's put it into a container carefully.

CL: (eyes closed) Yeah, I put it in like this. (She draws a box with printed flowers.)

TH: Good. Well, anything else?

CL: (She lies down for awhile, and suddenly speaks.) Oh, yes, there is. Mum says "tidy up." It makes me mad. (She explains those situations. Therapist listens to her for awhile.)

TH: I see. It is . . . when you recall that, how do you feel?

CL: Er . . . (She closes her eyes; a little later, she gets up slowly.) I become irritated. I feel like something like that. (Saying that, she draws lines something like earthworms with a brown crayon.)

TH: (pointing to the drawing) You are irritated. Then, do you want to put this into something, too?

CL: Yes. (She lies down and doesn't get up for quite awhile.)

TH: Can't you find a good one to put it in? Can I help you?

CL: Yes, I'll put it in a can. (She closes her eyes for a time) Yeah. (She draws a can and puts the word "irritate" into it.) It's going to be swallowed up by a vacuum cleaner. This is supposed to be a can of greenpeas. (She lies down but doesn't look at ease, or cleared.)

TH: That irritation has been surely put in, don't you think?

CL: No, unlikely. It's not safe. (She closes her eyes for awhile, then springs up and puts the can into a plastic bag in the drawing.) Now it's okay. (She throws herself down on her back.)

TH: Is there anything else . . . or nothing?

CL: (a few minutes later) That's all.

T: So how do you feel now?

CL: I feel great! (She looks bright, and looks at the therapist's eyes wonderingly.)

TH: You feel cleared, don't you?

CL: I feel something like after toilet. (She draws a water closet flushing and then on the back of the picture she draws some lines with a blue crayon, and writes, "I'm cleared.")

In the seventh session the play therapist continues to describe how she introduced focusing:

In the playroom, the girl and I were playing on the trampoline. The girl played and chattered aimlessly. Then we sat on the trampoline and chatted. Her conversation changed from one topic to another very quickly, and she was restless. She did not seem involved in what she was saying. But she could not stop chattering because she was so tense that it was beyond her control. When she finally became silent, she was at a loss and ill at ease.

We played on the trampoline, hand in hand, a long time, but she became restless when the movement stopped. We did focusing while sitting on the trampoline.

CL: Isn't there anything? When there's nothing to say, I'm uneasy. (She shakes her body continuously on the trampoline. Her restlessness was transmitted to me.)

TH: Take your time. It's okay. You can tell me when you remember something. I don't mind waiting.

CL: But I can't stand for unless I spit out something! (She shakes the trampoline violently.)

TH: (Therapist wants to do something for her, wholeheartedly.) What is it like?

CL: Um,m. . . . I feel that I have to say something. (She falls flat on her face on the trampoline.)

TH: (lies down by the girl) Are you uneasy?

CL: I think I shouldn't stop talking, you know. (Therapist sees the girl make a fist.)

TH: Do you think that is better? When you think about not talking, do you get uneasy?

CL: (She sits still) Yes. (Her body was rigid on the trampoline, therefore the trampoline kept swinging.)

TH: Then how about saying, "You can stop talking," to your uneasiness?

CL: (A few minutes later, she stops shaking the trampoline.) Yeah . . . I feel calm. (Her body looks relaxed and her fist is untied.)

TH: Really? Then set your eyes on that calm feeling for a while.

CL: (She lies down on her belly on the trampoline and, surprisingly, gets up in a few minutes.) I feel like, that's it.

TH: Oh, you feel that's it. Why don't you draw that last feeling?

CL: Yeah. (At first she draws a girl's wondering face and above it she writes, "That's so." Then she draws a quilt on the back of the picture explaining that her feeling is fluffy and warm.)

At the conclusion of these therapy sessions, her uneasiness disappeared. She was experiencing herself fully even when she had troublesome feelings in later sessions.

At school, she tried to belong to the tennis club and established good relationships with new friends. By the follow-up interviews, the therapist knew she had adapted herself well to her school life.

Discussion

How did this client change? The following is the writer's summary of the major change steps made by the client as described by Murayama and Yuba:

1. Prior to the method used (focusing with drawing in play therapy), the girl was always nervous and had great difficulty in centering herself on her feelings. She bore herself in a vague manner in play therapy. She *was* her uneasiness. By the above method, she gradually learned to attend to herself and have a bodily awareness of how she carried her problems. She became directed inwardly and her nervous state calmed down. She learned to concentrate herself.

2. After she experienced her problems through focusing and put them into the drawings of containers, she came to know what it is like to be released from her problems. She felt this new refreshed sense of lively energy and spontaneous wondering. She showed presence of mind as her nervous attitude dissolved.

3. In addition, she was able to express herself easily with her therapist. The client and therapist had many shared meanings and experiences. She was also more expressive and feeling oriented with schoolmates; she changed her school situation.

4. These changes resulted from her new ability to get a felt sense of herself. This enabled her to accept and enjoy experiencing herself not only in therapy but also outside of it. For her it was an awesome, great, new experience.

5. Focusing with drawing is a useful method to facilitate this process. The use of drawing in play therapy is not new; the unique characteristic of focusing is its emphasis on how the child experiences the drawing as well as the drawing being the reflection of what the child feels, or is feeling toward it. This connection to a felt bodily sense is extremely important to produce change-steps no matter what technique or modality is used. It is a cardinal principle of focusing that change does not occur unless this takes place. Implicit in drawing is some concrete control of one's feelings by the act of externalizing them, putting them outside oneself, no matter how vague or unformed or unshaped they may appear.

Focusing with a Five-Year-Old

Jonathan was five years old. He was extremely bright and already possessed a good vocabulary. His parents had been divorced a couple of months prior to his being brought to the mental health center, where I became his play therapist.

Jonathan was an only child. Jonathan and his mother lived with his maternal grandmother, who babysat him during the day while his mom worked. The grandmother was a very indulgent, permissive person, according to the mother. When he visited his father one day each week, he received firm limits; however, Jonathan was being encouraged by the father to live with him. The effect of this, according to the mother, was to upset Jonathan when he returned home and to leave him with confused and angry feelings. The mother felt she could not compete materially with what the father had to offer and was concerned about the lack of an adult male role model in his life.

She brought him for therapy because she was aware that he was conflicted and she wanted the child to have an opportunity to work out some of his mixed feelings in therapy to prevent what she felt could result in greater difficulties later in his development.

There were 15 sessions in all, and only excerpts are presented to highlight some of the focusing steps with a very young child. We had had one preliminary interview with both Jonathan and the mother, who had been having therapy sessions with another therapist. I also had had a brief encounter with Jonathan in the waiting room. It was suggested to the mother that Jonathan may want to bring one of his favorite toys or stuffed figures with him to the first session.

When he entered the playroom at the first session, holding his stuffed figure (which he called Timmy), he ignored the family of doll figures in the dollhouse by the door and chose to play with the animal figures next to the dollhouse on the table. He chose the lion figure and used it to frighen and knock the other animal figures off the table. He did this several times. The therapist followed his play closely as Jonathan was seriously involved. He did not engage with the therapist directly at first; he seemed very intense. Therapist comments were extremely limited and literally based: "You pushed them all away"; "You pushed them off the table"; "You don't want them close to you."

He ignored the therapist's comments and, after the fourth time knocking all the animal figures off, he paused briefly. Then he ran to an adjacent room and took all of the figures off a shelf and set them up carefully on a low table; he then knocked them off onto the floor. He quickly looked at the therapist, then took a ball and threw it at the wall. He was very forceful in his manner.

He ran to the first room and picked up a pair of boxing gloves and addressed the therapist for the first time directly, "What are these for?" The therapist informed him that they were for hitting the wall or punching at something. Surprisingly, he put them down immediately and asked the therapist his name. He then asked for the therapist's assistance in the use of the watercolors. He worked on one picture carefully and asked if he could give it to his mother. Then he explored the use of the finger paints, but soon pushed the jars aside.

He pointed to Timmy and said, "Timmy was afraid." Since the child was talking about Timmy, the therapist also talked about Timmy. "How does

Timmy feel now?'' Jonathan responded, ''Timmy is still afraid, but not a lot; not like he was.'' The therapist asked Jonathan to point to where Timmy felt scared. He pointed to Timmy's midsection. The therapist suggested, ''Jonathan, would it be okay with you if you held Timmy while he's afraid?'' Jonathan held Timmy for awhile patting him a little. (He is not the intense, forceful child he was.) The therapist suggested again, ''Can you make a clay ball to show how scared Timmy is now?'' Jonathan set Timmy aside and made a clay ball. The therapist encouraged Jonathan to check with Timmy, to sit with Timmy to see if he was still scared. Jonathan sat quietly for a moment with the clay ball in hand: ''Yeah, he's still just a little scared.'' ''Jonathan, is it alright with you to pretend you are holding Timmy's scary feeling in your hand, that the scary feeling is in the clay ball?'' the therapist asked. He answered, ''Yeah.'' The therapist asked, ''Does that feel better to Timmy, to know that you have his scary feeling in your hand?'' ''Yeah,'' he responded. The therapist asked, ''How far away do you think you can put Timmy's scary feeling in the room? Use the clay ball to show me.'' Jonathan thought for a brief time. ''I know,'' he said. He walked to the door leading to the small toilet room that divided it from the adjacent playroom. He turned to the therapist and smiled quickly and disappeared into the adjacent room. The therapist decided not to follow him. Within a short time he returned. ''Do you know how far away I put it?'' he asked. ''Nope,'' the therapist replied. ''Come on,'' he said, ''I'll show you.'' He led the therapist into the next room and pointed to the corner of the room. The clay ball was there. The therapist asked him to check with Timmy to see how Timmy felt now. Jonathan airily stated, ''Oh, he's okay. He's not scared anymore.'' The therapist asked Jonathan to see whether Timmy felt good or whether something else might be bothering him, not feeling okay. ''Okay,'' he said. They both walked into the main playroom and he sat by Timmy. Jonathan suddenly asked, ''What time is it?'' The therapist told him the time and also mentioned it was almost time for him to leave the playroom to join his mother. He asked, ''Will I be able to come back?'' The therapist responded, ''How do you feel about coming back?'' Jonathan answered, ''I like it here.''

The above excerpt illustrates the introduction of focusing to a very young child as well as a point that is extremely valuable and perhaps unique to focusing. People often become accustomed to dealing with difficult, hard, confused, painful feelings by deflecting or avoiding them in some way. Focusing encourages a person to be gentle and friendly to these difficult feelings. The Reverends Campbell and McMahon (1985) relate focusing to spiritual growth, and describe this as a vital element in the focusing process. They relate the process of being gentle and friendly to unpleasant feelings while focusing as crucial to spiritual as well as psychological development.

Transactional analysis theory is based upon the notion that an individual has, as one of his ego states, a child-state. (The other states are adult and parent). It is as if a person who is emotionally hurting or troubled has a hurting child within who needs someone to sit with him. The person who is troubled may not find a solution to the problem, but being with the troubled child within a friendly caring way is at least not neglecting or abandoning him.

The experience of being with a scared or sad place without any compulsion to control, attack, or eliminate those uncomfortable, unpleasant feelings, is not a frequent one. In the above session, the therapist introduced focusing to the child deep into the session when some of his intensity had already diminished and when Jonathan had begun to engage the therapist directly. He was asked to sit with his favorite stuffed figure much as an older brother or parent might sit with a frightened child. In addition, he was asked to concretize the scary feeling by making a clay ball. The very act of holding this symbol of his inner frightened place in his hand provided a different relation to his discomfort and possibly some measure of assurance that he was in control. It is also important to note that the therapist had checked again with Jonathan after the clay ball was formed to see how Timmy felt. The reason for this was to help Jonathan stay with his felt sense and not get distracted by the activity of making clay balls for its own sake. The crux of focusing, no matter what the age, is the felt sense, not the technique.

In the third and fourth sessions, Jonathan began playing with the people figures in the dollhouse. He arranged the top floor, especially the bedroom, with just the mother figure and the child figure in it. On the bottom floor was the figure of an adult male that was ignored. Most of the sessions were conducted on a client-centered baseline following the child and reflecting the child's meanings and feelings using the child's own main symbols.

In the fourth session, Jonathan turned to the adult male figure for the first time and, with an angry look, threw him down and disarranged all the furniture in the dollhouse room. Then he stepped on the figure and abruptly began to work with clay. He made a long, rounded shape, then broke it up. Then he picked up the male figure off the floor and placed it in bed with the female figure; the little boy figure was placed in the other room in the dollhouse. Jonathan appeared calm and the angry look was gone.

What is significant in the above sessions was that the child had strong, angry feelings that appeared to be related to anxieties he was attempting to manage related to his family situation. The child needed the space to conduct and control his own therapy. He needed neither interpretations nor the intrusion of a technique; he made his own change-steps.

In the sixth session, Jonathan stated that he felt sick inside, like he wanted to throw up. He had awakened during the night and had seen his mother and a strange man naked outside his room in the hallway. He was frightened but there was more to his nausea than fear; there seemed to be a twisted feeling there—like an emotional knot—not easily definable. He seemed to want to verbalize about it, but couldn't put it into words. He seemed stuck and frustrated. A doing activity (i.e., physically doing) did not seem like an option for him; he needed to be with what was bothering him but to unbottle his feelings also.

"Jonathan, what part of you feels the strongest?" the therapist asked. Jonathan said, "My fists." The therapist asked Jonathan to make a fist, and let himself feel the fist. The therapist asked, "Can you feel what you feel when you make a fist anywhere else in your body, Jonathan?" He said, "In my shoulders." The therapist urged him to check how strong he felt in his shoulders. The therapist then asked, "How about anywhere else?" He answered, "In my legs." "So you feel strong in your legs, too. Stop and feel your legs being strong," the therapist said. After 15 seconds of waiting, the therapist said, "Jonathan, let your fists, your shoulders, your legs, and all the parts of you that feel strong be with your sick stomach; pretend it is like they are visiting a sick friend; can you do that?" The therapist continued, "Would your sick stomach welcome someone strong and friendly to be with it?" Jonathan said, "Yeah." He even managed a little smile. There was a silence. "How do you feel now?" asked the therapist. "I thought the man was going to hurt my mommy!" blurted Jonathan.

In the remainder of the session Jonathan was able to verbalize some of his feelings of being afraid, of the way his world was jarred without having concepts that could help him explain what was happening. He used finger paints to express his feelings later in the session as he unbottled his emotions. At the end of the session he was sufficiently free or released from his problem that he could invite the therapist to show him how to make paper airplanes out of some of the finger paintings.

The excerpt illustrates a subtle existential as well as a therapeutic point. The person is always more than his behavior or any thing he can say about himself. A planet can be viewed through a telescope, but there is a vast cosmos surrounding it. The leaf implies a tree, and feelings imply situations, happenings. There is always an implicit sense of a situation, of another person, and so on. The feeling remains encapsulated, stuck, unless the feeling sense once again— and in a fresh way—joins what it is a sense of.

Jonathan was stuck, but he sensed so much more than he could express at the moment. He was in his fear and whatever else he was experiencing. It was as if the situation owned him, rather than he owning the situation. He felt overwhelmed and helpless. The therapist felt centered in Jonathan's need and was directive. He literally helped Jonathan to get in touch with some of his own strength, in effect, reminding him in an experiential way that he was more than the helplessness that filled him. Once Jonathan began to sort out his own feelings the therapist returned to his client-centered baseline.

Several months after the termination of therapy sessions with Jonathan, his mother requested an appointment with the therapist. She came to share her observations of changes in him and to express her appreciation.

She noted that he laughed more, was more fun for her to be with, and seemed much more stable and content whenever he returned from visiting with his father. She stated that he asked her, occasionally, whether he could visit the playroom. The therapist met Jonathan and his mother in an unplanned way a year later. Jonathan was very excited to see the therapist and his mother stated that he had begun school and was making a good adjustment.

Focusing with Adolescents

The following case is presented in an oversimplified manner in order to illustrate the way focusing assisted an adolescent, referred by the Probation Department, to get in touch with and to clarify vague bodily experiencing and sensations prior to acting-out behaviors.

James was a 14-year-old who was 1 of 10 children. His mother was a passive, compliant woman who was very dominated by her husband. James' father was subject to explosive outbursts, blackouts, and so on. He was compulsive and perfectionistic, especially as related to the family image in the community. He was very concerned about the way his family dressed, how they behaved in public, and so forth. He saw no dichotomy between his own open affairs with women in his neighborhood and his strict behavioral expectations of his family.

James had done well in school academically until a year before when his grades had begun to slip. He was liked by teachers and other students. He had been apprehended previously for shoplifting, but he admitted in therapy that he had shoplifted several times, always alone.

In the first session, he appeared more self-assured than the therapist expected based on the intake report, although he respectfully looked at the therapist waiting for him to take the lead. The therapist met his gaze, and gently instructed, "Just take your time, and scan to see where you want to begin." A minute can seem like a long time in this kind of silence. He seemed to look up for help. In this situation the therapist decided to use a focusing opener that he has found useful, "James, I want you to say to yourself, 'Gee, I feel great,' and then put on the desk—just like you would put groceries out of a grocery bag, or newspapers out of a heavy bag—all the things that bother you, that stand in the way of your feeling good."

He put out two problems: (1) He expressed concern that he keeps stealing even though he had no intention of doing so and it makes him sad (tears welled in his eyes), and (2) He felt unwanted by his father. Asked which was the problem that was the hardest for him right now, he answered, "The stealing." He continued, "If I could straighten up, dad would not be so mad at me."

In his last statement, the first sign of the critic was manifested. It is not helpful to allow the critic to take over one's inner space for several reasons: (1) It doesn't solve the problem; (2) It makes an already difficult situation harder, and (3) It is seldom that, if all the pieces that bring you to where you are psychologically could be known, one would be found to be totally responsible for what came to be. James went on to blame himself for making his father angry with him and not want him. He strayed somewhat from how he felt about his shoplifting and began to get held back from further processing by his critic.

The therapist invited him to return to his feelings about his shoplifting. James said, "I don't know why I do it. I don't need the stuff I take; most times I give it away." He was a puzzle to himself. He often looked down sadly with his chin on his chest.

The therapist asked him to listen to his feelings just like he would listen to his Walkman with his earphones on. He urged James to imagine himself and how he felt prior to entering the store and then as he entered the store, but especially before he entered the store. James looked downward with his eyes half closed. After awhile he said, "Cranky, I feel cranky inside, like something crankin' me around." The therapist just resonated the handle. "Cranky," the therapist quietly repeated, "So it's like cranky, is it?" He said, "Yeah . . . no. It's like something crankin' me!" This was different than being cranky and he wanted the therapist to hear the difference.

The above shows how a person can sense something undefined yet know what it is not. Obviously, in such instances, the person is matching what he feels against an unclear experiencing base that informs and directs one's processing.

"James, just be with that feeling of being cranked for awhile. Be with it in a friendly way. If something bubbles up from there like a picture or a word or a person, let me know when it happens," the theapist gently directed. After about a half-minute, tears welled up in James' eyes, overflowing onto his cheeks, as he sat with his head downward. He said, "It's my dad. Yeah. . . . I was mad at my dad." The tears came more freely. "I want him to do things with me and he never does. I want to go fishing and he won't go. I want to go to games with him and he won't go. He doesn't want me!"

James had made an important bioconnection between the hunger he had for his dad's closeness and approval and his shoplifting. His acting out was no longer to be a puzzle to himself. As the sessions continued there were many ups and downs in James' life. Eight sessions later he reported that he was doing very well in his relationship with his father. His father was playing basketball with him and it had been a "long time since I've thought of stealing."

In the 11th session the client reported that he was given a free sample (later verified) from a nutrition store. When he got home his father would not believe he had not stolen the sample and he withdrew all privileges. He was also worried that when he would begin high school he would get into fights and the teachers would not like him. His confidence was beginning to unravel again.

In the next session James reported that he was hit in the face by his father for ironing without permission. He wanted to find an alternate living situation. The Probation Officer was assisting him in this matter. James was very depressed.

Fortunately, the father did care and entered treatment himself with another therapist. In the next few sessions James began to be optimistic again about his relationship with his father. His father allowed him to structure his own discipline when he left home without permission; he got off to a good start at school; he was taking up basketball and swimming (an activity he was afraid of). He was in the process of terminating; three sessions prior to terminating he came to the session, greeted the therapist, and sat quietly.

The therapist and client sat in silence a long time, possibly 15 minutes. It was a comfortable, even enjoyable, silence. It felt like sharing but the therapist did not know where this quality came from. Because such a long period had passed without anything being said, the therapist said, "James, I feel comfortable and even enjoy this quiet time with you but I do have a need to check with you as to how it feels to you. Is your inside as relaxed as your outside looks?" James nodded, and smiled. The entire session was wordless with only one more gentle check made by the therapist to make sure this way of using his session really fit where James was psychologically.

The therapist can only speculate about what this silent session meant to James. Coming from a home where there were so many in the family, perhaps, for once in his life he could share a quiet space, a time when he could just be without any expectations on him or anyone pushing him to do something. Perhaps it was a relief from the instability or chaos that could erupt at any time at home.

Whatever was occurring, it seemed to be enjoyed. It was very important that James was able to share a totally at-ease situation with an adult. Without words, this was a powerful and friendly silence. For James it may have been too good to be true, having been either depressed, angry, or frightened of an adult most of his life.

Three sessions later, James terminated therapy although the therapist felt he might return at a later date due to his uncertain relationship with his father. Two years later the therapist learned that he was in jail for stealing after a good adustment in school and home, and he was going to be sent to a boy's school. According to school officials, who liked James and thought he had an outstanding basketball career ahead of him, his relationship with his father had worsened again

Focusing and Graduation Anxiety

Every year in a comprehensive community mental health center, as graduation approaches, one can expect a certain number of self-referrals who are suffering from graduation anxiety. These are usually short-term cases. Typically, the adolescent is frightened or panicked at suddenly being faced with job and career responsibilities, leaving home, and the separation from friends. Complicating this situation is that he cannot be open with his concerns with parents or relatives as they are so proud of his accomplishment and seem to have no doubts that he wll succeed. The youth does not want to disappoint their joyous moment and their sense of success as parents, especially. Those nearest and dearest to him may not have the faintest hint that he is scared.

The following are excerpts from a therapy session with a young person who referred himself. He stated that he was having some mild suicidal ideation.

The curious feature of his situation was that he was working two jobs and had already bought his own very expensive automobile, so he had demonstrated both his ability to take care of himself and his sense of responsibility. The following example shows how important it is for the therapist to be open for surprising turns as the client takes his own direction from processing his feelings. Also, it will re-emphasize that focusing is introduced gradually in the context of the therapy session by taking advantage of interactional opportunities to sensitize the client to relate to how he feels about a problem. Focusing must fit easily and naturally within these interactional opportunities. If in any way it does not, the therapist returns to the client-centered baseline that is a precondition of therapy.

The client's presenting problem was that he had some mild suicidal ideation. He was so anxious about graduating and going through the ceremony that he had thought about overdosing on pills his mother had in the home. (His father had died when he was in his first year of high school.) He had not shared this problem with his mother.

A major conflict for him was that he would soon be separating from friends he had known since childhood. He detailed their plans: one was joining the Navy, a few were going to the same college, and so forth. He was remaining home to work. As he said, "I knew it was coming someday but now that it's here, it's awful! I can't stand the idea of not seeing them at school or going over to their homes or just calling them up."

The therapist responded in a client-centered way except that he did take advantage of a couple of pauses to ask the client gently, "Can you make a friendly place for that in front of you, a large friendly place there where you can see it, kind of like a mural in front of you?"

After a while, the client's intensity diminished, and suddenly he began to weep quietly. (The therapist did not know what was going on.) The client said, "If my father were alive, I know I'd be able to go away to school! Why did he have to die?" Very gently, as he continued to weep, the therapist asked him if he could make a special friendly place for all the hurt and anger he felt for his father not being there to help him, right there in front of him. He cried more freely, as if his body were releasing all the pent up anger and hurt it had held in while he manfully took up the slack in his household. And when he stopped crying, he very softly, without any intensity, stated, "I miss him very much. I worked so hard at not missing him for such a long time. He was a good father and he would be proud of me. It's hard for me to go through this ceremony without him out there!" He cried again. The therapist watched the body closely as well as being sensitive to other dimensions of what was being expressed. When the client stopped crying again, his facial expression was relaxed, his breathing fuller; generally, he seemed untwisted and whole, that is, at peace with himself.

At the end of the session (the remainder of the session was spent in reflecting in a client-centered way) he had resolved that he would go through the graduation ceremony. He was surprised at how much better he felt, and he stated he would like to leave the option open for returning for a second session and would telephone if he needed it. The therapist was not called for an appointment, but he did get a graduation invitation.

In the above excerpts, the therapist did not depart much from being client-centered in his reflections. However, he did sieze interactional opportunities—a few long pauses—to urge the client to: (1) Make a large, friendly place for all that was involved in his conflict, and (2) To put it all in front of him, out there, where he could see it all.

That he could be friendly to feelings that trouble him, that cause him distress, that make his life difficult may come as a surprise and a relief. In the above example, it certainly helped to open the way for underlying feelings that were difficult for the client, feelings he had avoided facing for a long period of time. When he could finally admit these feelings, he no longer felt incomplete; he felt more wholly human.

OBSERVATIONS IN FOCUSING WITH ADOLESCENTS

Although the writer has done therapy with many self-referred teenagers, very often in a comprehensive community mental health center adolescents are referred against their will by parents, Probation Departments, schools, and others. In a few instances, it has been helpful to the client for the therapist to maintain a stance as a technical companion in a phased exercise. This has the effect of maintaining an initial distance while still working on the problem with the focusing procedure. It has proven to be very reassuring in those instances as there also appears to be a safe psychological environment created by the structured exercise. At the same time, the steps can be done while the youth closes his eyes; this also contributes to having some control in the unwanted situation. There is no clear criteria for this as yet, except the therapist's intuitive sense of the person. Generally, the writer has proceeded much as he would with an adult in the therapy hour. The exception would be those younger adolescents who use the therapy hour in the playroom and/or in the office.

SUMMARY

Focusing consists of specific steps of instruction to enable someone to attend to the bodily sense of a problem; to get a word, phrase, or image that helps hold onto that bodily sense; and, through further specific steps, to process the problem experientially. The experiencing body is central to focusing, and each interaction of the focuser is aimed at helping the person become aware of how he experiences his problem, and not just the details of the problem. This approach can be used to make any method or modality more effective, including play therapy and working with adolescents. The focusing technique applied to children and adolescents is relatively new, and the literature regarding it is scant. However, the few published reports, and the personal communications to the writer, suggest very strongly that focusing can be used to benefit children as young as 3 years of age as well as adolescents.

With younger children, there appears to be more interest by focusers in helping children to clear a space (Step 1) and getting a felt sense (Step 2) as well as receiving (Step 6). All the steps are valuable although these seem to be most useful at lower age levels.

There are three cautionary notes that need to be observed. First, the relationship is more important than the technique and the child may discontinue a focusing step whenever he chooses to do so. Second, the goal is to reach the inner felt sense of the problem in a bodily way and the strategies used to achieve this, such as the clay balls, pictures, and so on, must not come to dominate the process. Last, it is crucial that the result feels good to the child.

Focusing with children and adolescents is a new and important method for catalyzing changes. Much more exploration with this approach needs to be done.

REFERENCES

Barba, D. (1985). Single case study of a female adolescent firesetter. *The Focusing Folio, 4*(2), 50–70.

Campbell, P.A., & McMahon, E.M. (1985). *Bio-Spirituality* (Vol. 17). Chicago: Loyola University Press.

Gendlin, E.T. (1966). Research in psychotherapy with schizophrenic patients and the nature of the "illness." *American Journal of Psychotherapy, 20*(1), 4–16.

Gendlin, E.T., Beebe, J. III, Cassens, J., Klein, M., & Oberlander, M. (1968). Focusing ability in psychotherapy, personality, and creativity. In J.M. Shlein (Ed.), *Research in psychotherapy* (Vol. 3. pp.: 217–238). Washington, DC: American Psychological Association.

Gendlin, E.T. (1981a). *Focusing.* New York: Bantam.

Gendlin, E.T. (1984). The client's client: The edge of awareness. In R.F. Levant & J.M. Shlein (Eds.), *Client-centered therapy and the person-centered approach* (pp. 76–107). New York: Praeger.

Levant, R.F., & Shlein, J.M. (1984). *Client-centered therapy and the person-centered approach* (Vol. 13). New York: Praeger.

McGuire, M. (1986). School project: Teaching clearing a space to elementary school children age 6 to 11 years. *The Focusing Folio,* (4), 148–61.

McMahon, E.M., & Campbell, P.A. (1985). Teaching children to focus. *An interview with Marianne Thompson* (Pts. 1 & 2). Coulterville, CA: The institute for research in spirituality.

Murayama, S. (1986). *Teaching clearing a space to elementary school children* (Vol. 3, No. 2). *The Focusing Connection.* Chicago: The Focusing Institute.

Neagu, G.V. (1986). Focusing and play therapy. *Association for Play Therapy Newsletter, 5*(1), 2-4.

Rogers, C.R., Gendlin, E.T., Kiesler, D., & Truax, C.B. (Eds.). (1967). *The therapeutic relationship & its impact: A study of psychotherapy with schizophrenics.* Madison: University of Wisconsin Press.

Rüdisser, F. (1986). Focusing in der schule oder Wärme in Bauch. *Focusing Informationen, 1,* 1-9.

Santen, B. (1984). Focusing as an initial therapy with 'borderline adolescent.' *The Focusing Folio, 3,* 15-36. (Original work published 1982).

Schaefer, C.E. (Ed.). (1976). *Therapeutic uses of child's play.* New York: Jacob Aronson.

Tomlinson, T.M., & Hart, J.T. (1962). A validation of the process scale. *Journal of Consulting Psychologists, 26,* 74.

van der Veen, F., & Stoler, N. (1965). Therapists judgment, inteview behavior and case outcome. *Psychotherapy, 2,* 158.

PART 3

Altered View of Reality Techniques

Techniques Involving Rituals
and Bogeyman Tactics

CHAPTER 10

The Therapeutic Use of Rituals with Children

AARON NOAH HOORWITZ

INTRODUCTION

Across cultures and throughout history, rituals have provided forms for change and transformation, forms that give people a sense of comfort and control in a world that is mysterious and to a large degree incomprehensible. They are used to provide milestones that help to construct the reality of a person's, a family's, or a people's history; they are used to heal or cause harm; and they are used to ward off danger. Rituals reinforce the myths, symbols, and social consensus to guide an individual or group forward.

Psychotherapy itself is a ritual of change, a contemporary rite with pre-scribed forms of belief and behavior. It is to some extent mysterious because the clients, and even the therapists, have only an imperfect understanding of exactly what the effective ingredients might be to cause a therapeutic change. Yet, we and our clients engage in prescribed sequences of behaviors in the belief that these sequences of behaviors will bring about the hoped for change. It is useful to differentiate between psychotherapy itself as a ritual of change and the particular methods used in a given form of therapy that are believed to catalyze change. Those particular methods might have effects that are quite independent of the effects of ritual. Yet some of these methods are themselves effective precisely because they are identical in form to ritual. Methods to be considered can be taken either from modern therapeutic practice, from exotic shamanic practices, or even from mundane everyday activities.

For example, there was once a doctor who was famous for curing warts by turning on an impressive machine and painting the warts a bright color. The machine and the paint were irrelevant to the cure except insofar as they helped

Drafts of this chapter were prepared simultaneously with those of a chapter on a similar topic, coauthored with John O'Connor, for publication elsewhere; although significant differences exist between the chapters, some similarities and identities are bound to occur. The other chapter cannot be cited because it is only in a preparation stage.

to constitute a therapeutic ritual. A witch does the same thing in preparing a love potion by muttering exotic incantations and asking the supplicant to bury an assortment of unusual ingredients at a crossroads. Wise old grandmothers craft a similar healing ritual when they get rid of the pain from a bumped knee by having the child jump up and down seven times, count to 20, and then pinch an ear. The examples are endless, whether they are exotic or mundane, whether they are taken from the shamanic and cultural practices that have been observed in other cultures by anthropologists, or whether they are taken from the formal and informal rituals existing in everyday life in our own culture.

The purpose of this chapter is to describe how rituals can be used with good effect in therapeutic work with children. Two case examples will be presented to illustrate the ways in which this can be done. First, however, it is important to articulate my understanding of ritual and the aspects of it that I believe to be responsible for therapeutic change. Second, I will turn to the reason that use of ritual is particularly appropriate as a modality for children. That reason consists of the stages of cognitive development characteristic of most children. Third, anthropological sources are discussed to obtain clues on practical principles that can be employed in the crafting of ritualistic interventions. A discussion follows the case presentations, in which the strategic function of ritual is discussed; specifically, how it interrupts problem-maintaining solutions to a problem. First, it is necessary to address the question of why it is that a ritual can help to bring about a change, whether that ritual be the general act of engaging in psychotherapy, or whether it be some specific sequence of acts that a therapist prescribes.

WHAT IS A RITUAL?

A ritual is a specific sequence of acts that are believed by a supplicant, a client, or a group of people to punctuate or promote a change in the life of an individual, a family, or a group of people. It may mark the end of one phase of life and the beginning of the next, or it may bring about a change, such as the solving of a problem. Both of these types are relevant to therapy with children.

The first, which provides some punctuation in the history of the person, may sometimes be used to alter the world view or reality of the family, much as a bar mitzvah or a wedding may alter a family's view of a child. This altered view may then facilitate behaviors and interactions that help the family to transcend the phase of life within which they had been living. The second type consists of a prescribed set of acts that are believed to bring about a change in a problem or maintain a desired status quo. Since these are the ones more commonly employed in therapeutic work and the ones that are illustrated in this chapter, the discussion will focus on this latter type.

A common characteristic of rituals is that they involve repetition of some action. This may consist of a specific sequence of activities that must be performed just right or the right amount of times in order to be effective.

A very crucial ingredient is the *belief* that the ritual will effect a change or maintain a desired status quo. This belief is enhanced when the set of acts constituting the ritual makes sense within the logic or belief system of the child, family, or culture (Hoorwitz, 1988). In our culture, therapists and other helping agents can utilize the pre-existing belief in clients that whatever the therapist prescribes will be helpful. It may be necessary for a therapist to enhance belief in the efficacy of a ritual if the ritual does not, on its face, possess an overriding appearance of validity.

Rituals also communicate a message about the process of change that is identical to a hypnotic message (Hoorwitz, 1988). The message is that if a set of prescribed acts are performed, then a desired or curative effect will be achieved. The relationship between the prescribed set of acts and the curative effect involves a causal link that is questionable when using formal logic.

This dubious casual link is contained in any suggestion that takes on the following form: "If you count to 10 slowly while concentrating on each number, then you can notice yourself feeling more relaxed and your eyelids becoming heavier." Counting to 10 slowly while concentrating on the numbers, by itself, simply does not cause the hypnotic effect. It is *presumed* to cause the hypnotic effect and it is this presumption, contained in the language of hypnotic suggestion, that facilitates the effect. The counting to 10 or the participation in a ritual are identical in the sense that they constitute a presumed cause for an intended therapeutic effect.

Another characteristic of rituals is that they tend to contain metaphors and symbols that stand for or that refer to events, actions, and objects not immediately present. In the most simple form, a ritual is intended to cause some effect and by doing so is assumed to share some identity with that effect. Therefore, rituals are inherently metaphorical or analogical for something else. In the most complex forms, every aspect of every act in a ritualistic sequence is replete with potent and redundant symbols referring to various aspects of a person's or a culture's history, values, and world view. When numerous and redundant enough, the symbolic resonance that the ritual creates serves to validate and perpetuate that history and world view. In the use of rituals with families, it is important to employ sequences of action and objects that symbolically refer to things meaningful to the family members. The purpose of the intervention may be to interrupt habitual problem-maintaining interactions, but this can be accomplished only if the intervention can be integrated within the values and world view of the child or family so that it reinforces the strengths of the family.

Rituals are also enhanced by appearing to be, to some degree, incomprehensible (Hoorwitz, 1988). This incomprehensibility may simply reflect an unclear causal link between the ritual and its intended effect. Rituals may appear more incomprehensible if they are exotic, possess unpredictable procedures, or if they engender mystery and confusion (O'Connor & Hoorwitz, 1984).

Incomprehensibility is important because it serves the hypnotic function of depotentiating conscious sets of expectation; that is, immobilizing a person's usual conscious set of strategies and expectations for negotiating reality demands. It distracts attention from, or depotentiates, these usual strategies that ordinarily might result in conscious and critical scrutiny of the dubious causal link between a presumed cause and an intended effect.

To the degree that this element of incomprehensibility exists, attention is distracted from the question of whether the presumed cause (i.e., the ritual) will produce the intended effect. It distracts from the question of whether the ritual does indeed contain an efficacious ingredient. Distraction renders the person more open to implied suggestions that change will occur and also allows time for the person's cognitive, autonomic, and other internal processes to respond to the suggestions for change.

The effects of distraction from a dubious causal link and of depotentiation of conscious sets have parallels in the field of hypnotherapy and also in tribal rituals observed by anthropologists. Distraction from a dubious causal link is a very minimal redistribution of attention and this minimal degree may easily go unnoticed as trance. Although only this minimal degree may be necessary to bring about a curative effect, hypnotists and shamans have developed procedures that bring about a maximal redistribution of attention.

Focusing attention on a spot on a wall, or on the repetitious sound of a metronome, or on a drumbeat in a tribal ritual, all serve to redistribute attention away from usual everyday considerations that help to maintain the generalized reality orientation that we consider to be normal consciousness. When the redistribution of attention is severe enough, a person has a subjective feeling of being in trance or in an altered state of consciousness. It has been observed that the effects of rhythmic drumming, which is prominent in spirit dancing in some North American Indian tribes, seems to be a major factor operating in the induction of altered states during spirit dance initiation (Jilek, 1982).

The same observation was made by Aldous Huxley (1961, p. 369) when he pointed out that no man can listen for very long to native drumming or Indian chanting before losing a critical attitude. He pointed out that if Western people were exposed long enough to the rhythmic sound of beating drums and chanting, every one of them would end up "capering and howling like the natives." These observations also help us to understand the role of repetition that exists in many rituals, whether it is the exotic repetition of tribal drumming or the mundane repetition of a prayer in a child's ritualistic warding off of anxiety.

The depotentiation of conscious sets can be considered equivalent to severe or sudden redistributions of attention. It is of interest that tribal rites exist that bring about this effect with dramatic and traumatic procedures. For example, the first act of initiation in spirit dancing in the Salish tribe consists of grabbing and clubbing the initiate (Jilek, 1982). This entails a surprise attack on the initiate. During an unexpected moment, he is seized by a number of shamanic aides who rush at him and lift him helplessly. He is then clubbed with power-filled canes and rattles, manhandled, and thrown into ice cold water. The psychological shock occasioned by the unexpected experience, not to mention the physical shock, probably disorients the initiate from usual reality considerations to facilitate an altered state of consciousness.

While these more exotic and dramatic applications of ritual, either in shamanic practices or in hypnotic procedures, facilitate recognizable alterations in consciousness in either the initiate or in the hypnotic subject, a recognizable alteration in consciousness is not necessary for a ritual to be effective. In therapeutic rituals, it is necessary only that the incomprehensibility of the ritual serves to distract attention from the dubiousness of the link between the presumed cause and the intended effect and that it enhances respect for the ritual.

This last point can be emphasized. The characteristic of incomprehensibility, in addition to serving a distracting function, can also lend an air of mystery that engenders awe and respect, which in turn can facilitate belief in the efficacy of the ritual. Also worth noting is the irony that rituals are likely to be most effective when they are incomprehensible and yet possess an overriding appearance of validity.

These, then, are the characteristics that I believe to be crucial in defining and understanding rituals that are used to heal. They are applicable to use with adults as well as children. There is, however, a factor that makes ritual a particularly appropriate modality for children. That factor consists of the unique stages of cognitive development through which children must pass and that render them particularly open to the effects of ritual.

CONSIDERATIONS ON COGNITIVE DEVELOPMENT

The primary reason that children are predisposed to use of ritual is that more primitive forms of logic are more accessible to them than to adults. It is not until adolescence that human beings develop what Piaget and Inhelder (1969) described as formal operational thinking, the formal propositional logic that we employ as adults. Some of these adult forms of logic are available during the stage of concrete operational thinking (from about the age of seven to twelve), but these can only be employed on objects that are physically present. The stage most characterized by magical thinking and a predilection to ritual is that described by Piaget as preoperational thinking (usually seen between the ages of two and seven).

Throughout these stages of development, children proceed from animistic and magical reasoning to a more scientific way of reasoning. However, a residue of the superstitious thinking of earlier stages may remain in adulthood. During times of stress and emotional upheaval, children and adults of any age may temporarily revert to or access aspects of preoperational thinking.

Preoperational thinking is characterized by syncretic reasoning, which means that a causal connection is believed by the child to exist between two events by virtue of them appearing together or in sequence. For example, a child might believe that God made her fall off her bicycle because she didn't wear a jacket like her mother told her to. Thinking at this stage is also animistic; for example, believing that the moon is alive because it follows you as you run.

Magical thinking is also characteristic of this stage. This means that a thought is equivalent to a deed in the mind of the child. That is, if children wish in anger that a parent was dead, they then feel as if they had performed the act and may feel as guilty as if they had actually attempted murder. Because they think something in their heads, they believe it is so in reality. There is confusion between an inner and an outer reality that would make a three- or four-year-old's thinking appear psychotic if in an adult body.

In view of these considerations, it is possible to see how magical ritual is a natural expression of preoperational thinking. When a child wishes her mother dead, and fears that as a result of the wish the event will occur, it is natural for the child to invent an equivalent ritual to undo the event. For example, she may use a doll to represent herself so that she can punish herself for the transgression.

As children enter the stage of concrete operational thinking, they develop new cognitive capacities for coping with the world and for defending against anxiety. They exercise these new capacities by making things, collecting things, counting things, and by many other activities that have the appearance of compulsive activity. It is natural at this stage to develop obsessions, compulsions, and idiosyncratic anxieties that reflect repeated sequences of thought or action. It should be evident, then, that this natural predilection for compulsive behavior at this stage serves to additionally predispose children to the use of ritual. Compulsion and repetition, combined with a bit of magical thinking, is all that it takes for the creation of a ritual that will undo whatever it is the child fears. For example, "I will be safe if I confess my sins and say three prayers in a row," or, "My stuffed animals won't come alive and be monsters if I put them all in the right places and count them up."

Examples of rituals that children naturally construct are endless. These are informal, idiosyncratic rituals, but children are equally interested in formal and in collective rituals. A trivial but well-known example of a collective ritual is that of not stepping on a crack for fear of breaking mother's back. Whether rituals are formal or informal, collective or idiosyncratic, they often reflect and organize childhood themes of fear, loss, injury, power, social concerns, play, revenge, retribution, and the undoing of vengeful acts or feelings.

They also often involve the use of a transitional object, that is, an experience or object that reminds children of an absent parent and thereby brings comfort. A good illustration can be remembered from the movie *The Godfather* when Don Corleone, as a young child, spent his first night in a lonely room on Ellis Island singing to himself a song his dead mother used to sing to him. A child's relationship with a blanket or a teddy bear can metaphorically replace a relationship with a missing parent. The development of rituals with the use of transitional objects helps children to feel more comfortable, to feel in control, to be active rather than passive, and to perform actions that diminish helplessness and powerlessness.

To summarize this section, rituals are particularly appropriate for children because the repetitive sequence in many rituals accesses the compulsive coping mechanisms that are so frequently used by children. More importantly, children are predisposed to accepting the validity of a ritual. They are less likely than an adult to scrutinize the dubious causal link between a presumed cause (i.e., the ritual) and the intended effect. To the degree that the child thinks with syncretic logic, or reverts to it, there is no doubt about the causal connection at all.

TYPES OF MAGIC

In the actual construction of ritualistic interventions, we can capitalize on the type of thinking characteristic of young children by drawing from anthropological sources that have identified types of magic, such as imitative and contagious magic. These have a natural appeal to the reasoning employed by children.

Imitative magical rituals (Frazer, 1959) utilize the law of similarity: like produces like. The assumption is that one can produce an effect by imitating it in a metaphoric or symbolic form. To illustrate, in some cultures the belief exists that a person can be injured by injuring an image or an effigy of the person, such as a voodoo doll. Another application of this principle is the belief that childbirth can be facilitated by dropping rocks or dolls from the genital region of a woman. To melt someone's heart, melt a waxen image. To cure jaundice, throw yellow objects away.

It is also useful to consider the principle involved in contagious magic. This principle contains the assumption that things that have been in contact continue to act on each other. The properties of one object are transferred to, or absorbed by, another. For example, after performing a complicated ritual, an Ndembu native suffering from a backache leaves his backache with a particular type of tree, and announces to the tree that he is doing so (Turner, 1967). An Indian initiate is struck with a power-filled cane in a spirit dancing ceremony and a power possesses him (Jilek, 1982). On a spirit quest, an initiate is visited by a vision of his totem, an animal-like spirit from whom he derives qualities characteristic of that animal. A child holds a rabbit's foot, absorbing from the object its luck.

In examining these two principles, one can see that they utilize characteristics that connect events, objects, or actions. They are not causal connections in any way, but because they can be used to categorize, organize, or relate events, it is possible to see how they could be viewed as causal. They are used as a way of establishing identity between events. Once this is understood, other principles or concepts can be identified that are used in the same way in ritual.

For example, the principle of polarity, like similarity, is found in many rituals (Turner, 1967, 1969). An illustration is the opposition of evil with a symbol of good, such as using a cross to ward off the devil. Another principle is that of symmetry or balance. For example, a runner disclosed that if he scraped a foot on the ground, he became anxious, and could only allay his anxiety by scraping his other foot as well. Related to symmetry and polarity is the existence of threesomes, triangles, or tripartite divisions in many religious themes and ritual practices. Expulsion and incorporation can also be used to organize discrete events. The use of rhyme, rhythm, and repetition also serve to connect and organize verbal material that may have no causal or even sensible semantic connection. Many examples of rituals are characterized by several of these principles at once.

The significance of these principles is that they suggest an identity between rituals observed by anthropologists in prescientific cultures and those that can be used to heal children's problems. More practically, these principles help to dictate the choice for objects or actions in a ritual. They do so because they are principles that connect discrete objects, actions, or events and thereby appeal to a child's type of reasoning. The causal connection, which exists in syncretic reasoning, is incomprehensible to formal logical thought because there is no formal causal connection. Yet because these principles do connect or categorize events, they help to provide a sense of validity for a ritual.

Utilizing these principles to help guide the process of crafting healing rituals for children and families, one can begin to generate possibilities. A timid and insecure child could eat his father's favorite cereal to be similar to his father, in order to help give him strength, courage, and confidence. A young girl who yearns for her absent father could be given a ring he wore as a transitional object that allays separation anxiety by making the father metaphorically present. A child with a headache can transfer the pain to a stuffed animal by touching the forehead with the animals. A child who hears voices can squeeze a doll and transfer the voices into the doll.

CRAFTING OF RITUALS

In crafting ritualistic interventions for specific problems, it is useful to consider all of the factors discussed in previous sections. The therapist must decide which actions will be employed and in doing so can use principles of contagion, imitation, and other principles that were discussed. It is important not to neglect the various ingredients crucial to the use of ritual, such as the ingredient of incomprehensibility and the implied hypnotic suggestion that change will occur by virtue of the enactment of the ritual.

It is also helpful to have insight into the reality or world view of the child and the family, including its symbols, myths, legends, motifs, and values. These can then be used to give validity to a ritual and to facilitate its integration into the history, reality, and everyday life of the family. When this is possible, it is more likely that a ritual will counter the habitual problem-maintaining sequences of interaction and buttress the strengths already existent within the family, providing some rough guide for the development of spontaneous and healthy forms of interaction.

CASE EXAMPLES

In this section, two case examples are presented that utilize ritual to address children's problems. The various considerations relevant to the use of ritual that have been discussed to this point are operationalized in these two case examples. In the first case, the problems of hallucinations and suicidal ideation are addressed by a ritualistic exorcism. (This case example is described in greater detail in Chapter 10 in Hoorwitz (1988). In the second case example, the more common problems of worry and separation anxiety are addressed by a ritual utilizing a transitional object.

Case 1: An Exorcism of Voices

Patricia K. was 12 years old when her parents brought her to a mental health clinic for help in addressing her auditory hallucinations, her suicidal ideation, and her headaches. She was the youngest of three daughters and had just been away from home for the first time, to a religious summer camp. She had been homesick at the camp and had also been terrorized by some of the religious notions concerning good and evil to which she had been exposed. Against the camp director's advice, she left the camp and returned home prematurely. After returning home, she reported that she could hear the camp director talking to her and that it terrified her. Her parents attempted to reassure her but this did not help. She also began to talk about killing herself and complained of severe headaches.

Neurological and medical problems were ruled out by her pediatrician and by a neurologist. She was treated at the mental health clinic by a social worker and by a psychiatrist, who put Patricia on a low dose of Mellaril. The treatment consisted primarily of helping her to feel safer at home and helping the parents to keep her going to school, which she had begun to refuse to do. However, over a period of a month, she progressively became worse and, after a suicidal gesture in which she stood in a crossroads waiting to be hit by a car, she was briefly hospitalized. At the request of the psychiatrist, I visited Patricia and her family in the hospital to attempt to address the problem.

In questioning Patricia and her parents, I learned that her development had proceeded normally and that there was no evidence of psychotic disorders in the family history. Patricia had been having trouble academically and the parents feared she might fail a grade as had one of her older sisters. The parents mildly disagreed about handling this problem, with Mr. K. being more firm and Mrs. K. being more indulgent. There had also been a mild disagreement about her attendance at the camp, with Mr. K. reluctant to allow her to attend a camp with a religious doctrine that was different from the family's religion, and with Mrs. K. persuading Mr. K. to allow it because Patricia anticipated a good time with a close friend who was attending. A pattern appeared to exist in the family in which Patricia was identified with Mrs. K., Mr. K. was more firm, and Mrs. K. tended to indulge Patricia and to extract from Mr. K. his reluctant permission to allow certain activities.

Patricia's demeanor was soft and cooperative, rather than defiant or uncommunicative, and she gave the appearance of being younger than her age. She was generally very obedient toward her parents, except when she forgot to do a chore or was lazy. She appeared also to be an impressionable child with a rich fantasy life.

Her hallucinations consisted of three types of message. One message from the camp director was that her parents would die if she did not come with him. Another was that she should kill herself because she was "no good," meaning both that she was sinful and that she was inadequate due to not being able to control the hallucinations. The third type consisted of the camp director telling her that she did not have to listen whenever an adult was reprimanding or instructing her; this message was conveyed with much profanity that Patricia herself would never consider articulating aloud.

I then asked Patricia if the camp director was talking to her at that moment. She answered that he was not, but that he was listening. I asked that she deliberately get the director to speak to her, in order to gain some control over him. She replied that he would not speak because he knew what I was up to. I answered that since he was listening, he would have to speak to her to tell her not to listen to me, and to let me know when she could really hear him. Patricia then said that the director was speaking to her and telling her, with much profanity, not to listen to me. I instructed her to close her eyes until she could hear this voice as vividly as she possibly could and only after hearing it this vividly could she rest for a few moments. She closed her eyes and listened and then finally opened them.

I then turned to Mr. K., who seemed pleased that some control over the problem was being achieved. I asked Mr. K. to take some control over the problem as well, by bringing on the problem by means of reprimanding Patricia. Patricia again pointed out that this would not work because the director knew what was being attempted. I told her that the director would not be able to help himself. I then asked Mr. K. to pretend to reprimand Patricia and I coached him to sound mean enough so that the director would have no choice but to speak again. He did this until it succeeded in getting the director to speak to Patricia. I then allowed Patricia to rest for a few moments, in preparation for the next stage of the intervention.

I then withdrew three small dolls from my pocket and showed them to Patricia, whose attention was immediately riveted by the dolls. I handed two male dolls to Patricia and asked her to decide which of them reminded her of the camp director enough to actually become that person in her imagination. After some thought and attention, she chose one and handed the other back.

She was then handed a doll of a little girl and was told that this represented a part of herself, the part that was inadequate and the part that was sinful; that is, the parts of her that she wished to kill. She was told to hold one in each hand.

She was then told that she could allow herself to hear the voice of the director as vividly as possible and that when she was ready to get rid of the voice, she could close her eyes and begin squeezing the doll. As she squeezed harder and harder, she was told, the voice could travel out of her and into the doll. After a few moments, she closed her eyes and began squeezing while I repeated the suggestion. I said that she could stop squeezing when the voice was completely out of her and completely in the doll. When she opened her eyes, she was asked to notice that she was sure that the voice was completely gone. She indicated that she was sure.

She was then asked to close her eyes and to notice those parts of herself she wished to kill. She was told that as she squeezed the little girl doll harder and harder, those parts of herself could be emptied from herself and go into the doll; she could stop squeezing and open her eyes when she was sure that those parts of her were gone and present only in the doll. She began squeezing and the suggestion was repeated.

After she opened her eyes, I asked her to close her eyes and squeeze both dolls, just to be sure that every last part of the director and the parts of herself she wished to kill had been drained from her. She followed this instruction for a few moments and then opened her eyes.

I then told her that she could now use the dolls to act out what she had been hearing in her head before and that she could say aloud what she had been only hearing before. I asked her to begin playing with the dolls in this way. I illustrated with an example, pointing out that she could have the doll of the director say to the doll of the little girl that she was no good and ought to kill herself, and that the little girl doll could respond in some way. She began doing this and was coached to do it properly, that is, to articulate a dialogue aloud rather than silently. She was told that she could develop an irresistible urge to play with the dolls more and more often, like a little girl, and that this could become a problem since she was no longer a little girl. I told her that when her parents and the medical staff were convinced she had developed a problem of playing with dolls like a little girl younger than her age, she could then be discharged from the hospital.

Her father was instructed to pretend to be angry with her for acting younger than her age and to tell her to shape up, while her mother was told to indulge and encourage the doll play, and to coach her to play properly; the parents were also told that they could pretend to argue about whether she was too old to play with dolls. The family was told that this was only a temporary solution to the problem until the next meeting.

Patricia begged to be discharged from the hospital immediately. She pleaded that she had already developed an irresistible urge to play like a baby and she said that her headache was finally gone. However, I said that it was too soon to be sure. It was decided at this point that she would be taken off all medication.

I met with the parents alone for a few moments to be sure they had the strength and commitment to follow through with the plan. Mrs. K. thanked me for somehow getting rid of a painful headache that had been plaguing her as well. She also asked if there was anything hypnotic about what I had done. I said that there was and Mrs. K. appeared to be pleased with this answer because she had been expecting something exotic from treatment, something like her own views of exorcism or hypnosis. She and her husband had feared that something hypnotic or traumatic had been done to Patricia at the camp, and they resented questions by helping agents that suggested that something in their family functioning might have caused the problem.

Patricia was discharged from the hospital the next day. I met with the family again a few days later, along with the psychiatrist. Patricia had continued to remain symptom free and was playing regularly with the dolls, though she did enjoy it. I instructed her to continue playing with the dolls as a precaution against the voice returning.

In answer to the family's request for an understanding of the problem, I then explained that I could not be sure of the seriousness of Patricia's problem, but that it was possible that she had been traumatized at the camp, as the parents believed. I also suggested that she was a very obedient and loving child whose wishes to grow up and be independent were very fearful to her; any wishes she had of expressing an opinion or of engaging in a behavior contrary to her father's wishes terrified her. I pointed out that this was, of course, unrealistic of her, since her father loved her so much. She needed to learn that her father could tolerate moderate attempts at independence on her part. To begin to practice, she was asked to sacrifice herself temporarily and to engage in mild acts of disobedience; her father was asked to catch her at these acts and to lecture her. Reluctantly, and with an imperfect understanding of why this was necessary, the family agreed to follow the instructions.

I met with the family for a third session two weeks later, at which time it was learned that Patricia had followed instructions, remained symptom-free, and was engaging in age-appropriate activities, such as going to school, to parties, and to friends' houses. I told her to stop playing with the dolls, to wrap them in a handkerchief, and to place them in a box with a top. I asked the family to bury this box in a cupboard somewhere. I also wrote out on a notecard the suggestions I had made about the symptoms leaving Patricia and entering the dolls. This notecard was to be stored in the box with the dolls, and if the symptoms recurred, Mr. K. could get the dolls and read the monologue to Patricia. This was intended as a first aid kit in the event the family could not immediately contact the psychiatrist. It was also intended to provide the family with some confidence in being able to handle the problem should it recur. It also brought closure to the problem by burying it with the dolls.

I did not meet with Patricia again, although I did consult with the psychiatrist who continued the therapy. At follow-up contacts four and nine months later, Patricia still had not reexperienced hallucinations or suicidal ideation.

Discussion

The specific interventions used in this case emerged from a particular formulation of the problem. First, it was considered possible that Patricia was suffering from a psychotic episode, but it was considered more likely that the hallucinations were more hysterical in nature. She possessed a vivid imagination and a rich fantasy life that may have predisposed her to being traumatized by ideas to which she was exposed at camp.

Her camp experience was also one that put ideas in her head in an out-of-the-home setting, a fear of many parents that was literally realized here. It may have been her first step at individuation, and thereby represented the prospect of ultimate separation that was too anxiety-provoking for her to bear. It also appeared that she was struggling with typical developmental conflicts concerning defiance and separation. This was especially supported by the contents of her hallucinations.

She was able to avoid addressing this difficult developmental conflict by developing a symptom that demanded she leave home but that constituted a developmental regression that permitted her to stay at home where she was treated as a sick or younger child. In general, the problem appeared to be metaphorical for the complicated process of an adolescent growing up and leaving home, being exposed to, but not equipped for, the insults of the world.

It may also have been metaphoric for a problem in one of the parents, as Madanes (1981) has suggested, such as headaches or other medical problems; or it may have been metaphoric for a problem between the parents that recapitulates the interaction around that problem, such as a parent's wish to separate from the other but inability to acknowledge it. Since these issues were unclear, it was important to attempt to preserve the typical family interaction around the problem in the temporary solution to the problem until these issues could be explored or until it was clear that the family would remain in treatment.

What was most clear was that Patricia was presenting symptoms that terrified both herself and her family. She and her family and other helping agents had done their best to alleviate the symptoms, but their efforts were failing. Her parents, who she had heretofore viewed as powerful, were helpless in solving this problem. This created a hierarchal incongruity in the family that was necessary to resolve (Madanes, 1981).

The author's demeanor and instructions at every point suggested to Patricia that a change in the problem would occur but would not occur by the usual attempts she had made to get rid of the problem, such as wishing it would go away or trying not to think about it. Unlike previous attempts to address the problem, consisting of behaviors by helping persons that did not help and that may have served instead to maintain the problem, I sidestepped Patricia's interactional style of engaging helpers in fruitless struggles. Instead, I began with a paradoxical intervention, asking Patricia to produce the problem. This not only served to help Patricia to feel that she had some control over the problem, but showed her that I had some control over it, which increased my credibility for subsequent interventions. This control was then temporarily transferred to a parent, who pretended to be angry with Patricia in order to control the occurrence of the voice. This realigned the incongruous hierarchy, in which a parent was simultaneously powerful yet helpless, to a congruous hierarchy, with a parent in charge of the problem.

The exorcism of the voices and of the suicidal ideation was highly ritualistic. It contained all of the ingredients discussed in the earlier sections of this chapter. It also appealed to notions of exorcism to which Patricia had probably been exposed in the media, so that it possessed a certain validity for her. It was characterized by both imitative and contagious forms of magic: imitative in the sense that the dolls were physical representations of herself and of the camp director; contagious in the sense that the dolls absorbed her problems by her squeezing them. The use of dolls appealed to the child in her, especially to those cognitive capacities that enabled her to regress to a preoperational stage of logic where magical thinking creates a magical reality, where pretend and play can seem real, where hallucination and delusion are normal, where syncretic logic dominates, and where thought of an action can become confused with having actually performed the action. This ritual was the crucial intervention used for alleviating the problem.

The next intervention, that of suggesting a developmental regression by means of doll play, constituted one side of the adolescent conflict between dependence and independence. It preserved the dependence expressed by the symptoms of hallucinations, suicidal risk, and headache. It also preserved the the parental interaction around the symptoms. This intervention has been described by Madanes (1981) as altering the metaphorical action. In this intervention there is an alteration from a painful problem that the family is helpless to control to a ritualistic behavior that represents a more manageable and less painful problem. This intervention, the task of continuing doll play, constituted an additional ritual, one that would succeed in sustaining a desired status quo, rather than a change. It was a repetitious ritualistic task that could be used to ward off the danger of a recurrence of the problem.

Asking Patricia to engage in acts of mild disobedience, in a deliberate fashion, and asking Mr. K. to catch and punish her, again in a deliberate fashion, was also a ritualistic intervention. It choreographed in a slightly distorted and exaggerated form the typical tug and pull between adolescents and their parents. It thereby punctuated a change in the family's evolution, from a stage in which the parents were dealing with a child to a stage in which they were dealing with an adolescent. It was intended to provide not only practice for this next stage, but a marker for its onset. If it could provide this, then the child's view of herself and the parents' view of themselves and of the child would be altered. This altered view of the family's reality could then dictate different behaviors and interactions than existed previously.

In the final stage of the intervention, the dolls were buried and put to rest in a ritualistic manner that put closure on the problem of hallucinations and suicide. Yet the burial preserved the power of the dolls and of previous ritualistic suggestions should they ever be required again. The way this was done empowered the parents to deal with the problem temporarily.

CASE 2: ALLAYING SEPARATION ANXIETY

Jenny was four years old when her mother contacted me with the complaint that Jenny had become weepy, fearful, and would not go to sleep in her own bed. These problems had begun shortly after Jenny's parents had separated, with the father moving out of the house. Jenny visited with her father every weekend, but it was not possible for him to see her during the week, due to the geographical distance that separated them. Although visitation was proceeding smoothly and the parents were fairly amicable with one another, my conclusion was that Jenny was suffering primarily due to the loss of her father from her daily life.

I spoke to Jenny about this in the presence of her mother, articulating for Jenny how her life had seemed to turn upside down since the separation and how difficult it was for her when her father wasn't readily available. I asked Jenny and her mother to arrange to have Jenny draw a picture for her father at least once a week and for Jenny to dictate a letter, to be mailed to her father. I also asked that arrangements be made for Jenny to speak on the phone with her father. These measures were intended to keep her father's presence alive for her during the week. I also asked for her father to be present at the next session.

At the next session, the problem was explained to Jenny's father and he appeared willing to do whatever was necessary to help. He had already begun to call Jenny during the week and Jenny had drawn a picture for him and mailed it. However, she continued to appear weepy and still had difficulty getting to sleep in her own bed.

I found out during that session that Jenny had a transitional object, a stuffed animal called Duffy that she often carried around with her. She no longer slept with Duffy, though she had used to do so. I told Jenny and her parents that Duffy could be used to help Jenny to remember that her father loved her, even when he was not there. Her father was asked to go home with Jenny and to take Duffy in his hands and to specifically say to Jenny that Jenny could hug Duffy whenever she needed to remember that her father still loved her and was thinking of her, and to then show Jenny how to hug Duffy. Her mother was asked to be sure that Jenny took Duffy to bed with her, and also to read a short story to her each night.

Thereafter, Jenny took Duffy to bed with her, mother read her a short story, and Jenny gradually got used to sleeping alone. Within a week, she appeared less weepy, more perky, and no longer had trouble getting to sleep. She herself explained to me that now she thought of her father whenever she looked at Duffy or played with him.

I explained to the parents the various effects that separation has on children of Jenny's age and gave them further advice on how to handle these effects. This was necessary because despite the alleviation of the presenting problem, Jenny still suffered the pain of missing her father and still suffered from an overall confusion and anxiety regarding the disorganization of her world.

Discussion

In this case, imitative magic was the principle employed: the stuffed animal, Duffy, was used to imitate or represent the absent father. Since a transitional object was used for this purpose, it probably already possessed capacities for representing an absent parent, capacities that Jenny had probably projected onto it repeatedly over time. Although Jenny had gradually become more independent of Duffy, she was now being asked to become more dependent on him, which can be considered to be a regression in development. Yet, this mild regression was judged a small price to pay if it could help to alleviate the specific loss of her father, about which she felt intense pain.

Due to Jenny's stage of cognitive development, it was unnecessary to include exotic or incomprehensible elements that would distract her from the dubious causal link between the ritualistic hugging of the stuffed animal and the curative effect. She was told that hugging the animal would cause her to feel better and she simply believed it. It was judged that her belief would be enhanced if she was able to make a vivid association between Duffy and her father. This was why he was asked to go home with her, to hold Duffy in his hands, to hug Duffy, and to explain to her how to go about hugging Duffy.

DISCUSSION

Discussion of Case Presentations

There are similarities and differences in the way magic was used in these cases. The use of dolls in Patricia's case was an application of the principle of imitative magic. The dolls represented parts of her that she wished to be gone from her. In Jenny's case, the use of an object that represented parental power and security was also an application of the principle of imitative magic. Applications of this kind are imitative in form in the sense that the objects represent or symbolize someone else with powers greater than the child's, powers that the child would like to possess. The imitative principle is more obvious in these particular cases because there is actual representation, as in the use of a doll; it may be less obvious, though equally potent, in cases in which there is symbolization of an object or person, as in the use of a father's coin or ring to symbolize (rather than represent) the father.

The principle of contagion is also relevant to these cases, but in a different way with each. In both cases there was an absorption by the dolls of the child's problems: in the case of Jenny, Duffy absorbed her fears; in the case of Patricia, the dolls absorbed her hallucinations, her sense of inadequacy, and her feelings of sinfulness. However, in the case of Jenny, there was probably a transmission from doll to person as well as from person to doll. She absorbed from Duffy the security and assurance that her father's presence provided. Patricia absorbed nothing from the dolls.

Ritual was used in a variety of ways in the case of Patricia, unlike the case of Jenny in which ritual was used in just one way. Its most obvious use in Patricia's case was in the transmission of the symptoms to the dolls. Because this had the appearance of an exorcism, it appeared more magical and exotic than most applications of ritual might be. Yet this case illustrates some other useful ways in which ritual can be applied. The prescribed doll play was intended as a separate and additional ritual that would maintain a status quo in that it would ward off the danger of a recurrence of the problems. The prescription of adolescent defiance and parental control over this mock defiance was intended to provide a ritualistic milestone or marker in the evolution of the family's development, marking the end of one stage and the beginning of the next.

Unlike Patricia's case, Jenny's case illustrates a more common and less complicated use of therapeutic ritual for a variety of typical problems in children. A father's ring, a mother's necklace, or an older sister's bracelet are typically used to represent a power greater than the child's. Such transitional objects as stuffed animals are also commonly used. These objects can then be utilized to either transmit power and security to the child, or to absorb fear, worry, pain, and obsession.

The Strategic Function of Ritual

It may be evident from the case illustrations that ritual also serves the strategic function of interrupting repetitive sequences of interactions in which the problem is occurring, both within the child and between the child and the parents. The child is afraid to go to sleep alone and fights the parent. The parent acts in ways that essentially tell the child that she should try to be brave and not think about what worries her. The child tries to be brave and not to think about her worries, but this only reminds her of her worries and she inevitably fails. The child gets into the parent's bed and the parent is too tired, exasperated, and helpless to put the child back to bed.

The child is in a struggle with the problem, trying to be brave and failing. Internally, the attempt to be brave only reminds the child of her fragility and aloneness and is a solution that only maintains the problem (Watzlawick, Weakland, & Fisch, 1974). The more powerful parent attempts to help by reassurance and advice to be brave, but these solutions also maintain the problem;

therefore, the powerful parent is also helpless, continuing to try to help the child and failing (Madanes, 1981).

What the parent is doing to try to help the child with the problem and what the child does internally to try to address the problem only serve to maintain the problem. It is essential to block these solutions or to distract the parent and child from them in order for change to occur. Ritual is an optimal means by which to accomplish this (Hoorwitz, 1988). It immediately draws attention and distracts attention from usual solutions. The child (and sometimes the parent) is given something concrete to do that is incompatible with a previous attempted solution that only maintained the problem (e.g., trying not to think about the problem and thereby reminding oneself of the problem). Attention is now focused on actions that the child believes will result in change.

The hypnotic effects of this arrangement may sometimes be sufficient to then produce change. However, other agents of change may also be operative. First, the simple fact that usual attempted solutions have been blocked may be sufficient to result in change. Second, other changes in the interactions in which the child is involved may result in change. For example, Jenny was now having a story read to her each night in her own bed by her mother, rather than having to derive the comfort of that contact by seeking her mother's bed. She was also having more frequent communication with her father. It is difficult to say whether these latter measures would have been sufficient by themselves to result in change. Even if they were sufficient, they were certainly augmented by the strategic and hypnotic use of ritual.

CONCLUSION

The utility of ritual in therapy is that it blocks usual attempted solutions to change that are maintaining a problem while at the same time it fosters the belief that change will occur. That is, it tells the client to change but tells the client not to change by means of usual solutions. Both of these functions are economically and elegantly condensed in the single act of a ritual prescription. At the same time it permits the application of any other potential agents of change that the therapist has confidence might effect change. While ritualistic interventions can be used effectively with adolescents, adults, and couples, as well as with children, they are particularly appropriate to work with children, due to the stages of cognitive development characteristic of children, as was previously discussed. Simply put, ritualistic thinking is as natural to children as is play.

REFERENCES

Fisch, R., Weakland, J.H. & Segal, L. (1982). *The tactics of change: Doing therapy briefly*. San Francisco: Jossey-Bass.

Frazer, J. (1959). *The new golden bough*. New York: Criterion.

Hoorwitz, A.N. (1988). *Hypnotic methods in nonhypnotic therapies.* New York: Irvington.

Huxley, A. (1961). *The devils of Loudun.* London: Chatto & Windus.

Jilek, W.G. (1982). *Indian healing: Shamanic ceremonialism in the Pacific Northwest today.* Blaine, WA: Hancock House.

Madanes, C. (1981). *Strategic family therapy.* San Francisco: Jossey-Bass.

O'Connor, J., & Hoorwitz, A.N. (1984). The bogeyman cometh: A strategic approach with difficult adolescents. *Family Process, 23,* 237–249.

Piaget, J., & Inhelder, B. (1969). *The psychology of the child.* New York: Basic Books.

Turner, V. (1967). *The forest of symbols: Aspects of Ndembu ritual.* Ithaca, NY: Cornell University Press.

Turner, V. (1969). *The ritual process: Structure and anti-structure.* Ithaca, NY: Cornell University Press.

Watzlawick, P., Weakland, C.E., & Fisch, R. (1974). *Change: Principles of problem formation and problem resolution.* New York: Norton.

CHAPTER 11

The Bogeyman Cometh

Theoretical Revisions and Further Applications

AARON NOAH HOORWITZ

INTRODUCTION

In a previous publication (O'Connor & Hoorwitz, 1984), an intervention was described in which a therapist played a bogeyman role in order to frighten and shock a defiant adolescent. The intent was to create an experience that would dislodge the adolescent from his usual view of reality and induce an altered view, rendering the adolescent more tractable to adult control. The prototype for an intervention of this kind was provided by Carlos Castaneda (1972) when he described how the sorcerer Don Juan advised that a parent should hire a derelict to leap out of hiding with a prompt punishment when a child misbehaved.

A theoretical rationale was extensively elaborated in the previous publication but only one case example was used to illustrate this bogeyman intervention. One purpose of the present chapter is to illustrate and discuss a more diverse range of applications, including nonadolescents, problems other than defiance, and cases in which the intervention failed or was inappropriate. Another purpose of the chapter is to tighten the theoretical rationale and to supplement it with a discussion of the hypnotic effects of the intervention and an explication in systemic terms of the way in which reality is viewed differently following a bogeyman experience. The original rationale is first summarized, with a brief description of the case previously presented, followed by theoretical revisions. Then, further applications of the intervention are presented in five case examples, followed by a general discussion.

RATIONALE

The intervention was originally developed to address the acting out behavior of defiant adolescents for whom usual solutions were ineffective. These adolescents were involved in relationships of conflict with caretaking adults that could be described as symmetrical in the sense that every disciplinary action taken by the adults was matched or outmatched by escalating misbehavior. These were adolescents who had not yet learned, or did not believe, that their misbehaviors would ultimately result in aversive consequences. The purpose of the intervention was to make those anticipated aversive consequences so vivid to the adolescent that it catalyzed an alteration in the adolescent's view of reality and a shift to a complementary relationship with adults such that the adults could provide guidance and the adolescent could accept it.

In the previous paper, we described the case of David, who was misbehaving in various ways, was defiant towards his caretakers and other helping agents, and who was increasingly assaultive to peers and adults. David's therapist and the staff of the group home where he lived contacted me with the request for some intervention that might prevent placement in a more restrictive facility. They believed that they had tried everything possible and were at their wits' end.

I advised the group home director to file charges against David for assaulting her, which would serve to bring the case to court and permit the opportunity for me to play a role as a consultant to the court. Specifically, this enabled me to play a role as a person who would be making a recommendation to the court about David's future. I then gave them an appointment for David to meet with me prior to his court appearance, and arranged that the meeting occur in an empty courtroom in the courthouse. Although the exact truth was told to David, the intent was for him to develop the impression that he was going to court. Prior to the meeting, I met with the group home staff and compiled a detailed list of David's misdeeds, with dates and times.

On the day of the meeting, I recruited some probation officers and others, chosen for their size and forbidding appearance, and told them where to stand in the courtroom and what to do in order to make the occasion appear to be formal and ominous. David was kept waiting in a holding room for a considerable amount of time with the intent of increasing his anxiety about the meeting. When he was finally brought into the courtroom by a large, gruff-looking man, he was seated at a long table across from me, while I shuffled papers as if David's presence were quite unimportant.

Finally, I looked up and slowly told David that he was in serious trouble for his assaults and his other misdeeds. He attempted to interrupt by minimizing what he had done. I did not directly respond to these arguments. Instead, I laughed at him and told him that it was he, not myself, who would have to pay the consequences for his behavior, and that I wasn't interested in excuses and rationalizations. I then began to list the intimate details of each of his misdeeds. This intimate knowledge stunned and silenced him.

I then told him that his misdeeds would result in a fate he would not like and that I was afraid that I would have to recommend something of that sort to the judge. I said that there was still time before he returned to court, but that I doubted he could learn to control his behavior before that time. He responded that he could; again, I laughed, and I expressed serious doubt. I did say that his only hope to control himself was to look to his caretakers for help. I then dismissed him.

The child care staff were privately instructed to stop trying to get David to behave himself and not to respond to any provocation. Instead, they were to look sympathetic and say they were sorry that I would find out about each misdeed, and to complain about my harshness and unfairness toward David. David quickly allied himself to the child care staff and to the therapist and was soon taking guidance from them. I called frequently and unpredictably to find out how he was doing, and David was told about these calls. By the time David appeared in court, he was responding appropriately to the rules in the group home and to interventions by his therapist.

This bogeyman intervention consisted of an integrated display of several characteristics that we believed to be essential to a bogeyman role. An almost identical constellation of attributes is often used to describe shamans, sorcerers, deities, demons, and monsters. These are: omniscience, hierarchical superiority, incomprehensibility, potency (or omnipotence), and capacity to create illusion. Together they were displayed in a way that was intended to bring about three systemic shifts in a person's relationships to others. These characteristics and the systemic shifts are briefly described below in terms of the way in which they are adapted to interventions with clients who are involved in symmetrical conflicts with others. For more detailed descriptions of these ingredients, the interested reader is referred to the original publication.

Omniscience

First, a bogeyman figure must display a form of omniscience, appearing to know more about the client than is usually possible for others to know. In David's case, I displayed an intimate knowledge of his symptoms, misbehaviors, and relationships with others. This lends credibility to the intervention and helps to assure that the bogeyman's message will be believed.

Hierarchical Superiority

Second, the bogeyman must be capable of assuming a structural position that is hierarchically superior to the systems in which the client is involved in symmetrical relationships with others. This position enables the bogeyman to impinge on the client's life while remaining immune to the client's symmetrical maneuvers that ordinarily engage others in futile symmetrical struggles.

Incomprehensibility

Third, the bogeyman's behavior must in some way appear incomprehensible or unpredictable to the client in order to violate expectation or to induce similar states of surprise, confusion, or wonder. The violation of expectation is intended to nullify the client's ordinary orientation to reality, thereby facilitating a receptivity to an altered view of reality and to suggestions for relating differently with others.

Potency

Fourth, the bogeyman has to have power to effect some change, such as to heal or to cause aversive events to occur, or at the least, the power to deliver a potent message that such a change is imminent. The major portion of the intervention may be an effective bluff, but there must be at least a minimal degree of potency so that the intervention not constitute an empty threat and so that consequences to misbehavior can be implemented if necessary.

Illusion

Fifth, as a craftsman, the bogeyman has to be capable of distorting the client's perceptions and beliefs about reality by means of illusion, misdirection, use of props and confederates, and orchestration of action. This capability is sometimes necessary to ensure that the previous four characteristics are operationalized with sufficient impact.

Systemic Shifts

There are three systemic effects that the intervention is intended to accomplish. First, it should signal, or punctuate, that the client's symptomatic behavior has reached an upper limit, a limit that will not be exceeded. Second, the intervention is a strategic attempt to interrupt the sequence of interactions in which the client is ordinarily engaged. The client must fail in attempts to engage the bogeyman in a symmetrical relationship by means of provocative behavior and must be forced into a complementary relationship with the more powerful bogeyman. This leaves the client poised for a "second order" rather than a "first order" change (Watzlawick, Weakland, & Fisch, 1974); specifically, a change in the client's view of reality and in the way the client relates to others. In the case of a defiant adolescent, it puts the adolescent in the position of being receptive to usual forms of treatment and to guidance from caretaking adults.

Third, the intervention is intended to reduce the symmetrical strain between the client and those with whom the client was experiencing conflict by forcing them to orient themselves in the same specific way toward the bogeyman. For example, an adolescent and caretaking adult will unite in opposition, confusion, or deference to the bogeyman, a union that reduces the symmetrical strain between them and facilitates complementary, supportive exchanges.

THEORETICAL REVISIONS

Tightening of the Rationale

The rationale for this intervention can be tightened by delineating the exact linkages that exist between the five characteristics of the bogeyman figure and the three systemic effects produced by the intervention. Although the five characteristics may produce an interactive or cumulative effect that contributes to all three systemic shifts, careful analysis suggests that certain of the characteristics are responsible for each systemic effect.

First, the characteristics of omniscience and potency appear to be the ones that enable the bogeyman to punctuate the notion that an upper limit has been reached and to convey the message that this limit will not be exceeded. The client may already have been told in a variety of ways that an upper limit has been exceeded, but the appearance of omnipotence and omniscience can impress the client in such a way that this message will now be viewed as valid.

Second, the hierarchical superiority of the bogeyman enables the bogeyman to refrain from responding to symmetrical maneuvers that the other person tends to habitually use and appears to be the characteristic essential for forcing the client into a complementary, subordinate relationship to the bogeyman. Hierarchical superiority is a concept drawn from the approach of structural family therapy rather than from strategic therapy; it is a concept that assumes the complementary relationship intended by this intervention. Yet it highlights the strategic necessity of interrupting a problematic sequence of interactions, in this case, interactions that happen to consist of a circular sequence of symmetrical, one-upmanship maneuvers.

Third, the systemic shift from symmetrical conflict to a relationship in which parent and child form a supportive, unified position in response to the bogeyman is most likely brought about by a combination of the ingredients of omniscience, potency, and incomprehensibility. When these ingredients engender resistance, they result in a union against a common enemy that can be described as a symmetrical relationship to the bogeyman; when they engender behaviors of deference and awe, the union of parent and child is in a complementary relationship to the bogeyman.

Hypnotic Effects of the Intervention

In the previous publication, the characteristic of incomprehensibility was described as serving the hypnotic function of depotentiating conscious sets, that is, dislodging a person from usual ways of understanding a situation. This cognitive condition renders a person uncertain of how to next respond and, therefore, renders the person receptive to a reframing of the current situation and to suggestions for future action. In addition to these effects, which are described in the previous paper, the characteristic of incomprehensibility makes it possible for an implicit hypnotic suggestion to be made that positive change will occur.

Clients generally come to a therapeutic situation with a belief that whatever the therapist does, even if they do not comprehend it, is aimed at effecting change. When the intervention is incomprehensible, an implied message is conveyed that some special ritual is in progress that will effect change; the characteristic of incomprehensibility highlights this implicit suggestion for change, makes it more salient, and gives the suggestion a form that is equivalent to an indirect hypnotic suggestion.

The implicit suggestion takes on something like the following form: "Because this particular ritualistic intervention is presently occurring, it will cause you to change, although you do not have to comprehend how this intervention causes the change." This suggestion is equivalent to such common hypnotic suggestions as the following: "If you listen carefully to my voice, you will go into a trance," or, "If you stare at that dot on the wall, your eyelids will soon feel very heavy." These messages are hypnotic because the relationship between the presumed cause of the hypnotic effect (e.g., the ritual of staring at the dot) and the hypnotic effect (e.g., the eyelids feeling heavy) involves a causal link that is often questionable and yet can facilitate the intended effect. Since the logic of such suggestions is so dubious, the suggestions are sometimes more likely to be believed or accepted when the causal connection between presumed cause and hypnotic effect is clearly incomprehensible rather than accessible to logical analysis.

The presumed cause may consist of either a mysterious ritual, a therapeutic task, the act of sitting in a therapist's office for 50 minuites per week, or the presence in one's life of the puzzling behaviors of a bogeyman figure. The useful effect of incomprehensibility is apparent when considering a supplicant who cannot comprehend exactly why a shaman's incoherent chanting might be effective for his head pain. The more incomprehensible is the presumed cause, the more it communicates that some ritual is in progress that will cause change to occur and that does not depend on the client's deliberate attempts to facilitate the change (Hoorwitz, 1988).

The characteristic of incomprehensibility serves several functions in these instances. It helps to distract the client's attention from consideration of the question of whether the ritualistic intervention does indeed contain an efficacious ingredient. It also distracts attention from the ingredients or influences that actually facilitate the change, ingredients that may be either contained in the ritual or independently applied, thus preserving and protecting those ingredients from a scrutiny or analysis that could reduce their potency. The distracting function of incomprehensibility also allows time for the person's cognitive, autonomic, and other internal processes to mobilize an idiosyncratic response to therapeutic suggestions for change.

What Is Altered in the Altered View of Reality

An issue that was not fully addressed in the previous paper is the nature of the altered view of reality that is produced by the bogeyman intervention. The idea of an altered view was repeatedly mentioned, both in that paper and in this chapter. But what exactly constitutes this altered view? What is it that alters?

This question can be addressed by considering the alteration to consist of a fourth systemic shift, but this time a shift in the way the symptom bearer views his relationship to the symptom, rather than a shift in relationships with other people. Although problems or symptoms have interpersonal functions, it is necessary to focus on an individual's personal relationship to a symptom in order to describe this shift as clearly as possible; this is why the term "symptom" will be used here rather than some other term with a more interpersonal meaning. Specifically, the shift is from a symmetrical to a complementary relationship with the symptom (Hoorwitz, 1988).

It is easier to recognize the symmetrical quality of the relationship between a person and a symptom in those who strive to get rid of their symptoms and fail to do so on their own. They are in an active, ongoing struggle with a symptom, a struggle that occupies the foreground of conscious thought and that is almost impossible to abandon. The very fact that the symptom bearer is in a struggle or conflict with the symptom implies a symmetry between symptom and symptom bearer. This is a symmetry of power in which the symptom possesses as much power to remain present as the symptom bearer possesses to be rid of it. It derives power from the symptom bearer's ongoing self-definition as a person either having or not having the symptom.

When the symptom bearer attempts to change by conscious deliberation (e.g., by gritting his teeth and trying not to quarrel with his wife, trying not to think about smoking a cigarette, or trying not to feel so depressed), the symptom and symptom bearer continue to have equal power because the bearer continues to define himself in terms of the symptom's presence or absence. That is, the commission or ommission of the symptom is still an open question, a conflict, a struggle: to smoke or not to smoke, to hold on to one's temper or to really let him have it.

Although it is more difficult, it is possible to recognize the symmetrical relationship between symptom and symptom bearer even in people who refuse to acknowledge their symptoms as problematic. For example, in Dickens' *Christmas Carol,* if Scrooge had attempted, before his conversion, to be less miserly, he probably would have found it difficult, if not impossible. The same is the case for many smokers, drinkers, defiant adolescents, or those with other ego-syntonic problems that they claim are not problems. They sometimes try to change, as an experiment, to show that they can, and find that they cannot.

It is necessary to give up the struggle with the symptom for significant change to occur. When one surrenders one's self-important view of oneself for a more humble one, the symptom loses its power and the struggle loses the meaning that it had. When this kind of change occurs, it is not only one's view of self that has changed; one's relationship to the symptom is also viewed differently. Scrooge no longer had to struggle with the question of whether to be miserly or not; the struggle was behind him. When this kind of change occurs, the conflict or question is now a moot point; it is remembered, but it has a place now in the background of awareness, in a subordinate or complementary position. It is in this way that reality is viewed differently. The person feels that he has suddenly grown beyond the problem, whether the problem was defiance in the family, smoking, drinking, or miserliness.

Giving up the struggle with the symptom and thereby shifting from a symmetrical to a complementary relationship with the symptom can be facilitated by a surrender to a more powerful force. Bateson (1972) noted this process in the Alcoholics Anonymous approach. The alchoholic experiences panic and recognizes that he is powerless in his struggle with the bottle, enabling him to surrender and to place himself in a supplicant stance toward a higher power that can help him. The bogeyman figure can play the role of this more powerful force in some instances. In bogeyman interventions, the bogeyman interrupts a sequence of symmetrical maneuvers and forces the person into a position of surrender to establish a complementary relationship. This shift in interpersonal relationships catalyzes a shift in the person's relationship to the symptom.

FURTHER APPLICATIONS OF THE BOGEYMAN INTERVENTION

The previous paper identified defiant adolescents as the clients most appropriate for this intervention because their defiance was so severe that usual solutions were ineffective. However, I have found that the intervention can also be effectively applied to adults, to couples, and to nonadolescent children, as well as to problems other than defiance. I have also learned that it need not be an intervention of last resort and can be applied early in the life of a problem.

In order to show a wider application of the concept beyond the single case described in the previous paper, several case examples are presented below. The adult problems will be omitted in this presentation in order to allow for a focus on children and adolescents in families. Presentation and discussion of failures will also be included.

CASE 1: THE INCORRIGIBLE BICYCLIST

Mr. B. was a behavioral psychologist who had tried, by means of several strategies, to break his seven-year-old son's habit of riding his bicycle in the street. When his son knew that there was a high probability of Mr. B. observing him, he kept the bicycle on the sidewalk; however, when Mr. B's attention was otherwise engaged, especially when he was at work, his son frequently forgot the injunction to stay on the sidewalk. Punishments, rewards, and other behavioral plans met with initial improvements, but inevitable relapses.

Being a good behaviorist, Mr. B. reasoned that his son was getting away with the misbehavior enough to be gratified by intermittent reinforcement, which tends to render a misbehavior resistant to extinction, especially when punishment of the misbehavior is also intermittent. He decided that he needed to improve on the immediacy and certainty of the aversive consequences of the misbehavior. Therefore, when he left for work one morning, he parked his car around the block, doubled back to the house, and hid in the bushes. When his son, riding his bicycle, rode down the driveway into the street, Mr. B.

leaped from the bushes with a yell and a prompt punishment. After one further repetition of the intervention, the misbehavior ceased to occur.

Discussion

Mr. B. explained the success of his intervention in behavioral terms, pointing especially to the immediacy and the certainty of the reinforcing event as the effective ingredients. A behavioral explanation of this sort is accurate and certainly more economical than a view of the event as a bogeyman experience.

However, while the immediacy and certainty of consequences play important roles, this sort of immediacy and certainty is highly unusual in such circumstances. To the child, his father springing from the bushes was a highly unpredictable and incomprehensible event; this incomprehensibility is one of the defining characteristics of a bogeyman intervention. That such an event should occur at the precise moment of misbehavior also conveyed an unexpected display of omniscience, another essential characteristic. Most of the other characteristics also appear to be integrated in this event. While a behavioral explanation is accurate, a more enriched and resonant understanding of the event can be achieved by viewing it as a multifaceted bogeyman experience.

The only ingredient that is absent is the bogeyman's effort to unite parent and child in some form of unified position, either by opposing them both or by putting them in awe of him. The reason it is absent in this case is that the parent was himself a bogeyman figure. The purpose of the maneuver is to reduce the symmetrical strain between parent and child and to facilitate complementary exchanges. The maneuver was not necessary here since the purpose was achieved when the bogeyman, who was the parent in this case, forced the child into a complementary relationship to himself. Mr B. was at first a parent who was locked in a symmetrical struggle with his child: each time his child rode the bicycle into the street undetected, the child matched or outmatched, in symmetrical fashion, Mr. B's attempts to control him. Mr. B. shifted the relationship to a complementary one by successfully catching and punishing his child each time the child attempted to misbehave, placing himself in the role of the catcher and his son in the role of the caught. In other words, Mr. B. arranged the situation in such a way that a symmetrical relationship was no longer possible.

Of particular interest is that Mr. B's son was atypical of those defiant adolescents for whom a bogeyman intervention was thought to be most appropriate. He was a preadolescent child whose misbehaviors could be characterized as mild and mischievous rather than severe.

CASE 2: THE TERRIBLE TWO'S

Mrs. L. informed me of an intervention she employed in her many attempts to control her toddler's exploratory and oppositional behavior. Lisa, two years of age, was continually overturning flower pots and other knicknacks and, more ominous, was frequently attempting to ignite an ornamental cigarette lighter placed on an end table in the living room.

Mrs. L. did not believe in compromising her own needs to the degree that she would remove the lighter and the breakables. She also did not believe in physical punishment. Therefore, she spent a great deal of energy and time in physically removing Lisa from circumstances of imminent breakage, to which Lisa promptly returned as soon as Mrs. L.'s attention was engaged elsewhere. When frustrated enough, she would violate her principles and slap Lisa on the hand. Lisa always responded with agonizing wails, signaling a degree of pain that caused Mrs. L. severe pangs of guilt and that did not deter Lisa in the least from a persevering and earnest pursuit of her endeavors at the earliest opportunity.

Mrs. L. decided at that point to stop trying to remove Lisa from the breakables and the lighter, since Mrs. L's yells and slaps were sufficient to achieve only momentary cessations of misbehavior. However, she did decide to try something different. Since Lisa tended to behave herself in Mrs. L.'s presence, she realized that the main problem was that Lisa misbehaved outside of her presence. Therefore, she decided to appear to disappear from Lisa's presence by hiding in a doorway, waiting for a misbehavior. By arranging that Lisa was playing near the lighter and some breakables, Mrs. L. did not have to invest a great deal of time in this intervention; a few minutes at the most.

When Lisa was on the verge of a misbehavior, such as touching the lighter, Mrs. L. leapt into the room with a yell. Although the intervention required some degree of investment of time and energy for a couple of days, Mrs. L. described it as fun. At last, she felt effective. In addition, it significantly altered Lisa's behavior. Although her exploratory behavior continued, she no longer attempted to touch the lighter and other breakables.

Discussion

In a case such as this, a therapist might have attempted to use behavioral methods to address the problem, which might have taken longer. To use a bogeyman approach with a problem like this might be viewed as an extreme approach. It could engender mistrust, fear, and timidity in a child. However, I believe that with a 2-year-old child the most probable effect is that the child will believe that the parent is omniscient and all-powerful. I do not consider that to be an undesirable effect for that particular stage of development.

A difference that exists between this case and the previous one is that, unlike Mr. B., Mrs. L. expressed some reluctance to take a firm stand and to stick to it. This reluctance permitted a repetitive sequence of exchanges that maintained the symmetrical relationship between Mrs. L. and Lisa. Mrs. L.'s reluctance to be firm makes her case typical of many parents who remain locked in symmetrical relationships with their children.

For example, when attempting to be firm, the parent wavers and the child takes advantage; the parent then gets fed up and overreacts with too much firmness, then feels sorry, backs down a bit, and allows the child to again take advantage. Uncertainty about the justice of a decision, guilt about possible inadequacy as a parent, empathy for a child's pain, worry that the firmness is too harsh or that the child will abandon or hate the parent as a result of discipline, can all contribute to a parent's reluctance to give up symmetrical relationships with their children.

In other variations, parents allow themselves to get into endless symmetrical arguments because they simultaneously feel a need to be fair and a need to win. They debate points endlessly as if their children were lawyers and will finally listen to reason. Another related variation is that of trading insults: attack and counterattack. Symmetrical relationships of these sorts can be exciting and stimulating, and this stimulation makes it difficult to resist or disengage from symmetrical maneuvers.

The needs contributing to symmetrical exchanges and the gratifications engendered by such exchanges are powerful factors maintaining the exchanges. Whether it be a need to win, a need to get even, or a need to assuage guilt, the parent may be reluctant to forego the hope of gratifying that need. Parents usually do not realize that they are not yet fed up enough with the kind of conflict they are complaining about to do something decisive to change it. The therapist needs to evaluate this issue carefully before advising a bogeyman intervention because the advice will be wasted if the parent is not yet ready to forego the advantages accruing from symmetrical exchanges.

CASE 3: A REGRESSED ADOLESCENT

Robert T. was almost 16 years old when he was referred by his probation officer to myself. Robert had been placed on probation due to a truancy petition filed by the school system for a school refusal of six month's duration. The probation officer (P. O.) was unable to get Robert to go to school or to regularly involve himself in a tutoring program; the P.O. was also unable to get Robert to regularly attend probation appointments, to involve himself in therapy, to seek needed medical treatment for a severe skin problem, and to participate in a daily physical education program that was intended to help improve his skin condition.

The P.O. was on the verge of making a decision either to place Robert in a residential facility or to drop the case and leave Robert alone. Despite his anger at Robert, the P.O. feared that placement might be harmful to Robert, who was quiet and shy, and feared that he might be "eaten alive" by the tougher population of residential facilities. Since Robert would shortly turn 16 years of age and have the right to quit school, the P.O. was tempted to give up on Robert and to drop the case. However, before giving up, he asked me to evaluate Robert with the hope that a fresh idea might emerge from the evaluation.

The evaluation revealed that Robert had stopped going to school 6 months prior to the referral, but the reasons he gave were vague, such as not liking the teachers. These were typical reasons given by adolescents. The most probable precipitating factor was the embarrassing skin condition, the onset of which had coincided with the school refusal. His mother, a single working parent, had made repeated but fruitless attempts to get him to go to and to stay in school, including punishment, bringing him to school, and reasoning with him. However, he spent each day at home, watching television, and occasionally socializing with a few friends and cousins who would visit him.

His demeanor was shy and reserved and his mood was depressed. He engaged in no antisocial or defiant behaviors, his only misbehavior being his refusal to attend school. He was never openly defiant toward his mother, the P.O., or other authority. Instead, he engaged in a maddening and repeated display of passive opposition by promising to go to scheduled appointments or to call for appointments regarding probation meetings, therapy, tutoring, and medical treatments, but always forgetting or showing up too late for the appointment.

His life was a striking contrast to that of six months before, at which time he was described as an exuberant, outgoing teenager who enjoyed school, peers, and the opposite sex. Although the legal system would soon have no jurisdiction over the truancy matter, my view was that since the school refusal constituted a violation of the law, the state had the right to intrude upon Robert's life and to address the reasons for the school refusal, namely, his depression and the regression in his development. In addition, the adults involved felt so defeated in their attempts to help that their helping behaviors assumed a chronic repetition of halfhearted attempts at previously unsuccessful solutions. If left alone, Robert's interactions with caretaking and helping persons would assume a repetitive pattern and the developmental regression might become permanent. The bogeyman intervention crafted for this case was designed to disrupt Robert's complacency regarding his regressed position and to mobilize him in a way that would permit usual solutions to take hold.

First, I contacted the school guidance counselor, the tutor, Robert's physician, the P.O., Robert's mother, the therapist he was supposed to be seeing, and the director of the physical education program he was supposed to attend. A rigidly scheduled tutorial program was arranged, as was a series of scheduled appointments with physician, P.O., therapist, and physical education instructor. More important, however, was that I established with each of the above participants the limits of each participant's responsibility and procedures for prompt communications to myself on whether or not Robert was meeting his commitments. Then a meeting was arranged for most of the participants, at which I confronted Robert with what was about to happen.

Robert first expressed some surprise at a meeting of this size. I responded by quietly pointing out that each of the participants were busy people and would not stand for Robert to continue wasting their time. I told him that he had come to the end of the line.

However, I spoke in a mild and sympathetic manner, in a monologue that is paraphrased here.

I know that you won't like what's about to happen now because your life will become very busy and disrupted and full of hassles. You may even hate it. But it's for your own good, to get you out of this slump. You now have a full schedule of appointments with your doctor, with your therapist, and with your probation officer, as well as tutoring every day and physical education every other day. I've written them all out and I have a copy for your mother. I'm going to keep track of whether you miss any of these, and I do mean any, because I'll find out within the day.

My tone of voice became apologetic at this point. I shrugged my shoulders and opened my palms in gestures of helplessness.

I'm sorry, but there's no other way. There won't be any more forgetting of appointments or showing up late, and no excuses, because I'll know, and if it happens, well, then I'll be recommending that you be placed in a residential facility where you will get an education after all. You have no choices anymore. Your only choice is to get into placement if you wish, and you can do that easily enough I'm afraid, if you want, by just missing a couple of these appointments.

For the first time, Robert became openly enraged and defiant. His words were something like the following: "You can't do this. You don't have the right to butt in like this."

I turned away from Robert and addressed the others, informing them that although they might sympathize with Robert's concern over how hassled his life would become, it was important to let me know about any missed appointments, even those about which Robert had conned them with plausible excuses. I extracted a pledge of commitment from each of them so that Robert would be aware of the comprehensiveness of the communicational network. Following the meeting, two of the participants privately expressed to me how stunned they had been by the meeting, which they had assumed would be an ordinary case conference, and wondered if I hadn't been too hard on Robert.

In the days following this meeting, I telephoned the various participants, including Robert, at unpredictable times, in order to keep intact the flow of communication and to assure Robert that he could no longer tell one helper one story and then a different story to another. The unpredictable calls to Robert also kept him on his toes, wondering what I might do next, and wondering when. Thereafter, Robert kept almost all, though not quite all, of his appointments. To his P.O. he expressed some surprise at how easy it was for him to change. He soon became attached to his therapist, gradually widened his peer relationships, eventually learned to express anger and defiance in small doses, passed his high school equivalency exam, and finally went to work.

Discussion

Although the intervention in this case has the appearance of an ordinary interdisciplinary case conference, the purposes were quite different than those for which case conferences are usually held. A case conference setting was used to orchestrate the action necessary to bring about a bogeyman experience for Robert. Since one of its purposes was that of disrupting Robert's complacency, it was similar to the approach of creating a crisis used by structural family therapists. However, the creation of a crisis was only one aspect of the case. The varied aspects of the intervention can be more aptly and comprehensively captured by the bogeyman concept.

The omniscience that I pretended to have was the most prominent of the ingredients employed in this case. Although I did not attempt to make my knowledge of Robert's whereabouts appear supernatural, my knowledge of him, by means of the complicated network of communication involving other helping agents, was certainly greater than what he usually experienced with other adults. The belief in omniscience was augmented by the presence of the several persons who would be reporting to me and by the subsequent unpredictable phone calls.

The power to impinge on Robert's life was also prominent, existing in my influence to facilitate a placement. While hierarchically superior, extremely firm, and able to impinge on Robert's life, I did not make a stern and blustering appearance; my sympathetic and apologetic manner was unlike the manner other helping adults had previously used to interact with Robert. The paradoxical combination of a firm and apologetic presentation may have engendered confusion and wonder. These as well as other seemingly incomprehensible aspects of the intervention were also intended to underline the implicit suggestion that the entire intervention had the power to effect change. My impression was that this suggestion was understood by Robert and that it took hold.

Robert's comment concerning how easy it was for him to change also suggested some confirmation for the hypothesis that Robert's relationship to his problem shifted from a symmetrical to a complementary one. The other systemic shifts also occurred. The most noticeable shift was the alignment of other helpers with Robert, due to fear that I was being too hard on him. They were no longer in the position of having to hound Robert. They could devote their energies to helping him and to saving him from my clutches. Thus, complementary relationships replaced symmetrical ones between Robert and the various helping persons with whom he was involved.

Of particular interest is that Robert was extremely atypical of the group originally identified as appropriate for bogeyman interventions. Rather than being a defiant person engaged in antisocial behavior, he was primarily a depressed and regressed adolescent whose only crime was his refusal to attend school.

CASE 4: A FAILURE

Susan D. was 14 years of age when her mother brought her to a mental health agency for help in controlling her behavior. Susan got into fights and was violent with her mother and other adults. She had run away several times, came and went as she pleased, was becoming sexually promiscuous, was abusing drugs, and refused to be controlled by her mother. She was soon placed with her uncle, who also began to have trouble with her. At that point, I became involved and played an elaborate bogeyman role very much as I had with David, described above. The intervention had an immediate impact and Susan's uncle and therapist were able to follow up with appropriate measures.

After several months of greatly improved behavior, Mrs. D. became envious of the uncle's apparent ability to handle the child. I did not, however, realize the extent of this envy at the time and did not adequately address it. Following a weekend visit at the mother's home, the child returned to her uncle's in an upset state. In the subsequent two days, she engaged in two assaults that were typical of her former acting out behaviors, she ran away once, and she began to drink and to break curfew. In standard bogeyman fashion, I took prompt and forceful action by coaching the uncle, the therapist, and others in ways that produced the result that Susan was arrested for the assaults and placed in a temporary detention facility.

This action had an initial humbling effect on the child. However, I had not anticipated the known fact that only natural parents were allowed to visit the detention center, was not aware of the strength of the mother's envy of the uncle, and underestimated the mother's ability to sour the child on the uncle's home as an appropriate setting. As a result, the child was isolated from the influence of her uncle and closeted with her mother. The mother allied herself with the child by scapegoating the uncle, blaming him for the child's problems. Rather than the temporary detention having the salutary effect intended, the child's defiance increased to the point that a more restrictive placement was required.

Discussion

The various ingredients integrated in this intervention are by now quite evident and need not be highlighted here. What is of greatest interest in this case example is the reason for failure. It can be accounted for by my failure to recognize the degree to which Mrs. D. would be envious of the uncle's success with the child, and the importance of addressing this by some means; also by permitting an opportunity to exist in the detention center for the mother to undermine the progress that had been made. This opportunity would not have existed if an alternative consequence to her assaults had been used, instead of the detention center, or if our energies had been directed to ensuring that a transfer in custody to the uncle had become legal.

CASE 5: A POOR CANDIDATE FOR INTERVENTION

Joanna D. was 14 years old when her parents brought her to court on a petition stating that they could no longer control her. The court referred her for evaluations by the Probation Department and by the Department of Mental

Heath. These evaluations revealed that Joanna was the oldest of three children in a middle class family and had been well behaved until she started middle school, at which time she experienced some difficulty adjusting to the new school. In addition, when she began to engage in minor acts of misconduct that are somewhat typical of adolescence, her mother responded with an unexpected firmness, which was mistakenly construed by Joanna as a sign of rejection.

With her cognitive-social development still immature enough for Joanna to view herself through her mother's eyes, she responded to this threat to her self-esteem by attaching herself to a lower class delinquent peer group that provided her with the affirmation she no longer believed her mother would provide; this peer group encouraged acts of truancy, theft, aggression, promiscuity, and drug abuse. Increasing levels of misconduct by Joanna were met by her mother with increasing measures of discipline. Due to the increasing intensity of hostility between Joanna and her mother, the escalations in discipline were sometimes unrealistic and unreasonable, such as restricting Joanna to the house for 2 months. Joanna would respond to this sort of discipline by a wrathful refusal to accept any restriction at all and sneaking out or storming out of the house. Mrs. D. would then escalate the disciplinary measures and Joanna would escalate her acting out behaviors.

With help from a therapist, Mrs. D. was able to secure Mr. D.'s support in her efforts to control Joanna. However, this alliance brought no increment in control over Joanna; instead, it created an increase in Joanna's rage, since she had always viewed her indulgent father as her ally and now felt betrayed by him. The parents energetically followed advice from the therapist, but the situation only deteriorated further when Joanna's brother and sister became targets for Joanna's anger and occasional physical assaults. Joanna refused to remain involved in family therapy and the family turned to school counselors and to a church group, but neither of these efforts resulted in any change in the problem.

During the evaluation, Joanna calmly pointed out that she was too old to be told what to do. She believed that the court would adjourn the case repeatedly and do nothing to control her. This belief had been fostered by her observation of peers who had been brought to court and whose cases had been repeatedly adjourned, usually with warnings and empty threats by the judges and other players in the system. Even her peers who had been placed on probation or in residential facilities had not appeared to her to have suffered from the experience. When faced with the prospect of placement, she stated calmly and matter-of-factly that she would not go, or, if forced into a facility, would run away.

The Probation Department concluded that Joanna was so uncooperative that it would be impossible to maintain her on probation. The probation investigator had told Joanna, as a last-ditch effort intended to elicit some cooperation or fear of placement, that she was definitely going to be placed, unless he could be convinced that there was a chance for him to work successfully with her. He also told her that he knew that she thought she was going to keep getting away with things, but this time she was wrong.

The probation officer consulted me and described his manner of interacting with Joanna as playing the bogeyman, a role with which he was somewhat experienced. She had responded to his bogeyman behavior by laughing and by refusing to acknowledge that he could have any impact on her. He asked me whether it might be possible to have more of an impact on Joanna if I were to craft a bogeyman intervention. I did not think it very probable. I advised the investigator to go ahead with plans for an appropriate placement that would more adequately meet Joanna's needs.

Discussion

This case was included for illustration because it is typical of a kind of child that therapists, probation officers, and courts often face. It is also typical of the kind of case for which a bogeyman approach is likely to fail at this advanced stage in an adolescent's history of defiance. The nature of the family interaction, the symmetrical escalation, the early adolescent depression, as well as other relevant factors, all might help to account for the problem; however, they are not the factors that make this case typical of one for which bogeyman interventions are ineffective. The factors that appear most crucial here are the rigidity of the adolescent's belief system and the absence of effective resources that would be necessary for application following a potent bogeyman intervention.

Joanna's belief that the system could have no impact on her life was too rigid to be modified enough to render her susceptible to parental control, therapeutic assistance, or other resources existing in her environment. Since the peer group she had embraced provided her with the affirmation she craved, it helped her to maintain a view of reality in which establishment figures could have no impact on her behavior. Even if a bogeyman intervention could have had some initial effect, it was doubtful whether the parents could summon enough energy to set and enforce limits without doing so in anger. The emotional atmosphere at home was intensely negative, with child and parents feeling betrayed by one another and fed up with one another, an interpersonal context that could easily precipitate explosive behavior. Although it might have been possible to craft a more potent bogeyman intervention than that attempted by the probation investigator, there would have been only a remote chance of any success and the degree of illusion and effort necessary in a case like this would have been enormous. Most likely, Joanna would have learned that the intervention was only one more bluff; this would have been unhelpful to her.

GENERAL DISCUSSION

Expansion of the Population

The most interesting aspect of this collection of cases is the expansion of the population for which the bogeyman intervention was originally considered appropriate. It was used successfully with preadolescent children and with those whose behavior could be characterized as mischievous and passively oppositional. It was also used at earlier stages in the life of a problem than formerly thought to be appropriate. For example, it was not used as a last resort in the case of the toddler Lisa. Although other interventions could have been worth attempting in that case, Lisa's mother developed an intervention that produced quick and lasting results.

It is interesting to speculate whether it would have been appropriate for a therapist to prescribe the intervention in the case of Lisa when other less drastic interventions might yet be tried. The negative effects of the intervention include the possible trauma experienced by the child and the child's resulting false belief that the mother was omniscient. Yet the trauma was probably no worse than that which most children experience accidentally and quite frequently; and I wonder whether it is really very harmful for a child of that age to believe her mother is omniscient.

Relative Prominence of Ingredients

Due to the use of the intervention with an expanded population, the intervention can be seen to take on different appearances in different kinds of cases, sometimes appearing hardly recognizable, as the bogeyman intervention that has been described in the rationale, and at other times conforming closely to that picture. These changes in appearance may be due to the possibility that the relative prominence of the various ingredients shifts according to the nature of each case. Only two of the ingredients seem to have high visibility in most cases: omniscience and power to effect change. Most of the rest of the ingredients, while present, do not always appear conspicuous.

Heavy reliance on two of the ingredients, illusion and incomprehensibility, tends to render the intervention easily recognizable as that of a bogeyman approach because these involve a histrionic performance. Good examples include the cases of Susan D., the incorrigible bicyclist, the toddler Lisa, and the case of David described in the previous paper. However, where these two ingredients are used more sparingly, such as in the case of Robert, the regressed adolescent, the interventions appear more mundane and may easily go unrecognized as bogeyman interventions.

Although it is not usually possible to verify whether reality is viewed differently in the sense that a person's relationship to the problem has shifted to a complementary one, this shift is assumed to generally occur in bogeyman experiences; it is more likely to be conspicuous in adolescents or in adults who tend to talk more about their inner experiences. Also, the implicit suggestion that the intervention constitutes an incomprehensible ritual that will effect change is assumed to exist to some extent in each application of the intervention, but the prominence of this suggestion depends on the degree to which the intervention takes on the appearance or format of a ritual.

It may be that not all ingredients are necessary to an effective application of the intervention. The cases in which a parent played the bogeyman role showed that it is not necessary to employ the maneuver of inducing awe or resistance in order to unite the parent and child in a supportive relationship. It was impossible to employ this maneuver in these cases because it was the parent who played the bogeyman role. It may be that any maneuver that results in a complementary relationship between parent and child is satisfactory. If further cases were examined, it is possible that other ingredients could also be identified as useful but not always necessary.

Failures

Failures are important to consider so that a search for their causes might yield contraindications and other sorts of guidance for future cases. In the case of Susan D., it was a collusion between parent and child, rather than conflict between them, that contributed to failure. My failure to recognize this soon enough and the logistical oversight concerning the visitation rules in the detention center help to explain the failure in this case.

In another case not reported here, the mother was very unwilling to keep her preadolescent child in the home setting and viewed him as a rotten child, expecting only misbehavior from him. She also provided very inconsistent discipline. A bogeyman intervention was employed and had an initial impact that surprised the mother. She was sure it would not last, continued to expect the worst from her son, and continued to provide inconsistent discipline. The only thing controlling the boy's behavior was his contacts with the bogeyman, and this was clearly insufficient.

Within two weeks, his misbehaviors were as frequent as previously. It was clear in this case that the mother's unwillingness to keep the child at home, her expectation of failure, and her inability or unwillingness to provide fair and consistent discipline were the primary contributing factors. The intervention probably should not have been attempted without there being backup resources in the child's environment to support the impact that the intervention achieved. Also, to employ the intervention in this case was misguided insofar as it affirmed the mother's view that the child was rotten or the one at fault; it would have been more appropriate to address the mother's rejection of the child and her inadequate parenting capacities.

These examples demonstrate that to reduce the chance of failure in each case, it is important to keep in mind that a parent's willingness or ability to take certain actions, if called upon to do so, is usually necessary to a bogeyman intervention. Therefore, it is usually not attempted when it is doubtful that the caretaker can follow through with requested action. It is also not attempted when it is clear that the child will interpret a display of omniscience and power as a bluff. The case of Joanna D., described above, is an example of a situation in which it was feared that even the most carefully crafted bogeyman intervention would be perceived as a bluff. Despite these various precautions and caveats, errors in judgment and factors beyond our control cannot always be anticipated, as in the case of Susan D.

SUMMARY AND CONCLUSION

The cases presented here have served to further illustrate the bogeyman approach. These additional cases have permitted an opportunity to search for reasons why the intervention may fail in certain instances. Hopefully, this sort of search will be helpful to others who may attempt similar interventions. The expansion of the population of clients and problems for which the intervention might be appropriate has had another interesting result: The intervention takes on a more ordinary, or less exotic, appearance than as previously described.

Earlier in the chapter, the theoretical rationale was tightened and then supplemented by further elaborating the hypnotic aspects of the intervention and by providing a systemic explanation of the altered view of reality resulting from a bogeyman experience. These theoretical considerations can help to more clearly identify bogeyman interventions as something more than just scare tactics and to differentiate them from other related interventions. They can also provide guidance in the crafting of related interventions that contain some of the effective ingredients of a bogeyman approach. As work in this area progresses, further insights and mistakes are bound to surface; therefore, further refinements can also be expected in regard to both theory and practice.

REFERENCES

Bateson, G. (1972). *Steps to an ecology of mind.* New York: Ballantine.

Castaneda, C. (1972). *Journey to Ixtlan: The lessons of Don Juan.* New York: Simon & Schuster.

Hoorwitz, A.N. (1988). *Hypnotic methods in nonhypnotic therapies.* New York: Irvington.

O'Connor, J.J., & Hoorwitz, A.N. (1984). The bogeyman cometh: A strategic approach for difficult adolescents. *Family Process, 23,* 237–249.

Watzlawick, P., Weakland, Ch.E., & Fisch, M.D. (1974). *Change: Principles of problem formation and problem resolution.* New York: W.W. Norton.

PART 4

Other Techniques

CHAPTER 12

Phototherapy

Using Snapshots and Photo-Interactions in Therapy with Youth

JUDY WEISER

INTRODUCTION

The power of ordinary snapshots to convey emotional meaning, to secure relationships across time and distance, and to symbolize personal metaphors, is the focus of this chapter. Phototherapy, an innovative use of a 150-year-old technology, uses people's personal photos and their interactions with these images as powerful adjunctive tools for counselors and therapists who wish to move beyond the constraints of traditional verbal-only therapy when helping people with their emotional or family problems.

Most of us keep snapshots around—without ever pausing to really think about why. The power of these "mirrors with memory," as Oliver Wendell Holmes called them (Akeret, 1973, p. 4), is so strong that they become treasured (or sometimes hated) parts of our lives, yet we rarely take the time to explore them in any great depth. Phototherapy involves not only taking time to examine the contents of those photographic images that we decide to take, pose for, hold onto, or respond to, but also noting what occurs in the process of interacting with them (as well as considering others' responses). Probing our photos to reveal what they mean to us, how they make us feel, what memories they stimulate, and how these answers reflect our personal makeup and underlying values can help us understand our particular uniqueness in how we know what we know, and better appreciate the importance of this knowledge for understanding ourselves and others.

How people respond to a photograph, or what and how they choose to record (or pose for), can reveal a tremendous amount about them; this is in addition to the information in the image itself. Each response to a photo is individually unique, based on people's particular constellations of past experi-

All photos in this chapter, with the exception of Figure 12.4, were taken by Judy Weiser.

ences blended with their psychological configuration and personality; their values, attitudes, thoughts, feelings, and expectations; and their family and cultural background, training, and traditions. Each photo is thus, at least in some ways, a self-portrait. The process of interacting with these insights-from-the-inside can be intimately revealing of people's feelings and personal realities.

Although this process of exploring the secret lives of photographs can be used by anyone on an individual path of personal discovery, these techniques can be of great benefit for counselors and therapists working with young people (or people of any age) to improve their ability to attend to their clients' emotional (and sometimes unconscious, or at least nonverbalized) needs using ordinary photographs as the medium of dialogue.

The following pages will show how using photos (i.e., self-portraits, pictures of clients or taken by them, their family snapshots, albums, and personal photo displays or collections) as therapy tools for exploring feelings and memories can greatly aid in therapy with children and adolescents. Using these phototherapy techniques permits us, to paraphrase T.S. Eliot, to return to the places that are our physical and emotional sources and to be able to know them, again, for the first time.

HISTORICAL BACKGROUND

To study the history of phototherapy, one must begin with the history of photography itself, as it was not long after people learned how to freeze time forever (the first daguerreotype appeared in the 1830's) and capture visual material onto film, that they began having emotional relationships with these artifacts. At first, only the rich could afford such special portraits; soon, however, the process became more affordable, and anyone who wanted to could find a way to have a photo taken. Large numbers of people became photographers or their subjects; some believed the resulting photos reflected the world the way it really was for them, while others were quite offended when their captured image was not at all what their imagination had embellished.

Some professionals who worked with disturbed people made particular use of the emotional contents of photography, such as British psychiatrist Dr. Hugh Diamond, who, in 1856, wrote what is probably the earliest formal documentation of photography used as therapy, and Dr. Thomas Barnardo, who published similar findings in 1870 (Gilman, 1976); such uses, usually with hospitalized psychiatric patients, continued erratically but with increasing frequency through the remainder of the past century and into our own. With the advent of smaller and simpler cameras in the early 1900s, the snapshot released people from the need for previously planned formality—and a universal hobby was launched. It is this casual and yet emotionally-filled nature of these artifacts that led such sensitive photographers as Minor White (1966), Gassan (1983), and Ralph Hattersley (1971) to use photographs as much more than simple documents, and that later led mental health professionals to begin to work with them as chosen tools.

Phototherapy itself as a formal field has evolved predominantly within the past decade or two. It is generally agreed that interest in the field was precipitated by a brief notice in *Psychology Today* (Zakem, 1977), in which Zakem and Stewart noted their Ravenswood Hospital Photo Therapy Project and asked for feedback. The response led to the first major International Symposium in Illinois in 1979. Other conferences and meetings have ensued; there is now an International Phototherapy Association, a journal, and an active network of therapists and researchers.

Despite its catchy name, phototherapy is not a therapy unto itself or a particular modality or school of thought; rather, it is a comprehensive system of techniques that has been found to work successfully—often in cases where nothing else has—using photography as a medium for communication, expression, and reflection. But everyone's particular conceptual and theoretical models are not necessarily the same; I do not want readers to assume that there is some consistent set of assumptions about therapy imbedded within the set of techniques called phototherapy. These tools can be used quite successfully regardless of personal preference of therapeutic modality (Adlerian, psychoanalytic, behavioral, Gestalt, Freudian, developmental, existential, phenomenological, systems, Rogerian, rational-emotive, Jungian, communications models, etc.), or client population/setting/restrictions. The next section is a condensation of some existential/phenomenological principles that I have found helpful in understanding therapeutic applications of photographic communication.

EXISTENTIAL AND PHENOMENOLOGICAL COMMUNICATION

Some basic concepts underlying my approach to phototherapy are conceptually housed within the domains of existential and phenomenological philosophy and psychology. Detailed analysis of how we perceive, create, and store meaning, and how this relates to photographic communication is beyond the scope of this chapter (see, for example, Weiser, 1975, 1983, 1985, 1987 in press; and Krauss, 1979, 1980, 1981, 1983a), but it is clear from studying these subjects that any act of perceiving filters and creates meaning in addition to, and sometimes different from, the physical or symbolic properties of the incoming stimulus. We contribute to (and thus change) the meaning perceived by our very process of perceiving it; others do the same with the verbal and nonverbal messages we send, no matter how clear we try to be. These selective filters have a personal-cultural base in which family can be seen as a type of subculture, and are always within situational contexts; as Bandler and Grinder (1975) have conceptualized it, the personally created map of reality being responded to is not the actual context-free territory itself, but is rather at least partially created by the perceiver as attention is paid only to what is noticed—in or out of our conscious awareness. In an example from visual perception, it is the difference between all the total input physically reaching the retina (*visual field*) and that portion of this information that is actually consciously or unconsciously seen (*visual world*) as the world that we know and recognize (Hall, 1969).

It is the nature of most human beings to try to make sense out of what we encounter; our senses are bombarded with input; and we try to figure things out as we take in vast fields of sensory data, selectively code it in such a way as to record and hopefully understand its meaning for us, store this meaning internally for future use, and sometimes attempt to reconstitute parts of it to create communications to others (and ourselves) that can somehow convey what we mean. If the message received is close to the one we intended, then we can claim to have communicated; using a mutually agreed upon set of codes and semiotics that make up our spoken language, we strive to take internal concepts and translate these into words that will manage to give another person a way to see what we mean, to understand in the same way we do. Often this succeeds; often again, especially in more stressful situations, it does not (or else we think we've communicated, but do not know for sure how to know for sure). Most usually the lack of congruency underlying this possible dissonance lies in the other-than-verbal domains, and trying to get a sharper picture of people's nonverbal messages and cognitive/comprehending processes becomes a major goal in attempts to better understand and communicate with them. If people could only become more comfortable with the idea that theirs is not the only way to see things (but that it is just as valid as any other), and feel secure in this enlarged conceptual ideology, then interpersonal communication on a small or large scale could be so much easier facilitated.

Perception deals with differences that make a difference; as we describe things, we bring into existence those things that we later accept as real. These concepts borrowed from existential philosophy have serious implications for therapy, where children, families, couples, or individuals may be operating in separate (sometimes invisibly different) perceptual/cultural systems and not even know it, and then become frustrated when natural assumptions are not automatically shared as one would expect. There really is no right or wrong existing independently in this world; there is only "different"—we, through our personal, societal, and cultural applications, add the values that label, in both verbal and nonverbal form. Each of us, inevitably, by our very own nature, impose our own personal/cultural map; we are our own selective filters. A grave error is made if we think that what we perceive is that reality itself, forgetting the effect of each person's unique process of perceiving, symbolizing, and taking meaning. This error is much too frequently made when working with youth of any age, in assuming they must always bend to fit our expectations, rules, values, and labels.

We create meaning through personal and cultural filters and interact with others who do the same. Our memories are coded, stored, and accessed nonverbally. Most of what we know of our own lives we know in an area where words do not go. We think, remember, and feel not in words, but in symbolized meanings that are more culturally universal, or part of the collective unconscious perhaps, but still cognitively structured by selective perception of reality and cultural/subcultural differences. Therapists who can internalize and incorporate these concepts into their operational style usually find their clients responding in a more spontaneous and intuitive manner, revealing from behind their verbal defenses and protective rationalizations information that they may have been unaware of at a conscious level. This aids clients in finding an enriched appreciation for their own personal uniqueness and backgrounds, a better understanding of their particular communication process and values (and therefore those of others), learning more about who they are, where they are, and, I hope, why they are: "By broadening his conception of the forces that make up and control his life, the average person can never again be completely caught in the grip of patterned behavior of which he has no awareness" (Hall, 1973, p. 187).

To study any techniques of counseling and therapy requires an exploration into the depths not only of perception, but also of communication itself, especially its predominantly nonverbal components. Whatever the reasons for referral for treatment, youths certainly exemplify a more narrow-band, selectively organized, and perceived reality, with many memories and feelings from earlier years still stored at the preverbal level they originally occurred within, and often not yet brought up to any level of conscious awareness, much less understanding, catharsis, and/or resolution. It is necessary, therefore, to appreciate the relatively more significant value of the other-than-verbal components of their communications and internalized meanings, their symbolic and metaphorical language, in order to more fully aid them.

Spoken/written language is frequently only an approximation in communicating what is really inside us; words can never completely convey the totality of what is intended or comprehended, nor can they give us back any true assurance that the person received our full communication as we wished. Most of our senses receive and transmit information unfiltered by intermediary symbolic linguistic interpretation; as our eyes take in the vast majority of all the knowledge we absorb, we can be certain that for most people the world is perceived and evaluated through a visual literacy far more complex than words could ever fully define or represent. I believe that most humans think, feel, and recall memories not in direct words, but in iconic imagery, thought-pictures (sometimes accompanied by kinesthetic or other cues), and visual concepts that comprise the cognitive maps that we try to encompass in our spoken or written representations, but that our words can never fully describe.

In order to get inside our heads, to really know how we think, how we know what we know, our values and beliefs, our reasons and traditions as we know them, there must be a way to tap into all this predominantly visual information in some nonverbal manner that is less directly intrusive than verbal or written enquiry. To more directly connect with the insides of people's minds and feelings, one must have additional tools that complement linear verbal methodologies, tools that somehow can manage to do this exploration of nonverbal terrain in a nonverbal manner providing a less intrusive or disruptive view of the person under observation. The moment we observe a behavior, we have changed it in that process of observation; the moment we label or define, we are imposing our own values and perceptions onto the meaning perceived. Any interpretive process automatically alters and limits; it is important to remember that such a process usually occurs naturally: spontaneously, unconsciously, and often totally out of our (or our client's) conscious awareness or self-reflective ability.

Communication is predominantly nonverbal, people's actions quite literally speak louder than their words. At its most simple and basic it deals with "the emission of information and its perception by humans and animals" (Poyatos, 1983, p. xvi). But all students of communication quickly realize that the majority of our messages are based heavily on nonverbal (and predominantly visual) components that we may not be all that conscious of, and these cues are by no means universal across cultures or generations, or even families or individuals. Difficulties can arise if the same reality produces different meanings or messages to people, especially if they don't realize this is happening, and proceed to act upon what they believe to be mutual agreement; this could be simply a statement of cross-cultural differences, or of more serious consequence if in the context of individual psychotherapy and reality testing. Basically, communication is based on shared understandings; if there is agreement that the message received and responded to is indeed the one that was intended when sent, then there is hope—but not a certainty—that we communicated successfully.

This, a more functional working definition, is the assumption I will use throughout this chapter, as discussion of most communication rests not on the more obvious spoken or written message, but rather on all the accompanying other-than-verbal cues, contexts, and out-of-conscious-awareness components; communication truly occurs only when both parties agree (consciously or subconsciously) that it has. "The term communication can almost never represent an absolute concept" (Poyatos, 1983, p. 13), nor a discrete event. Any attempt to freeze a slice of time in order to examine the communication process at that moment would fail to completely encompass the full dynamics of what was going on, although a photograph would certainly stimulate more recall than a verbal-only memory. In examining psychotherapeutic contexts, it is clear that this functional definition is the only one useful in the realities of the counseling setting, as successful communication is always so situationally defined.

It therefore becomes clear that we must enlarge our awareness (and our clients') to include appreciating the dimensions of nonverbal communication, as it affects so much of what is dealt with in therapy through cultural and familial contextual revelations. These beliefs, value systems, feelings, and so on, are coded nonverbally, not translatable solely through words.

I have found that most people arrive in my office confused and in some sort of emotional pain. They are not seeing things the way they think they should (or the way someone else is demanding); how they have been conducting their life is not succeeding well enough according to their expectations; their very being is felt to be unacceptable or dysfunctional, often being labelled such by a referring person. They often feel personally threatened, their "feelers are all curled in" (as one client described it) to protect themselves, and their defenses are well-entrenched. Under these circumstances, where change is needed, it is clear that it must be initiated from within to be trusted. Usually their nonverbal messages and expressions of emotional affect are targets for work in improving communication and interaction, on the level both of self and with others. People can usually use feedback on how others see them, especially in finding out what is perceived above and beyond the message they think they are sending when they act and talk. (These areas apply equally well to the therapist's affect and effect on the client, as well as the reverse.)

Psychologists may think our field deals only with the treatment of individuals, but in practice these are not isolated interchangeable digits that exist apart from the process of time, family, and culture that has produced them. To help individuals in therapy, one must get into their nonverbal communications and cultural mandates; to do otherwise would be to sabotage the therapy's long-range effects by suggesting context-free change (which cannot possibly occur without consequences to their family and cultural lives).

Phototherapy techniques, I believe, can help clients begin and proceed along the path of learning from trained therapists how to examine their own nonverbal visual messages through looking at the photo-artifacts that stop and still these communications so that they can be held and examined for exploring what they say about them, what values and feelings they reflect and express, how it is that they know these things to be true (and thus how they are evaluating the messages of others as well as having expectations of them), and how to appreciate these differences between themselves and others without feeling threatened or perceiving any necessity to demand or enforce change.

In working with youth in therapeutic settings, when the broader general goals are to enable children and adolescents to become more flexible in dealing with issues they encounter, improving their problem solving abilities and self-image by better understanding the underlying values being communicated, "to be able to re-frame their problems (and lives) by having an improved and more conscious cognitive perspective along with an increased ability to tap into it for clarification" (Ostiguy, 1986, personal communication) I would suggest that these nonverbal concepts and communications are best worked with through nonverbal tools. Photographs and the process of taking and interacting with the prints are increasingly being used to give youth "a better picture" of themselves and to bring their lives "into sharper focus." Since "seeing is believing," and "a picture is worth a thousand words," "seeing for yourself" can be a powerful tool when input from others is not relevant or accepted.

Phototherapy skills, when used by a competent professional helper, can well make use of our commonly accepted substitution of the phrase "I see" to mean "I understand."

PHOTOGRAPHY AS THE MEDIUM OF CHOICE

Why use photography as the therapeutic medium? What is it about photographs and the process of interacting with them that make this choice so special? Since the only way people can take in any information from their environment at all is through their sensory organs (roughly 85 percent of which is visual input), our understandings and memories evolve from processes that are not verbally-contexted, that have a predominantly visual component inexorably bonded to each moment experienced or remembered. As people need to better comprehend their nonverbal knowledge and values, we must somehow be prepared to guide them toward better understanding of this visual, and usually unconscious, language and its metaphoric and symbolic representations.

Since so much of our perception and communication with the world and people around us is uniquely and personally filtered, mental health professionals can increase the range of their possibilities of helping by making use of the unique advantages (and somewhat paradoxical interaction with reality) provided by photography as a tangible yet personal organization of experience. The following points summarize the implications photography provides as relevant for therapeutic interventions:

1. Photography and its products are nearly universally encountered, socially acceptable, and personally relatively nonthreatening. Most people have had contact with photographic imagery—although perhaps not all have encountered cameras, most have seen snapshots or magazine or billboard visuals. Most people keep snapshots around them of past events, places, people, even of themselves; these are usually accepted as commonplace items, very natural parts of one's life, items that are usually safe for mutual discussion, even with nonfamily members, as they can be found in the personal environments of almost everyone, nearly everywhere, even if just through calendars, magazines, advertisements, and so on.

2. Photos are tangible documents of actual times and events that have really happened in front of the camera and thus can be discussed as the equivalent of (or stand in for, or symbol of) that actuality. Most people know that photos are supposed to represent (literally, re-present) the real-life moment that was actually taking place in front of the camera at the very second of the picture-taking; after all, if it wasn't there in the first place, we couldn't have captured it on film. We frequently use such photo documents to prove that something did indeed once really occur: "Look! The snow that year was so

bad it covered the house," "See, your father did once have a full head of hair," or to stress the truth of things that are usually biased by personal interpretation, political agenda, or other standard manipulations (i.e., "Your facial scars really don't show to others; look at this photo and see for yourself," or for a more global example, how the recent famine in Africa became real and personally horrifying once photographic images of its effects on children were brought directly into our minds). We often use photos as unarguable proof of the reality of a fact or event in space or time; if there is a photo of it, then it must certainly and indisputably have happened (i.e., the camera cannot lie).

3. Not only do people see photos as a way to prove a given reality or actuality, but in most spontaneous encounters with snapshots, we see them as that very reality itself. By this, I mean that immediate, unconscious, cognitive-perceptual leap our brain provides us when we encounter a photograph face-to-face: in viewing a photo, most of us unconsciously perceive ourselves being there at that very moment the camera documented the scene, our eyes jumping into the scene at the location of behind-the-camera as if we were really there in person at that very time. In our minds, we are integrally and inseparably part of it, at the very moment it was frozen in time; we are there at that time, even if it occurred generations ago, and we experience its moment as now, the associated feelings and contexts as present ones. We are usually not consciously aware that we are viewing a piece of paper with stuff smeared on it in patterns existing only in two dimensions; instead, we see the image as if it was a real, three-dimensional slice of life, and as if we were actually part of that scene (either in it, standing next to the photographer looking at it, or somehow behind or inside the lens itself). The fact that a mechanical device was used to place the scene onto lifeless flat paper is usually unconsciously overlooked (and therapeutically irrelevant), as we visually and emotionally connect with the image's actual contents (and our perceptions of their meanings) as if they were still alive and in process in the present. What the camera sees, the eye sees, and thus we see.

4. Most people take and keep photo-artifacts that have the most intense emotional meaning to them (i.e., memories of places, people, or times that have strong feelings associated with them). Conversely, most people will not keep photos around them that they strongly dislike or feel ambivalent or uneasy about. People very rarely will photograph things that do not matter to them, and in later viewing photos that they have taken, they will usually not keep the ones that have no personal meanings connected. Snapshots that do not matter rarely matter enough to be kept or given to others.

5. People take and keep photographs for very uniquely personal reasons; what they see when viewing a photo (theirs or someone else's) is a perception based not only on the stimulus image's content itself, but also (and far more so), based on the sum of what they are bringing to that moment of perception: a blend of their background experiences, personality, family system and history, cultural and societal values, and so on; that is, the totality of everything

that has happened to them right up to the very moment of interacting with that frozen moment of time that they or someone else decided to keep forever. A snapshot represents a selective and personally symbolized reality—in some ways a metaphor of ourselves; egocentric and ethnocentric values, perceptions, and expectations inseparably filtering what is chosen to be photographed, when, and how. And all photos do represent an actual choice (though not necessarily a conscious one): what is selected, how it is composed and mentally/visually organized, which photos are kept, which photos make it into albums or are discarded or given as gifts. Although the camera does document what is in front of it, it is the person who decides when the right moment is and what or who to include, as well as whether it is worth keeping. The resulting photo in and of itself has no meaning—in our perceptions or imaginings we actively participate in the meaning created.

6. When taking a photo, people usually have a goal in mind, though not always a conscious or verbalizable one; during this process—and after, when viewing the photo—they usually have a strong idea of what they were hoping to have captured, and how well they succeeded. They may be pleased by finding they got what they wanted (or better than they expected) and can explain where in the image this success is visible; or if not, they can often be helped to bring to conscious awareness what the facet is that is felt to be missing, that should have been there but was not, that would be needed to really make the photo complete. This can easily lead to exploring what would have to change in the image for the originally-desired portion or message to be there after all, answers describing the visual message (and accompanying meanings) the person perceived to be lacking. These visual expectations are directly connected to underlying values and personal sense-making systems.

Thus, in considering all the above truths about photographs and the act of photographing, a curious blend occurs, a combination of documentary proof at the same time as a presentation of a personal selective reality, often presented in a symbolically represented language, that then conceptually returns upon itself full circle to again be a more real proof; a mutually dependent relationship of seeing and believing. This somewhat paradoxical identity gives rather ordinary snapshots the power to allow complex examination of a frozen slice of time fixed forever onto film as fact, and yet at the very same time permits the appreciation of the varieties of realities possible from a single stimulus, demonstrating to people the power of personal metaphors and meanings as they interact with it or attempt to explain it to others using, not word-associations, but photo-related ones. When viewing several photos selected for reflecting upon, or taken by, a person, what we are really seeing is their own self-portrait in a more abstract form, that is, those things that they have noticed, attended to, and given special interest. When considering one or two snapshots offered for examination, we can certainly learn a bit about people; when we have the opportunity to see dozens and dozens, we can begin to notice for ourselves what we perceive to be repeating patterns and reoccurring themes.

Although one definitely should not make assumptions about a person by viewing only a few selected snapshots, questions could certainly be asked and responses noted for holding in reserve until more are seen and repetitions and patterns begin to emerge. If photos are posed, then what we see in viewing the later snapshots is the photographer's selectively organized world; however, if a collection of photos are all candids, then we are seeing the random moments that were actually going on that someone chose for special reasons for remembering. Indeed, if the person is selecting the image contents, and doing so repeatedly and consistently over time, then we are being shown a symbolic representation of their state of mind (and their perceived reality) at those times, and can use this to enquire of them about how they feel this represents their very personality; sometimes the recurrences and deeper patterns point out to photographers themes and issues and feelings that they may not have even been aware of at the time of photographing. Photographs are not only footprints of our minds in terms of where we may have been, but also perhaps of where we might be heading, though not necessarily realizing it yet.

PHOTOTHERAPY LITERATURE REVIEW

Rigorous research in the field has, unfortunately, been sparse and usually more phenomenological or hermeneutic in orientation; true evaluations depending upon reliability and validity are difficult to design when working with nonverbal domains of selectively perceived and presented realities.

Fryrear (1980, 1983) has attempted the most comprehensive review to date on phototherapy literature. Citing previous less formal attempts to systematize the various research, writings, and smaller reviews on phototherapy by Stewart (1979a,b; 1980), Zakem (1978), Loellbach (1978), Levinson (1979), and others from past *Phototherapy* journal articles, Fryrear proposed a framework for organizing the phototherapy territory into 11 broad encompassing areas (and then provided many article and book citations within each category): evocation of emotional states, elicitation of verbal behavior, modeling, mastery of a skill, facilitation of socialization, creativity/expression, diagnostic adjunct to verbal therapies, a form of nonverbal communication between client and therapist, documentation of change, prolongation of certain experiences, and self-confrontation. For a more thorough literature review, readers can consult his first chapter in *Phototherapy and Mental Health* (Krauss & Fryrear, 1983), where he enlarges on these citations. I would recommend a few additions to his list: awareness of one's system of personal symbology and metaphors, establishing one's place within one's family system and sibling constellation, study of archetypes, awareness of cultural and historical roots, and several others. As this list is really only a starting point, and makes no assumptions about being complete, we can use it more as a springboard for appreciating the diverse applications possible using photographs as therapeutic tools.

The abundant literature in the field, however, clearly points out the many beneficial results these techniques have satisfactorily provided those conducting the projects. There have been numerous articles and several books published, most on applications of a specific technique with a particular age group or environmental setting.

THE TECHNIQUE IN GENERAL

Photography can be approached actively (i.e., taking photos, collecting them, or completing assignments) or more passively (i.e., viewing, re-viewing, reflecting, musing, or imagining upon our own snaps or those taken by others—even years later). Photography has for too long been a passive form on another level: letting people see photos, but not demanding any involvement or feedback from them, as if they were simply interchangeable viewing units; this has often been obvious in more formal gallery exhibits, where photography as an art was exhibited.

Photography, however, is more than just art alone. There has been a change in its usage by people other than artists: using photography as communication as well as art, conceptualizing photography as a verb, as well as a noun—an active process that is itself at least equally important as its product, the photograph itself. If probed with the right kinds of questions, a photograph can reveal much more than its image contents, not only about what is photographed, but also about the photographer or photo-keeper or photo-responder; not only the contents, but also the process; not only what is kept or documented, but also why and how.

As photographs are representations of how we see the world, and how we choose to interpret it to others and ourselves, they convey nonverbally how we perceive and create meaning. They are very real to people (as one client told me, "My photos *are* me"), and they take on a real living quality at times (as when we remove the snapshot of an ex-friend or lover from our albums or wallet, when we grieve the photos if lost in a house fire or if a purse or wallet is stolen); that is, they take on a prescience beyond their simple paper/chemical existence. As mentioned above, when we re-view a photo, the moment is now; this re-creation in present time and emotions allows us to get back in touch with the feelings as if they, too, were happening this very moment; thus, we can work with them in an immediate sense. This very immediate intensity that allows such deep therapeutic investigation is balanced by the facet of the photo being at arm's length; because they are so commonplace and somewhat less threatening than direct confrontation, they allow a distancing and objectifying of oneself and others that somehow allows a bit of safety or protection into the process, and this in turn allows probing into deeper levels than usually allowed verbally. By putting a frame around things, photos assist in simplifying and partializing, thus stilling the process of life into more manageable and comprehensible units of meaning, which we can study more privately or hear others' responses about without losing the identity and safety of our own perceptions.

This use of photographs as stimuli, as catalysts, to reconnect one with a visual memory and its associated feelings that were bonded to the actual experience of that moment (though stored at an unconscious level)—this is photography as communication; when used by professionals in the mental health fields as a way to help people when words are not enough—this is called phototherapy. The techniques involved are based on using photographs (and the process of taking or imagining photographs) as beginnings, as ways into people's other-than-verbal emotional spaces; there is not, however, any independently existing simple list of rules of how to proceed, but instead an increased awareness of how to ask the kinds of questions that use people's ordinary snapshots for the power that they contain and an enhanced sensitivity in noticing the full depth of their responses. Phototherapy basically requires that one learn to listen to what else goes by while the client is answering with supposedly factual information, a way not to read photographs *for* the person, but rather to somehow see between the lines, making therapeutic use of what they share, both verbally and nonverbally, consciously and unconsciously, based on photo-explorations.

A photograph should not mean, but rather suggest or guide; for therapeutic goals, one does not aim for some kind of rigid code of external objective interpretation, but rather an awareness of the open-ended explorations allowed by using photos as our tools to help us better achieve our goals. The client should not be photographing or selecting in order to meet outside expectations, either stated or implied. Photographs should be very sparingly analyzed, and not defined in any absolute terms; we must be careful when establishing a methodology of photographic therapy not to try to establish a fixed language. Very simply, when asking questions using phototherapeutic techniques as a stimulus (as discussed below), most therapists discover client progress in areas where, in the past, verbal-only techniques have run into walls of defenses, rationalizations, and excuses. In the last century, photography has developed into a very powerful medium not only of art, but of communication; in the hands of therapists who are trained in how to best make use of what Van Vliet so poetically calls this "stopping to respond to what the eye discovers" (Fryrear, 1980, p. 9), they can become valuable tools for helping people get a sharper focus of what is going on inside themselves and in their interactions with others.

A photograph is much more than just the individual parts of its image; the whole is so much more than just the sum of its parts. Phototherapy begins with this foundation, and then proceeds to utilize both symbolism and projection as the basic techniques or tools for treatment. Photographs taken by clients concretely and symbolically portray objects that are directly related to their mental state and to their own personal-cultural map of reality, showing actual objects as well as symbolically presenting equivalents of that person in visual representation. Photographs taken by a client or drawn from the family album offer examples of the ways the world is defined, represented, and remembered by the individual. "Photographs not only record a point of view; they also encourage the maintenance of that point of view in memory and imply a mindset. . . . Photographs indicate parameters, rules, norms, and values; they allow clinicians to see who is where, with whom, and what they are doing. Photos show a system [or family or cultural context] operating with a hierarchy and rules" (Krauss, 1980, p. 10). Since the gap between our own perceptions and the perceptions of others plays such a major role in many counseling situations (and problem definitions), "such a reality check could have broad uses in therapy" (Stewart, 1980, p. 17); examining differences in our own perceptions as they change over time, as well as how they compare with those of others, could provide great psychological benefit.

The term "expressive" or "arts" therapies is used to describe those ways of working with people in their more visual, emotional, metaphorical, nonverbal, holistic, and right-brain domains. Using such therapies usually results in clients responding in more spontaneous/intuitive and less protected or defended manners. In general, all people—even those without problems—could use these same tools to explore themselves on their own and to find an enriched appreciation for their own personal uniqueness, a better understanding of their particular communication processes, and possibly that of their family, friends, and neighbors; photo-communication is not the sole domain of mental health professionals, but rather a universal language with which they can tailor special use.

As with all of the various expressive therapies, phototherapy shares in the conceptual framework the implication that our creative expressions are actually projections from our inner selves, that we are individually unique, and that we perceive, code, store, retrieve, and put forth information in ways that reflect our personal makeup. People wishing to understand and help us would do well to look at our creative output and perceptions in order to have a fuller picture of who we are inside. Phototherapy should thus be viewed as a set or system of creative techniques, rather than a conceptual model of therapy, an interweavable collection of tools that can be used individually or collectively, not in isolation, but as adjuncts to verbal therapy to provide the therapist with additional flexible alternatives that can be used in conjunction with any theoretical methodologies therapists might choose as their preferred modalities.

It will be seen from the following section elaborating on and illustrating each specific technique of phototherapy, that as people discuss the layers of unfolding meaning around a simple photographic image, they are actually dialoguing with themselves, bringing to light their perceptions, expectations, values, and personal symbols; as they share information about themselves, and perceptions of others doing the same, they can usually communicate more fully. The innovation lies in using photography (process and product) to guide our self-exploration and discovery, our communications with ourselves and others, that will, I hope, lead to the reduction of barriers and prejudices, expectations and judgments of ourselves and others that so often get in the way of our mutual understanding and acceptance.

SPECIFIC TECHNIQUES, WITH CASE ILLUSTRATIONS

Just as I described photography above, phototherapy tools can themselves be used passively (reflecting upon an image; studying the contents and reactions to those photo-stimuli; researching other lives and worlds whether from visual artifacts, family albums and films, or constructed documentation), as well as actively (actually photographing, either spontaneously or toward some goal; using the photo as a starting point for interactions, dialogues, constructions, and confrontations with self or others). Phototherapy can be seen as both passive and active, and occasionally both at the same time.

When clients take photos, or respond to pictures they have selected to look at, or explore how they wish to be photographed, they can provide insight into their own values, emotions, expectations, and cognitive styles; as they become more aware of feelings, and less verbally protected or guarded, they become more flexible and adaptive in their interactions. With photography and visual literacy so permeating our society, and with the keeping and valuing of snapshots so nearly universally commonplace, working a selection of photographs with a client can be a much less threatening way of opening blocked areas, as it stays somewhat one step removed from the person inside.

As with so many techinques based conceptually on holistic or systems orientations, these tools suffer a bit from having to be taken apart for analyzing each section as disjointed separate entities; phototherapy is so much more than just examining each technique on its own and then adding them all together. Most practitioners use these techniques in various combinations, intersections, and overlays, in tangible or even abstract forms, as they really are components of an integrally related system.

Projectives

When we look at photos, ours or other people's, we respond to them; and regardless of any intentions we might have to the contrary we nonverbally interact with them as well; thus, we actively take part in the meaning we perceive (based on our own personal and cultural filters for interpretation), and we subconsciously take the meanings we need at that time emotionally. Besides what we think the photographer intended us to get from the photo, we cannot help but be affected by our own unique background experiences and values. Viewing photos usually results in some sort of response—feelings, memories recalled, thoughts about the subject content. We can place ourselves in the photo, to explore alternative possibilities, consider options in the role of photographer, project emotions and scripts onto the image coming from our own life, create themes, stories, or larger contexts if wished. Responses to photo viewing, taking, or gathering assignments reflect our cognitive structuring and valuing of our world, and can thus increase our tolerance and appreciation for the differences and differentness we might encounter in others.

The following examples will illustrate a few of the numerous possibilities:

In telling me about the seated child in Figure 12.1, surrounded by grown-up bodies, various clients have responded: "He's scared; he's been bad, and they're making him sit there till his parents come to get him and then he's going to be punished," and "She's a runaway and just got caught stealing a sandwich, and they're gonna take her to jail and beat her up!" These two were further probed for how they imagined the child got into the situation in the first place; what will happen to the child next ("What will the next photo in the story show?"); what they thought the child was thinking, feeling, hoping, expecting, and so on; what they would tell that child; what they thought that child would say or do if able to speak or move; and so on.

Figure 12.1.

In the answers to the questions I asked about the child, I was able to hear them respond not only for the subject in the photo, but also in some ways what they themselves would do under similar circumstances. Therefore, if the therapy relationship were trusting enough, I could also ask more direct questions, such as: "Could this photo have been of you at some point in your life?" or, "If that were you, what would you be feeling or thinking; what would you do; how did you get into this situation?" and thus probe that youth's 'inner spaces' more directly, while at a safer arms-length distance.

For example, with this same image, one nine-year-old girl responded to this photo by saying the little girl was lonely, and she was worried, because her Daddy had gone off and left her, and she was afraid he wasn't ever coming back to find her. This interpretation bears greater import when understanding that this child was in therapy trying to resolve her feelings about her parents' recent separation'as well as her father's subsequent lengthy hospitalization. Asking questions such as, "What would she say if she could speak?" or, "If her Daddy could hear her and know how she was feeling, what do you think she'd tell him?" can lead to further depth of how she was making sense of it all. Similarly, to probe her expectations and feelings, I asked, "If you had a magic wand, and could make everything right again for this little girl, what would you do? How would that photo look?"; not surprisingly she answered, "I'd have the whole family together in the other photo, everybody all there, all of them hugging her, so she'd know it was all okay again!" We then worked with the notion of collage as a metaphor for blended/separated families still retaining an integral identity.

Any snapshot, my own, theirs, or even pages torn from magazines, visually aids the imagining or projecting by taking it out of the realm of the totally abstract, and enabling the therapist, if desired, to continue on in a first-person probe. This projective process works equally well should there be no problem to probe, simply as a means to make contact, share a moment of time and place, and allow the client to realize that the therapist is willing to pretend, play, and take part in fantasy (which usually produces therapeutic information eventually).

For another example, still using the same photo-projective stimulus discussed above, a teenager once responded, "These people are all lined up for a rock concert to start; they've been standing there for hours, and this little guy is pooped. He trusts that it will be worth the wait, 'cause he trusts his older brothers who are keeping people from stepping on him, but he doesn't really know what a rock concert is in the first place, and he's beginning to pout!"

Our further discussion led to his own personal family role of having to take care of his 10-year-old brother after school, and how they have a great relationship, which he actually enjoys (although he'd never admit this to his buddies). Should I have wished to enquire further, I could have led with such questions as, "What do you think your brother would say about this photo himself, and what do you think he would think about your version?" or, "If you could change anything in this photo, what would that be?" or, "What do you think that child would rather be doing?" Each answer would be full of information, and each could possibly trigger a long discussion, depending on which of the branching paths I might have wanted to explore.

Differences in values or backgrounds can surface, as when parents, siblings, and youthful clients all examine selected photos and give their individual and equally correct responses.

In an example of this, a family I was seeing seemed to be having difficulty realizing their own interrelated roles and shared responsibilities in the pattern of events that precipitated the emotional breakdown and recent suicide attempt of the 16-year-old son. I wanted them to realize how each of them was coming from differing values and expectations and how this presented an inconsistent reality and conflicting messages to their son/brother. I believed that until I could get them to respect the validity of each other's position and realize that shared communication was still necessary and possible, I wasn't going to be able to get them to depolarize enough to make any progress. I had them each write responses to five photos, and then share these with each other; when it was clear that no one could be wrong (as an absolute term), they began to question how it was that they each saw the same thing differently, and began to explore the underlying feelings represented by each answer, and what would have to change for each to also perceive what another saw.

As one of the five photos, the one of the brick wall (Figure 12.2) produced a range of perceptions and responses: "Looks like somebody forgot to set the brakes," the father laughed. "It's obviously a brick wall tumbling down, a breaking of a wall, a destruction, possibly an accident—but it's a collapse that's in perfect order somehow, almost looking like it was etched out and looks and feels quite comfortable." Mother saw it as, "a high mountain valley of stone, a thin river cutting through and down; if it were to mean a person, then I'd find it sort of vulnerable, a breaking out of something private, not meant to be seen, but sort of an awkward 'oops' feeling that wasn't supposed to happen."

The daughter said it felt like her stabbed ears after being subjected to her brother's incessant loud stereo music, but softly added, "It was *too* quiet when he was away in the hospital." The son, the original focus of the therapy, described the image: "It's like a wall of frozen anger . . . and you have to take it apart slowly, brick by brick by brick . . . starting to trust people again, starting to believe what they say. It's the wall between me and other people, the wall I've built myself, by choice. I was aware I'd put it there, to keep people at a safe distance, and that way nobody could hurt me again 'cause they couldn't get close enough . . . wonder how many more bricks there are to go . . . how high it really is . . . ."

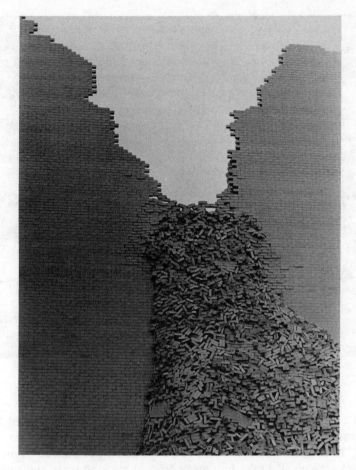

Figure 12.2.

There is never any way to predict ahead of time exactly what the responses might be to a given snapshot. I am no longer surprised when an image that I originally took in a humorous or tender frame of mind produces in a client an emotional response that is far from what I might have expected:

One day at the local zoo, I photographed a scene (Figure 12.3) that I wanted to save, as it symbolized to me the joys of childhood play, imagination, and make-believe pleasure that I as an adult too rarely encounter. When first placing it on the wall of photos in my office waiting area, I expected responses reflecting this, and did, indeed, hear several comments such as: "Oh, the innocence of childhood fun"; "They're in never-never land with Peter Pan, or with some pirate ship exploring some desert island somewhere"; and, "They're off on some adventure a million miles away; time is standing still, and they have absolutely no awareness that there's anyone else around.

Figure 12.3.

When one almost-teenager paused to look at this image, I asked him for his response. "It's like they've adopted that elf right into their family like a brother," he smiled. "What would you do if that elf came alive?" I innocently asked back. "Well, I'd take him away from there, and treat him to lunch at MacDonald's; I'd feed him green food and ask him if he knew E.T. [from the movie of that name]; then I'd take him home to show my Mom." Easy answers so far, I thought, and so I continued, "What would she think of all this? What would the elf say? What would happen?"

His choice of where to go in answering, quickly resulted in my becoming a much more serious listener: "Mom would think it was great, but then she and me would have to find a big enough hiding place for him before Dad got home, cause there might be trouble." "Why?" I gently queried. "Because if Dad was drunk like he usually is, and saw this elf thing in his way, he'd kick him and beat him up. Better if I hid him under the bed with me and my little brother till I can tell for sure if we're gonna get hit or not." Needless to say, a lengthy counseling process ensued with this family as it dealt with admitting out loud that there were previously-denied problems and abusive situations, and then beginning to do something about it.

Painful and abusive situations are the ones most usually guarded and protected by the family system and one's psyche; children are cautioned not to tell anyone what goes on at home, and if not dealt with therapeutically, such memories of distorted truth and the confused feelings associated with them can lie dormant and out of control, surfacing only when one's unconscious is suddenly triggered, where one sometimes finds oneself wondering if such things actually happened in one's past or not, whether they are true memories of actual events and valid feelings, or did one for some reason only imagine them, or assume one's own guilt in precipitating them. Such memories and feelings that are not consciously stored or verbally accessible often remain out of conscious awareness altogether, surfacing only when a sensory stimulus like a smell or a visual input brings them forth spontaneously and intuitively, without the usual defensive safeguards and verbal rationalizations that so often cloak their deep pain and power. To release such material for working with, one must bypass those usual verbal channels, and sneak inside somewhat sideways in an immediate process that touches the feelings before the conscious mind can cover or deny them with words. It is often much safer to talk about the people in the photographs, even including oneself in such images, than about oneself directly, where such information may prove too threatening to a vulnerable or insecure identity. Photo-projectives can provide such a catalyst, touching below awareness, and yet manageable because of their tangible distancing and symbols.

I might also add that in most child and adolescent work I have usually found my particular clients to be in a general position of self-perceived powerlessness, victims of the treatment of protective system in terms of self-assertion or self-confidence. Using projectives is one way to give back a bit of that power, as the client's perception and interpretation is, by definition, unable to be a wrong one, and in being viewed as equally valid, a bit of relaxing and giving up of extreme positions can occur as they allow others the right to have their particular viewpoint as long as their own is not threatened. This can be a beginning step toward therapeutic goals.

This type of projecting upon a photo-stimulus is really what goes on with all the various phototherapy techniques; the moment one views any image (e.g., on paper, in a viewfinder, in an album, or even on a magazine page), one is partially creating the information perceived; the moment one takes a picture, one is projecting uniquely personal (and cultural) frames and selective filters. Even imagining or remembering photos not in one's hands is a form of projection; meaning is so idiosyncratic and individual that photos take on a life of their own almost apart from our process of visual perception. Photos can sometimes provide a given meaning at one particular time, and a completely different message or feeling upon another viewing later—which can often be a great shock, or even yield a sense of betrayal—compared to the original meaning we took at first glance:

One young lady, Elaine, brought me a photo (Figure 12.4) she selected from her personal family album, as an example of her childhood and its events. "This particular photo has a lot of meaning for me for many reasons," she explained. "I value the closeness of it, the physical placement of the three

Figure 12.4. (Private collection, E.M.)

females (myself at age five, my sister at age eight, and my mother). The picture was taken a year before my parents broke up, and it is the only document I have of a real family outing. I also see a lot of affection in my mother's eyes for the photographer (my father), which I have rarely seen in other photos. The three of us (or rather the four of us) appear to be a very close family (which is rather a false view, but still one I really cherished for its idealism)."

We explored the image, discussing each person, the setting, the feelings, and the memories recalled. While I attended most to these major facets, and didn't really notice smaller details such as a shoe or a tuft of grass in the scene, Elaine suddenly stopped to stare angrily at the folded pages of what she identified as a newspaper on a rock at the far left edge of the image. "My rosy view of this scene really changed just now, as I became aware of the newspaper that is sitting beside my mother on the rocks. And the more I begin thinking about the symbolic significance of that newspaper, the more it really bothers me—that my mother may well have not really been there with us at the outing as I had originally perceived; generally she preferred to read than to do things with us. This speaks to my desire for a mother who would put her parenting before her intellectual life, as my mother did not. It also speaks to my unarticulated desire for a mother that really loved my father. So my anger was really directed at the newspaper for destroying my perception of the occasion as a happy, intimate family outing."

When asked what would happen if the offending newspaper were not there, were somehow cropped out of the photo, she replied, "It wouldn't be right to crop it out as it represented an honest view of the situation." However, a few months later, when Elaine was making a collage of old photos for her mother's birthday gift, she debated for quite some time as to whether to cut the newspaper out, which she ended up doing, "partly due to the space restrictions of the collage itself, but mostly because I decided to honor my vision, realistic or not.''

Ideally, I would have liked to have been able to let Elaine share her perceptions with her mother, who now lives far away, and have a mutual discussion occur about what those times were really like (and similarly share with her father as well); as demonstrated later in album work, finding others' memories and attached feelings belonging with an image from one's personal past may also shed light on their versions of what was going on at that time, allowing one an altogether different perception than one may be invested in maintaining. It would probably be enlightening to discover her mother's, sister's, and father's versions of "how" that photo means to them.

A different form of projective technique can be in studying selection criteria, such as in having a person examine a grouping of several photos of persons or places in collage, at one time. People can make comparative judgments and give verbal answers based on nonverbal knowledge when asked about what they are seeing in front of their eyes (and very often revealing what is behind their eyes as well). When asked to examine a group of several portraits, and try to state which of them is, for example, a schoolteacher, a homosexual, a drug dealer, an ex-prisoner, or a nice person, that is, whatever one would wish to concentrate on for therapeutic reasons, most people, if comfortable with the setting and questioner, will risk guessing a response or two; if working with a particular population group, such as youth, the images and questions certainly could be arranged and organized to reflect this more specialized focus (refer to example in the addendum at the end of this chapter), thus finding out how clients are making their decisions, based on nonverbal reasons. This somewhat of a parlor-game procedure takes on serious import in therapeutic settings, as people are probed, not for their direct choice answered (it matters little if their guess is actually correct or not), but more for how it was that they knew their answer, what do they think would have to change for them to have responded differently, where did they conceptually go inside their minds, and how did they scan those nonverbal photo-inputs for the nonverbally noted information cues on which they based their responses.

I have found that the best way to probe such areas is to ask not only for direct answers (such as who is X, or which is Y) but to immediately ask such companion questions as, "Why do you think you chose that answer?"; "Where do you think you got the information from in the photo (your visual reasons and what perhaps these represent) that you based your answer upon?"; "How do you think you knew that?"; "If I changed this or that in the photo [to partialize different facets of the image], do you think your answer would still be the same? If not, why not?"; "How do you think your friend's (mother's, father's, sister's, brother's, or psychologist's) response might be different? Why might that be?" and so on.

Using this procedure, all sorts of clues to values, prejudices, and evaluating systems can reveal themselves; answers appear spontaneously, naturally (as if obvious to everyone), often casually as contexts for responses (but with great therapeutic weight), such as: "He can't be the homosexual—he looks so rugged and outdoorsy," "I didn't pick that girl as the one who might be the paralyzed person because she looks so happy," or, "The boy with the turban is the thief, *of course*" (italics added to reproduce vocal stressing), "That girl couldn't be an Indian—she's dressed too nice and doesn't look poor enough," or, "That guy couldn't be my friend—he's wearing an earring!" All of these comments have, unfortunately, actually been made to me, by either clients of mine, or participants in my workshops, in response to projecting upon photo stimuli, stated as if the answers would be equally obvious to everyone. No matter how these responses may make us cringe, they are the true, gut-level, real feelings behind the mask of people's public politeness, and if we are ever to change how humans really feel about one another, we must get into those places beyond their words to see how they mean what they say, to help them separate out differences from perceptions of threat or forced change. Cameras don't take pictures; people do: Their reactions upon examining these visual metaphors (their own or other people's) are what we need to work with and share with them in order to produce real change that will go beyond surface levels, changing people who have been long stuck in roles into live, flexible, personally unique and treasured individuals.

Examining the use of photographs as active and passive projectives in some ways sums up the whole of phototherapy, as no matter the form they take (self-portrait, family album recollections, pictures taken by or of a person, videos, etc.) the therapeutic concept is to use them all as discussed above, to project upon, think about, respond to, and interact with actively and passively as well. In some ways, describing phototherapy techniques could be succinctly defined with the above section; however, although the others may have the same conceptual base, there are some differences and additional benefits in considering how to weave the projective approach with other formats. Therefore, I will continue with the following descriptions of how phototherapy works with photos taken by the client, photo-assignments, photos of the client by others, self-portraits, and historical/album/photo-biographical, and other more minor types.

Photos Taken By (or Collected By) the Client/Assignments

When we decide to snap a picture, the decision process (our hopes, goals, desired outcomes, and how we arrive at that particular choice in order to fit all our criteria) can indicate what is important in our unique value and belief system. If it did not work out as we expected, what went wrong and what it would take for it to become a successful photo, can be equally revealing. A well-trained probing of the chosen moments of time we ourselves personally select to record can provide information, consistent themes, interests, personal metaphors, and symbols (that we possibly might have been completely or partially unaware of at the time of shooting). Even those casual, candid, "me-at'' shots (''me at the beach,'' ''me at school,'' etc.) can reveal personal and family information, just by paying attention not only to what is in them, but also to the relationships and qualities that provide those nonverbal meanings. There are reasons why we choose to look at or take a particular photo, and although we should not overdo any interpretations from a single image, from a split second taken from life, and make too much of just that one moment, there are ways that our photos speak to us from deep inside, especially if we find particular ones consistently attracting our attention.

One warning, however, tied to the earlier warning about not trying to interpret a whole lot just from one given image: If a therapist is viewing a particular image taken by a client, or even a picture of that person, one should be very careful making any assumptions about what one is looking at, until finding out whether the photo was posed by the photographer or the subjects, or whether it indeed represents a spontaneously captured, truly unposed candid moment in time.

I was quite surprised one day to find in a boy's family album a very recent snapshot of his two usually hostile parents sitting arm-in-arm on their front porch. Recalling that he had stated that they hated each other, and had hardly spoken in two years of separation, I was about to challenge his view of their reality, because, after all, there was the photo ''proving'' to me their ''obvious'' closeness. He introduced the photo to me as, ''This is my parents; you asked me to bring in photos of them, and I had none at all of both of them together at the same time, so last week, when Dad was dropping me off at Mom's, I bribed them each with their favorite candy bar to let me take just one photo of the two of them together (I told them my psychologist wanted it, and that helped convince them, but that was just my excuse). Anyway, I took it outside, so that the neighbors could also maybe see that there was still hope.'' His dream was clearly demonstrated in that pose.

Conversely, finding repeated occurences of images in past albums can provide cause for re-examination of what might be distortions of actual events or feelings.

When a 15-year-old client, who had been adopted at birth and was now conducting a major search for her birth mother, told me she had been adopted by a couple who actually haven't ever really loved her, I suspended disbelief, and worked initially with her as if that personal reality were possible (though, having seen her adoptive parents interacting with her, I found her claims hard to believe). When she brought in several albums containing early childhood photos of her with this family, I saw image after image of hugs, cuddles, joy, and comforting—what to me seemed a very loving home for her and her siblings.

When I confronted her with my perceptions (owning them as my own, as she certainly had a right to her own very different view), she began to cry, and admitted that she'd lied about the past mistreatment. ''I guess I just couldn't accept how much it hurts them for me to be looking for my real Mom; I think I made it all up inside my heart without my mind really knowing I was doing this, because I had to have some reason inside me to explain why it was so important to me to find her and ask her why she gave me up. No, they aren't cruel to me; they love me, and really, I love them, too—it's just that how can it be that if all that is true, why am I hurting them with my search? I just don't understand." With this information now at a conscious level, it provided a breakthrough in communication with her adoptive parents who decided to help her with her investigations, as they were less threatened by them and could accept her feelings.

A creative therapist can give various photo-taking assignments to pair with certain desired goals, to tighter define certain concern areas; more open-ended creative projects can yield personal insights as well. Clients can be asked to simply, "Go out and use up a complete roll of film, and bring me the prints next time we meet"; these prints can be a rich source for finding out what is important to that person. They will photograph what has seemed important to them to document; with no structured assignment ("No, I don't care what you shoot, just bring me the prints when you're done") a person simply makes nonverbal personal choices, as well as more subtly reflecting how they handle tolerance of ambiguity. Discovering how and why they took the pictures that they did gives clues to their inner (and possibly unverbalized) priorities, needs, and interests; even finding out any differences between what they actually got, compared with what they thought they would get, can be beneficial.

If used later along in a therapy process, a tighter structuring of assignments along more specific themes or issues can be focused upon, such as working on a relationship by assigning the two people to photograph each other (building trust, and trusting risk), or asking a third person to get some shots of the two of them together to find nonverbal discussion occurring as interactions about how, where, and who to be for the photo, feelings about sharing a common visual space, becoming in the togetherness a unit, an entity, with some common definition, as well as possibly realigning a power structure as the photo-taker has relatively more control in directing, if allowed to. Also, certain topics can be assigned ("Go photograph things that make you angry," "things you would like to change in your world," "the you nobody knows," "who you'd like to be in 10 or 20 years," or "who you were when you were little," etc.); the topic assigned can thus mirror and complement the work that is going on in therapy, as clients learn to see better the makeup of their perceptual and evaluating systems. When the photos are discussed with the therapist (who can nonjudgmentally share his or her own and sometimes differing perceptions, or guide the conversation toward specific targets), clients can begin to understand how values and expectations color and influence what is seen and perceived, and appreciate how their photos can speak to them from inside themselves in ways their conscious awareness cannot, or, perhaps, will not.

Actually, even an imaginary list of what one would shoot if given a certain assignment can reveal information about how people view their world. Instructions such as, "What photos would you want to take for showing your parents what your group or foster home now is like?" or, "If you were in charge of the rules at home, and you photographed those changes you made, what kinds of differences would I see; what would such photos show me?" Just the imagined lists of visual fantasies can be therapeutically useful.

Photos of the Client Taken by Others

In examining how other people see us, we get some idea of how we present ourselves to the world; in dialogue with others (or with their photos of us) we gain valuable clues as to the identity we convey, our public face. This is often a safer channel for interpersonal feedback, as different interpretations of the same photo can be compared (because, of course, it is the photo under scrutiny, not the person). In realizing that each person photographs us differently, we can begin to appreciate the flexibility of our identity and our possibilities, as well as recognizing the limitations and dangers of labeling others.

When we view pictures of us taken by others, we sometimes see parts of ourselves that we were not aware of ("I really do look different from my twin," "I do look grumpy in this picture; I knew I was upset, but I didn't realize it made me look mad," "I look older or more competent than I expected I would," etc.). In asking photographers to tell us why they photographed what they did, or why they picked this particular one from the whole roll of possibilities to have enlarged and presented to us, we learn how each values different parts of our identities. One boy was extremely pleased to receive a snapshot taken of him catching a fly ball at his class's recent baseball game; he exclaimed, "Boy that's the first picture I've ever got that proves I finally did something right for a change!"

If people cannot be comfortable allowing their photo to be taken, perhaps we should examine the deeper layer of the relationship being tested. If there's no emotional closeness or trust, people will probably not be willing or able to spontaneously share the frame of film. People often use photos of themselves to speak to others for them, to explain who or how they are, choosing the ones that best present the facets of themselves that they want communicated. One mother, who was in charge of her family's album, brought me her selection that showed examples of her children only when she was in the photograph with them, hoping to show me with photos "that cannot lie" what she could not fully express verbally to her satisfaction: that she was a good mother. Thus, how one makes a selection out of many snapshots of themselves for a particular theme or reason can reveal the underlying values at work in making those choices. To then title that collection, or to state its theme, or to ask those photos to talk for themselves, can uncover that nonverbally stored information that is so essential to the communication being hoped for. Even exploring who clients might want to give a photo of themselves to, or perhaps, more valuable, who they would not want to have their image (and thus power over them, in terms of unfinished business) can also be quite potent an investigation.

Thus, helping clients explore their photo-posing behavior can reflect both their individuality and their familial contexts and backgrounds, as they demonstrate how they hope to be seen and remembered. How we pose reflects our view to (and stance for) the world, our public or private selves metaphorically represented in our bodies, faces, and surrounding artifacts. Asking us how we wish to be photographed (and thus preserve our image permanently), when, with whom, where (whether in formal portrait sittings, or in quick spontaneous snapshots), by whom, and so on, can shed light on our inner perceptions of ourselves and our relationships with those around us. It is also helpful to consider for whom a photo is being taken: each of us would probably pose very differently for a portrait intended as a gift to our mother or father as contrasted to one for a friend, driver's license, job application, school graduation, or lover's wallet. Who we are to the people in our lives is reflected in the guidelines we use for how to dress, pose, show expression for them to later see in the snapshot, and is also communicated by our reasons for including various props, decorations, settings, and so on. Candids capture life, unposed, as it is really being lived and freeze this forever; thus, they catch whatever was actually going on at that very moment, with all its surrounding details. With enough photos to suggest patterns or generalizations across specific situations, people, or times, they can demonstrate one's usual or typical behavior or affect in those given kinds of moment or situations, whether posed or unposed, and thus assist the study of the entire family system.

Self-Portraits

At the core of most therapeutic work with children and adolescents, probably more so than with any other age group, lie the concepts of self-image, self-esteem, self-acceptance, and self-confidence. Self-portraits allow for powerful accessing of these concepts, and thus people often find them the most threatening and risky kinds of photos to encounter. Carefully guided while at perhaps their emotionally most vulnerable moments, clients can explore, confront, and dialogue with themselves, while documenting for themselves any changes that are occurring—whether with still photo self-portraits, video therapy self-confrontation, or photos by others that are perceived as unfiltered; these are the most intense and powerful of all photo-imagery, as one is usually most invested with one's own image.

The strictest definition of a self-portrait is one that is taken solely by oneself, where the presence of another person remains totally irrelevant to the process. In phototherapy, one can be a bit more tolerant about such a tight definition; any photo that one takes of oneself, through any means, is accepted as a self-portrait; this could include situations using delayed timed-release shutters, cable releases that allow self-triggering, mirror shots, or even one person telling another the desired moment for getting them right, as they want. Any photo that is of a person, where that person has had total control of the setting, moment of shutter-release, and other such affecting details, is an acceptable definition for therapy purposes; this can even include stand-ins, visual metaphors, equivalents, or symbols for the self (i.e., masks, environmental objects, collages, etc.) As this is, therefore, a combination of projecting, with photos of the client by the client, the illustrations and discussions in the above three sections can effectively be applied to self-portrait techniques.

Certainly, when finding that one's clients choose to present themselves in what appears to the therapist to be a self-destructive pose, one should not hesitate to immediately explore further until one is ethically reassured or initiates further treatment. Generalizations about not taking too much meaning from only one given photograph should, in this kind of situation, be treated on a par with the client's vaguely offered suicide threats, wherein ethically no such threat should be totally ignored, and one should probe until one is certain no dire consequences are going to happen due to not taking someone seriously enough.

Figure 12.5 is one such example, where I was at a treatment center's group home, having several children pose for self-portraits to be sent to their families as a Christmas greeting. The others posed in friendly or clowning manner; this boy, who had been playing alone as a cowboy, took his time and carefully posed for my camera as shown. Needless to say, after finishing all the photos, and sending the others out to play, I sat down with him for a while to check

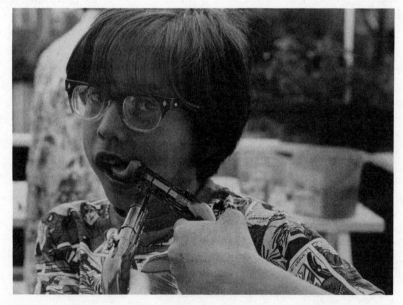

Figure 12.5.

things out. This photo may have been totally innocent, perhaps mocking an earlier-viewed television program, or something he had private reasons for choosing, but until I probed his feelings and discussed further what may have prompted this pose, I could not just leave and assume that all was well. (It wasn't; he was very depressed.)

Self-portraits deal with reflections of self-image, and when one's inner picture is poor or distorted, it is very hard to receive positive feedback.

Debbie, a Deaf Native Canadian Indian girl with whom I have worked comprehensively over the past decade (Weiser, 1975, 1981, 1983, 1987), brought me her package of high school graduation photos, taken a few weeks earlier, to help her decide which ones to keep and which ones to send up-coast to her family, as she had not personally visited them in several years. I had been trying throughout these years to help her improve her feelings about herself; we had worked a great deal with her self-portraits as well as with my photos of her, trying to explore her feelings about herself through her reactions to her self-image. She had usually responded to her photographed self very critically or neutrally; never in all those years had I found her response to be one I perceived to be accepting, pleased, or in any way positive: if she didn't frown at it, or put herself down in some way when describing the image, she simply had nothing at all to say about it, expressed little interest in seeing it, and consistently barely tolerated discussing it.

On the particular day that she brought in the school photos, we were also videotaping the session; Figure 12.6 is taken directly from that tape, Debbie holding the snapshots in front of her for me to see, with me pointing to one

Figure 12.6.

particular image. When I began to express my personal pleasure at how many of them seemed to turn out so nicely, she interrupted me to say (in sign), "Aren't they pretty?" Somewhat in shock, after having waited so many years to eventually hear this evident leap in self-esteem, I replied, "Yes, I agree they are! What did you think when you opened up the envelope?"

She mimed a face indicating pleased astonishment, and replied, "I saw them; it really was me, and I felt, Oh my God!—I'm beautiful!; I want to send them to my Mom; she doesn't know I'm pretty; now I can show her and she can see for herself!" Since we were taping, I have been able to occasionally reinforce this spontaneously made self-perception in replay to Debbie and to her family, and because it is visual and speaks for itself, she doesn't have to feign any embarrassment or invent any defensive explanations. She believed herself to be pretty; we have proof that even she cannot deny, no matter how depressed she might be feeling.

Such a luckily videotaped vignette demonstrates the immense power of direct self-perception unfiltered by the well-intentioned contributions offered by others, to let a client see for themselves what perhaps the whole world can see, but they cannot yet accept hearing: that they are acceptable in some way, not just to others, but by whatever standards they have been judging themselves; they have indeed met their very own (and highest) expectations. It is a momentous occasion for therapist and client alike and, at least in the above case, one that neither will likely ever forget.

Historical/Album/Photo-Biographical

Family photos, home movies, and now family videos offer proof of that group's existence over time, documenting permanence as well as change over time, continuity, roots, traditions, values, and degree of freedom for the individual within it all. These snapshots can give insights to the full system of several generations, relationships, and networks—to see ourselves and our contexts and thus to better appreciate current situations and feelings, and perhaps to recognize where expectations are coming from. As long buried and well-defended emotions will respond less guardedly to a visual stimulus, photos can be used to reconnect us with memories and feelings around past events, people, places, and times, allowing us to respond as if that moment was right now again, no matter how long ago it actually occurred.

Photo-biographical information can be tapped for not only factual and historical information, but it can also be examined for the patterns and relationships demonstrated or suggested in the prints. As with all the other techniques mentioned above, working with family photos really involves all the other techniques as well. In family album work, loosely defined as the book(s), collections, boxes, drawers, bags, or whatever that people keep their family photos in, one also finds a less-than-formal definition of family, more reflective of the full support network and system of relatives and sometimes friends that comprise it. As one of my clients so eloquently put it, "My family? My family is everyone who's in my family album, including my dog." Therapists trained in family systems work often use a family tree or a map of several generations (called a genogram) as a focus for inquiry; this process can often be aided by pairing the names and dates with photo-examples from clients' albums, to give the names faces and the people personal, rather than just role, identities. Those interested in any of the family systems approaches to therapy will find a wealth of potential information about triangles, power alignments, differentiation/fusion, alternating generations, sibling constellations, and other such dynamics suggested by and available for further probing from family photo-stimuli.

Usually when working with a family, rather than with an individual model, what is sought are those patterns of interactions among the various members, patterns that have existed and sometimes still exist across time and generations, mirroring and repeating; it is no wonder that album snaps are so helpful in this search, as they are candids documenting whatever was going on at that time. Who regularly stands next to whom can point out power structures, alignments, and alliances; distances between people that repeat photo after photo can demonstrate emotional closeness or separation; discoveries such as these must, however, be tempered with such warnings as those given previously, that one cannot interpret anyone's album for that person, but must use the repeated observances as foundations for guiding the line of questioning, blending the quest for factual data with more open-ended emotion-tapping kinds. For example: "I notice that in all these photos, your Mom is always standing with or touching or close to your brother, whereas you are always standing apart, with there often being quite a space separating you from the others. Would you tell me a bit about the relationship you have with your family, and does my comment have any meaning for you in light of this?"

In their ability to freeze action, photos can be used to still the dynamics of the family system and allow them to be scrutinized. Not only does one learn of the past, and changes over time and place and persons, but in re-experiencing the photos while looking at them, current feelings and behaviors can be better understood and appreciated, and the therapist can gain the ability to reconnect clients with previously blocked and buried material. Memories are sometimes dressed up, remembered differently than they really happened. Looking back at photos from those times can do a lot to help correct psychologically limiting distortions and misrepresentations, clarifying hazy details. They are an undeniable record of the past and of change, that no amount of verbal filtering can completely cover up.

Two years before finishing high school, and terribly bored with it all, Alan wanted to drop out: He had a sensible-sounding plan though it needed his parents' approval. He had already secretly been accepted for the shipbuilding apprenticeship program, and had contacted the local night school about finishing his degree through their work-study arrangement. Feeling very proud of his untypically thorough planning, he approached his parents for permission, and was devastated to find his father surprisingly furious and upset with the idea. He had anticipated their agreement, as they had discussed his school problems recently, and were hoping for some redeeming plan.

In our next family session, he again brought up the idea, as he was very upset. As the family had also brought along their generation-old collection of photos at my earlier request, I decided to find out what Alan's father had been like at the same age (hoping for at least some defusing of polarities and an attempt to step into each other's shoes for enough time to explore what was really going on in this particular crisis).

As Father began to show Alan what his own teenage years had been like, the photos of the old farm, the desolate environment, the long walk to school, the one-room schoolhouse, and as he shared the many feelings now brought back from those days, he looked rather taken aback, and told Alan, "I guess I was angry with you because to me, school was my only chance out of that awful place, and when my own Dad died, and they pulled me out of school at age 15, I thought my world and any chance I'd had for escaping it had ended forever. I swore then that any kids I ever fathered would never have to leave school, that they'd never have to suffer what I had. I guess all this got in my way when I heard you say you wanted to drop out; angry bells started ringing in my head, and it's only now that I finally realize why. Tell me again what you're planning and this time I'll really listen to you; maybe we can work something out." With tears in their eyes, they hugged silently and began talking.

SUMMARY AND CONCLUSIONS

In summary, therefore, I suggest that the goal for improved communicating for our clients, and also for ourselves as well, is to examine what we know, to discover more about the parts we might not yet be so aware of, to learn more about how we know these things (and thus ourselves) internally, to find out how (and where) we uniquely perceive, code, and store information, and to bring all this to a more conscious level—and in doing so, to learn more about the rich complexities of our fellow humans and how to better relate and communicate with them as well as with ourselves. It is suggested that one way to begin is to pay closer attention to what is being sought out to photograph, to pose for, to keep, to visually respond to, and to converse about both internally and with others, sharing and comparing responses. If clients can learn how all this happens internally, and realize that the same thing is going on inside everyone else; if they can begin to appreciate how much more is going on than just the verbal parts of their interactions and how much power resides in the nonverbal, emotional, and often out-of-awareness facets of everyone, then we are well on the way to their improved mental health.

I would like to add a slight caution, however; although these techniques appear to be simple, and perhaps, universally applicable, more intensive training must be provided for therapists who wish to appropriately use them to their full potential. Anyone attempting to employ these tools in the research or understanding of others must have used them first for their own personal self-discovery and exploration, in order to know not only how each technique works in action, but also how each actually feels, to fully appreciate their power to tap deeply stored emotions and memories.

To implement phototherapy, no special skill in the craft of photography is required, either for the therapist or for the client. As long as the intended user understands what a photograph is and represents, and has a self-image that will not be shattered by intense self-examination, these techniques can be useful with almost any age or type of client. It is crucial, however, that the therapist's training be especially thorough in achieving fluency with working in those more abstract, nonverbal, and/or metaphoric domains that the photographic catalyst stimulates.

It is not terribly complex to integrate phototherapy techniques into one's repertoire of helping skills; it simply requires training, practice, an understanding of the ethical components involved, and, most importantly, an open and curious mind, combined with a firm commitment to work within the value system of the client rather than interpreting, and thus defining, meaning for that client (as well as trying as best as possible to keep one's own personal agenda out of it all). One must learn and then practice the concept that there really is no right and wrong in this business of psychotherapy; there is only "different," and that the therapist as well as the client can learn to expect, understand, and appreciate these differences as a model of healthy interactions.

In counseling children and youth, I would offer the suggestion that rather than being able to walk in their shoes for a day in order to really experience the world as they do, let us instead ask to step behind the lens of their cameras in order to see what (and how) they see; to pose for them under their direction of how we should be (or pose) for the camera; to reflect with them upon the meanings, feelings, memories, and thoughts stimulated by a photo-catalyst (and nonthreateningly share our differences); to explore albums or photo-taking assignments with them as they explain why they took a picture in a particular way, and what, if anything, was missing that should have been there; to get a view into their family and its values represented in their photo collections, albums, and personal displays by discovering what they deemed important enough to be permanently kept or chosen to share with us; to sensitize ourselves to the nuances and messages of their nonverbal behavior as they pose for a self-portrait as they want it to be; and, finally, to ask them for their reactions to our own photos that we think we know so well ourselves, and thus discover how different and unique each human mind and its perceptions can be. Far more than the proverbial thousand words is reflected in those tiny lenses when a person (not a camera) takes a picture; photographs are a powerful visual frame of reference quite unlike any other available for our use in helping people.

ADDENDUM: HOW TO DO PHOTOTHERAPY

As I have stressed throughout this chapter, there can be no formal list of instructions on how to do phototherapy; regardless of the techniques selected, the purpose of use, the audience, or the setting, users of these various means of photo-exploring must realize that where one goes depends upon why one would want to be going there in the first place. Like all good tools, these techniques are only brought to life through the hands of the users. At its most basic level of operation, phototherapy consists of asking questions, questions that are open-ended and able to draw out feelings as well as thoughts, nonverbal feelings and memories as well as standard verbal response clichés. The skill is in not only learning how to ask the right questions, but also in knowing how and when to use which combinations of techniques in order to reach particular goals with each client.

As the concept of projecting underlies all the techniques, and the image content of all photos is really only a starting point, a stimulus or catalyst bringing forth personal memories, thoughts, and feelings; perhaps readers would like to experience photo-projecting for themselves, to get a clearer picture of how it all happens. If so, please consider what responses you have to the questions accompanying the photographs that follow, which have been selected to appeal to child and adolescent clients.

The very first moment you are aware you have an answer, try to introspect how it was that you knew that, why you think that answer came to your mind, what facet of the photo gave you that knowledge, and what would have to change in the image for you to uncover a different response.

Try sharing your reflections and comments in dialogue with significant others in your life, or with your clients.[1] Examine the group of informal portraits that follows; reflect upon these people portrayed and try answering (and sharing your answer in discussions with others) the following questions for each one:

Who is this person? What are they doing? Where were they when this photo was made? How do you think they were feeling at the time the snap was taken? When you look at this photo, what thoughts and feelings come to mind? How would you title this photo? What do you think was going on in the photo and

---

[1] I would be interested in receiving readers' responses, reactions, comments, feedback, anecdotes, and so on. Please address all correspondence to this author c/o: PhotoTherapy Centre, 1107 Homer St. (Suite #304), Vancouver, B.C., Canada, V6B2Y1.

Figure 12.7.

what do you think happened next, after the photo was snapped? Do they remind you of anyone you know?

What is each person's background; what is their home like, and their family
(and how did you decide that)? Would you think any of them shy, friendly,
hard to get to know, a television star, a prize student, handicapped, in any
kind of trouble, orphans, delinquents, owners of pets, and so on (one could
get endlessly creative here, depending upon which areas were to be worked);
if so, why—what in the photo made you think that? What is their favorite
food, movie, thing to do, relative, animal, place to go, and so on.

If they (this photo) could speak, what would they (it) say? Which ones (if
any) would you like to meet, or have as friends or neighbors; why do you
think you picked those choices? If you could say something to any of these
people, what would you like to say to whom? Why? If you met any of them,
where do you think they would want to take you (and would you go)?

Why do you think the photographer took any of these snapshots? If you
could rephotograph them, how do you think your photo might end up different? Are there any other questions you feel like answering? (*Note:* I have arbi-
trarily chosen to demonstrate questions in reference to photos of people; however, the same procedures could also be used with scenics, still-lifes, family
group photos, pets, houses, and so on; i.e., whatever would be of use to the
client to respond to or interact with.)

REFERENCES

Akeret, R.U. (1973). *Photoanalysis.* New York: Simon & Schuster.

Bandler, R., & Grinder, J. (1975). *Structure of magic* (Vol. 1). Palo Alto, CA: Science
& Behavior Books.

Fryrear, J.L. (1980). A selective non-evaluative review of research on photo therapy.
Phototherapy, 2(3), 7–9.

Fryrear, J.L. (1983). Photographic self-confrontation as therapy. In D.A. Krauss &
J.F. Fryrear (Eds.), *Phototherapy in mental health* (pp. 71–94). Springfield, IL:
Charles C Thomas.

Gassan, A. (1983). *Report: Minor White workshops, and, a dialogue failed.* Sun
Prairie, WI: Baumgartner Press.

Gilman, S. (Ed.). (1976). *The face of madness.* New York: Brunner/Mazel.

Hall, E.T. (1969). *The hidden dimension.* Garden City, NY: Doubleday Anchor.

Hall, E.T. (1973). *The silent language.* Garden City, NY: Doubleday Anchor.

Hattersley, R. (1971). *Discover yourself through photography.* New York: Association
Press.

Krauss, D.A. (1979). The uses of still photography in counseling and therapy: Development of a training model. Unpublished doctoral dissertation, Kent State University,
Ohio.

Krauss, D.A. (1980). A summary of characteristics of photographs which make them
useful in counseling and therapy. *Camera Lucida, 1*(2), 2–12.

Krauss, D.A. (1981). Photography, imaging, and visually referent language in therapy: Illuminating the metaphor. *Camera Lucida, 1*(5), 58–63.

Krauss, D.A. (1983). Reality, photography and psychotherapy (Chapter 3), and, The visual metaphor: Some underlying assumptions of phototherapy (Chapter 4). In D.A. Krauss & J.F. Fryrear (Eds.), *Phototherapy in mental health* (pp. 40–55, 56–70). Springfield, IL: Charles C Thomas.

Krauss, D.A., & Fryrear, J.L. (Eds.). (1983). *Phototherapy in mental health.* Springfield, IL: Charles C Thomas.

Levinson, R. (1979). Psychodynamically oriented phototherapy. *Phototherapy, 2*(2), 14–16.

Loellbach, M. (1978). *The uses of photographic materials in psychotherapy: A literature review.* Unpublished master's thesis, George Williams College, Downer's Grove, Illinois.

Poyatos, F. (1983). *New perspectives in nonverbal communication.* New York: Pergamon Press.

Stewart, D. (1979a). Photo therapy comes of age. *Kansas Quarterly, 2*(4), 19–46.

Stewart, D. (1979b). Photo therapy: Theory and practice. *Art Psychotherapy, 6*(1), 41–46.

Weiser, J. (1975). PhotoTherapy: Photography as a verb. *BC Photographer, 2,* 33–36.

Weiser, J. (1981). *Using photo albums in therapy with "special needs" families.* Unpublished manuscript written with major contributions from Dr. Alan Entin.

Weiser, J. (1983). Using photographs in therapy with people who are "different." In D.A. Krauss & J.L. Fryrear (Eds.), *Phototherapy in mental health* (pp. 174–199). Springfield, IL: Charles C Thomas.

Weiser, J. (1985). Training and teaching photo and video therapy: Central themes, core knowledge, and important considerations. *Phototherapy, 4*(4), 9–16.

Weiser, J. (In press). See what I mean? Photography as nonverbal communication in cross-cultural psychology. In F. Poyatos (Ed.), *Cross-cultural perspectives in nonverbal communication.* Lewiston, NY: Hogrefe.

White, M. (1966). Equivalence, the perennial trend. In N. Lyons (Ed.), *Photographers on photography.* Englewood Cliffs, NJ: Prentice-Hall.

Zakem, B. (1977, September). Newsline: Photographs help patients focus on their problems. *Psychology Today,* p. 22.

Zakem, B. (1978). *Phototherapy: A developing psychotherapeutic approach.* Paper presented at the Raveswood Community Mental Health Center, Chicago, Illinois.

CHAPTER 13

Making Life Books with Foster and Adoptive Children

JOANN HARRISON

INTRODUCTION

"As a teenager, I couldn't look into the mirror without wondering, Where did this face come from? Who do I look like?" The young woman glanced tentatively at the clinician before continuing, "I searched the faces of people on the street looking for someone whose face resembled mine. It finally came to a head when I married and became pregnant. My doctor asked me lots of questions about my family's health history. I couldn't tell him. That's when I decided to search for some answers."

As children move through the foster care system and into adoption, large portions of personal history are lost. They may not know who they have lived with, what their family background is, if they have brothers and sisters, why their parents placed them, or even their original names. This information that most of us take for granted is very important to identity formation and to general life adjustment. The result of not having it are children with confused realities whose fantasies and conflicts keep them from adjusting adequately to family life.

A life book is a written record that gives this information back to children. It is therapeutic in that it explains what has happened, helping them accept their situations. A life book is a useful tool for children who have been separated from their families, regardless if the plan is return home or adoption.

The life book is the most common tool for preparing children for adoption, according to a study of adoption disruptions (Partridge, Hornby, & McDonald, 1986). Life books are used 58 percent of the time to prepare children. Although there are no statistics that isolate the effectiveness of the life book technique, the study does state that preparation of children for adoption is critical and that not enough effort has been put in this direction.

The effective preparation of children for adoption is not only significant in the initial placement and later finalization of that adoption, but it is also significant to the ongoing maintenance of the adoption. In 1985, an unofficial survey of over 100 group care facilities throughout the country was initiated by Kay Donley, Executive Director of New York Spaulding for Children. It was learned that about 10 percent of children in those facilities have come from threatened adoptions, those where the child cannot be maintained in the home due to placement problems. About half of the children were placed as infants and half were placed as special needs children. Experienced practitioners strongly suspect that the preparation of these children was not complete and that it was not reinforced over a period of time. The children did not understand their situation, did not have enough information about themselves, and were not able to talk to their adoptive parents.

The life book concept has been used since the late 1960s by social workers and therapists. Most existing information about life books is how-to in nature. The concept frequently appears in literature dealing with foster care and adoption.

According to Aust,

The life book process is the beginning of a re-education of the child's beliefs in a manner congruent with Ellis' Rational Emotive Therapy. That is, in helping a child understand the reality of his life to date, one must find and dispute the irrational, negative beliefs the child holds about himself and his parents in order to allow him to see himself, his life and the future in a more positive and realistic way (1981, p. 558).

Aust further states that,

Growth in most of the children completing a life book has been shown in the child's having a more positive self-concept; a more realistic and accepting view of self, parents and environment; a better understanding of where he has been and where he is going; improved memory; more appropriate social behavior; an increase in academic skills; a more realistic "cover story" for his situation, rather than one involving fantasy or self-blame; improved interpersonal relationships; and increased tolerance of separation and change (1981, p. 559).

Life book techniques presented here are just a beginning. As you, the professional social worker or therapist, work with individual children, you will see ways to tailor your approach to the differing needs of each child, and you will generate new approaches to meet new situations.

THE FACTS AND HOW TO TELL THEM

A child's life book should cover the significant events of the child's life. While a life book can include an endless amount of material, there are several critical issues that need explanation in order for children to understand their situation. These include the reason that the birth parents placed the child in foster care or for adoption, that placement was not the child's fault, and that the child has a right to parents. Children need to know the role of social workers and the courts, what happened to their siblings, and the role of foster care. If the plan is adoption, they need to know why the foster parents did not adopt them and that they have the right to participate in adoptive planning.

In addition to these key issues, it is helpful for children to know the facts surrounding their birth, some descriptive and health information about their development, and information about the places where they have lived and when they lived there. For children who are going home, the life book should include plans and issues concerning this return.

A bigger question for most professionals is not what to put in a life book but how to say it in a way that will not further damage the child's self-image. You clearly need to be sensitive and compassionate, presenting the information as positively as possible. But, you also need to be direct, accurate, and specific, so the child will understand and accept the information. Most clinicians' initial attempts to be both sensitive and direct are so ambiguous that the message is lost. It helps to practice with someone who can give you feedback before you talk to the child. Children have such a strong ability to deny what is painful that you have to be sure you give the message clearly. Eight-year-old Aaron was told by his clinician that his mother could not take care of him because of her drinking. He accepted this explanation superficially. Months later, to his clinician's dismay, he said he wanted to go home to take care of his mother. His explanation was that his mother could not be blamed if she could not take care of him. The clinician had to then explain to Aaron that his mother had been given a fair chance but had chosen not to stop drinking.

Separation from Birth Parents

It is crucial that children know why their birth parents placed them into foster care or for adoption. If they are not told the reasons, they will invent reasons to satisfy their need to know. What children invent is potentially much more harmful to them than hearing the truth. Since children assume the blame for placement, the child needs to know that placement occurred because of the parents' problems rather than anything the child did. Many children assume that they are bad and do not deserve parents. Children need to hear that all children, including them deserve to be cared for by parents.

Carrying the guilt for a placement loss is something children will continue to do even after they have been assured that the parent had the problem. When children hear that their parent was unable to care for them they will sometimes assume there was something about them that caused the problem. Children need to hear that the parent could not care for any child. When this is not the case, as in circumstances where parents give up only one child, you need to spend time talking about the reasons why only that child was placed.

When talking to children about separation, avoid vague generalizations like, "Your mommy was sick," or "Your mom had a lot of problems." These raise questions in a child's mind about what might happen if the adoptive parents get sick or have problems. Also avoid glowing comments like, "Your mother couldn't care for you, but she loved you so much she gave you up for adoption." Such an explanation does not ring true. People do not give away those they love.

It helps to talk about the underlying reasons a parent may not be able to follow through, especially in situations where the obvious reason has a stigma attached. It is also important to talk about feelings the birth parent has concerning placement. This helps the child see the parent as a whole person. It benefits the child's self-esteem to know the decision was not easily made.

A sample description of a six-year-old's separation might sound like this:

You lived with your mom and dad until you were four and a half. Your family had happy times like Christmas and birthdays and when you got your dog. It would be nice if things could always be happy but you had troubles too. Your dad had a hard time growing up. His mom and dad mistreated him, and he did not learn how to treat children. He was worried about grown-up things like money and his job. When he worried, he would drink too much to try to make himself feel better. When he drank too much, sometimes he would hit you and your mom. Your mom was not able to protect you or herself. This made all of you very sad. You were very afraid of your dad. Now, it's every child's right to grow up safe. Because you were in danger, the court asked the social worker to find a home where you could be safe until your mom and dad could learn how to take care of you without hurting you.

A sample description of a 10-year-old's separation might sound like this:

When you were eight, your mom and dad began to have some serious problems. Your dad left home. Your mom didn't have a job or any way to take care of the three of you. She had to depend on others for a place to stay and food to eat. She felt overwhelmed. That is a feeling people have when they have more to do than they can handle, and they don't know how they are going to do it. She didn't feel very good about herself. When people don't feel good about themselves, they sometimes don't make good choices about the things they do or the people they spend their time with. Your mom had trouble making good choices, and she got into trouble with drugs. This made her feel even worse. By this time, your mom was very worried about what would happen to all of you. She felt she could not take care of you and take care of herself at the same time. This was hard for her and she had a lot of strong feelings. She was angry this had happened and sad and afraid of what the future held. She wanted you children to have the things you needed. So, she asked the social worker for help.

If you are working with the child at the time of termination, you may have the opportunity to involve the birth parent in telling the child why he is being placed. This is ideal in many ways. The message comes directly from the parent. The parent takes responsibility for the problem and the parent gives the child a positive message about living a happy life and attaching to new parents. Most parents want to do the best thing for their child, and many parents are willing to participate in such a goodbye session if you prepare them well. You should agree on what is actually to be said before the session, with care taken that the message is not a mixed one. The child should be told that this is a final decision. Sometimes, in the actual session, you will need to support or assist the parent if the parent has difficulty talking. If you do this, you should always get the parent's verbal or nodded agreement. What is said should later be recorded in the life book.

One concern children have about background information is whether they will turn out like their parents. Exploring these fears helps put the child at ease. With children who are afraid that they will abuse their children like they were abused, you might say:

> Your mom was mistreated when she was growing up, and she never learned how to treat children. She expected too much, and she also never learned how to control her own feelings. Her mom didn't teach her some of the things she needed to know to be a grownup. But things are different for you. Your new mom knows how to care for children, and every day she cares for you, you'll learn something new about how children should be loved and cared for. She teaches you these things by telling you and by showing you. And, there's another thing she teaches you. It's how to take care of yourself so you will have good feelings about you. This will let you have good feelings about your children. Your mom also teaches you how to solve problems so that you don't get stuck when you are angry. Every day you are with your new mom, you grow stronger and learn more about how to be a happy grownup.

You may feel that not giving full information will protect a child from these worries. But most children have at least partial information about their parent's problems. By not discussing it fully, you put the children at risk to fulfill their fears.

Besides separation information, it is helpful to a child's identity formation to have as much other information about the parents as possible. This should include a physical description, health information, interests, education, and strengths. Information should be given about the birth father even if he is absent or uninvolved. Also include information about grandparents and other relatives.

Foster Care

Children need to know that foster care is intended to be a temporary setting until the child can return home or be adopted. Foster parents are not permanent parents but those who care for children until arrangements can be made. Children are frequently placed into foster care when they are too young to get the details. Children need to know every place they lived, how long they were there (with specific dates), who the parents were, and why they were moved. Dates may not be of interest to young children, but later in life they will want this information. Time becomes more concrete if you tie it to events or to the child's age. You could say, "When you were three, you lived with the Smiths. That's when you broke your arm."

Special care should be taken to deal with the reasons for moves from foster homes. Children with multiple placements experience a series of rejections that significantly affect their ability to attach. If the move was not related to the children themselves, they still get the message that someone or something else was more important to the foster parents than they were. They need to know how the decision was made.

If the child's behavior did contribute to the move, the child needs to know that so that he can understand how people affect one another. A sample description of a move related to a child's behavior might sound like this:

> When you went to the Barker's you were 12, and you were still pretty angry with your mother. You were so mad you couldn't get it out fast enough. Sometimes it seemed you lashed out at them because she wasn't there to lash out at. You were also used to being out on your own a lot without many rules. It was hard to begin to be part of a family, especially when you were so angry. You just weren't ready yet. The Barkers were pretty confused about the whole thing, too. They didn't know how to help you, and they were afraid you would hurt one of the younger children. They didn't want to put one of the others at risk.

As with separations from birth parents, it is best if you can involve the foster parents in talking to the child about the reason for the move, especially when a child is attached to foster parents who have decided not to adopt. The child experiences this as another rejection. Because foster parents frequently have guilt feelings, they often give the child a mixed message. This causes the child to deny the reality of the situation and makes it harder to attach to the adoptive family. Getting the foster parents to tell the child of their decision in your presence makes sure that everyone hears the same message, and it gives you and the parents a chance to do some esteem building. It also lets you help the foster parents give the child permission to detach from them and to reattach to another family.

This is usually a painful process for foster parents who may be uncomfortable talking about these things. Foster parents may need your help knowing what to say and how to say it before they can talk to the child. More information is given about involving parents in the techniques section of this chapter.

Brothers and Sisters

Children experience trauma from the loss of siblings as well as from the loss of birth and foster parents. This loss is especially dificult for children who have cared for younger siblings. These parental children often show adult responsibility toward younger brothers and sisters. Their guilt at not knowing what has happened to their siblings and not insuring their siblings' safety can cause them to not attach in their new placement.

Children also feel guilty if they have strong negative feelings toward a sibling and something happens to that child. This guilt is amplified if separation occurs at the same time. One girl was deeply embarrassed that her sister was retarded. She made fun of her and refused to interact with her. The two children were separated. This girl expressed continued concern and guilt over her sister's welfare for a number of years.

It helps children to know where siblings are and if they are with a stable family that is taking care of them. Explore with children the circumstances of separation, getting their perceptions and clarifying the facts. A sample description of a sibling separation might sound like this:

> It seems that you're a little hard on yourself about your problems with Ricky. It's true that you and Ricky fought a lot, but that was Ricky's problem as much as yours. Neither of you were getting what you needed from your mom and it's only natural in that situation that you would be rivals. It's also only natural that sometimes you might wish Ricky wasn't around. I bet that maybe Ricky felt that way sometimes too. But your wishing it didn't make it happen. Your separation happened for a very different reason.

Where possible, it is good to initiate or to continue contact with separated siblings. Some adoptive parents who are unwilling to do this are willing to provide a picture of their child for the sibling.

Courts and Social Workers

Children typically have two emotional responses when they think of the court. One is fear; the other is blame. Children need to know that the court's role in their lives is that of protection, not punishment. The court is responsible for making sure they live in homes where they will be safe and get the things they need. Children also need to understand the court's position with their parents. The court did not cause the problem. The child needs to understand that the parents were given a fair chance. A child who blames the court or the social worker rather than accepting reality will have a much harder time adjusting.

Children also need an explanation of why they have a social worker and what that person does. When the plan is for the child to return home, tell the child that the social worker is the one who will help him and his family learn to live together again. If the plan is adoption, tell the child that the worker's job is to find him a family that he can grow up in and to help him learn to live with them. If the child has a separate therapist in addition to a social worker, tell the child the therapist's job is to help him learn about his feelings and to help him understand others' feelings.

Going Home to Birth Parents

As you work with children, it is helpful to make them aware of the progress of their birth family and the direction things seem to be taking. In this way you prepare the children for the next step. As the time arrives for them to return home, you will want to explore their expectations and fears in the life book. You will want to share with the children how things have changed and why you feel their parents will be able to take care of them now. You may want to initiate a dialog between them and their parents about the return. In this way they can share expectations and begin to use problem solving techniques to deal with the rough spots. They may each want to say what they would like to see happen differently and how that might happen.

You will also need to help the children with their feelings about leaving their foster families. It will help them to know that it is normal to have both happy and sad feelings about leaving a foster family to go home.

Adoption

When adoption becomes the plan, you will want to explore and work through the children's feelings about how this might affect them. Start with a definition of adoption and tell them the similarities and differences between adoption and foster care.

It is of utmost importance that the child contribute to the adoption plan. Children who are placed for adoption against their will are at high risk for disruption. In making an adoptive placement, it is best if the child is enthusiastic and asks to be adopted. At the least, the child needs to have agreed that of the alternatives, adoption is the best plan. The child should know that adjusting to a new family is hard work and that the child will be responsible for some of that work. It helps if the child knows some of the specific adjustments people make when they start living with one another. If they know what to expect and agree to the plan, they will be much more interested in making the plan work.

Children's concerns about adoption may center around loyalty to birth parents or attachment to foster parents. The life book process itself should thoroughly explore these feelings and bring children to a point where they can discuss the reality of their situation and their need for a life plan.

Other concerns that children have are sometimes irrational ideas that do not appear connected to adoption itself. For example, children in a temporary shelter may say they prefer foster care over adoption because they will have to move. They obviously will need to move anyway. Underlying these feelings is usually a fear of change and a fear that the adoption will not work out. You can neutralize some of this fear by presenting adoption matter-of-factly. The child needs to know that all adoptions do not work out, but neither do all foster care placements. If the adoption does not work, the child can try again. The child needs to be committed but not overly anxious.

Part of the children's contribution will be deciding what type of family they want. You can guide them in this by using the information you know about them. Since children are not always realistic about what they ask for (a family with money, horses, a pool; a family that never disciplines), you can have the children list their wishes by their importance in the same manner that you would discuss their Christmas list.

If an adoption disrupts, use the life book to talk about it. You will want children to tell you their idea of why the adoption did not work. Again, because children take the blame for placement failures, you will probably need to clarify for them what happened. As with a move from birth parents, it helps to address the underlying causes.

Other Information

You may include whatever information you or the child want. This may include information about friends, schools, pets, or activities. Children are especially interested in their births, and this information helps in identity formation. Put in the same type of information that you know about your own birth—date, time of day, place, weight, and length. Including developmental information is good for children also. It assures them that they were normal and did the things that all children do. Foster children often have a need to be like other children. If the child has a handicap, you will want to discuss the effect that handicap has but also give reassurance about all the ways the child is normal.

TECHNIQUES

Covering the facts is the essential foundation of doing a life book. You will soon discover, however, that helping the child deal with perceptions and feelings about those facts is even more critical. A number of techniques can help the child sort out and express emotions, as well as help you be more effective during the process.

Getting the Parent's Help

A foster or adoptive parent's help is a powerful resource. It creates a therapeutic, supportive atmosphere. In this way, your professional effectiveness can be stretched greatly. Involving parents is also a sound time management technique in agencies where case loads are high. You and the parent can divide tasks.

Since doing a life book aids in bonding, it assists both parents and child in the attachment process. It prepares adoptive parents to work with their child after the adoption has been finalized when you are no longer involved.

Children reprocess information about themselves as they move through developmental stages and as their ability to understand more sophisticated concepts increases. Involving parents in doing a life book gives you a chance to teach the family how to handle separation and placement issues at these stages. Joint work with a parent creates a bond between you and the parent that increases the chance that the parent will use you for support and build on systems you start together.

Many parents' initial response to dealing with a child's life issues is fear. They may logically explain that the child is doing so well that there is no need to dredge up the past. Foster parents fear that doing a life book will increase acting out behaviors. Adoptive parents fear loss of the child—that doing a life book might rekindle a child's interest in the birth family. A child's silence about feelings or family is often interpreted by parents as a sign that all is well. A more accurate interpretation is that the child is denying the situation or that the child is aware of the parents' discomfort in talking about the issues. It is easier for the child to fantasize about the facts than to risk the parents' displeasure.

Helping a child work through feelings about the past can actually help the parent claim the child. To gain a parent's assistance, you must first deal with that parent's fears. Listening techniques help identify those fears and reframe the parent's attitude. Most parents participate positively once they understand how much it helps their child. Children frequently regress as difficult topics are covered. Once committed, parents can see this as a normal part of the life book process. Your role becomes one of support to both parent and child.

Getting the Child's Help

Children benefit most from life books when they are actively involved in creating them. Some children eagerly join in life book work while others are reluctant. Reluctance is usually a sign the child does not yet trust you, or a desire to avoid the discomfort of talking about painful issues. Trust can be gained by using listening techniques, responding on the child's level and showing interest in the things the child does. It is important to respect the child's feelings by accepting rather than denying them. A child's perceptions may be very different than an adult's. It is better to accept what children say about their experiences than to discount them by not believing them. Exaggerations serve a purpose and can be dealt with once your relationship is strong. With disruptive children, it helps to make a time contract, possibly with a reward at the end of the time.

Encourage the child's participation by doing activities that are interesting and fun. Encourage children to share information about themselves that may not be in your records. Give them some control over the project by letting them choose activities. You may even let them choose when you talk about topics. For example, a logical and nonthreatening way to start a life book is to start with the child's birth. However, children may want to start with their present lives. Respond to the child's imagination and spontaneity and do not let yourself be hindered by preconceived ideas of what the book should look like.

Involving the child is also a wise time management technique. You can give the child assignments that may be written or experiential in nature. Thus, the project can move ahead without your direct involvement. Assignments can include writing part of the book, doing a collage, writing a story, using a tape recorder or working on a problem.

Life book sessions should be frequent enough to keep the child interested. Begin working on a life book as soon as you begin working with the child. Starting early will give the child more time to understand and accept what has happened. Children, like adults, need time to process feelings. Starting at the time of adoptive placement is much better than not starting at all, but it will not give the child the time needed to fully accept the situation.

Start with Feelings

Most foster and adoptive children have no experience identifying and dealing with their feelings. However, their feelings profoundly affect their behavior. These feelings are all entangled in a confused ball of emotion. Children need to sort out and understand their own feelings before they can deal with others. One established way of helping a child learn about feelings is through feeling faces (Fahlberg, 1981). Draw some simple faces expressing common feelings on pieces of paper. These faces may express happiness, sadness, anger, fear, or confusion. Confusion is usually defined to the child as having more than one feeling at a time. You may then ask the child to identify the emotion by looking at the face. You can ask the child what might be causing these faces to show these feelings or what events in life might cause these feelings. You might also ask children to demonstrate what they look like when they have these emotions. You can ask them what they might do or act like when having these emotions. In this way, through repetition, they start learning to identify their own feelings, those of others, and how people act when they have certain feelings. From this beginning, you can use the faces as you go through the child's life history. The faces are especially helpful in working with children who are not very verbal. If the children's emotions are strong and they are not able to talk about them, they can still communicate with the worker by pointing to the pictures.

Using reflective listening with children also helps identify feelings. This technique is very powerful in maintaining rapport. In this way, you are able to nurture the child and convey caring and respect while continuing work on the book. By using reflective listening, you can discover where the children's fears are in a way that makes them feel protected. Reflective listening used over a number of sessions will often help a hesitant child work through any reluctance about discussing feelings. This technique can be easily taught to children by using puppets and asking them to talk to the puppet and tell it what they are feeling. Children often pick up the technique just from watching a clinician use it.

Identifying feelings in this way is a good first step to problem solving. Helping both parent and child learn this technique assists in their adjustment to one another.

1. What is the problem? _____

_____

2. What do I want from the situation? _____

_____

_____

3. How can I get it? _____

_____

_____

4. How will my solution work? (List the possible pros and cons of the proposed solution.)

_____

_____

_____

_____

Figure 13.1. Problem solving worksheet.

Problem Solving Models

Making a life book not only helps clarify children's feelings about their history but also helps them adjust to their present placements. Teaching both child and parent specific problem solving strategies can help them jointly solve problems. The child can also use them to resolve problems independently. A problem solving worksheet is shown in Figure 13.1.

Step one allows problem solvers to define the problem clearly. Step two gets them to say what they want. Step three gets them to generate possible solutions. This process allows children and/or parents to see that there is at least one solution to every problem. It creates investment in the solution because the children thought of it themselves and because they have the chance to choose the best alternative.

Step four is designed to serve as a check. By listing the positives and negatives of each potential solution, the problem solver is able to visualize if the solution will work or not.

You can also help a child solve problems through the type of questions you ask. Questions that begin with the word "how" encourage children to look within themselves in a nonjudgmental way for information that will answer the questions. Such questions include, "How could you work that out?" or "How long will you be doing that?" If you want to help children control their feelings, you can ask, "How does that make you feel?" "How do you want to feel?" and then, "How could you make that happen?"

An example of this is work that was done with eight-year-old Brenda. She and her adoptive mother had frequent battles over eating, especially over Brenda's dislike of eggs. The clinician was present for one of these battles and asked Brenda how long she thought she and her mother would be fussing over eggs. When Brenda said she didn't know, the clinician asked if Brenda thought they would be fussing about eggs when she was 24. Brenda laughed and said no. The clinician then asked her if she thought they'd be doing it when Brenda was 16. Brenda again said no. The clinician kept on in this manner until Brenda said it would be somewhere between 9 and 11 (Haley, 1973). She then said it would be at her ninth birthday. The clinician said "Okay, it will be at your ninth birthday. I suppose it could even be before that, maybe even by Thanksgiving or Christmas or maybe before the end of the school year. But it will happen by the time you are nine." This conversation took place in October and at Christmas, Brenda approached the clinician at a gathering and whispered, "I eat my eggs without fussing now." The clinician showed that she was impressed and asked, "How did you figure it out?" Brenda said, "I put cheese on them. I like them with cheese."

Children can also be taught to problem solve by using behavior charts (see Figure 13.2). A behavior chart can be kept anywhere, but the life book provides privacy. Behavior charts can be used for such things as helping children remember to do their chores, helping them control behaviors, or helping them deal with emotions appropriately.

Foster and adoptive children have had little control over their lives and are often desperate to establish control in any way possible. These children have little experience in solving problems appropriately. By teaching children problem-solving techniques, you teach them that they can control their lives in a way that will give them positive reinforcement from others. This raises their self-esteem.

Writing Technique

The actual writing of the life book can be handled by you, the child, or both. The amount children will be able to do will depend on their skill level, handicaps, degree of hyperactivity, or their enjoyment of writing. Since many foster and adoptive children have difficulty with academic skills, you may wish to involve the child in some other way. One way that is fun for the child is for you to write the narrative and leave places where the child can fill in the blanks.

An interesting way to handle part of the writing is to do a time line. This is a dramatic way to show the order of events in a child's life; children readily become involved in them. A time line can be a one page, topic outline of the child's life, or it can be the basis for the whole book. One clinician made a time line out of pieces of lightweight cardboard and taped them together so they stretched across the room. When folded, this time line formed the life book. The child was fascinated by the unusual format and willingly helped write and illustrate her book.

Another way to handle some of the book writing is to do a genogram (Hart-

	Sunday	Monday	Tuesday	Wednes-day	Thursday	Friday	Saturday
I did not express my anger by hitting.							
I did not express my anger by talking back.							
I did not express my anger by misbehaving at school.							
I express my anger by saying calmly how I feel.							
I express my anger by exercise.							
I can say calmly what I want.							
I problem solve with others.							

Figure 13.2. Behavior chart.

man, 1978). A genogram is a type of family tree using circles to represent females, squares to represent males, and a network of lines to show family ties. As the genogram is assembled, a wide variety of information about the individual family members is written close to that person's circle or square. The genogram becomes a map of the family, on which family patterns are easy to recognize.

Illustrations

The best way to illustrate a life book is with photographs. Since most children do not own many photos, part of making a life book is searching for pictures. Former foster parents and birth family are the most logical people to have family pictures. These people are usually very cooperative and generous when they know that donating photos will help the child. Even hostile birth parents are sometimes willing to help. One birth mother let the clinician borrow and copy a family album that contained photos and many family documents.

In the absence of existing photos, the clinician and child can generate some together. These photos may include pictures of the hospital where the child was born, homes where the child lived, current and past caretakers, friends, pets, and pictures of the child.

When photographs are just not possible, a life book can be illustrated by using copies of parent figures and family scenes from children's books. Children like to contribute their own drawings to the life book. They also like to experiment with art supplies. You can use this interest to keep a child involved in illustrating the book. Artwork completed by children usually has some emotional content. This gives you the opportunity to explore the child's feelings about the person or event that is drawn.

Using Collages

Creating a collage helps children express their feelings while documenting their history. According to Harrison, Campbell, and Chumbley, "Collages may include certain themes or periods in a child's life. For example: My family looks like this; these things make me happy; I am afraid of these things; this happened when I was 4; I feel this way about my mother; this is how separation from my birth family makes me feel" (1984, p. 19).

Younger children respond well to collage making but usually need precut pictures to choose from. Collages can be varied by adding scraps of material or colored paper to them, or by drawing or painting on them.

Story Telling

A good way to help children express their feelings when they are unable or unwilling to talk about them is through story telling. Give children a situation and ask them to tell you a story about it. Ask them what the main character is thinking or feeling.

You can reverse this situation and tell the child a story using animals or other children as the main characters. During the story you can identify feelings the characters have. This gives you the chance to identify these feelings as normal ones that anyone would have. Or, you can ask the child to tell you what the story characters are feeling.

Metaphors work very well with children. They can be used to elicit feelings, make a point, or suggest behavior. An excellent example of a separation meta-phor is *The Suitcase Story* (Wenger, 1982).

Teenagers can use their creative skills in story writing (Harrison et al.): "Ask the teen to construct a story based on a theme in his life. These may include: What bothers me? What makes me happy? How I would like my life to be; how my feelings have changed about my birth mother" (1984, p. 43).

Writing Letters

Much often goes unsaid between foster or adoptive children and those who care for them. Writing letters or notes can be very therapeutic to children who have not been able to express their feelings. Letters are not as direct an expres-sion as face-to-face contact and are easier for many children who cannot han-dle direct exchanges. One little girl, age eight, wrote "I love you" notes to both adoptive parents and left them where they would discover them. This child was never able to express positive feelings face-to-face.

If you help children with the letters, you have the chance to help them clarify what they want to say and how they say it. Letters might express disap-pointment or anger to a birth parent for leaving, or concerns and hopes about going home. Letters may simply be a means of maintaining contact with signif-icant people.

Former caretakers are usually very willing to help you do something positive for the child. Many are willing to write the child (through you, if requested) describing the time that the child lived with them. This type of letter might discuss events, developmental stages, and the family's positive feelings about what the child contributed to family life. Letters like this build self-esteem.

Although some letters will be mailed, some will be written simply for their therapeutic value and will be kept in the life book. You and the child need a clear agreement about which letters will be mailed. In some cases, especially concerning birth parents, it might not be appropriate to mail a letter. Other-wise, the child should make the decision about mailing letters.

Making Lists

An easy way to help children sort feelings is to make lists. This gives you a chance to see what the child's perceptions are, to reassure the child about issues, and to help clarify values. Writing lists in the life book gives you and the child concrete information to look at when discussing issues.

You might ask the child to make a list of things that answer these questions: "What does it mean to be adopted? How do you have to change? What makes you afraid, angry or worried? How can you show your feelings?" (Harrison et al., 1984 p. 43).

Making lists can help clarify values. One sibling group spent a considerable amount of energy making negative comparisons between their new adoptive family and their foster family. Their adoptive mother worked and the foster mother did not. The adoptive parents occasionally went out together without the children. The foster parents never did. The adoptive parents lived in the city and ate things like shrimp. The foster parents lived in the country and shrimp had never touched their lips.

The clinician first got the children to make a list of all the things a family had to do for their children if they were a good family. The children agreed that a good family did things like feed the children, give them a bed, and a place to live, never beat them, make sure they go to school, teach them to swim, and give them hugs. Then the clinician got the children to make a list describing the adoptive parents and one describing the foster parents. Once the lists were down in black and white where no one could forget what was on them, the clinician compared the list of what makes a good family to the two lists describing the two families. Both families fell into the category of good families and the children had to admit that shrimp eaters could be good parents. The clinician made the point that two families could be good and still be different. The clinician was then able to address the issue of differences free of the children's accusations that the adoptive family was not a good one.

Puppets

Puppets are natural tools for the exploration of children's feelings. They are especially helpful for children who do not express themselves easily. Using puppets can give you an idea of the child's expectations of family life as well as the child's fears and concerns. You can, through the puppets, model effective family relationships. Puppets can also help in esteem building. Many children who cannot accept praise from others can often accept it in a less direct way through a puppet.

One key to puppet play is to switch roles with the child often in order to get a complete picture of the child's perceptions. This also gives children a chance to stretch their perceptions as they play others beside themselves. Roles might include clinician, the child, a parent, a teacher, or someone the child is having difficulty with. Information that comes from puppet play may prompt you to design other life book activities to deal with those issues.

Children so readily engage in make believe that almost anything can be used for a puppet—old socks with eyes sewn on, popsicle sticks with faces pasted on, as well as more traditional animal and people puppets. One inexpensive and very versatile raw material is the paper bag. Several lunch-size paper bags can make a whole family, frequently at no cost. The fold in the bag forms the mouth. The child can color the faces to represent family members or friends.

Other toys such as cars, trucks, and people figures can often be used to accomplish the same goal. These are especially helpful with very young children in acting out their moves to new homes.

Children also find it easy to play roles with paper dolls. You can use the kind found in stores or make them out of paper and cardboard. Paper dolls are interesting because they can be dressed for different occasions. One child's mother's difficulties increased when she became pregnant for the fourth time. The clinician used paper dolls and represented the pregnancy with a maternity dress.

For older children or teenagers, role plays without puppets can help explore complex issues such as communication. In this way you can help children sort what they want to say to others and how they might appropriately say it. Children learn that they can affect the behavior of others in a positive way.

Materials

Life books can be easily made with the materials available at most agencies: paper, markers, pens, and a notebook. The best notebooks are those that can be taken apart and reassembled. With these the child can rearrange the information as well as add to it indefinitely. Materials selected should be sturdy enough to withstand repeated handling by a child. Some clinicians like to use magnetic photo pages because the plastic offers some protection to pictures and mementos pasted into the book. Children enjoy playing with these pages.

Materials can get expensive, especially if you purchase a ready-made photo album. Sometimes parents will provide these. Remember that the important things about a life book are issues and feelings you discuss with the child, not how it looks. Do not let lack of a handsome album deter you.

CASE STUDIES

ANGELA

Angela, who was not very verbal and of borderline intelligence, was 17 when her clinician started a life book with her. She had been in foster care most of her life. The clinician had just completed a workshop on doing life books and this was her first book. She was enthusiastic in spite of others' comments that working with Angela was quite an ambitious project. Since the information the clinician had was contradictory, she decided to start by doing a life line. Angela, contrary to what others had indicated, was thrilled to get the attention and to have someone talk to about her life and her feelings.

They did the life line on a big piece of newsprint, using a marker to write the life events and magazine pictures to illustrate it. Angela's first picture selection was a photograph of a rose being struck by lightning. She stated that this was how she felt when she lost her family. She then selected a picture of a bottle of whiskey to symbolize why the family split up. In this manner, Angela and her worker went through a number of major life events. They ended the life line with a magazine picture of an attractive, poised young woman who looked like she could conquer the world. This was Angela's idea of her future life. From this start, the clinician and Angela continued on to make a life book.

Angela had been separated from her siblings. In the process of completing the life book, the clinician arranged for Angela to meet with these brothers and sisters. Sometimes, when separated siblings meet, they are unable to communicate with one another. They may appear disinterested and seem to have nothing to say. This was not the case when Angela met her siblings. She took her life book and they had a meaningful visit, sharing their feelings and talking about the common events in their lives. The life book gave them a way to talk that positively affected their future relationship. In the course of the visit, Angela said, "You must make a life book! It will take the pain away."

KEITH

Twelve-year-old Keith was placed into foster care with two siblings at age six and became a valued member of the foster family. At nine, he and his siblings were placed into an adoptive home. Keith clashed strongly with the adoptive mother whose authority he challenged on every front. This placement lasted about a year and disrupted. The children were placed in another adoptive home. Keith was defiant and had numerous school problems. Although he had a life book and understood how things in his life had happened, he had taken a macho stance and refused to acknowledge his feelings.

Keith's situation was complicated by the existence of a birth grandmother who maintained contact with the children. This woman was understandably upset that her daughter had given up her children. However, she was unwilling to take the children herself because she had remarried and her new husband did not want children. This grandmother's contact was limited by distance to about one personal contact a year. The rest of her contact came through birthday and Christmas presents and occasional phone calls. With this limited contact, the grandmother was able to give the children mixed messages that were strong enough to keep Keith from attaching to his new family. Through persistence, his clinician was able to discover the problem. Keith admitted that he did not want to be adopted; he wanted to live with his birth family. An explanation stating they could not take him was not enough.

Keith's clinician used the life book to talk about mixed messages and all the feelings his grandmother had about his placement for adoption. She told him how disappointed the grandmother was that her daughter had given up her children and that what the grandmother really wanted was for her daughter to be a responsible mother and to take her children back. The clinician also told Keith that his grandmother had a hard time giving up her fantasy that this would happen. The clinician then told Keith that his grandmother was in a difficult position. Part of her wanted to take the children. However, she had decided that this was not the best decision for her now because of her age and health and because her husband did not wish to take three children into his life at this time. The clinician also told Keith that his grandmother felt somewhat guilty about the decision she had made. She told Keith that when a person makes a decision that affects someone else and she feels guilty about it, she will give mixed messages about it. The clinician told Keith that when dealing with others, you need to watch what they do and not what they say. Doing that is often hard because you want very much to believe what they say.

After this discussion and explanation, Keith was able to start looking at the new adoptive family as the family who did what they said they would do; that is, take care of him. Keith and his family could then work on adjustment issues free of the emotional pull of his grandmother. Keith was eventually adopted by this family and was able to maintain a more useful interaction with his grandmother.

MARTY

Marty and her two siblings were placed for adoption when Marty was six. She was the oldest. After placement, she began to have school problems, and she started to lie. She also held back emotionally. Her mother said that when they questioned Marty about her school transgressions, she got a "glazed look on her face" and would not talk.

The clinician worked for four sessions with Marty on a life book. Since Marty appeared to have complete amnesia about the events of her life and her feelings, the clinician had to tell her everything and describe how other children felt when similar things happened to them. The clinician also guessed what Marty must have been feeling and told Marty her guesses. This is an effective technique with children.They will almost always tell you strongly if you have guessed wrong.

At the second session, the clinician introduced the feeling faces and also increased her nurturing behavior with Marty. Marty was not able to talk much but was able to point to the faces to express herself. Her main feeling about the adoption was fear. Her mother's no-nonsense approach, which worked quite well with the second of the siblings, contributed to Marty's fear.

By the third session, Marty was ready to work on her book and she was able to whisper to the clinician that "maybe she was afraid." The clinician used this as a springboard to problem solving by asking Marty if they could talk to Marty's mother about this. Marty agreed, and at their fourth meeting, clinician, child, and mother were able to discuss Marty's situation.

Marty and her siblings were adopted by this family. Their clinician sees them once a year at an agency party. Marty remembers the clinician and eagerly seeks her out to talk.

HOWARD

At 14, Howard had been in a number of foster homes, through two adoption disruptions and in two psychiatric facilities. He had been severly abused as a young child and had some significant physical problems because of it. On one hand, he could be a mannerly, sensitive person who liked to talk about his feelings. On the other hand, he was aggressive, threatening, and suicidal. He had never emotionally detached from his birth family. He had a rudimentary life book and expressed a desire to work on it more.

One key to Howard was that he wanted to talk about his feelings, and he needed help in problem solving. Since return to birth parents was not feasible, the clinician's first step was to get Howard to separate the essence of what he wanted from its connection to his birth parents. Howard was not able to understand these concepts, so the clinician took a risk and told Howard what he wanted, "I know what you want! It's to be loved for being Howard, not for doing well in school or for any of that other stuff. You want some one who will love you for being Howard." Since Howard knew he could not return home, it was a fairly easy step to talk about how this person could be anyone. The clinician wanted to address Howard's school behavior, so he said this anyone could be anywhere. It could be a teacher or a friend of the teacher. It could be the uncle of the girl who sits behind him at school. But Howard would not get to meet that someone if he did not treat that teacher or that girl well. By doing this, the clinician linked meeting the one who would love him for being Howard to treating those around him well. Since Howard usually got into trouble when he was feeling pressured and could not talk about his feelings, he was encouraged to identify people that he could talk to as well as to identify his own internal signs that he needed to talk.

The agency did not have a regular foster setting for Howard and was not likely to get one. The most feasible course of action seemed to be recruitment of another adoptive home. The clinician knew that this would only work if Howard was in full agreement. She wanted Howard to come to this conclusion on his own and to ask to be placed for adoption. Since Howard was in a temporary home, the issue of where he would live was frequently at hand. When asked directly what he wanted, Howard, of course, said he did not know. The clinician told Howard that he did know but he did not know he knew. The clinician also told Howard that he had the answers to questions but he did not know he had them. The clinician told him that, in time, he would find himself discovering the answers to these questions. The clinician also gave him a time frame by saying that Howard would surely have these answers by the end of the school year and maybe before—maybe by Christmas, maybe by St. Patrick's Day, but certainly by the end of the year. This gave Howard something to mull over—that he had the answer to questions. It also gave him a time frame. It was not long before Howard said that the reason he did not want an adoptive home was that he was afraid the same thing would happen, that he would lose control, lose the placement, and have to go to another psychiatric facility. The clinician suggested that Howard held the answers to these questions also. She also continued using more conventional problem solving methods with him. In the early spring, Howard asked the clinician to find him another adoptive family. Before placement, she helped Howard identify what he wanted from his family and how best to ask for it.

The clinician accomplished this by giving Howard suggestions and letting those suggestions grow. She reinforced her verbal messages with related life book activities.

CONCLUSION

A life book presents a unique opportunity to professional social workers and therapists. It is an opportunity to give children information about themselves that they do not have and to clarify misinformation, feelings, and values that they do have. It is a chance to shape the child's view of reality in a positive direction and help to prepare the child for a future life, be it a return home or placement for adoption. It is a chance to achieve real communication with children that will have a profound impact on their lives. Each child in care deserves this chance to understand and accept the events of his life.

We cannot stop at the completion of the life book, however. More needs to be known about the long term implications of foster care and adoptive placements: How will these children fare throughout their childhoods? What causes adoptive placements to sometimes dissolve years after placement? What additional work can be done with these children and families before and during placement to minimize this trend? Can continuing life books be helpful to parents and children years after placement? What is the best way to work with children who lose their families again in their teen years? These questions suggest the need for even more comprehensive preparation of children for moves they face. They also suggest the need for more information and more research.

Hopefully, this chapter has given you ideas for working with the children you know. Hopefully, too, it has touched your imagination and given you new ways to meet the individual needs of those children.

REFERENCES

Aust, P.H. (1981). Using the Life Story book in treatment of children in placement. *Child Welfare, 60*(8), 535–536, 553–560.

Fahlberg, V. (1981). Adoptive children/adoptive feelings. [Film developed by University of Georgia.] Washington, DC: U.S. Department Health and Human Services, Children's Bureau.

Haley, J. (1973). *Uncommon therapy, The psychiatric techniques of Milton H. Erickson, MD.* New York: W.W. Norton.

Harrison, J., Campbell, E.; & Chumbly, P. (1984). *Making history: A social worker's guide to Life Books.* Louisville, KY: Kentucky Cabinet for Human Resources, Department for Social Services.

Hartman, A. (1978, October). Diagrammatic assessment of family relationships. *Social Casework,* 465–476.

Partridge, S.; Hornby, H.; & McDonald, T. (1986). *Legacies of loss; Visions of gain; An inside look at adoption disruption.* Portland: Human Services Development Institute, University of Southern Maine.

Wenger, C. (1982). *The suitcase story: A therapeutic technique for children in out-of-home placements.* Detroit, MI: American Orthospsychiatric Association.

CHAPTER 14

Child Therapy and Animals

A New Way for an Old Relationship

MOTHER HILDEGARD GEORGE, O.S.B.

Carol is a normally developing five-year-old, the middle child of three girls in a loving family. Her youngest sister was born five months ago; since then Carol has had crying spells, often tells her father he does not love her as much as he loves the other siblings, and invents tales that shock the neighbors and nursery school teachers into thinking she is a neglected child.

Jamie is a six-year-old impoverished, innercity child, who has been in residential treatment at a school for emotionally disturbed children. He appears to be confused at times, is enuretic, and is generally fearful of his environment.

What do these children have in common? Both are candidates for animal-oriented child therapy.

INTRODUCTION AND THEORETICAL BACKGROUND

Only in the past few decades have experts of many disciplines been coming together to study the relationship between humans and animals. It is significant to note that the bulk of literature on the human-animal bond dates from the late 1960s.

Modern people have become so alienated from nature that, unlike primitive peoples, we cannot see the gifts other species contribute to our well-being. Because our modern society is so withdrawn, from nature, we have closed our eyes to the healing qualities of a relationship with the many guises of nature. Animals are a necessary part of the ecosystem of which humanity is but one part. Animals are a natural resource that can be tapped for people's physical and emotional development.

The Animal and Normal Child: Research

There is little research on the relationship between the normal child and animals, or on the effects of animals on children's development (McCulloch,

1983). Most of the work to date has been with abnormal children. My interest lies mainly in the area of helping children with problems that occur during normative development.

The physical, mental, and emotional development of the child is often interwoven with disagreeable events. The child experiences, on the one hand, confidence, acceptance, and success, and on the other hand, doubt, rejection, and failure. Even though negative experiences develop inner resources, they also produce tension in the child. This tension can cause a slowdown or a delay in development. According to Erikson (1963), such specific developmental tasks as trust, self-esteem, autonomy, responsibility, and empathy for others, are learned in the first six years of childhood.

I feel more professionals need to be concerned with the prevention of major problems in children: to help the small child develop his ego,[1] his sense of self-worth, his ability to know he is capable of many things, and his strength, so that if his world does crumble around him (divorce, a new sibling in the family, illness or loss of a parent, or even entrance into school), he will not crumble with it.

Since a small child learns best by example, he can develop an awareness of the needs and feelings of others by seeing how adults care for and relate to animals. The child can practice a variety of interactions with the animal, which can later be incorporated into relationships with others. Guttmann (Messent, 1985, p. 391) says that an animal can teach children behaviors not easily acquired by usual learning techniques, such as social behavior (sharing and responsibility for others) and a capacity to communicate nonverbally. His study showed that pet-owning children scored higher in being able to ask for needed help and were also given a higher status by their peers. A study by Kidd and Kidd (no date) found that the human-animal bond is established in children before their first birthday. It is interesting to note that a lot of the behavior between a small child and an animal resembles the parent-child relationship. Ten Bensel and Robin (1985) say this process of "infantile parentalism" suggests one way in which children cope with the loss of their childhood. Children as young as age three can learn nurturing behavior from animals.

Studies in the past few years (McCulloch, 1981; MacDonald, no date) have shown that animals help children develop self-esteem, a sense of achievement, socialization, cooperation, and nurturance. Many authors (e.g., Salomon, 1981; MacDonald, 1979) cite the value that the child receives from loving something that offers love and reassurance back without criticism. The animal is willing to give its love, does not talk back and argue, and provides a continuous nonjudgmental relationship.

According to Levinson (1969), animals provide the gentle, warm conditions children need but are so often deprived of. The animal provides stability in

[1]The masculine form of pronouns will be used throughout this chapter in the traditional mode in order to make it more readable.

the child's life, as well as helps the child develop motor skills and language (Condoret, 1977; Salomon, 1984). Some researchers (Salomon, 1984) feel that children see themselves in the animal, or regard the animal as an extention of themselves (ten Bensel & Robin, 1985). Animals help children learn about birth, death, and even toilet training (Levinson, 1972; Condoret, 1977). The animal also helps the child see what is involved in a relationship in terms of give and take.

Children learn responsibility from a relationship with an animal. They can begin to accept responsibility for their own actions as well as responsibility for the needs of others.

Katcher (1983) writes that animals help preserve our mental and physical equilibrium by providing kinship, intimacy, safety, and consistency. Condoret (1977) found in his studies of kindergarten children that the animal helps children develop imagination. The child can identify with the animal or project his desires onto the animal. According to Ross (1981), caring for an animal may be the first step in developing a concern for other people that comes from the opportunity to love and to be loved. Ross (1983) also relates how, at Green Chimneys (a residential school for emotionally disturbed young children in Brewster, New York), children are seen to work through their feelings of jealousy, rivalry, and possessiveness when they relate to an animal.

Studies by Bryant (1986) have shown that children talk to dogs when they are sad, happy, afraid, and angry. They even share their secrets with dogs. Her studies show that animals can help children develop companionship, affection, reliability, and intimacy, and can enhance self-worth. Katcher (1985) has demonstrated how the presence of an animal in an unfamiliar room with a stranger present can have a calming effect on children to the degree that the child's blood pressure (systolic and diastolic) is significantly lowered. He feels that the animal's presence reduces stress and tension because the sight and sound of the undisturbed animal is a sign of safety to the child.

Further studies of Condoret (1977) showed that animals bring out the personalities of children and improve their receptiveness to the environment and to others around them. He also found that enuresis disappeared in some of the children when they assumed responsibility for an animal.

According to Messent and Serpell (1981) the most important health-related aspect of the human-animal relationship is, most likely, play. The noncompetitive qualities of the animal's play can be important for developing children. Animals are better playmates than toys are because animals constantly bring children back into the reality of the relationship. Animals meet the developing needs of children, as they are active and energetic playmates and help to release tension and energies in the child. The animal also helps the child to explore more readily (Soares, 1985).

Animals stimulate touch; this leads to conversation and hence to socialization. Katcher (1981) feels that children today do not get enough chances to touch and be touched in a comforting way. The average middle class child is put to bed with a soft toy or blanket and not the touch or body of another human. Between the ages of five and eight the child must then give up this object that has become his second self. This transitional object enables the child to make the transition between mother and home, and the outside world. Animals can act as transitional objects (Soares, 1985) better than toys can because they help the child create his ego, overcome insecurity, and experience the environment in a way that a blanket or teddy bear cannot.

Animals also help children in a society that seems to frown upon excessive emotional expression. Hugging, fondling, petting, and kissing an animal is usually accepted.

Ross (1983) also found that children who develop sympathy for animals tend to be less destructive and more careful of other animate and inanimate objects. Animals help the child develop a respect for all life.

Stressful events in the life of the child, such as the birth of a sibling or the illness or death of a family member, may be eased by an animal. Ten Bensel and Robin (1985) found that animals play different roles in the lives of children, depending upon the child's stage of development and his needs. At one point in a young child's life the animal can represent a parent, while at a later stage the animal can become the child.

Animals are also very important for children who are physically ill. McCulloch (1981) says that when children are hospitalized, the things they love the most are taken away; these are the very things that could contribute to their recovery and happiness. Chronically ill children have personalities that are developing; animals can help maintain a fairly normal psychosocial development. This is true for the mentally ill child as well.

Katcher (1981) feels that animals decrease depression, loneliness, and social isolation, because they can be cared for by the child. They decrease anxiety when the child can touch, watch, and exercise them.

According to Levinson (1984), contact with soft furry objects, animate as well as inanimate, reduces tension and produces relaxation, because opiate receptors are blocked in the limbic system through the production of endorphins (complex biochemical reactions in the brain). Endorphins act as morphine does, by creating euphoria.

History of Animal-Facilitated Therapy

Animal-facilitated therapy, usually called pet-facilitated therapy (PFT) since most of the work is with pets (the author uses farm animals as well, and so calls it AFT), began in England in 1792, at York Retreat, which was founded by the Quakers. The mental patients of this institution were given rewards for improvements in their behavior that came about by caring for farm animals.

This was a major innovation in the days when harsh physical punishment was the usual control used with these patients. In 1867, pets, farm animals, and wildlife programs were integrated into treatment at Bethel Treatment Facility in West Germany (McCulloch, 1983).

It was not until 1942, in Pawling, New York, at the Air Force Convalescent Hospital, that the use of animals for the physically and mentally ill was introduced to the United States. The soldiers cared for the farm animals and worked in wildlife programs. Even though the program was termed a success, it was discontinued after World War II.

The whole idea for the use of pets in therapy with children can be traced to the pioneering work of the late Dr. Boris Levinson. He was Professor of Psychology at Yeshiva University, and a psychotherapist, who accidently stumbled on the efficacy of this treatment when he left his dog, Jingles, alone with an uncommunicative, difficult child for a few minutes. When he returned to the room he found the child in deep conversation with the dog. From then on Jingles became a part of this child's sessions, as well as sessions with other children. In 1961, Levinson presented his ideas at a Conference of the American Psychological Association. While most were enthusiastic, he was teased by some professionals who asked him how much of his fees went to the dog. To date, Levinson's book (1969) is the only one written on the subject of children and pets in therapy, though many professionals in medicine, psychology, social work, and related fields are using his ideas and methods. Experts can now see the beneficial effects of an animal in therapy with children. I found AFT necessary in my own work with emotionally disturbed and learning disabled children as a springboard for my theories of therapy using animals with the normally developing child.

BASIC METHODS AND PROCEDURES

Research on the Use of Animals in Child Therapy

Levinson (1969) found that animals could be useful in the psychological assessment of the child. Young children are often hard to assess because of their lack of a stable personality structure. Tests can show a child's IQ, school abilities, and personality traits, but often fail to show how the child interacts in day-to-day situations and relationships. The animal can give the therapist valuable clues, as it catches the child off-guard in his relationship with another living being. Even if a parent is in the room, the child can be guarded and defensive.

The animal helps the therapist see what the frustration tolerance of the child is and how involved with another the child can become. It also shows what kinds of relationships the child has with others. Condoret (1977) found that the child's relationship with the animal sometimes reveals disturbances in the child, especially any deep-seated relational difficulties the child has with parents and/or peers. The use of the animal enables early detection of problems. Daniel and colleagues (1986) wrote that interaction with the animal can be the opportunity that allows for therapeutic change in social interactions.

Children are often better able to discuss family problems, as well as their own developmental issues, when an animal is present. Death, aggression, insecurity, and negative feelings can be more easily expressed by way of the animal. It is the author's experience that the therapist gets more information (verbal and nonverbal) out of a child a lot faster when an animal is present; hence, the therapeutic process need not be so long. The animal helps the child relax and forget he is in therapy and, therefore, be more expressive of his true self. It can also be a fun time for the child and the therapist.

Gonski (1985), in her social work, uses German shepherds to help foster children see the relationship between themselves and the dog—which must also be cared for by someone other than its own family. For her, the dog functions as a problem solving agent and helps the child to see what behavior is acceptable as well as what limits are necessary in a relationship. She finds that her German shepherds can elicit conversation from even the most hostile child. Peacock (1986) found that interviews in which her dog is present are more relaxed and the child is more cooperative and able to enjoy the session. The dog serves to reduce tension and provides an atmosphere of warmth and trust. Levinson (1969) found that as the child relaxes, the therapist is able to build more rapport with the child and put more therapeutic demands on him. Also, because the therapist is freed of some of the responsibility of meeting the child's basic affectional needs, which are supplied by the animal, he can work on a higher level in the therapy process.

The animal gives the child more opportunity to feel master of the situation during therapy, which is important for building his ego and self-esteem. Interaction with the animal also allows the child to regress in the process (Levinson, 1969). The child can act like the animal, crawling on all fours and making noises like the animal. He does not need to use words to communicate to the therapist. His actions speak for themselves.

In terms of the milieu, the use of animals certainly provides a larger environment (and some might rightfully argue, one that is harder to control) in which to observe and interact with the child. When an animal is used in the therapist's office or playroom, the child and therapist can take the animal for a walk outside. This allows the therapist to see how the child relates to the surroundings and to other people, as well as how he handles the animal. When animals are used from the farm, the therapeutic milieu becomes greatly expanded.

Some might argue that the presence of an animal in a therapy session takes away from the relationship between the therapist and the child, but Corson and Corson (1974) found that this is not so. Rather, the animal strengthens self-reliance and psychological well-being, resulting in more interaction between persons.

Levinson (1969) recommends the use of animals with the young, nonverbal child, the inhibited, the autistic, the withdrawn, and the culturally and socially disadvantaged. He feels that this type of therapy is not too effective with the extremely bright, verbal child, or with those with organic, acting out, character disorders. However, it is my experience that the bright, verbal, advantaged child, as well as some acting out children, are excellent candidates. Teenagers also often enjoy work with an animal, especially the farm animals.

Children can conquer fears through a working relationship with the animal and the therapist; they can also be helped to develop a sense of security that assists them in overcoming other problems. The animal is a mirror for the child (as a good therapist should be) in which he sees himself as loved and wanted—not for what he should or might be—but for what he is (Levinson, 1969, p. 46).

Some children see normal developmental tasks as a challenge, while others experience them as threats. Levinson feels that the animal helps in the development of children who experience relational difficulties. Berl (Levinson, 1969, p. 75) says that emotionally disturbed children who have experienced difficulties in forming relations with others relate more easily to animals. Disturbed children are often more afraid of human, physical contact because they had been hurt so much by significant others. Levinson (1969), however, points out that contrary to popular belief, children do not identify more with animals than with humans. The advantage of the animal is that it acts as a transitional object for the child. The child forms a relation with the animal first, then with the therapist, and finally with other people.

Why does the child respond to an animal when he does not respond to another human? Levinson felt that the animal is an expression of the unconscious self. Savishinsky (1983) wrote that animals help us combine the unconscious with the conscious in a controllable manner. Rynearson (1978) said that animals help us resolve our inner conflicts. Bettelheim (1977) wrote that they resolve conflicts through dreams and fantasies.

Okoniewski (1984) found the emotional distance between man and animal less than that between two humans. This could well explain why the emotionally disturbed child, who has been so hurt by relationships, or who has not developed a capacity for relationships with other people, is better able to relate to an animal.

The author has found that when an emotionally disturbed or learning disabled child sees how difficult it is for an animal to master certain tricks or to acquire developmental abilities (such as a calf weaned from its mother trying to learn to drink from a bucket), he becomes more patient with his own struggle to master developmental tasks or to overcome problems. It has been found at Green Chimneys that the child who is disruptive in the classroom and has a hard time concentrating or sitting still, often blossoms on the farm. Once the child establishes a relationship with the animal and knows he can do things well with it, the confidence is transferred to the classroom and to relationships with others.

Technique and Goals

The animal-facilitated therapy technique differs according to the environment, the animals used, and the therapist's mode of treatment. A dog in an office would be handled differently than a goat in a barn. When an animal is introduced into the session, I usually let the child become comfortable with the animal. If the child is timid or fearful (which is not common), I introduce the animal and talk for it. The child can assume the role of the animal or put the animal in a role he chooses for it. The animal can be his alter ego or his complement. The animal can be mother, father, sibling, friend, or enemy, depending upon the child's needs and wishes. All the while, the animal is teaching the child, helping the child learn new things about himself and his environment.

It is necessary for the therapist to select the proper animal for the child. At times I will let a child select the animal he wants to work with. If a child asks for a lamb, I will direct the child to a lamb I am sure will respond. It is also necessary to assess the capabilities of the child in responding to an animal chosen. For example, it would be harmful for a three-year-old to be with an uncontrollable calf; a soft kitten or lamb would be more appropriate. An older child who is rough and acting out would be better off with a larger animal than with the soft furry kitten. It is also necessary to define goals for the animal: What must it do to help the child in the therapeutic process? If a child needs a warm, loving, friendly animal that would respond to his moods, then a dog would be good. If the child needs to develop self-esteem, then a farm animal he can train himself does nicely.

Levinson (1969) said that questions can be asked of the child through the animal. The therapist can ask the child about his own family pet and the relationship others in the family have with the animal. This information gives the therapist many initial clues into family relation dynamics. The child is able to chat about something close to him, with which he feels comfortable. If there is no pet in the family, the child can be asked what kind of animal he would like to have. The presence of the animal in the therapy session makes this conversation real for the child. The child does not feel so threatened when the therapist asks questions through the animal. In fact, the child usually forgets he is being questioned.

Even the child's dreams can be interpreted by talking about the animal's dreams. I had a five-year-old girl who was unable to talk about the nightmares that frequently woke her. One day, the Newfoundland was lying at our feet and groaned in her sleep. I asked the child what she thought the dog was dreaming. Of course she told me one of her own nightmares.

Small children also love to be interviewed by the animal. The child does not feel that he is directly confronted by a strange adult as the therapist asks questions through the animal. For example, "Gypsy is three years old. She would like to know how old you are."

Qualifications for the Animal

The characteristics of the animal's personality are most important for the success of the therapy treatment. If one is trying to strengthen the ego and self-esteem of a child, one would not choose an animal that always leaves the child feeling like the underdog. Rather, an animal should be chosen that gives the child ample opportunity to be master of the situation. The animal should be sensitive to the child's moods. Different breeds of dogs, for instance, have different temperaments. Gonski (1985) feels that German shepherds are ideal for her work because they are loyal, easily trained, intelligent, protective of children, and work well with children who experience lack of love, low self-esteem, and hopelessness. The author has found the Newfoundland to be the most gentle, intelligent, and least aggressive of all dogs. Even small children are not intimidated by its size, and its woolly fur conveys a teddy bear quality. Even lambs in our farm's flock have different temperaments. Some are very approachable while others run when anyone comes near them.

The animal should be well-trained if it is to be used in the playroom or therapist's office. When therapist and child are interacting it would serve no good purpose to have an animal roaming the room and getting into things.

Many feel that the animal used should be a purebred so that the temperament is fairly predictable; however, I know of therapists who use mixed-breed dogs and the animals are excellent. The therapist has trained the animal well and knows what to expect from it. I find that our purebred Cheviot sheep are high strung and often nervous, whereas those of mixed breeds are often the most docile and comfortable with children.

In the farm environment, the training of the animal can be left to the child as part of the therapeutic process. Kilgour (1984) and Diesch (1984) say that all farm animals domesticated by man are social by nature; this means that man can enter into a social relationship with these animals by taming them at certain critical stages within the animal's development. Farm animals make good pets. I milk a Holstein cow who follows me like a dog and loves cherry pie. It is very important that those working with animals do not ignore the psychology of the animals themselves.

Fox (1981) has shown that animals have emotions and reactions not unlike man: fear, anger, anxiety, jealousy, guilt, and depression. (While he does not mention happiness, most of us have experienced this in our favorite pet.) The brain centers that mediate emotions are identical in man and animals.

Dogs or cats need not be the only animals considered for use in a playroom or office. Fish (tropical or plain old guppies), birds, hamsters, rabbits, and rodents are all good choices. Practically any animal that can be tamed can be used. I know one therapist who, on occasion, uses a monkey. The animal must be nonaggressive at all times, tolerant of children, and quick to respond to the commands of therapist and child.

Qualifications for the Therapist

It is necessary to note that to be successful in animal-oriented therapy, the therapist must possesss other qualities than therapists not using animals. Levinson (1969) said that the therapist must be willing to give up part of his functioning as a therapist to the animal, who is virtually cotherapist. This means that the therapist must have a strong ego and not be threatened in any way by the child's relationship with the animal. The therapist must be mature and also willing to accept a childishness in himself in relation to his response to the animal. Most of all, the therapist should understand animals and the bond they have with man. In 1972, Levinson questioned over 400 psychotherapists and found that one-third used animals in their therapy sessions, primarily dogs. According to Lockwood (1986), many lack the proper knowledge of the bond relationship. Seminars and workshops are now held on the importance of the human-animal bond and it is given more emphasis in veterinary schools across the country, thanks to the work of Dr. Leo Bustad (Dean Emeritus, Washington State University). Mercy College in New York offers a PFT training program that is certified by the State.

It is understandable that using a well-trained, beloved dog in the playroom is not as demanding as using farm animals. I was once called upon to work with an 11-year-old boy and donkeys; I said yes only because I had a good background with horses. Another time, I used a crippled horse with an acting out, disturbed preteen. She became very sensitive and nurturing to the animal and was able to carry these feelings over into her relationships with other members of her family with whom she was experiencing difficulties.

When an animal is used in psychotherapy, the need for language is reduced. While it is often easier for the child to express himself through acting out with the animal, the therapist must depend more on the posture, tone of voice, and facial expression of the child in interpreting what the child is trying to communicate. This means that the therapist must be trained in the dynamics of body language—as should any good play therapist.

Practical Intervention Utilizing Various Therapy Modalities

It is important to note that all writers agree that animal therapy is adjunctive to other therapy modalities. The author has found that it fits well with logotherapy, Gestalt, child-centered therapy, and reality therapy, to name a few. It is also good in teaching the child to relax, as the animal and child can lie down together on the floor when the child uses breathing exercises.

Today more and more preschools and elementary schools are using animals in the classroom because of their positive effects on children. Hope Center

School (Polt & Hale, 1985) for retarded children in Denver, uses dogs and cats in the classroom. They found that the children developed nurturing skills through grooming, feeding, and petting the animals. The children also learned cooperation with others by sharing. At the top of the list of improvements was an increase in the children's self-esteem and confidence in themselves.

The use of animals in logotherapy can help children find meaning in their lives in day-to-day issues and situations. Logotherapy (from the Greek: to find meaning, soul) was developed by the Austrian psychiatrist Viktor Frankl (1962) after his experience in German concentration camps. His experience of suffering and death convinced him that there was one ultimate purpose for man's existence: each man must search to find meaning in his own life. He noted how some people curled up to the wall and died, while others seemed strengthened by the same experience, as though they had found an inner faith to keep them going. Frankl concluded that if one has developed an inner spiritual freedom, no one can take it away. Frankl felt that modern man experiences an existential vacuum, because he has lost the meaning of life. This meaning can be restored and the emptiness filled by doing a deed (achievement and sense of accomplishment), by experiencing a value (such as a relationship with another), and by suffering. If man has meaning in his life, he can find meaning in suffering, since it is an inescapable part of life, as is death. For Frankl, suffering itself has no meaning, but with the right attitude one can become a better person through suffering.

Frankl saw man as a unity of body (physio-dimension), mind (psycho-dimension), and spirit. He felt that other modern therapy modalities did not address themselves to the spiritual side of man and thus they split man's wholeness. When Frankl spoke of the spiritual dimension of man, he was not speaking of a religious dimension but of a specifically human dimension that allows a man to choose what kind of person he will become and how he will live his life. The spiritual dimension of man allows him to reach beyond himself, seek his life tasks and take pleasure in accomplishing these tasks. Because of this inner freedom, man also has a responsibility to others. For Frankl, love is the highest goal of mankind, and it can change one's life significantly.

In logotherapy, it is the therapist's role to help the child learn to solve life's problems and to fulfill life's tasks. Because it is one of the most eclectic methods (there are neither steps nor rigid methodology), the therapist needs to be creative. Frankl himself admitted that it is not a panacea but should be used in conjunction with other therapy approaches. It is useful in helping the small child come to accept certain realities (loss or suffering and pain) as part of the process of living. If the child has an inner sense of his own value and worth, he will not be defeated by outside circumstances. For this reason, the author feels logotherapy is an important adjunct to other therapy modalities, especially when animals are used. The animal helps the child fill a void in his life, by creating practicals whereby the child can care for and help another living being (doing a deed). The child also learns responsibility in this care of another. The child experiences a value by loving and receiving love from the animal. Such philosophical questions can be asked as, "Who am I?" "Where am I going?" and, "Why?" by first helping the child see who the animal is. The animal also brings love and hope to the depressed and discouraged child, as well as to the chronically ill child who has to cope with unavoidable suffering.

Used in child-centered therapy, which focuses on the feelings of the child, animals help the child experience a warm, caring environment. Child-centered therapy, also known as nondirective therapy and person-centered therapy, was developed by Carl Rogers (1965), the originator of the first truly American system of psychotherapy. According to him, children have worth and dignity in their own right and thus deserve respect. They have the capacity and the right to self-direction and, when given a chance, they can make wise judgments. They also have the capacity to deal with their feelings, thoughts and behavior, and have the potential for constructive change. According to Rogers, children act out when their basic needs of love and belonging are not met.

Child-centered therapy deals with the organization and functioning of the self. The therapist becomes a mirror to the child that reflects the child's inner self with warmth, acceptance, empathy, and trust. After the therapist reflects the child's feelings and behavior, the child is then able to explore the effects he has on others. Thus, negative feelings and behavior can be changed. The main goal of the therapist is to help the child become more autonomous, sure of himself, and spontaneous. The child learns to accept his own values and judgments rather than those of others. The therapist uses active and passive listening and reflects the child's thoughts, feelings, and behavior by verbally rephrasing what the child has just said or done, so the child knows the therapist understands. The therapist also helps the child clarify what he is feeling and doing. This is not a confrontative method, and the therapist sets limits for the child only when necessary.

One of the prerequisites of child-centered therapy is a warm, caring environment in which the child may explore his emotions and verbally act out the consequences of alternate behavior and feelings. We have already quoted research that shows that the presence of an animal gives the child a feeling of unconditional positive regard. The interaction between the animal and the child also gives the therapist more chance for reflection of the child's behavior and feelings, as the child is better able to freely express his real emotions and thoughts. Self-worth and esteem as well as empathy are increased. The animal is nonintervening and can be either a mirror to the child or can be the alter ego. The animal helps the child explore the environment. It also helps the child separate fantasy from reality. Children can play act with the animal, tell about its dreams, or invent stories about it. My experience is that a child often has greater imagination lying in the hay with a baby lamb in his arms than when in the therapist's office.

In Gestalt therapy (Polster & Polster, 1973), which centers on the here and now feelings and behavior of the child, animals help give the child contact with the rest of the environment. The needs of others are seen and responsibility is increased as the child learns to care for the needs of the animal. The child sees himself in his here-and-now behavior with the animal.

Gestalt therapy (from the German word meaning form, or a whole that has properties that are more than a sum of its parts) was developed by the late Fritz Perls. It sees the healthy person as one who can maintain concentration and awareness without being swallowed up by environmental stimuli that constantly bombard him. According to Perls (Polster, 1973), in order to be well-adjusted, one must develop a responsibility for one's life and a response to one's environment. The aim of Gestalt is to help the person focus on one need at a time until that need is met and the Gestalt completed. In order to be able to satisfy each need, the person must be able to determine just what his needs are, and how he can gain those needs.

Body language is a major factor in Gestalt therapy; Perls felt the body is better than words as an indicator of the truth. Children can become more aware of their behavior and feelings through activities that allow bodily contact. Because the relation with the animal is nonverbal, much body language is used. The child can act out with the animal and invent fantasy games. He can learn about the animal's body and senses and compare them to his own (e.g., breathing). This makes the child more aware of his own body, and there can be lots of safe touching between child and animal.

Reality therapy focuses on the child's having his basic needs of loving and being loved fulfilled. It was developed by William Glasser and is perhaps one of the few therapy modalities that began with children in mind. Glasser (1969) feels that problems arise when the child's basic needs are not met. Like Frankl and Rogers, he feels that children have the ability to learn to fulfill their needs and to become responsible. People who become responsible have a better image of themselves. Glasser believes that people become mentally ill when they behave irresponsibly. He feels the moral issue of right and wrong is too often ignored in other therapies.

According to Glasser, reality is the willingness to accept the natural and logical consequences of one's behavior. When one tries to avoid the consequences, reality is denied and irresponsible behavior occurs. The unconscious is ignored in reality therapy, because Glasser feels it is fertile ground for excuses for our misbehavior. He looks at *what* is going on, not at *why*. For him, this therapy is a teaching process rather than a healing process; the therapist is to teach the child better ways to meet his needs.

As in all therapies, the therapist must first establish a warm and trusting relationship with the child. The child's present negative behavior is looked at in a nonpunative way. The child evaluates what is going on in his life and how he is helping himself. The therapist then helps the child find alternates to his behavior in order to get his needs met. Glasser is strong on commitments and feels that for the therapy process to be effective, the child must commit himself to trying an alternate action of his own choosing. Logical and natural consequences are also used to help the child see what will happen if he does or does not do a certain thing. Glasser feels that when a child is given responsibility and learns success for doing it right, he develops self-esteem.

When an animal is used in reality therapy, the focus is on the child's loving and being loved. The child is also able to feel in control of situations with the animal, learns to problem solve in relation to another, and starts to accept another's rights. The child learns from the animal that there are limitations necessary in all relations, and he sees the consequences of his behavior toward the animal and, thereby, learns responsibility. The child also develops self-control and respect for the rights of others. Even the smallest preschooler can see what happens when he mistreats the dog; he soon learns the appropriate way to treat it. The child can make a commitment to the animal in terms of its care and then chart his progress, so that he will have a feeling of accomplishment.

EXAMPLES OF ANIMAL-ORIENTED CHILD THERAPY

A few brief examples from the author's practice will show how the relationship between child and animal affects the therapeutic process.

MARTA

Marta was an eight-year-old diagnosed as an emotionally disturbed child of a strict and abusive mother. She was aggressive and hyperactive, sexually precocious, and had temper tantrums. In her first few months at the residential school no one could get her to talk about her relationship with her mother.

In the first session with a small furry rabbit, she held him in her lap and stroked him, telling the therapist that the rabbit's ears had been chewed by the mother rabbit. (The rabbit's ears were normal.) The therapist asked her why this was so. Marta responded, "The mother rabbit chewed the baby rabbit's ears all up. She wanted the baby to leave home." The therapist then asked, "How did the baby rabbit feel?" In answering, Marta said, "Sad. The baby rabbit loves the mother rabbit but the mother rabbit no longer loves the baby." This dialogue about the rabbit was an opener for Marta to then talk of her own feelings about the mother who badly beat her.

PETER

Peter, an eight-year-old, was diagnosed as developmentally delayed. The major goals for him were to increase attention span and to show appropriate behavior in interaction with peers. He was extremely hyperactive when initially brought to the barn. Everything distracted him and he darted from one animal pen to another, wanting to play with them all at once. The therapist felt that play with animal puppets in a quiet room would be a good introduction to later work with real animals. After 6 weeks of focused attention with cow and rabbit puppets, Peter was brought back to the barn where he chose a miniature rabbit to work with. He was able to hold the rabbit for about 10 minutes during the first session, combing and petting it. With each ensuing session he was able to stay focused on the rabbit for longer periods of time. In the first few sessions he handled the rabbit roughly and had to be reminded how to hold it. After several months, Peter was able to care for the rabbit on his own every day, feeding and watering it and occasionally brushing it. He appeared to be more focused, calmer in his movements, and better able to relate to his peers. It cannot be denied that the whole atmosphere of the residential farm-school contributed to his improvement, but having an animal of his own was a big factor.

JAMIE

Jamie came from a broken home. He was eight years old, neglected, and the youngest of four children. He was tested with an IQ of 85, and often appeared to be confused or fearful of his surroundings. In his first months at the school, he was often angry and aggressive with his peers and acted out in class. It was very difficult to talk to him, even though he appeared to be cooperative and friendly in therapy sessions. The goals for this child were to improve ego-functioning and socialization skills.

On my first day with Jamie, we went to the barn where he was allowed to choose the animal he would like to interact with. He chose a four-month-old kid goat. He was shown how to groom her and put a lead on her. In the second session, I showed him how to feed her from the hand. He was fearful and dropped the food at her feet. I showed him she had no upper teeth and could not bite him, but it was not until I placed my hand under his hand that he was able to hold the food for her. After that he fed her often, sometimes getting carrots for her. After three weeks, he walked the kid outside the barn on a lead. I then told him that he, who was still very quiet, had to talk to her and tell her what he wanted her to do. When she was good he had to praise her and when she was bad he had to tell her so in a stern voice; however, he was never to hit her. He often had to be told that he was the master of the goat and had to set limits for her.

Talking to the goat was the beginning of his talking to me. Within a month he was asking me questions about the goat. Later he began to talk about himself and how he was feeling. He was reported as being more vocal in class as well as interacting better with peers. In fact, his teacher and child care workers said everyone liked him. His building of self-esteem was noted one day when he took the goat for a walk near his class, which was out for recess. He said to each one as they came over to him, "See how good I can handle her!"

CAROL

Carol was a normally developing five-year-old who began having difficulties integrating herself within the family after the birth of a sister. She told tales to gain sympathy from outsiders and cried more than usual. She often told her father that he did not love her as much as he loved the baby, even though he tried to spend more time with her than before the birth.

Carol was brought to the farm and given a newborn lamb to work with. Her mother was able to bring her a few days before the lamb's birth so that she could brush and feed the ewe. Hours after the lamb's birth, her mother brought her back. She held it and was able to help place it under the mother so that it could nurse. Carol came to work with her lamb once a week, caring for it and playing with it in a pen filled with hay. A special bond developed between her and the lamb and the therapist was able to make analogies for the child to see the lamb as similar to herself. (A new lamb will come next year, but the mother will love this one still.) After only six weeks, Carol's mother reported that she was crying less, asking to help feed the family dog, and relating more to the baby sister. After three months, therapy was discontinued but Carol still comes to play with her lamb.

MICHAEL

Michael was a charming six-year-old boy, with two older sisters and a younger brother (age four-and-a-half). The younger brother was "all boy," whereas Michael was loving, docile, sensitive, and passive. He easily gave in to his younger brother who was already physically stronger. He cried when the sibling took his things—which was frequently. It was felt that therapy with an animal would benefit him in strengthening his ego and self-esteem. He arrived at the same time as a newborn Jersey calf. For weeks, Michael came to feed him, groom him, and play with him. As the calf grew stronger (and harder to deal with physically), so did Michael's self-esteem and sense of accomplishment. Because the Jersey was the smallest in a herd of Holsteins, Michael could see a relationship between himself and the calf. He was able to tell me how, even though the calf was smaller than some calves born after it, it could hold its own in the herd and seemed to be content. After a year of working with his calf, Michael is a different boy. He is still sweet and sensitive to others, more so than his peers, and he is now able to see his own giftedness. Because he is more accepting of himself, he is more accepted by his peers.

SUMMARY AND CONCLUSION

The research and work of incorporating animals into my practice has shown me that animals are appropriate for therapy with emotionally disturbed, learning disabled, and normally developing children experiencing stress. The animal can be a model, mirror, and teacher for the child. Because the animal is nonjudgmental, it can serve to enhance the child's sense of self-esteem. The child is better able to express his feelings and to learn to solve problems by working with another living being that needs to be cared for. The child can explore and express his feelings without feeling guilty or fearing punishment. An animal also helps the child incorporate suffering and death because he can see that other beings have pain and are sick and die. The animal helps the child feel mastery over situations. Some therapists feel that a child should not be challenged in the therapeutic process; others feel that challenges of this sort (e.g., chasing two donkeys) strengthen the child's self-esteem. The animal helps the child see the consequences of his behavior in the relationship. If he hits the dog, he may be bitten or the animal may go away from him. The child strokes the animal and it usually responds with affection. The animal, in effect, helps the child get involved in a relationship that will have far-reaching effects in later life.

The animal helps the child who nurtures it to better understand his own relationship with his parents. He will be better able to see that rules and limits, in addition to love and affection, are necessary in all relationships. Perhaps one of the most important contributions the animal makes to the therapeutic process is that it is a significant other in the life of the child. Today, when there are so few extended families, children need all the significant others in their lives they can find. Toys do not fill this role.

While there should be playing in each session, one never knows what will happen when child and animal get together; the therapist must be prepared to go with the flow and relax, while at the same time being deeply involved in the therapy. There must be a lot of spontaneity. The animal eliminates boredom in the session and makes it more fun for both the child and the therapist.

The animal helps the relationship between therapist and child develop faster. The child can say, "Look how she is treating that animal, maybe she'll be nice to me, too; I'll take a chance." The practicalities of using animals—pets as well as farm animals—are as limitless as the creativity of the therapist. It is the author's experience that the use of animals with already existing therapy modalities is much richer and more fruitful than the therapy by itself, and there is better chance of ego-development in the child—a major goal of psychotherapy.

REFERENCES

Bettelheim, B. (1977). *The uses of enchantment.* New York: Vintage Books.

Bryant, B. (1986, August). *The relevance of family and neighborhood animals to social-emotional development in middle childhood.* Paper presented at the Delta Society International Conference, Boston, MA.

Condoret, A. (1977). The child's relationship with household pets and domestic animals. *Bulletin of the French Veterinary Academy, 50,* 481–490.

Corson, S., & Corson, E. (1974). Pet-facilitated psychotherapy. In R.S. Anderson (Ed.), *Pet animals and society* (pp. 19–36). London: British Small Animals Veterinary Association.

Daniel, S., Burke, J., & Burke, J. (1986). Educational programs for pet therapy in institutional settings. New York: Mercy College.

Diesch, S. (1984). Companion animals on the farm. In P. Arkow (Ed.), *Dynamic relationships in practice: Animals in the helping professions* (pp. 257–267). Alameda, CA: Latham Foundation Publications.

Erikson, E. (1963). *Childhood and society* (2nd ed.). New York: Norton.

Frankl, V. (1962). *Man's search for meaning: Introduction to logotherapy.* New York: Washington Square Press.

Fox, M. (1981). Relationships between the human and non-human animals. In B. Fogle (Ed.), *Interrelations between people and pets* (pp. 23–40). Springfield, IL: Charles C Thomas.

Glasser, W. (1969). *Reality therapy.* New York: Harper and Row.

Gonski, Y. (1985). The utilization of canines in a child welfare setting. *Child and Adolescent Social Work*, 93–105.

Katcher, A. (1981). Interactions between people and their pets: Form and function. In B. Fogle (Ed.), *Interactions between people and pets* (pp. 41–67). Springfield, IL: Charles C Thomas.

Katcher, A. (1983). Man and the living environment: An excursion into cyclical time. In A. Katcher & A. Beck (Eds.), *Perspectives on our lives with companion animals* (pp. 519–531). Philadelphia: University of Pennsylvania Press.

Katcher, A. (1985, March). Physiologic and behavioral responses to companion animals. In J. Quackenbush & V. Voith (Eds.), *The human-companion-animal bond, The Veterinary Clinics of North America: Small Animal Practice*, 15(2), 403–410.

Kidd, A., & Kidd, R. (no date). *Children's attitudes towards pets.* Unpublished manuscript.

Kilgour, R. (1984). The role of human-animal bonds in farm animals and welfare issues. In R. Anderson (Ed.), *The pet connection, Proceedings of Conferences on the Human-Animal Bond, University of Minnesota and University of California, 1983* (pp. 58–74). Minneapolis: Center to Study Human-Animal Relationships and Environments, University of Minnesota.

Levinson, B. (1969). *Pet-oriented child psychotherapy.* Springfield, IL: Charles C Thomas.

Levinson, B. (1972). *Pets and human development.* Springfield, IL: Charles C Thomas.

Levinson, B. (1984). "A quiet revolution [Foreword]. In P. Arkow (Ed.), *Dynamic relationships in practice: Animals in the helping professions* (pp. 1–20). Alameda, CA: Latham Foundation Publications.

Lockwood, R. (1985, Spring). Pet-facilitated therapy grows up. *The Humane Society News*, pp. 4–8.

MacDonald, A. (1979). Children and companion animals. *Child: Care, Health and Development, 5*, 347–358.

MacDonald, A. (no date). Role of pets in the mental health of children. (Unpublished manuscript).

McCulloch, M. (1981). The pet as prothesis: Defining criteria for the adjunctive use of companion animals in the treatment of mentally ill, depressed outpatients. In B. Fogle (Ed.), *Interactions between people and pets* (pp. 101–123). Springfield, IL: Charles C Thomas.

McCulloch, M. (1983). Animal-facilitated therapy: Overview and future direction. In A. Katcher & A. Beck (Eds.), *New perspectives on our lives with companion animals* (pp. 410-426). Philadelphia: University of Pennsylvania Press.

Messent, P., & Serpell, J. (1981). An historical view of the pet-owner bond. In B. Fogle (Ed.), *Interactions between people and pets* (pp. 5-22). Springfield, IL: Charles C Thomas.

Messent, P. (1985, March). Pets as social facilitators. In J. Quackenbush, & V. Voith (Eds.), *The human-companion animal bond, The Veterinary Clinics of North America: Small Animal Practice, 15,* (2), 387-393.

Okoniewski, L. (1984). A comparison of human-human and human-animal relationships. In R. Anderson (Ed.), *The pet connection* (pp. 256-260). Minneapolis: University of Minnesota.

Peacock, C. (1986, August). *The role of the therapeutic pet in initial psychotherapy sessions with adolescents.* Paper presented to Delta Society International Conference, Boston.

Polster, I., & Polster, M. (1973). *Gestalt therapy integrated.* New York: Brunner/ Mazel.

Polt, J., & Hale, C. (1985, Spring). Using pets as "therapists" for children with developmental disabilities. *Teaching Exceptional Children,* 218-222.

Rogers, C. (1965). *Client-centered therapy.* Boston: Houghton-Mifflin.

Ross, S., Jr. (1981). Feelings: Children and companion animals. *Ross Timesaver 23* (41), 13-15.

Ross, S., Jr. (1983). The therapeutic use of animals with the handicapped. *International Child Welfare Review, 56,* 26-39.

Rynearson, E.K. (1978). Humans and pets and attachment. *British Journal of Psychiatry, 133,* 550-555.

Salomon, A. (1981, June). Animals and children: The role of the pet. *Canada's Mental Health,* pp. 9-13.

Salomon, A. (1984, October). Children's modes of communication with the animal. Paper presented at the Child in Social Context Conferences, Winnepeg, Canada.

Savishinsky, J. (1983). Pet ideas: The domestication of animals, human behavior, human emotions. In A. Katcher & A. Beck (Eds.), *New Perspectives on our lives with companion animals* (pp. 112-131). Philadelphia: University of Pennsylvania Press.

Soares, C. (1985). The companion animal in the context of the family system. In M. Sussman (Ed.), *Pets and the family: Vol. 8. (3/4). Marriage and Family Review,* pp. 49-62.

ten Bensel, R., & Robin, M. (1985). Pets and socialization of children. In M. Sussman (Ed.), *Pets and the family: Vol. 8 (3/4). Marriage and Family Review,* pp. 63-77.

CHAPTER 15

"Let's Make a Movie!"

Videotherapy for Children

JOAN K. HAM

"Let's make a movie." Lives there a 10-year-old with imagination so dead that he can fail to thrill to this appeal? We thought not and embarked on a new use for video equipment in a mental health clinic.

Children who were suffering in the wake of a divorce were chosen for group therapy to help them with their problems. In the course of the therapy, they created movies to help themselves and others understand and cope with the issues they had in common. This chapter will review the grounds on which group therapy of this type was chosen for these children, the course of the therapy, the making of the movies, and an assessment of the project.

THE TECHNIQUE

Planning for the groups

The groups were integrated into clinic treatment for children at Unified Services for Children and Adolescents (USCA) in Troy, New York. The clinic is part of the Rensselaer County mental health system and serves the entire county, encompassing a wide range of problems and socio-economic groups. A therapy project for children and their parents living through a divorce was organized and conducted by Dr. Aaron Noah Hoorwitz, Linda Ford, M.S.W., Dr. John O'Connor, and this author. Dr. Hoorwitz was the principal therapist for the children's group and developed the curriculum for both the children's and the parents' groups (Hoorwitz, 1984).

Many of the children who are brought to our clinic exhibit unfortunate reactions to the divorce of their parents: they are sad, angry, acting out, withdrawn, confused, and rebellious. Each child and family was seen individually by a therapist to assess the situation and to bring relief through standard family therapy or individual psychotherapy. It seemed to us, however, that the children and their parents might also be helped by meeting together in a group so that they could benefit from the support of others in similar situations.

Not all children of divorced parents are appropriate for group treatment. In some cases the children are clearly suffering from the failure of parents to address their own issues or to resolve the ongoing conflict between them. In many instances, individual therapy for the parents and mediation between the parents is more important and more useful than treatment of the child.

Preschool children and early latency age children can be best helped by providing advice to the parents. In addition, these younger children are not strong candidates for the group process. Their social skills are not sufficiently developed, they cannot grapple with issues in a group context, and they cannot make use of or offer peer support. Early latency age children can make use of individual play therapy, or just talking, to work through their own problems around divorce. Some of them can be helped through directive storytelling and cognitive restructuring if their pain is too keen to allow direct expression or indirect expression through drawings and play.

Late latency age children and adolescents, however, are able to verbalize their feelings and experiences to a group and to receive comfort and support, knowing that they are not alone in their grief and pain. These were the children we sought for the group. Wallerstein and Kelly (1980) recommend that treatment occur after the initial shock of the separation of the parents and before the family as a whole has reorganized and readjusted to new situations and new patterns of life. Therefore, we endeavoured to include children whose parents had been divorced within the previous two years. We hoped to maintain a group of between 8 and 10 members and, therefore, began with 10 to 15 members, expecting that some would not stay through the course. Group size ranged from about 7 to 15. The group started with a contract for 8 weeks, but the children and their mothers needed more time than that; 12 weeks has become our norm. We included children ages 8 to 12. Younger children were, as stated above, not ready for the group, and adolescents might, we believed, corrupt the group by being too sophisticated for the activities planned.

The children's group met simultaneously with a parents' group. Fathers were invited to that group, but in fact it became a group of mothers. There were several reasons for having the groups at the same time. Both the children and the mothers were in need of talking about their situations, their pain, and their problems, and they needed to talk with others going through the same experiences. We wanted to separate the children and parents because we did not think it would be helpful to the children to hear all of the necessary adult discussion, and we wanted the children to be comfortable in revealing themselves. We hoped to coordinate the work of the two groups. For example, the issues discussed with the children could be presented to the parents in such a way that the parents would better understand the children and could be coached to respond appropriately if the children began to use the new skills they had acquired in the group. It also occurred to us that if the mothers were coming at the same time for purposes of their own, attendance in both groups would be improved.

The Curriculum

The purposes of the group were defined as group support, identifying and naming problems, and developing ways of coping. The overall sequence had six themes: building group cohesion, initiating expression of feelings in general, presentation of the problems of divorce as they related to others, sharing individual experiences and concerns, reinforcement of concepts and strategies through the making of a movie, and termination.

The children were introduced to one another and to the therapist, and various games for getting acquainted were part of the first sessions. Simple snacks were served to make the group setting seem more informal and friendly and less like school. The setting was the playroom at the clinic, where tables, chairs, toys, and other objects could be easily moved about at will. This room is also the room in which our videotaping equipment is located; when we began to make the movies, it was not necessary for the children to adjust to a new locale. We tried to achieve a balance between a relaxed and comfortable atmosphere on the one hand, and structure and guidance on the other.

At the beginning, the children were encouraged to talk about feelings in general; they drew pictures illustrating sadness, anger, and loneliness. With the help of the therapist, they talked together about the pictures. The intent was to help them to learn to talk about and identify their own feelings as well as those of others.

During the following meetings, some of the same activities were continued; to these were added stories told to the children about other children suffering through a divorce. For example, they might be shown a picture of a little boy looking sad, and they would be told some details about this boy (his name, his age, what kind of house he lived in, what grade he was in school, etc.); the details were chosen to elicit an empathic response from the children. Then it would be explained that his parents had recently been divorced. The children would be asked why they thought he was so sad. The children were quick to identify numerous issues. They said that he missed his father, that he was worried that the divorce was his fault, that he was hoping his parents would get back together, and so on. Many of the important issues facing children of divorce were raised in this way: reunion fantasies, guilt about the divorce, longing for the absent parent, worry about the absent parent, anger at both parents, infantilization and parentification of the children, loyalty conflicts, being asked to spy for or carry messages for the parents, developing a relationship with a parent's new opposite-sex friends.

Gradually the focus shifted from identifying the feelings to discussing the behaviors of the children in the stories. One girl was portrayed as very withdrawn and sad and spending a lot of time by herself. There was a story about a boy who got angry at everyone, threw things around, and refused to study at school. The children were asked what negative effects these behaviors resulted in for the story children, and whether or not their behavior was helpful to them in any way. Alternative patterns were explored by asking what else the children could have done. When good solutions were suggested by the children, these patterns were reinforced by having each child repeat the solution or by brief role plays.

As a first move toward having the children focus on their own issues, they were asked to draw pictures of their families before the divorce and after. Children who were willing to do so were then invited to present their pictures to the group and to talk about what had happened, how things were different now, and how they felt.

When the children were able to talk fairly freely about their own situations and about those things that distressed them, the therapist suggested that a TV show could be made by the children to illustrate the problems they had been talking about. This suggestion was enthusiastically received. The children were shown the equipment and the means by which the film could be made. They would be performing in the playroom with the furniture and props they already knew so well. Since the camera was actually out of sight behind a one-way window, there was little sense of getting up on a stage in strange circumstances, yet there was all the excitement of being "on television."

From the therapist's point of view, the videotaping provided something new and interesting to bring into the group sessions. It transformed the children by eliciting a degree of enthusiasm that had never existed in the usual modes of therapy. It was also a way of including all the members of the group, and, most important, it was a way of solidifying and rehearsing the concepts and ideas that had been stressed since the beginning.

In the next section I will describe the contents of two of the taping sessions. This may help to illustrate the organization of activities during such sessions, as well as the behaviors and feelings displayed by the children.

CASE ILLUSTRATIONS

EXAMPLE 1

In one tape, the children decided to illustrate the problem of being caught in the middle between conflicting parents and the problem of being used as a messenger. The group as a whole sketched out the rough outline of the plot, what scenes there would be, and what characters would be needed. Parts were assigned by the children with the guidance of the therapist, and enough parts were created so that every child had a role, however small. Shyer and younger children were given lesser roles; one person took two roles. The narrator was seen as a critical role, and one of the older, more articulate, outgoing, energetic members of the group was chosen by the children themselves. The plot was established by the whole group, and the therapist asked questions that helped them make the issues concrete.

The scenes in this tape were as follows. *Introduction:* The narrator presented the characters and performers and gave the title of the show. *Scene one:* Two children, a boy and a girl, are playing and the mother comes to them to say that their father will be coming soon to pick them up. Mother has a list of things for them to tell the father: a bill needs to be paid, a bicycle needs to be fixed, she wants the children home at a certain time. The children are sent off with admonitions to be sure Father gets all these messages.

Scene two: The children are in the car with the father. The children present the messages from the mother. Father is annoyed and snaps at the children, giving them angry messages to take back to the mother. The children are miserable. Father picks up his girlfriend, and there is a discussion about where they should all go.

Scene three: At McDonald's, the girlfriend tries to act like a mother and announces that she is the mother of the children when she is with them. The children argue with her about whether they will drink milk or soda, as they struggle with the issues of whether or not they will accept her authority. The father does not see what is happening between his girlfriend and his children, and does not protect his children.

The dialogue was made up spontaneously by the children. The therapist only allowed them to rehearse once because he did not want to lose the freshness of their responses by turning them into a rote recitation. There was no effort to create a polished performance, or even to have the plot reach some resolution.

After the show was over, the whole group gathered in a circle around the therapist. He praised their efforts in detail, emphasizing both the show itself and the understanding they exhibited about problems of divorce. Together they reviewed the central dilemma: what to do when parents put you in the middle. Eventually one of the children said, "I can't handle it when they do it. I'm just a little kid." The therapist seized the opportunity to use this apt phrase and added it to the idea of confusion that the children often alluded to. "I feel confused, I'm just a little kid," offered the therapist, and the children concurred that the sentence summed up their experience. He asked several individuals to say it aloud and then asked the group as a whole to say it as a means of rehearsing what they might actually say to their parents.

EXAMPLE 2

The second skit had as its theme the pain children feel when they are asked to take sides between the parents. A narrator again introduced the topic, the characters, and the actors, and announced the scene changes. The first scene was at the mother's house. Mother is complaining to her new boyfriend about the father. She complains that the father tells the children she is no good; she complains that she has to pay all the bills, that she has to do all the work. The boyfriend listens sympathetically. Then the mother begins to question the children about what the father says. One of the children admits that the father asks if mother is doing anything around the house because she never did anything before. Mother begins pumping for information to the intense discomfort of the children.

The second scene is at the father's house, where the father is complaining to his girlfriend about the mother. They agree that the mother is lazy, does not clean the house, does not wash the dishes, and runs around with other men. Father asks the children if the mother says anything about him at home. One child says the mother is a pain because she is always asking questions. Father asks more about the mother's boyfriends, how often she goes out. Finally the boy says, "You're just like her. You ask all these questions!" Father replies that he is right and she is wrong.

The third scene shows the two children playing with trucks and talking about their dilemma. "Who's right? Who's wrong?" they ask each other. "Why do we have to be on a side?" One suggests that it would be easier just to take a side, one or the other, but neither really wants to do that. "It's like there has to be a wrong," says one child. The older child remarks with a sigh, "It's too bad you're so young." The younger brother agrees that he can't help very much.

In the discussion afterward, the children expressed their frustration. "The kids in the middle feel pushed to take a side." "The kids didn't understand why they had to solve it." "When the kids hear the boyfriend or girlfriend saying the parent is right, they think maybe that parent is right." "Why can't we just not have to pick sides, just love each other at the same time and talk to each other and be who we are." This last sentence became the lesson from this skit: don't pick sides, try to love both, talk to both, and be who you are.

THE ROLE OF THE THERAPIST

The therapist helps to guide, direct, and encourage. The presence in the group of a few children who are capable of imagining and creating a scene is, of course, invaluable to the therapist. Such children quickly take charge, get ideas from others, and the project begins to take shape. When there is a child who is very domineering and begins to tell everyone what to do, the therapist must step in to ensure that the show will be a group effort. On occasions when all the children are rather shy and quiet, the therapist may have to be more directive, drawing out ideas from the children and coaching them. One of the reasons for waiting until a good group spirit has been formed before embarking on a videotaping exercise is that one hopes the children will have developed ways of working together that are constructive, so that the dominant child is somewhat muted and the shy children are involved. The most useful stance for the therapist to take is to attempt to play a minimal role, interfering only when necessary and only to make a specific correction. The more that the children feel that this is their project, the more enthusiastic and proud they are.

The praise of the therapist is the fuel that maintains energy and pride. This praise can be expressed indirectly when the therapist shows enjoyment of the spontaneity, jokes, and liveliness of the children. The therapist can praise them for their ideas, their acting, and for whatever details seem particularly apt and pleasing. Above all, it is useful for the therapist to praise them for their understanding about the problems of divorce. One way of helping the children overcome sadness and anger is to help them see themselves as experts on the problems that plague them. Knowledge, and the sense of owning knowledge, is one of the great factors in building self-esteem and belief in one's ability to cope. The situation may still be difficult, but at least the children can name their pain and have some understanding of what is happening to them.

Showing the Tapes

The children were led to believe that their tape would be used to help other children. They liked this idea very much and readily gave their permission for the tape to be used. The therapists, however, had second thoughts about using the tapes in this way. If the tapes could be used in an entirely different community, they might indeed be useful. Since Rensselaer County is not heavily populated, there would be reason to fear that other children would know some of the children in the group and would use the tape in unpredictable ways. We worried about confidentiality for these children and their parents and decided not to use the tapes with other groups.

Another major question facing the therapists was the potential use of the tapes with the parent group. Parents like to see their children perform, and children like to have parents in the audience. The tapes showed the issues very clearly and were a lot of fun. In many ways, they seemed an ideal teaching tool to use with the parents. On reflection, however, it was deemed that there might be pitfalls. Parents would need careful preparation. Parents need to be familiar with the issues depicted so that the tape could become a means of making the issues live. Parents would need to be warned that if a daughter portrays a mother, that daughter is not necessarily representing her own mother. She is playing a part established by the group and acting out the script. Parents would need to be warned that the situations, characters, and problems presented are indeed generic and not specific, so that they would not feel that their personal lives were being acted out on the screen for all to see. We felt that the therapists working with the parents would have to be the best judges of the utility of showing them the tapes. There may be groups that would enjoy the tapes and make good use of them, but there could also be groups in which particular parents would not be able to use the tapes constructively. In the groups we have had, we have only once shown the tapes to parents. The parents were clearly uncomfortable and stiff, and we have decided that we would probably not do that again.

The children, of course, have always wanted to see their own show, and this was always arranged. The children enjoyed it immensely; there were shouts of recognition, lots of giggling, and laughter. Reviewing the tapes also provided the therapist with the opportunity to bring up issues not yet fully discussed or to reiterate some of the lessons on the tape. This is an optimal means by which to help clients work through problems without the pain usually involved. The fundamental lessons for children of divorce can be said over and over in one way or another: the divorce is not the child's fault; parents should learn to talk to each other directly and not use children in the middle; children need to learn to live with their situation and get on with their lives; hoping that the parents will get back together is usually a false hope; a child can accept love from those who offer it and try not to grieve over what is not or what can never be. These messages can be talked about, acted out, observed, and reinforced through the combination of other projects and videotherapy.

DISCUSSION

Evaluation of Treatment Effects

The primary purpose of the group and the videotherapy was to provide helpful clinical experiences for the children. Nevertheless, we tried to do what was possible to provide material for research and to buttress our own sense of success or failure with factual assessments. Initially we tried to begin with a full developmental assessment of each child, but this process proved cumbersome and detrimental to the formation of the group. It was necessary to begin the group with the enthusiasm that existed and not dissipate that energy by requiring lengthy testing. We tried to develop a measure that could be used before and after treatment, and finally developed one with such questions as, "Do you find it difficult to concentrate at school?" and "Do you find yourself fighting with your brother and sister?" Children were to respond with "Not at all," "A little," or "A lot." The examiner read the questions aloud so that no child would be struggling with the reading of the questions. The answers were weighted and summed. Nine was the lowest possible score; 27 was the highest. A low score indicated that the child acknowledged little stress or such bad feelings as anger, confusion, or sadness. Scores over 20 suggest that the child is suffering from many painful feelings. The measure was given at the first session and again at the last of the 12 meetings. The number of children in the group varied from 10 to 15, but the number who took both tests came out in the end to be only 4, a very small sample. The results of the testing are presented in Table 15.1.

In Table 15.1, the means of the pre- and posttesting are presented, together with the variances for each. A one-tailed test was used as a t-test for correlated

TABLE 15.1. Pretest and Posttest Results

	Mean	Variance
Pretest	14.75	11.18
Posttest	12.50	2.75

means. The result was statistically significant ($t = 2.18$, $d.f. = 3$, $p < .05$). The direction of change was the one we desired and suggests that the children were less stressed by the end of the therapy sessions than they had been at the beginning. The answers of the four children who were present at both tests reveals that three of those four did show a decrease in pain from beginning to end. The results of the pretest for the 12 children tested at that time was 15.25; the 7 children posttested resulted in a mean of 12.50. Since both of these means are close to the means for the children present at both sessions, our conclusions have some support, despite the small sample. It does appear that the children were less sad, angry, and confused at the end of the group than they were at the beginning.

These figures are, of course, unable to bear close scrutiny. It would be useful to compare them with figures for a control group, either a group on a waiting list with no treatment, or a group that met to discuss issues of divorce but did not have videotherapy as part of the activities. It is not clear at this moment whether or not we will be able to accomplish this research at our clinic.

We also assessed the success of the group in a less formal way by noting the remarks made by children at the end of a group with and without video-therapy. During the last two sessions, children were asked to discuss what changes they had noticed in themselves and what they had gained from the group. The nonvideo group typically commented:

"It helps to talk about it with other kids who have the same problems."

"You don't feel like you're the only one."

"I liked the soda and cookies."

The children who participated in the video group are similar in their responses, but to us, at least, they seem more enthusiastic.

"It's real fun to do stuff in front of the camera."

"It gives you ways to solve your problems."

"I know all about divorce now."

"I don't think about it all the time anymore, just sometimes."

"I know how to stay out of the middle now."

"I learned that the easy way is to take sides. It's better not to, but it's harder."

We hope to develop more comprehensive and accurate means of assessing the utility of our program as it evolves.

Potential for Use with Other Groups

Videotherapy has been a useful tool for us in working with children of divorce, and we have asked ourselves whether it might also be used for other special problems. Children with learning disabilities, for example, could make tapes in which they tried to explain to others how their disability makes it difficult for them to perform certain tasks. These children could also illustrate typical interactions with the world that cause them difficulty and they could experiment with various ways of coping, of helping others understand their difficulties, and of finding ways to negotiate these situations. Scenes could be drawn from home, school, and community.

Similarly, attention deficit disorder children could demonstrate their understanding of their own disability. They could act out the strategies they were learning in the group for succeeding better at tasks in the classroom, for controlling their impulsive behavior, and for developing social skills.

Children of established single parent families could also use the process in ways similar to those used by the children of divorcing parents.

Distressed and disabled children of many sorts could use group support to talk about their feelings and to develop the self-respect that could help them in the outside world. Making a movie could help to solidify and reinforce what they have learned. It could also give them the satisfaction of accomplishment in making a "movie" or "TV show."

In all these instances it should be clear that careful preparation is required. The group must develop cohesion and spirit so that the children are comfortable with one another and are able to talk about their own experiences and feelings. There needs to be discussion in the group of the issues facing them so that when the time comes to make the movie, those issues will be focused on and utilized. The therapist needs to be careful to let the project be done by the children; a smoothly polished performance is not the goal. Thorough preparation should lead up to the making of the movie so that this project becomes the climax of the sessions. The children should have the sense that they prepared for something, they did it, they reviewed it, and now it is time to say goodbye.

We believe that late-latency age children are the ideal group for videotherapy. They are sophisticated enough in their understanding of shows, they are not yet as self-conscious as adolescents, they are able to organize group activities, and they have the verbal skills and language concepts necessary. Younger children would, no doubt, also love to be in a show, but more adult guidance and supervision would be needed. Adolescents might also enjoy such a project if they did not see it as too childish; if they thought the movie would be used for the benefit of others, they might be more willing to be involved.

CONCLUSION

Many clinics and mental health services and practitioners across the country are using video equipment to enhance the quality of their services. Videotherapy is thus becoming more possible. It worked very well for us with several late-latency groups of children struggling with the problems of divorce. Making a movie seems to engender enthusiasm and excitement that role playing usually does not. All the advantages of role playing are present; in addition, there is the possibility of playing the scenes back for further comment and discussion.

We look forward to hearing how the technique is applied by other therapists in different situations. When properly prepared by the therapist, videotherapy calls forth the energies and innate spontaneity of the children. It provides a suitable project for, and climax to, a series of meetings, and serves to underline, reinforce, and teach therapeutic lessons.

Author Index

Subject Index

Page numbers followed by *t* or *f* indicate tables or figures, respectively.

Dentistry, pain control in, with hypnosis, 156
Dermatitis, hypnotherapy for, 152
Developmental delays, animal-oriented therapy for, 413–414
Differential therapeutics, 2–3
Dimension of Self-Concept, 182
Divergent Product Test, 183
Divorce, children of
  issues facing, 421
  videotherapy with, 419–420
Doll play, 16
Drawing, 16. *See also* Story-drawing
  with focusing, in play therapy, 277–282
  serial, 98–132
    background of, 98–99
    case examples, 106–130
    counselor's behavior during sessions, 104–105
    counselor's role in, 116–118
    directive technique for, 106, 118–125
    methods, 103–106
    nondirective technique for, 105–118
    partially directive technique for, 106, 126–131
    patterns, 99
    setting for, 103
    stages of, 102–103, 131
    symbolic themes, 100–102
    termination images, 131
    themes in, 131
Dreams, interpretation, 407
Drumming, rhythmic, effect of, 300

Eclecticism, 1–2
  technical, 3
Eczema, hypnotherapy for, 152
Encopresis, hypnotherapy for, 149
Enuresis
  and animal-oriented child therapy, 402
  hypnotherapy for, 156
Epilepsy, 199–200
Experiential psychology, 267
Expressive therapy, 352

Fairy tales, 9–10
Fantasy, 10, 16
Fantasy enactment, 103
Fantasy play therapy, 43–67. *See also* Imagery interaction
  case studies, 52–64
  combined with behavior modification, 62–64
  controlling child-therapist relationship in, 54–55
  directiveness in, 64
  goals of, 65
  grief work in, 57–59
  interventions in, 65
  intervision in, 65
  with mentally handicapped children, 61–62
  to overcome trauma, through brief mother-child treatment, 56–57
  research findings on, 45–47
  as silent growing experience, 59–61
  supervision of therapist in, 65
  therapist's role in, 64
  trust in, 55–56
Fears, relaxation training for, 161, 185–186
Feelings Checklist, 183
Finger painting, 16
Focusing, 266–293
  with adolescents, 287–289, 291
  with adults, 268
  applications of, 266, 273
  with drawing, in play therapy, 277–282
  felt sense in, 267–269, 285, 292
  with five-year-old child, 282–287
  and graduation anxiety, 289–291
  handle in, 269–270
  in home, 275–277
  literature on, 273
  procedure for, 268–270
  in schools, 273–275
  steps of, 268–270
    with children, 270–272
  theory of, 266, 267–268
  with younger children, 292
Formal operational thinking, 301

DATE DUE		
MAY 0 6 1991	FEB 2 1 1998	
NOV 1 5 1991	JUN 0 5 2002	
MAR 1 4 1992	AUG 1 5 2002	
DEC 1 0 1992		
DEC 1 8 1992		
APR 0 3 1993		
DEC 1 3 1993		
SEP 1 7 1994		
DEC 0 3 1995		

(*continued from front*)

Women in the Middle Years: Current Knowledge and Directions for Research and Policy *edited by Janet Zollinger Giele*

Loneliness: A Sourcebook of Current Theory, Research and Therapy *edited by Letitia Anne Peplau and Daniel Perlman*

Hyperactivity: Current Issues, Research, and Theory (Second Edition) *by Dorothea M. Ross and Sheila A. Ross*

Review of Human Development *edited by Tiffany M. Field, Aletha Huston, Herbert C. Quay, Lillian Troll, and Gordon E. Finley*

Agoraphobia: Multiple Perspectives on Theory and Treatment *edited by Dianne L. Chambless and Alan J. Goldstein*

The Rorschach: A Comprehensive System. Volume III: Assessment of Children and Adolescents *by John E. Exner, Jr. and Irving B. Weiner*

Handbook of Play Therapy *edited by Charles E. Schaefer and Kevin J. O'Connor*

Adolescent Sexuality in a Changing American Society: Social and Psychological Perspectives for the Human Service Professions (Second Edition) *by Catherine S. Chilman*

Failures in Behavior Therapy *edited by Edna B. Foa and Paul M.G. Emmelkamp*

The Psychological Assessment of Children (Second Edition) *by James O. Palmer*

Imagery: Current Theory, Research, and Application *edited by Aneés A. Sheikh*

Handbook of Clinical Child Psychology *edited by C. Eugene Walker and Michael C. Roberts*

The Measurement of Psychotherapy Outcome *edited by Michael J. Lambert, Edwin R. Christensen, and Steven S. DeJulio*

Clinical Methods in Psychology (Second Edition) *edited by Irving B. Weiner*

Excuses: Masquerades in Search of Grace *by C.R. Snyder, Raymond L. Higgins and Rita J. Stucky*

Diagnostic Understanding and Treatment Planning: The Elusive Connection *edited by Fred Shectman and William B. Smith*

Bender Gestalt Screening for Brain Dysfunction *by Patricia Lacks*

Adult Psychopathology and Diagnosis *edited by Samuel M. Turner and Michel Hersen*

Personality and the Behavioral Disorders (Second Edition) *edited by Norman S. Endler and J. McVicker Hunt*

Ecological Approaches to Clinical and Community Psychology *edited by William A. O'Connor and Bernard Lubin*

Rational-Emotive Therapy with Children and Adolescents: Theory, Treatment Strategies, Preventative Methods *by Michael E. Bernard and Marie R. Joyce*

The Unconscious Reconsidered *edited by Kenneth S. Bowers and Donald Meichenbaum*

Prevention of Problems in Childhood: Psychological Research and Application *edited by Michael C. Roberts and Lizette Peterson*

Resolving Resistances in Psychotherapy *by Herbert S. Strean*

Handbook of Social Skills Training and Research *edited by Luciano L'Abate and Michael A. Milan*

Institutional Settings in Children's Lives *by Leanne G. Rivlin and Maxine Wolfe*

Treating the Alcoholic: A Developmental Model of Recovery *by Stephanie Brown*

Resolving Marital Conflicts: A Psychodynamic Perspective *by Herbert S. Strean*

Paradoxical Strategies in Psychotherapy: A Comprehensive Overview and Guidebook *by Leon F. Seltzer*

Pharmacological and Behavioral Treatment: An Integrative Approach *edited by Michel Hersen*

The Rorschach: A Comprehensive System, Volume I: Basic Foundations (Second Edition) *by John E. Exner, Jr.*

The Induction of Hypnosis *by William E. Edmonston, Jr.*